Aho-Girl

\'ahô͵gərl\ *Japanese , noun*.

A clueless girl.

2 | Hiroyuki

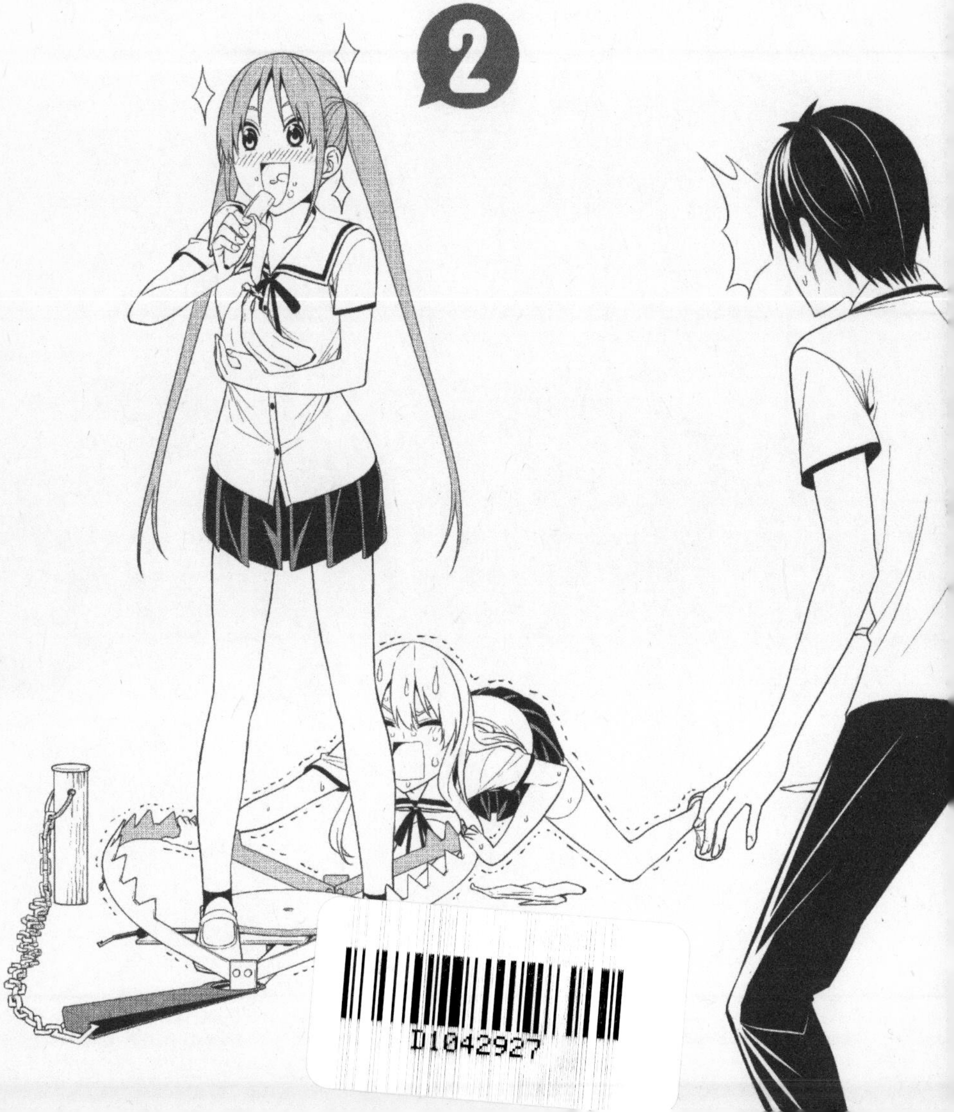
2

CHARACTER PROFILES

AHO-GIRL's Cast of Characters

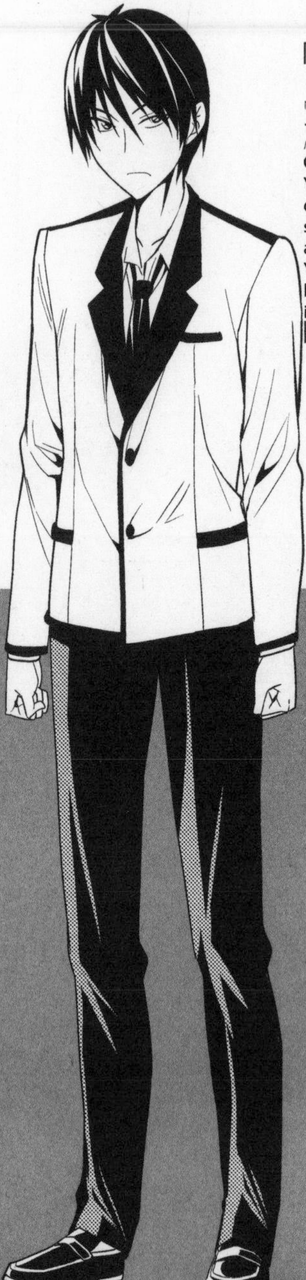

Name **Akuru Akutsu (Akkun)**

Memo

Childhood friend of Yoshiko, who lives next door. Plays the aggravated straight man to Yoshiko's absurdity. Tries to cure Yoshiko of her stupidity, but despite all his effort, it's not going very well.

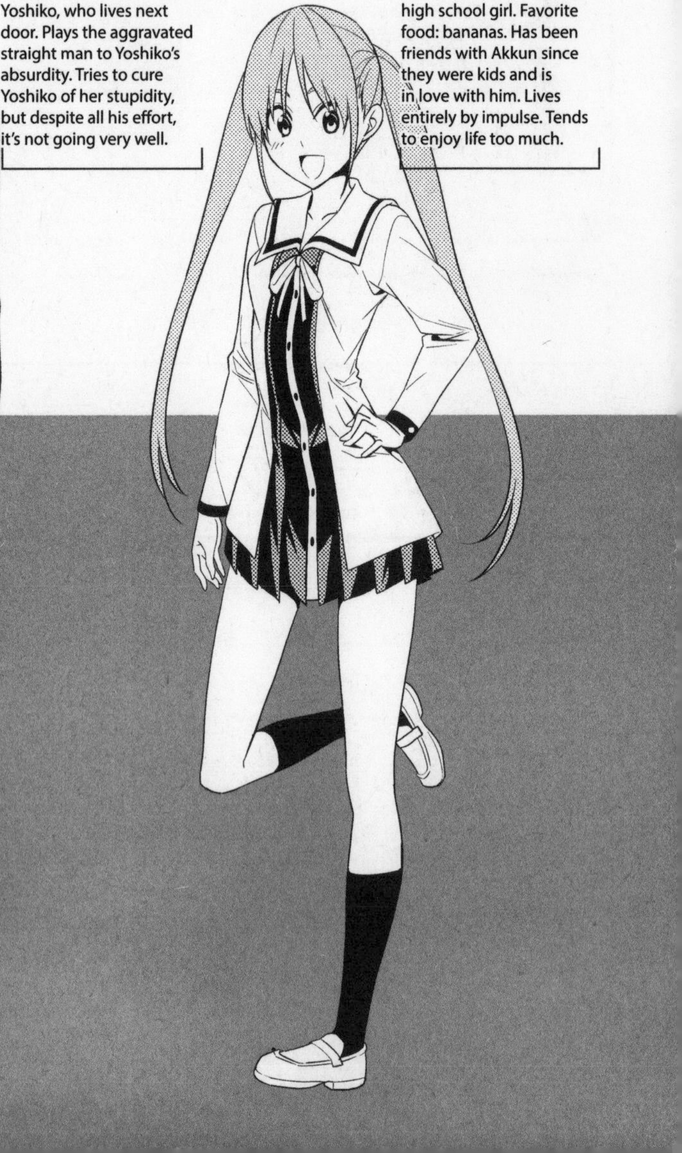

Name **Yoshiko Hanabatake**

Memo

An inexpressibly clueless high school girl. Favorite food: bananas. Has been friends with Akkun since they were kids and is in love with him. Lives entirely by impulse. Tends to enjoy life too much.

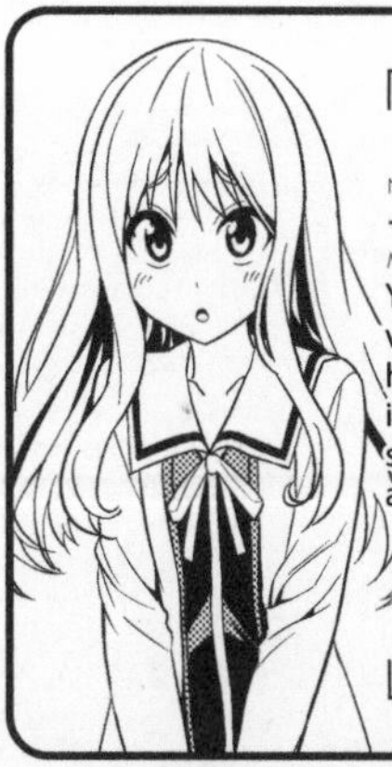

Name **Sayaka Sumino**

Memo

Yoshiko's friend. She's a very kind girl. She knows her kindness lands her in all sorts of trouble, yet she remains kind. Worries about being boring.

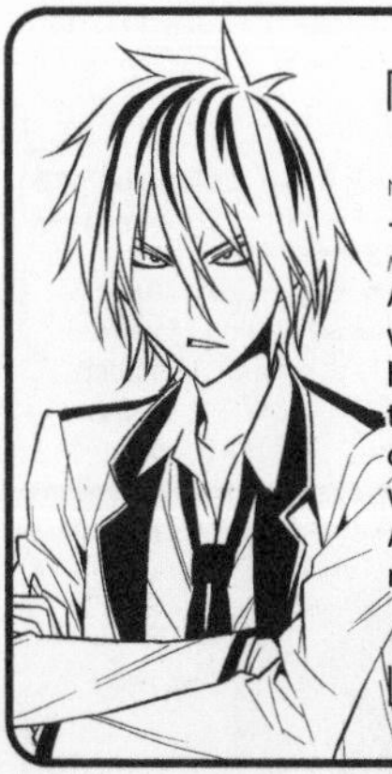

Name **Ryuichi Kurosaki**

Memo

An unfortunate hooligan who knows nothing of human kindness and therefore was easily won over by Yoshiko. Seems to want to be friends with Akkun, but there's not much hope for that.

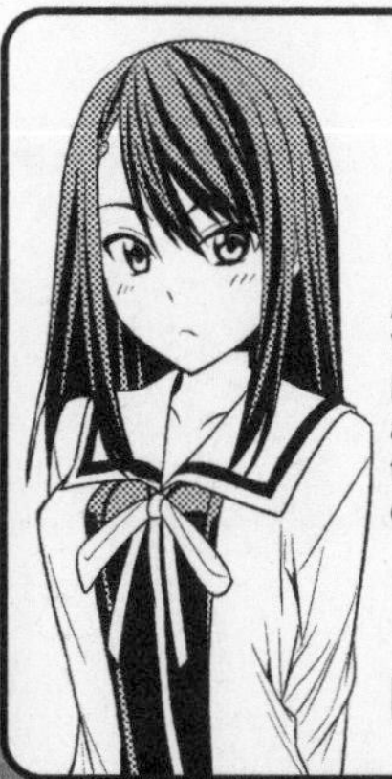

Name **Head Monitor**

Memo

An upperclassman at Yoshiko's school. Has fallen head over heels for Akkun and begun to stray from the moral path, but she doesn't realize it. G cup.

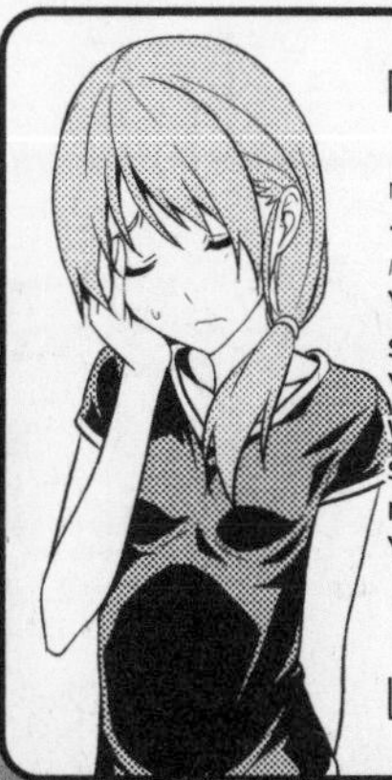

Name **Yoshie Hanabatake**

Memo

Yoshiko's mother. While she does worry about Yoshiko, she's far more worried about her own sunset years. Will use any means necessary to fix Yoshiko up with Akkun.

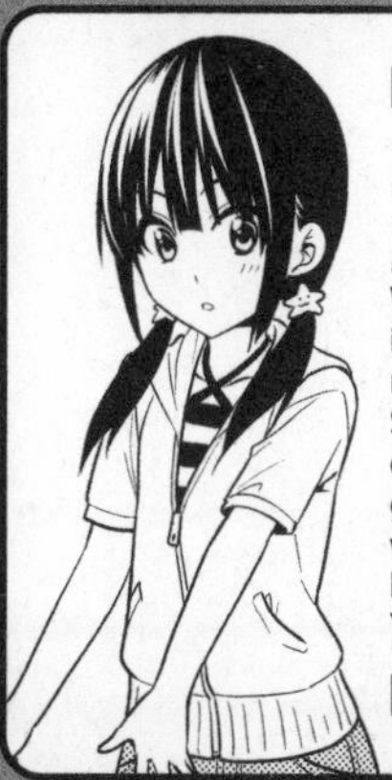

Name **Ruri Akutsu**

Memo

While her brother Akkun is an overachiever, Ruri's not quite so fortunate. She is constantly dismayed by her terrible grades. Perhaps the day will come when all her hard work pays off. Hates Yoshiko.

HIROYUKI
PRESENTS
AHO-GIRL
VOLUME.2

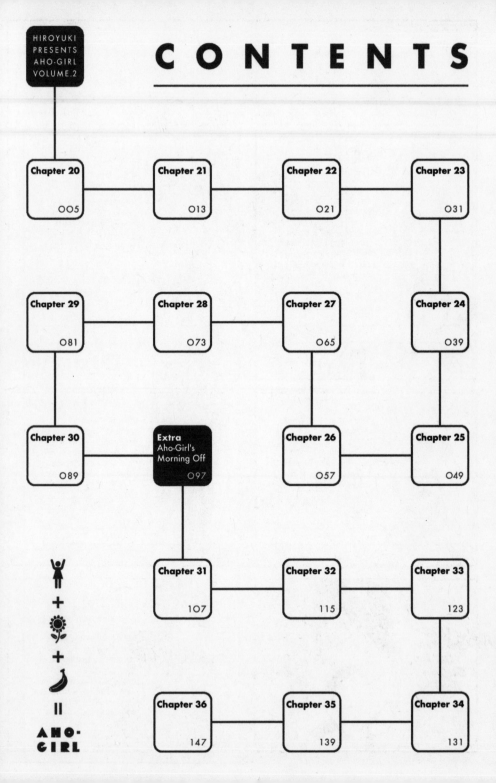

CONTENTS

HIROYUKI PRESENTS AHO-GIRL VOLUME.2

AHO-GIRL

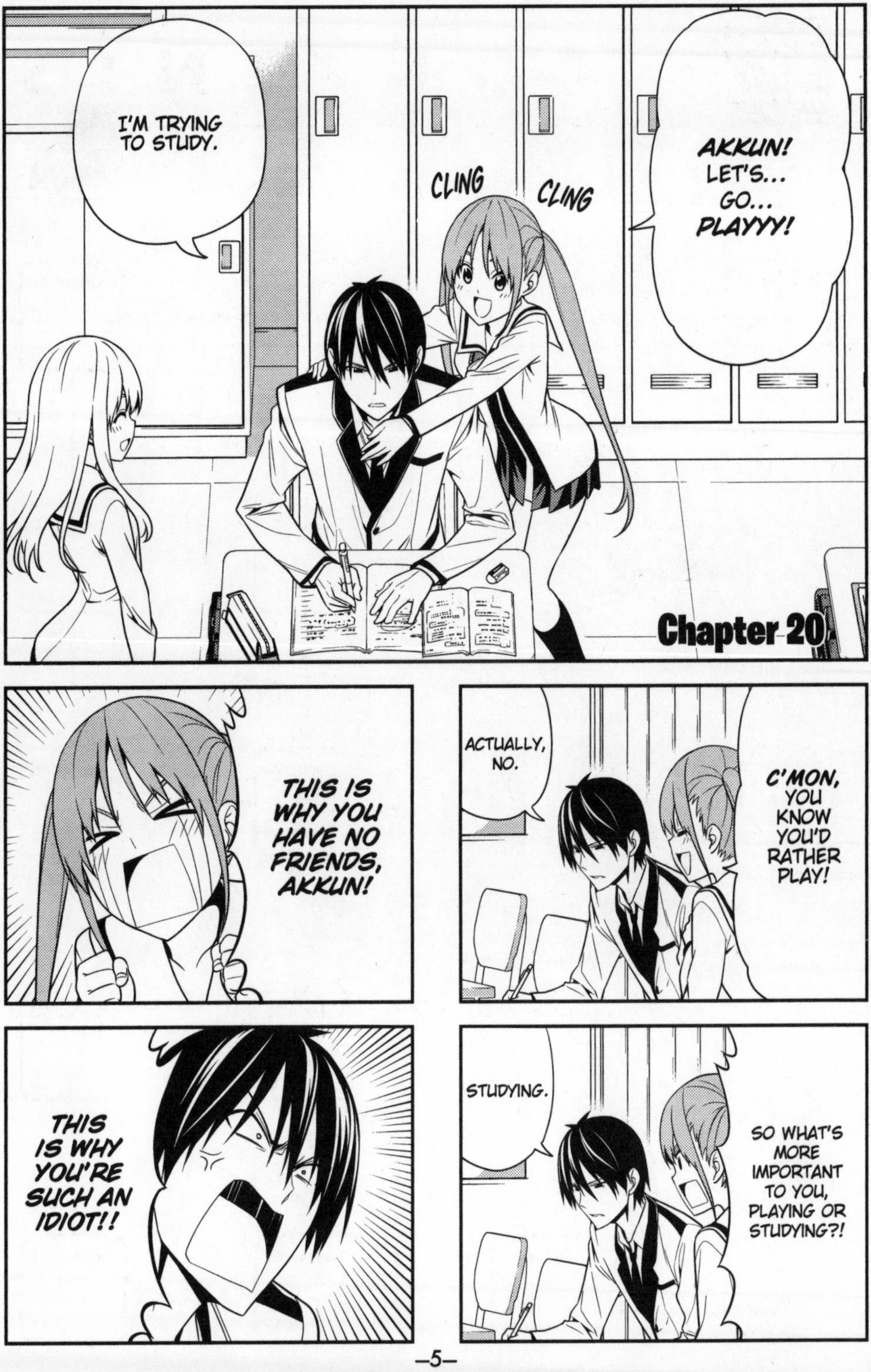
AKKUN! LET'S... GO... PLAYYY!
CLING
CLING
I'M TRYING TO STUDY.
Chapter 20
C'MON, YOU KNOW YOU'D RATHER PLAY!
ACTUALLY, NO.
THIS IS WHY YOU HAVE NO FRIENDS, AKKUN!
SO WHAT'S MORE IMPORTANT TO YOU, PLAYING OR STUDYING?!
STUDYING.
THIS IS WHY YOU'RE SUCH AN IDIOT!!

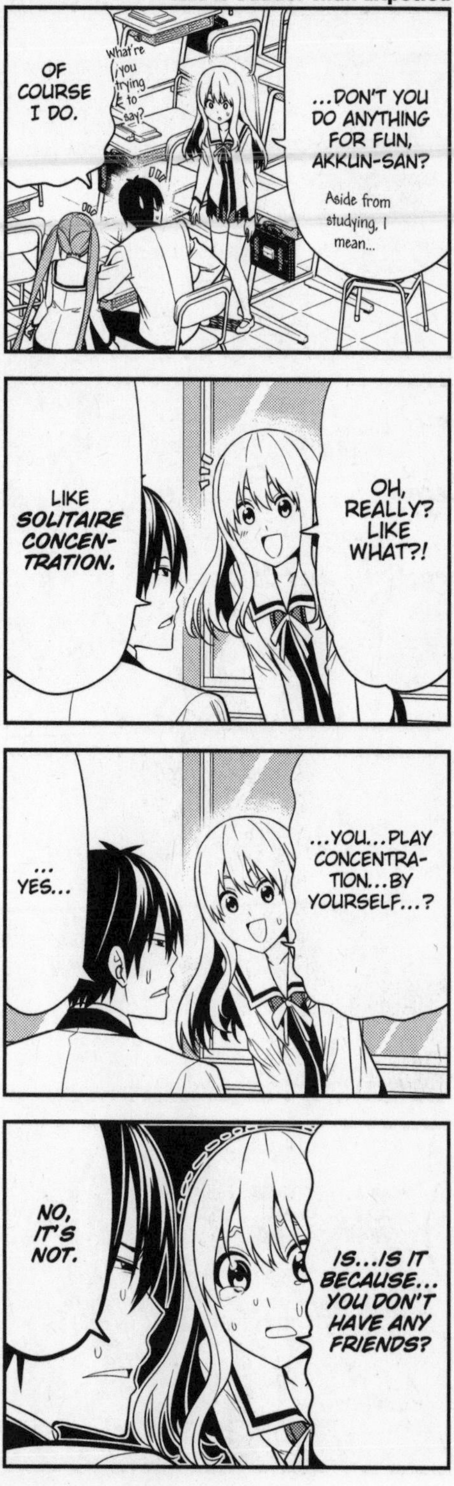
...DON'T YOU DO ANYTHING FOR FUN, AKKUN-SAN?
Aside from studying, I mean...
OF COURSE I DO.
What're you trying to say?
OH, REALLY? LIKE WHAT?!
LIKE SOLITAIRE CONCENTRATION.
...YOU...PLAY CONCENTRATION...BY YOURSELF...?
...YES...
IS...IS IT BECAUSE... YOU DON'T HAVE ANY FRIENDS?
NO, IT'S NOT.

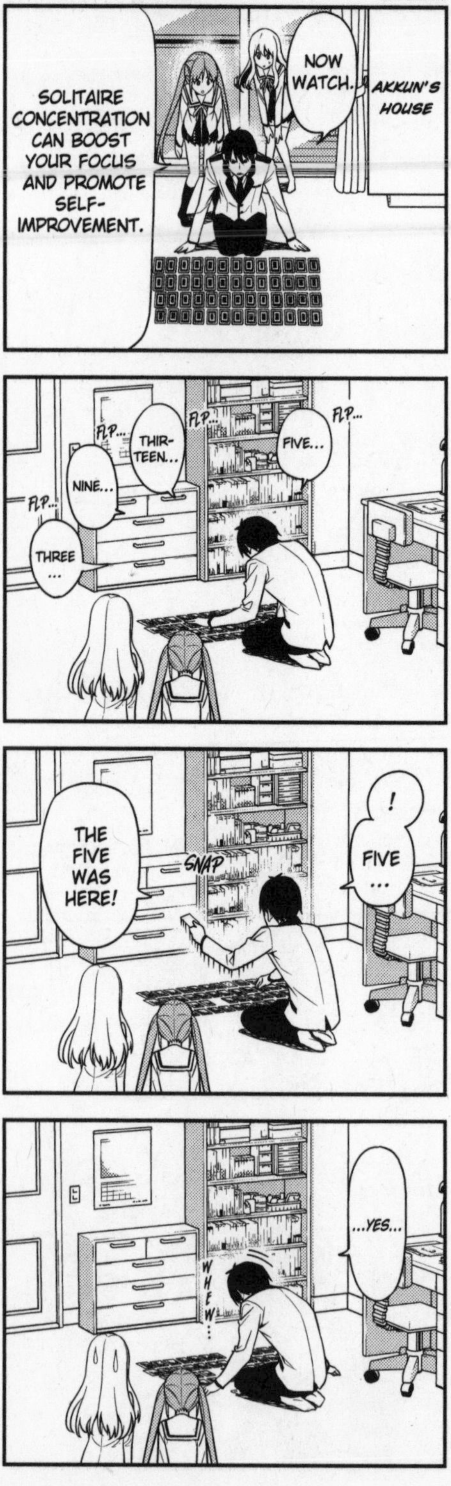
AKKUN'S HOUSE
NOW WATCH.
SOLITAIRE CONCENTRATION CAN BOOST YOUR FOCUS AND PROMOTE SELF-IMPROVEMENT.
FLP...
FIVE...
FLP...
THIRTEEN...
FLP...
NINE...
FLP...
THREE ...
!
FIVE ...
SNAP
THE FIVE WAS HERE!
...YES...
WHEW...

He's a Little Intense

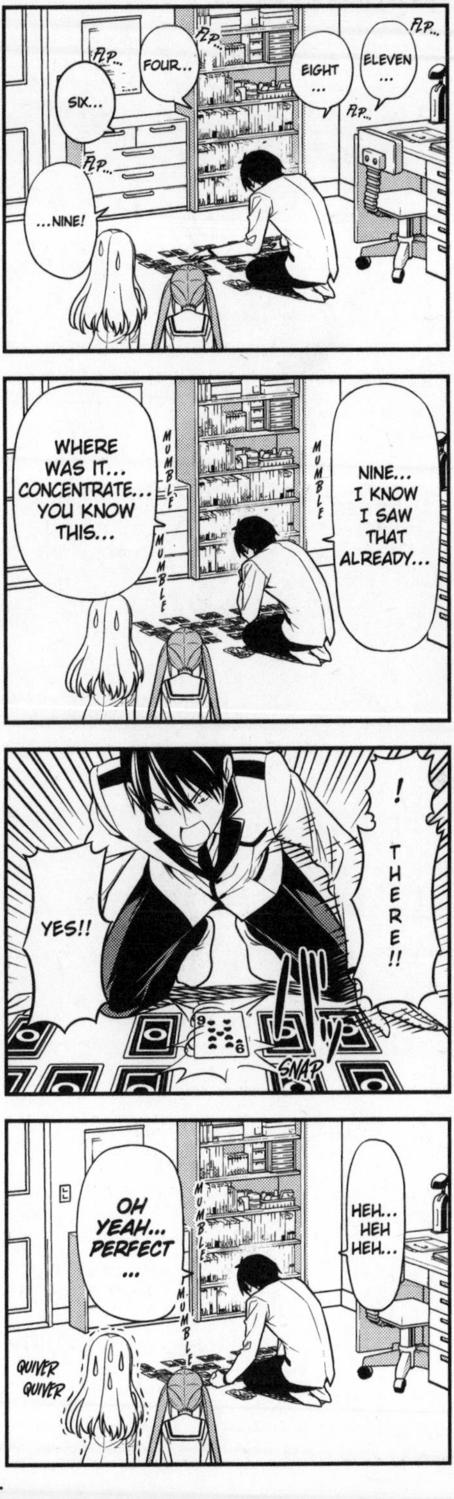
FLP...
ELEVEN ...
EIGHT ...
FLP...
FLP...
FOUR...
FLP...
SIX...
FLP...
...NINE!
NINE... I KNOW I SAW THAT ALREADY...
MUMBLE
MUMBLE
MUMBLE
WHERE WAS IT... CONCENTRATE... YOU KNOW THIS...
!
THERE!!
YES!!
SNAP
HEH... HEH HEH...
MUMBLE
MUMBLE
OH YEAH... PERFECT ...
QUIVER QUIVER

He Must Be So Lonely!

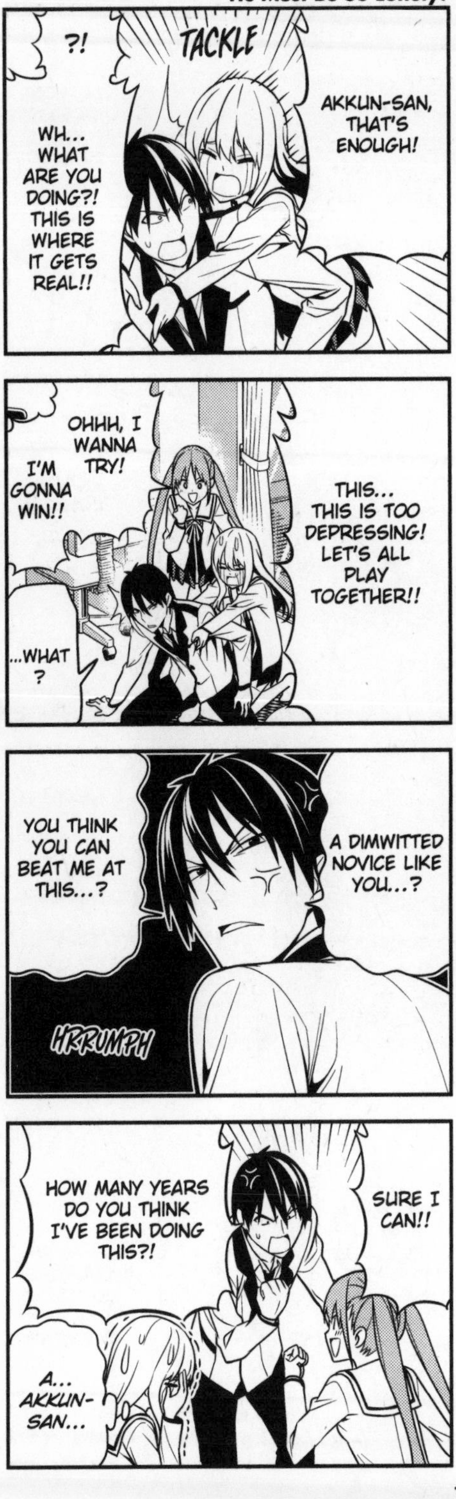
AKKUN-SAN, THAT'S ENOUGH!
TACKLE
?!
WH... WHAT ARE YOU DOING?! THIS IS WHERE IT GETS REAL!!
THIS... THIS IS TOO DEPRESSING! LET'S ALL PLAY TOGETHER!!
OHHH, I WANNA TRY!
I'M GONNA WIN!!
...WHAT ?
A DIMWITTED NOVICE LIKE YOU...?
YOU THINK YOU CAN BEAT ME AT THIS...?
HRRUMPH
SURE I CAN!!
HOW MANY YEARS DO YOU THINK I'VE BEEN DOING THIS?!
A... AKKUN-SAN...

A Wild Yoshiko Appears!

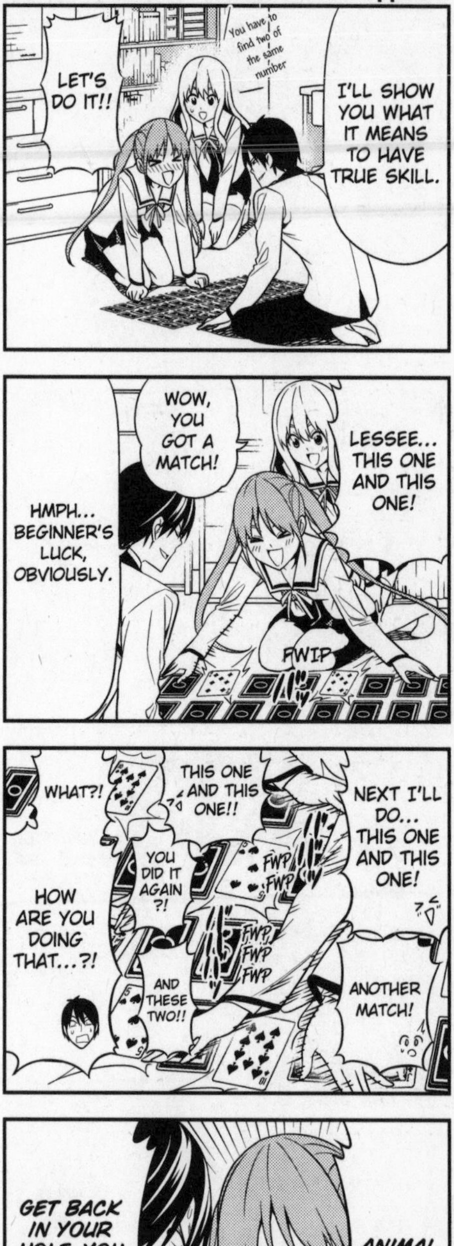
I'LL SHOW YOU WHAT IT MEANS TO HAVE TRUE SKILL.
You have to find two of the same number
LET'S DO IT!!
LESSEE... THIS ONE AND THIS ONE!
WOW, YOU GOT A MATCH!
HMPH... BEGINNER'S LUCK, OBVIOUSLY.
FWIP
NEXT I'LL DO... THIS ONE AND THIS ONE!
THIS ONE AND THIS ONE!!
WHAT?!
FWP FWP
YOU DID IT AGAIN?!
FWP FWP FWP
HOW ARE YOU DOING THAT...?!
ANOTHER MATCH!
AND THESE TWO!!
ANIMAL INSTINCT!!
GET BACK IN YOUR HOLE, YOU SNAKE!!

It's Super Effective!

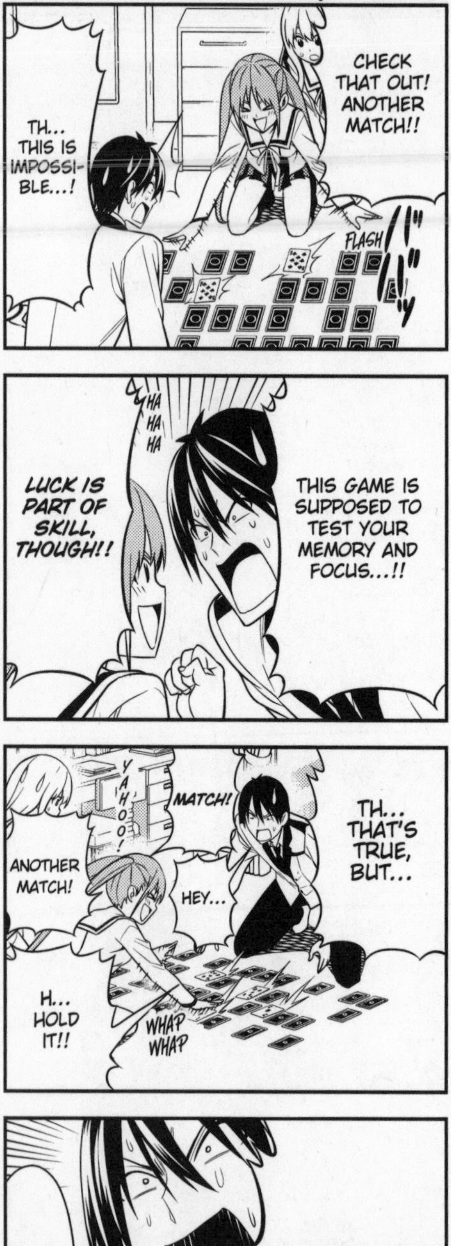
CHECK THAT OUT! ANOTHER MATCH!!
FLASH
TH... THIS IS IMPOSSIBLE...!
THIS GAME IS SUPPOSED TO TEST YOUR MEMORY AND FOCUS...!!
HA HA HA
LUCK IS PART OF SKILL, THOUGH!!
TH... THAT'S TRUE, BUT...
MATCH!
YAHOO!
HEY...
ANOTHER MATCH!
WHAP WHAP
H... HOLD IT!!
Y...YOU'RE CHEATING!!
AKKUN-SAN...

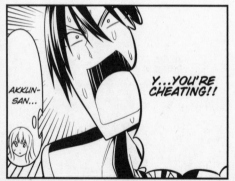

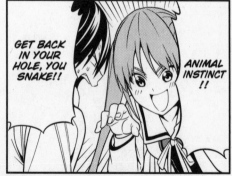

Rattled

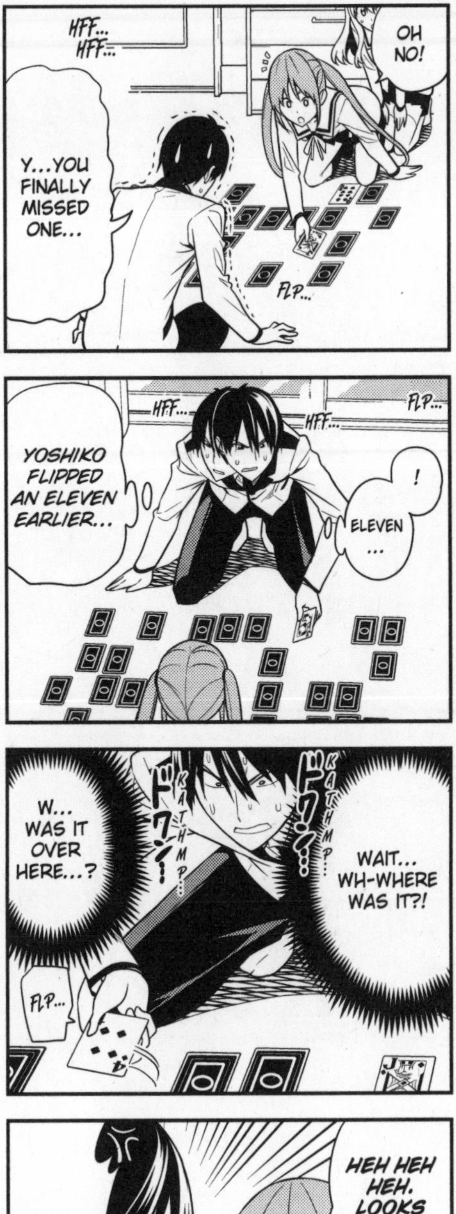
OH NO!
HFF... HFF...
Y...YOU FINALLY MISSED ONE...
FLP...
FLP...
HFF...
HFF...
!
ELEVEN...
YOSHIKO FLIPPED AN ELEVEN EARLIER...
KATHMP...
WAIT... WH-WHERE WAS IT?!
KATHMP...
W... WAS IT OVER HERE...?
FLP...
HEH HEH HEH. LOOKS LIKE YOU NEED A LITTLE MORE FOCUS, HUH?
SHUT YOUR BANANA HOLE!!

So I Can Be Myself

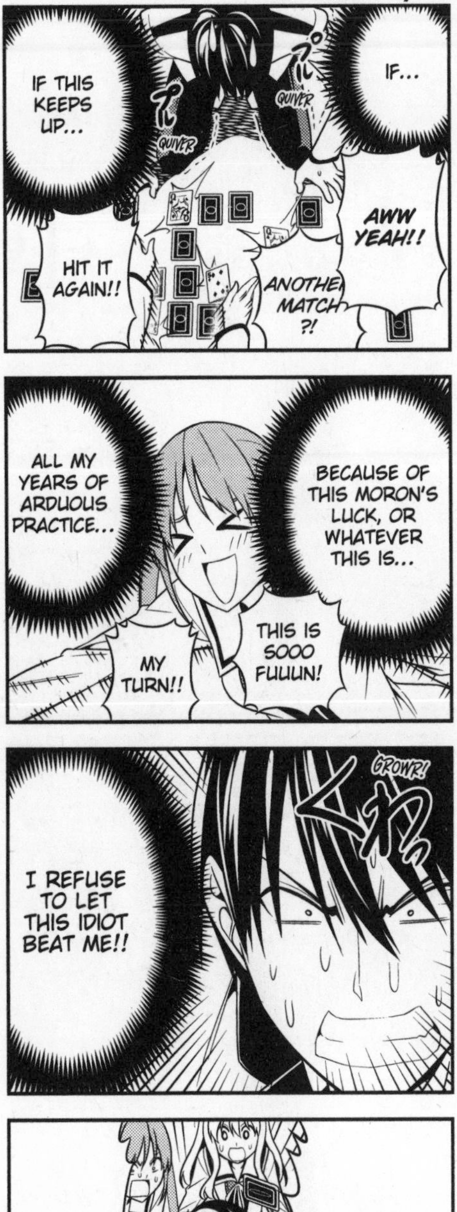
IF...
QUIVER
QUIVER
IF THIS KEEPS UP...
AWW YEAH!!
ANOTHE MATCH ?!
HIT IT AGAIN!!
BECAUSE OF THIS MORON'S LUCK, OR WHATEVER THIS IS...
ALL MY YEARS OF ARDUOUS PRACTICE...
THIS IS SOOO FUUUN!
MY TURN!!
GROWR!
I REFUSE TO LET THIS IDIOT BEAT ME!!
OH... OH NO! GOSH, MY HAND SLIPPED!!
H... HEY! NO FAAAIR!!
SCATTER

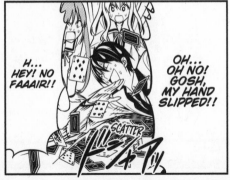

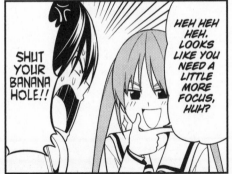

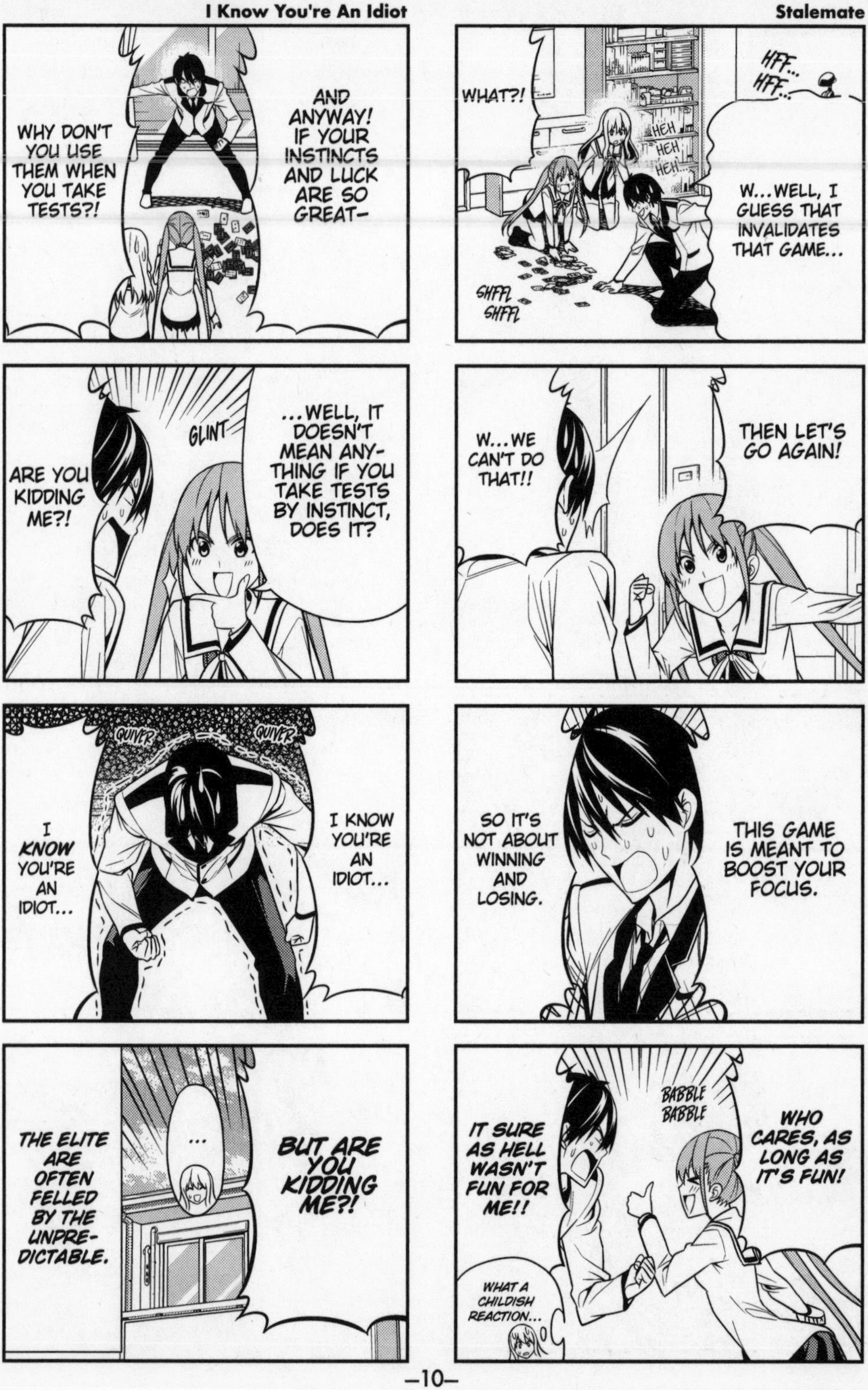
Stalemate
HFF... HFF...
WHAT?!
HEH HEH HEH...
W...WELL, I GUESS THAT INVALIDATES THAT GAME...
SHFFL SHFFL
THEN LET'S GO AGAIN!
W...WE CAN'T DO THAT!!
THIS GAME IS MEANT TO BOOST YOUR FOCUS.
SO IT'S NOT ABOUT WINNING AND LOSING.
BABBLE BABBLE
WHO CARES, AS LONG AS IT'S FUN!
IT SURE AS HELL WASN'T FUN FOR ME!!
WHAT A CHILDISH REACTION...
I Know You're An Idiot
AND ANYWAY! IF YOUR INSTINCTS AND LUCK ARE SO GREAT-
WHY DON'T YOU USE THEM WHEN YOU TAKE TESTS?!
...WELL, IT DOESN'T MEAN ANYTHING IF YOU TAKE TESTS BY INSTINCT, DOES IT?
GLINT
ARE YOU KIDDING ME?!
QUIVER QUIVER
I KNOW YOU'RE AN IDIOT...
I KNOW YOU'RE AN IDIOT...
BUT ARE YOU KIDDING ME?!
...
THE ELITE ARE OFTEN FELLED BY THE UNPREDICTABLE.

Defend the Inner Sanctum

GO, GET OUT OF HERE!
EEEK!!
POIK
B...BUT AKKUN-SAN!
IF YOU WANT, I'LL PLAY THAT GAME WITH YOU WHENEVER YOU WANT!
THANKS SO MUCH!!

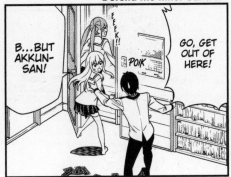

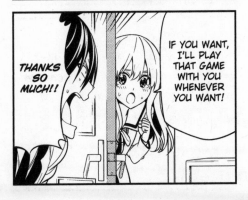

(Men may be tortured, men may feel sadness, because of)

Aho-Girl

\\'ahô,ɡərl\\ *Japanese , noun.*
A clueless girl.

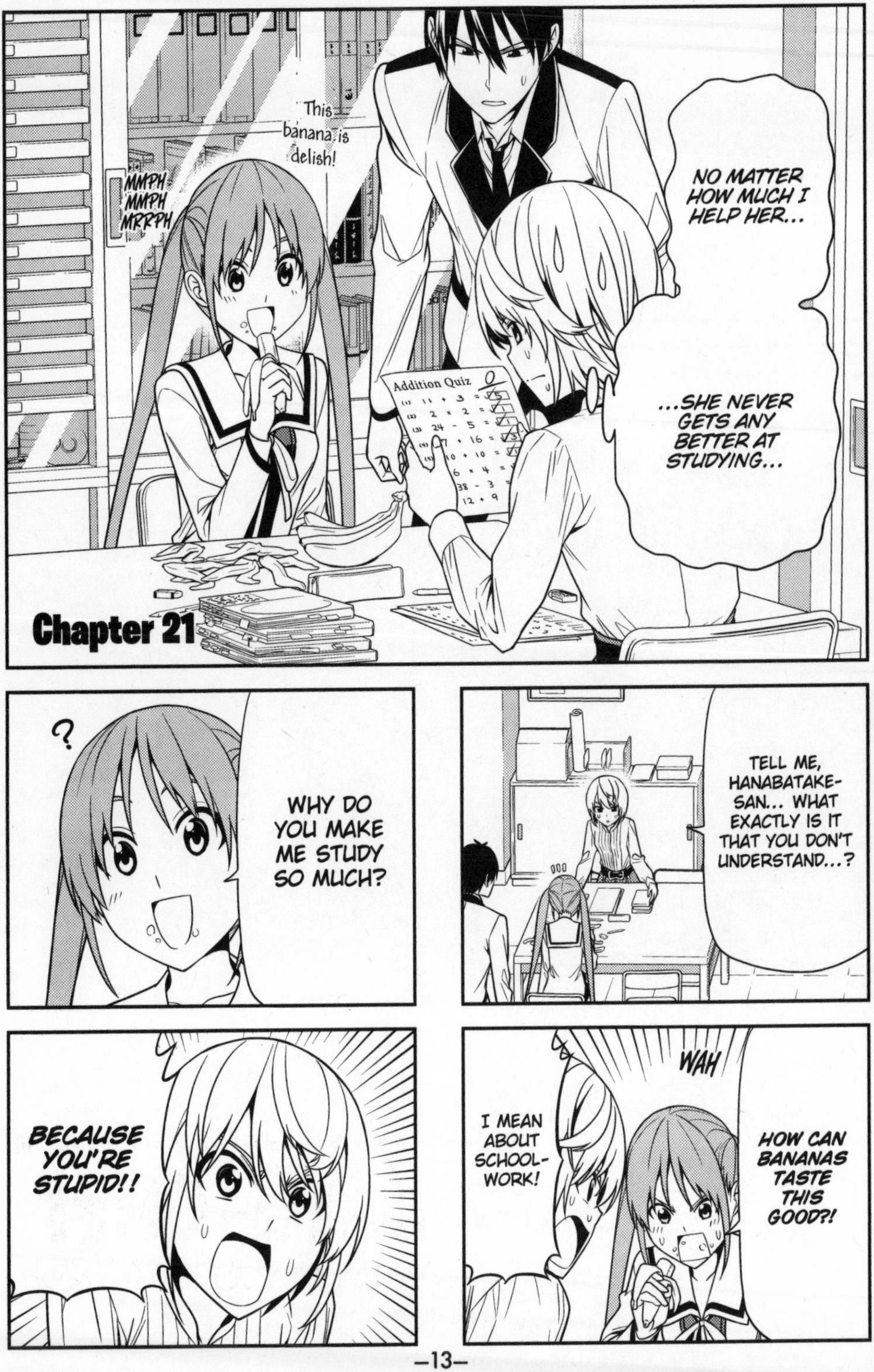
NO MATTER HOW MUCH I HELP HER...
...SHE NEVER GETS ANY BETTER AT STUDYING...
This banana is delish!
MMPH MMPH MRRPH
Addition Quiz
Chapter 21
TELL ME, HANABATAKE-SAN... WHAT EXACTLY IS IT THAT YOU DON'T UNDERSTAND...?
?
WHY DO YOU MAKE ME STUDY SO MUCH?
HOW CAN BANANAS TASTE THIS GOOD?!
WAH
I MEAN ABOUT SCHOOL-WORK!
BECAUSE YOU'RE STUPID!!

Akkun's Shown Her So Many Times...

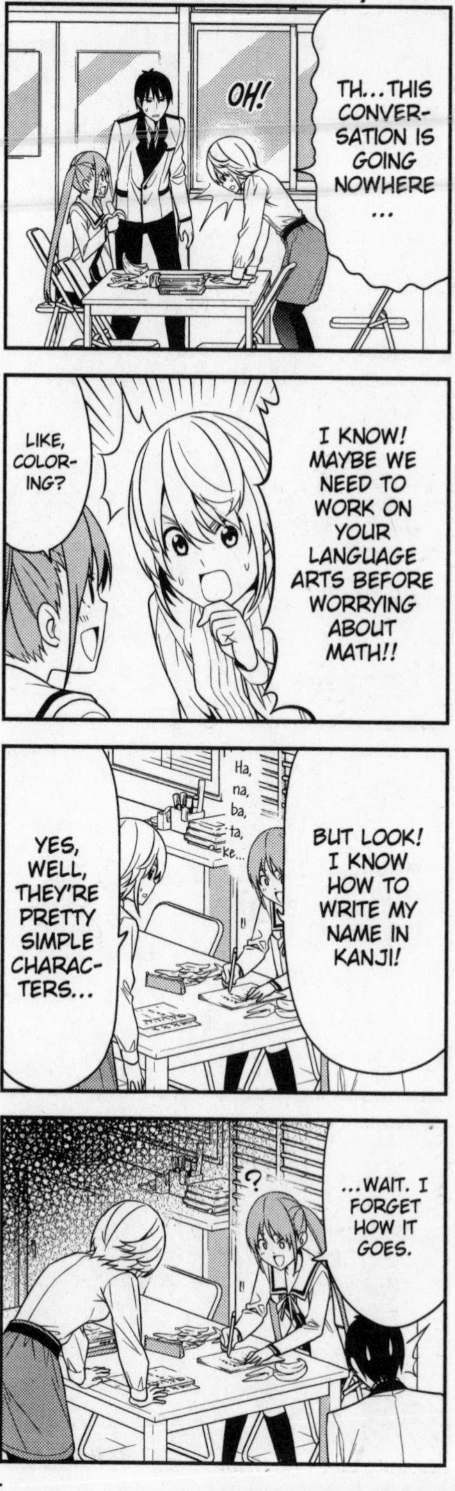
TH...THIS CONVERSATION IS GOING NOWHERE ...
OH!
I KNOW! MAYBE WE NEED TO WORK ON YOUR LANGUAGE ARTS BEFORE WORRYING ABOUT MATH!!
LIKE, COLORING?
BUT LOOK! I KNOW HOW TO WRITE MY NAME IN KANJI!
Ha, na, ba, ta, ke...
YES, WELL, THEY'RE PRETTY SIMPLE CHARACTERS...
...WAIT. I FORGET HOW IT GOES.
?

Relying on You

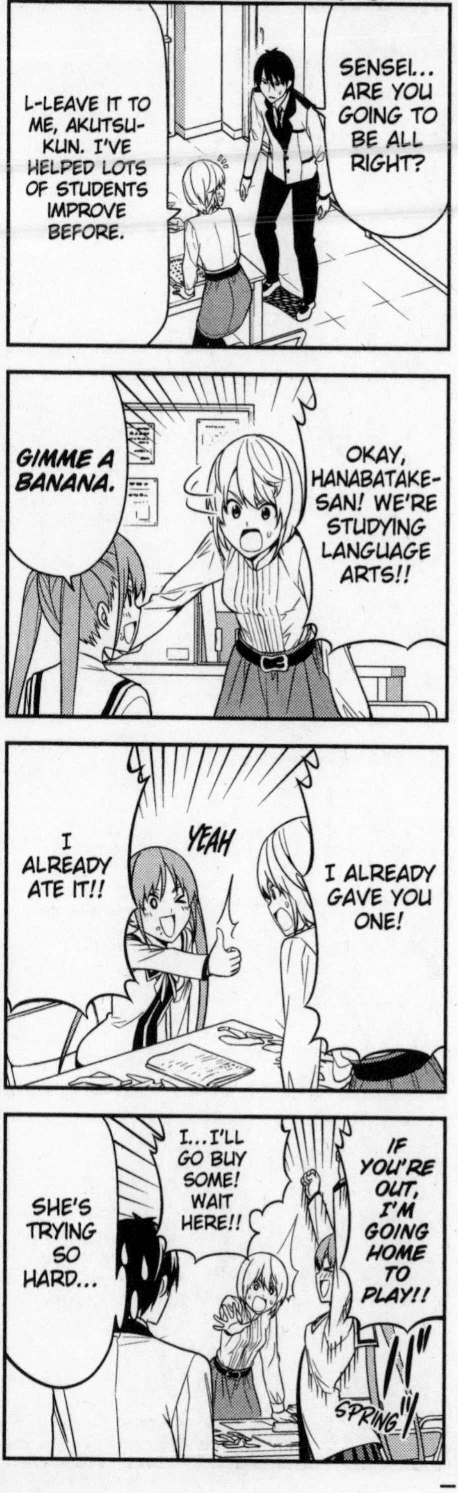
SENSEI... ARE YOU GOING TO BE ALL RIGHT?
L-LEAVE IT TO ME, AKUTSU-KUN. I'VE HELPED LOTS OF STUDENTS IMPROVE BEFORE.
OKAY, HANABATAKE-SAN! WE'RE STUDYING LANGUAGE ARTS!!
GIMME A BANANA.
I ALREADY GAVE YOU ONE!
YEAH
I ALREADY ATE IT!!
IF YOU'RE OUT, I'M GOING HOME TO PLAY!!
SPRING
I...I'LL GO BUY SOME! WAIT HERE!!
SHE'S TRYING SO HARD...

It's Got a Pronunciation Guide on It

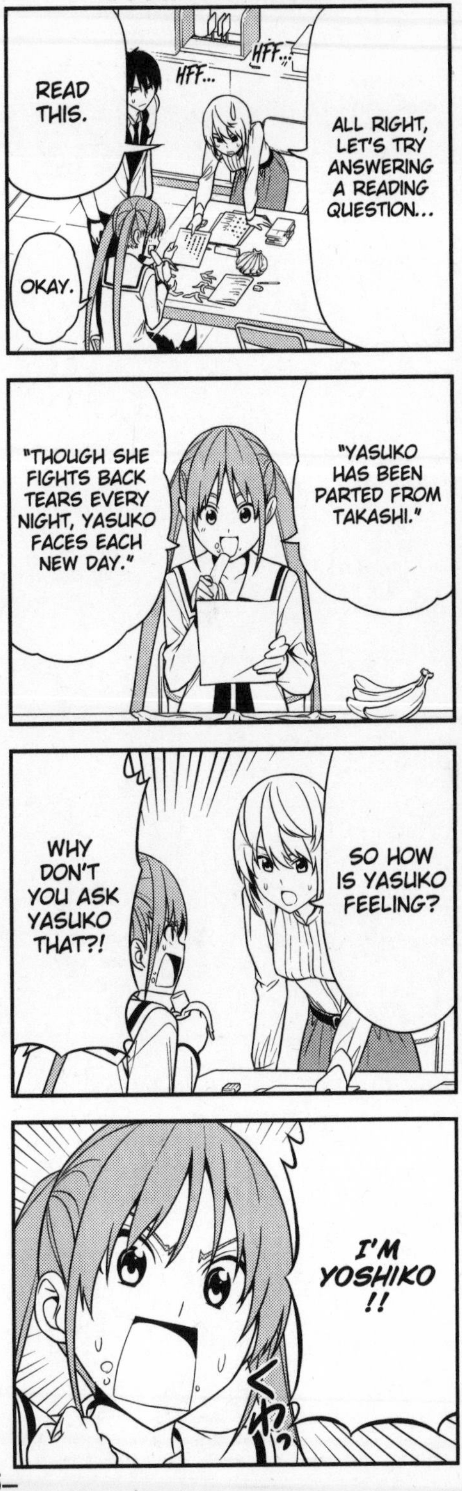
ALL RIGHT, LET'S TRY ANSWERING A READING QUESTION...
HFF... HFF...
READ THIS.
OKAY.
"YASUKO HAS BEEN PARTED FROM TAKASHI."
"THOUGH SHE FIGHTS BACK TEARS EVERY NIGHT, YASUKO FACES EACH NEW DAY."
SO HOW IS YASUKO FEELING?
WHY DON'T YOU ASK YASUKO THAT?!
I'M YOSHIKO!!
くわっ

Reading Comprehension

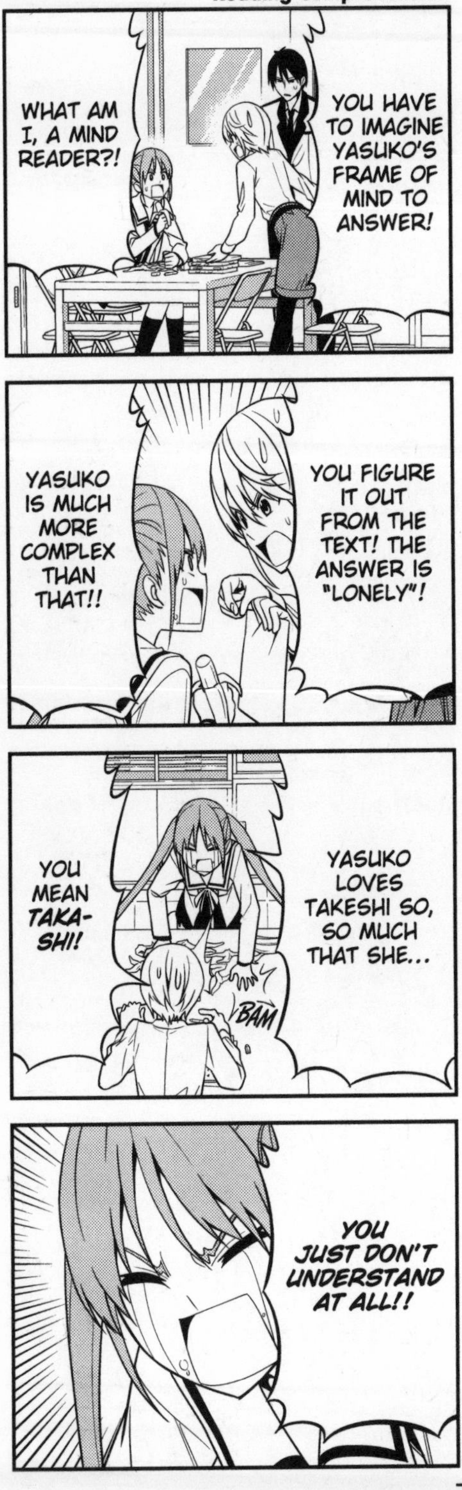
YOU HAVE TO IMAGINE YASUKO'S FRAME OF MIND TO ANSWER!
WHAT AM I, A MIND READER?!
YOU FIGURE IT OUT FROM THE TEXT! THE ANSWER IS "LONELY"!
YASUKO IS MUCH MORE COMPLEX THAN THAT!!
YASUKO LOVES TAKESHI SO, SO MUCH THAT SHE...
BAM
YOU MEAN TAKA-SHI!
YOU JUST DON'T UNDERSTAND AT ALL!!

Question

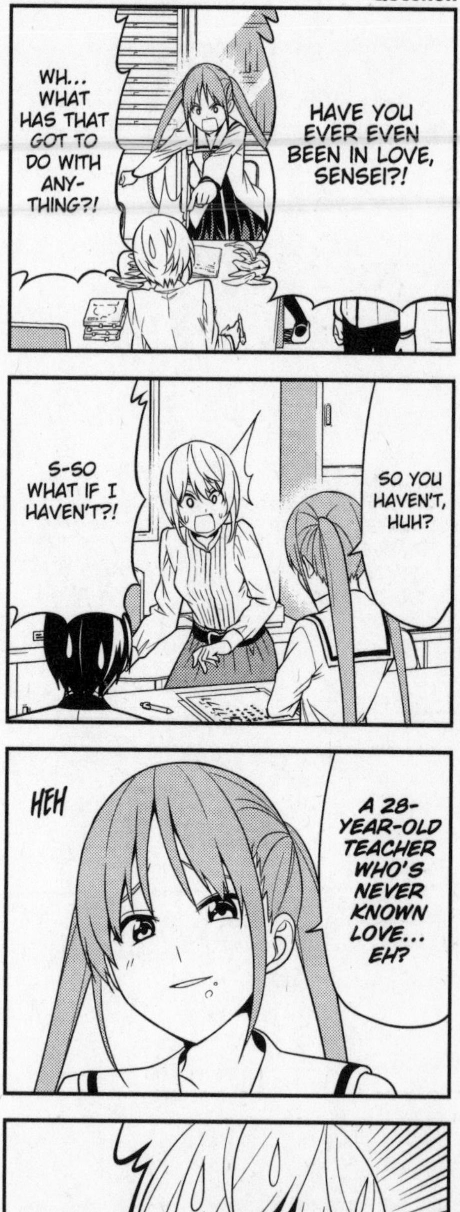
HAVE YOU EVER EVEN BEEN IN LOVE, SENSEI?!
WH... WHAT HAS THAT GOT TO DO WITH ANYTHING?!
SO YOU HAVEN'T, HUH?
S-SO WHAT IF I HAVEN'T?!
A 28-YEAR-OLD TEACHER WHO'S NEVER KNOWN LOVE... EH?
HEH
SO WHAT?!

The Shocking Truth

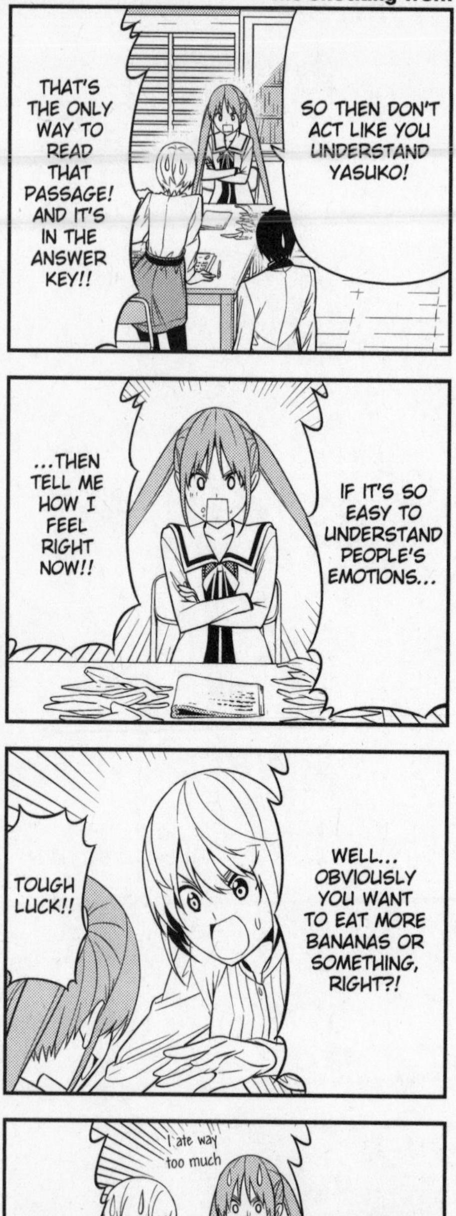
SO THEN DON'T ACT LIKE YOU UNDERSTAND YASUKO!
THAT'S THE ONLY WAY TO READ THAT PASSAGE! AND IT'S IN THE ANSWER KEY!!
IF IT'S SO EASY TO UNDERSTAND PEOPLE'S EMOTIONS...
...THEN TELL ME HOW I FEEL RIGHT NOW!!
WELL... OBVIOUSLY YOU WANT TO EAT MORE BANANAS OR SOMETHING, RIGHT?!
TOUGH LUCK!!
I ate way too much
IN ACTUAL FACT, I'M SO FULL I KIND OF WANT TO PUKE!!
HOW WOULD I KNOW THAT?!

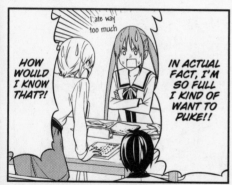

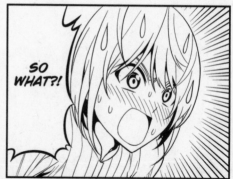

An Idiot's Wisdom

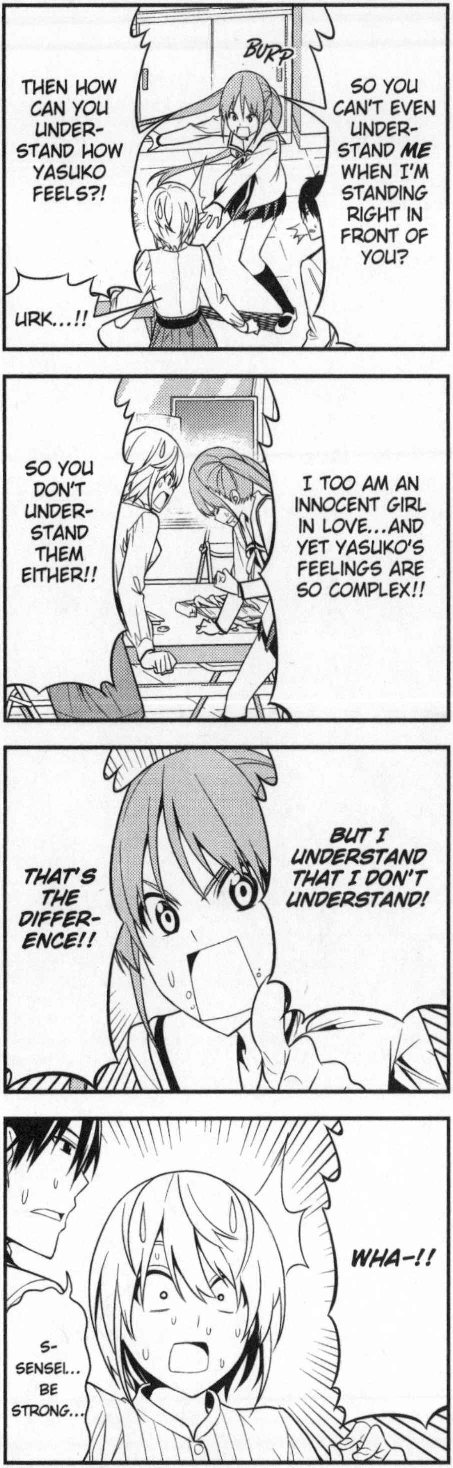
SO YOU CAN'T EVEN UNDERSTAND *ME* WHEN I'M STANDING RIGHT IN FRONT OF YOU?
BURP
THEN HOW CAN YOU UNDERSTAND HOW YASUKO FEELS?!
URK...!!
I TOO AM AN INNOCENT GIRL IN LOVE...AND YET YASUKO'S FEELINGS ARE SO COMPLEX!!
SO YOU DON'T UNDERSTAND THEM EITHER!!
BUT I UNDERSTAND THAT I DON'T UNDERSTAND!
THAT'S THE DIFFERENCE!!
WHA-!!
S-SENSEI... BE STRONG...

We're Not Making Oranges or Machines Here

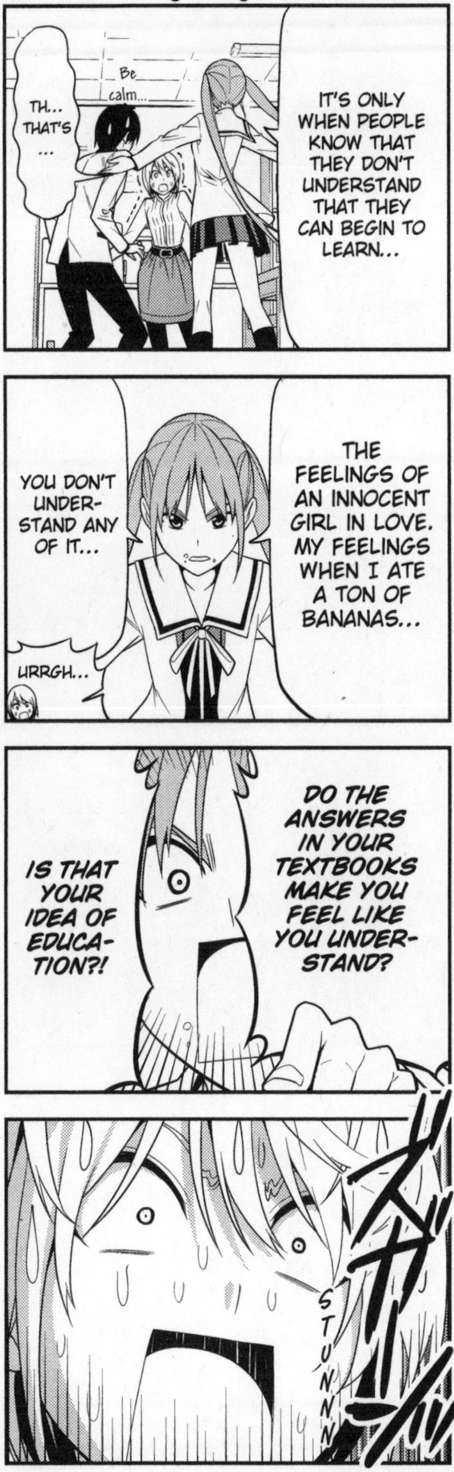
IT'S ONLY WHEN PEOPLE KNOW THAT THEY DON'T UNDERSTAND THAT THEY CAN BEGIN TO LEARN...
Be calm...
TH... THAT'S ...
THE FEELINGS OF AN INNOCENT GIRL IN LOVE. MY FEELINGS WHEN I ATE A TON OF BANANAS...
YOU DON'T UNDERSTAND ANY OF IT...
URRGH...
DO THE ANSWERS IN YOUR TEXTBOOKS MAKE YOU FEEL LIKE YOU UNDERSTAND?
IS THAT YOUR IDEA OF EDUCATION?!
STUNNNN

Fall to Temptation

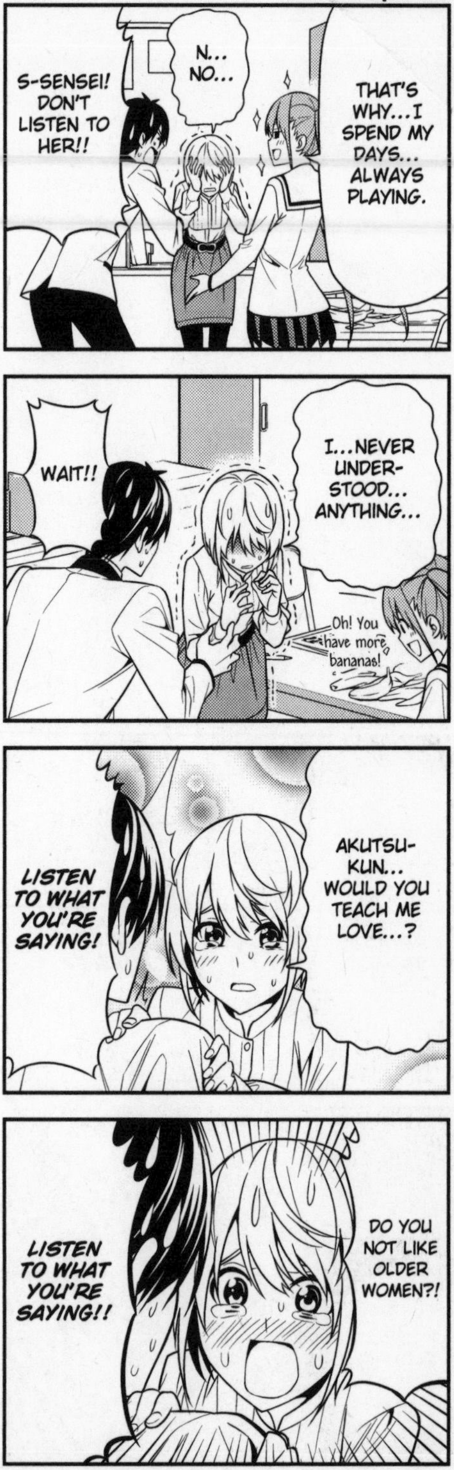
THAT'S WHY...I SPEND MY DAYS... ALWAYS PLAYING.
N... NO...
S-SENSEI! DON'T LISTEN TO HER!!
I...NEVER UNDERSTOOD... ANYTHING...
WAIT!!
Oh! You have more bananas!
AKUTSU-KUN... WOULD YOU TEACH ME LOVE...?
LISTEN TO WHAT YOU'RE SAYING!
DO YOU NOT LIKE OLDER WOMEN?!
LISTEN TO WHAT YOU'RE SAYING!!

Guidance

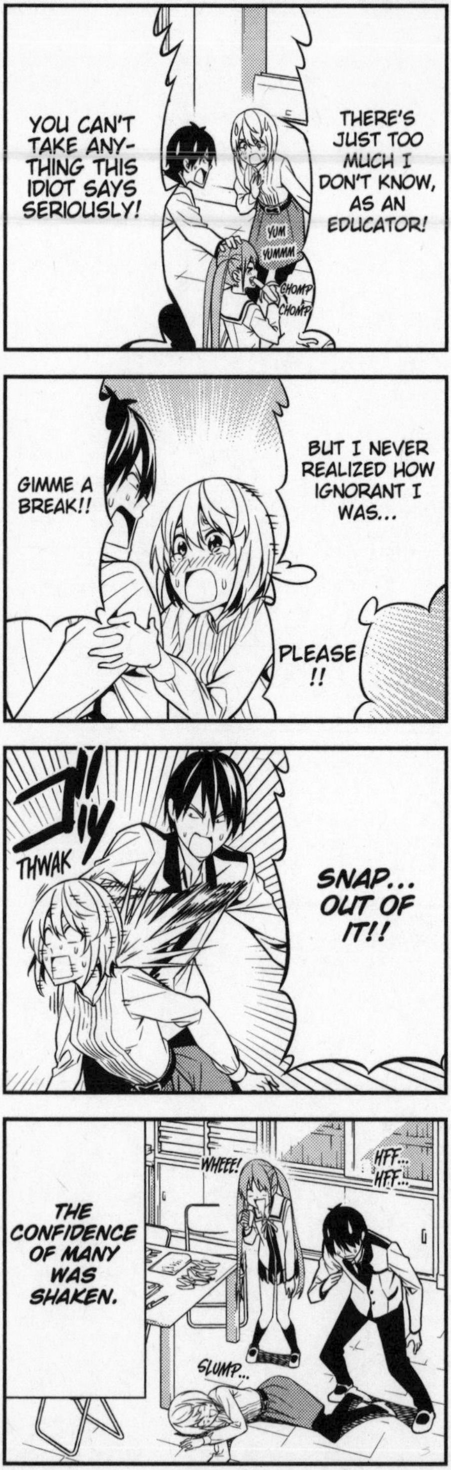
THERE'S JUST TOO MUCH I DON'T KNOW, AS AN EDUCATOR!
YUM YUMMM
CHOMP CHOMP
YOU CAN'T TAKE ANYTHING THIS IDIOT SAYS SERIOUSLY!
BUT I NEVER REALIZED HOW IGNORANT I WAS...
PLEASE!!
GIMME A BREAK!!
SNAP... OUT OF IT!!
ゴッ
THWAK
WHEEE!
HFF... HFF...
SLUMP...
THE CONFIDENCE OF MANY WAS SHAKEN.

There Doesn't Seem Like Much Chance of That

PLEASE, SENSEI...
IF YOU GIVE UP, THERE WON'T BE ANYONE TO TEACH YOSHIKO TO STUDY...
TWITCH
TWITCH
...P... PLEASE...

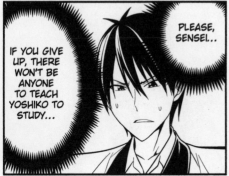

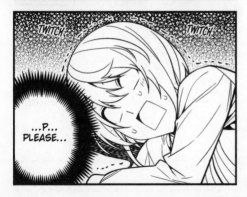

Name	**Teacher (Atsuko Oshieda)**

Sex	
Height	**158 cm / 5'2"**
Weight	**49 kg / 108 lbs**
Blood type	**A**
Birthday	**02/18**

Memo

Homeroom teacher for Yoshiko and Akkun's class. Teaches math.

She is passionate about education, but because she takes everything very seriously, she ends up accepting Yoshiko's idiotic arguments far too readily.

Has always attended all-girls schools, and so has no romantic experience. She hasn't given much thought to it until recently…

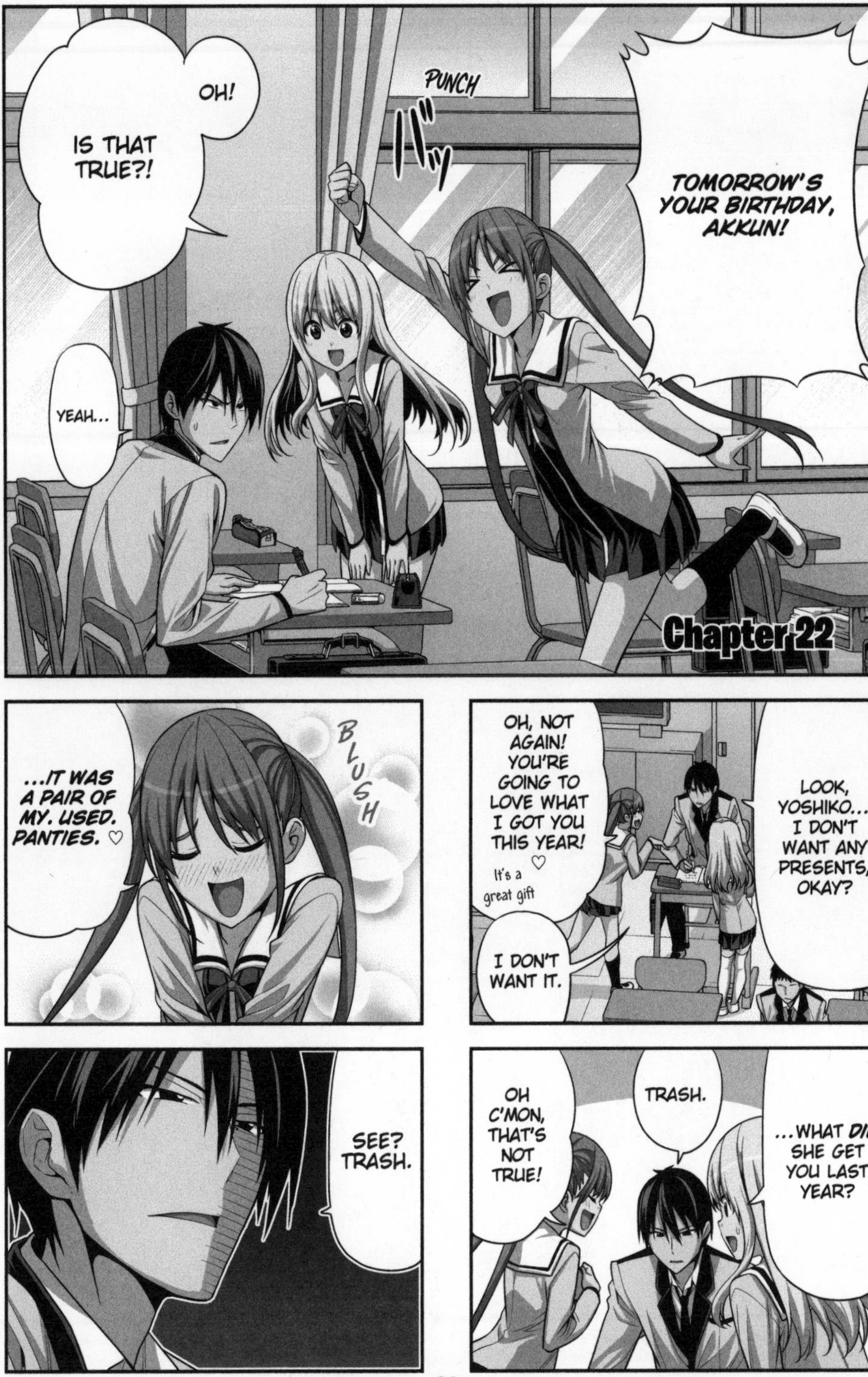
TOMORROW'S YOUR BIRTHDAY, AKKUN!
PUNCH
OH!
IS THAT TRUE?!
YEAH...
Chapter 22
LOOK, YOSHIKO... I DON'T WANT ANY PRESENTS, OKAY?
OH, NOT AGAIN! YOU'RE GOING TO LOVE WHAT I GOT YOU THIS YEAR! ♡
It's a great gift
I DON'T WANT IT.
BLUSH
...IT WAS A PAIR OF MY. USED. PANTIES. ♡
...WHAT *DID* SHE GET YOU LAST YEAR?
TRASH.
OH C'MON, THAT'S NOT TRUE!
SEE? TRASH.

His Parents Are Busy People

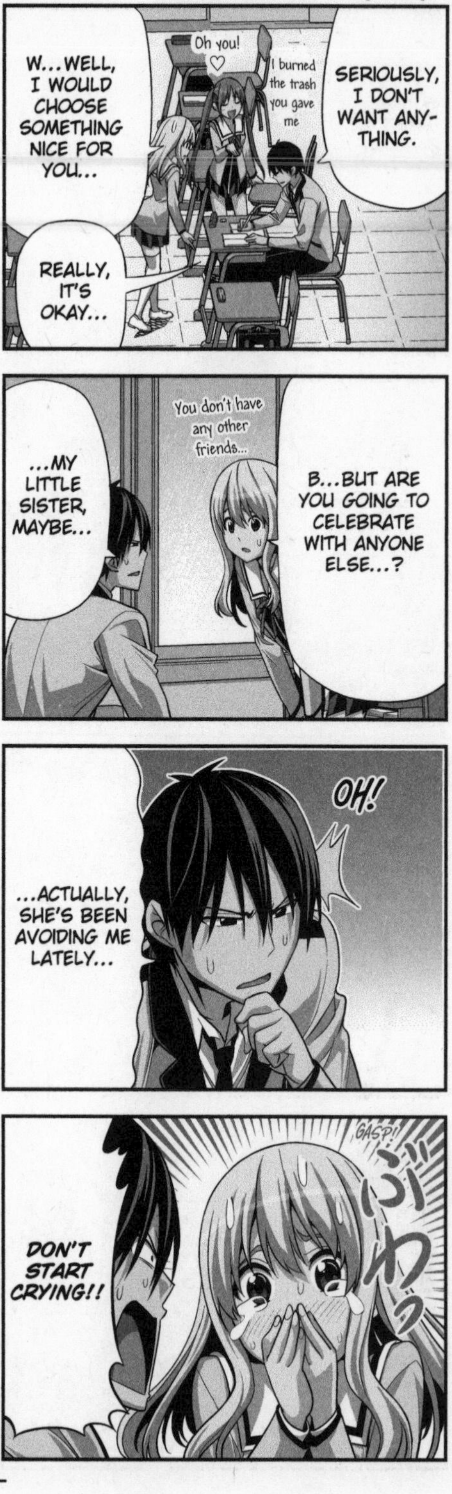
SERIOUSLY, I DON'T WANT ANYTHING.
I burned the trash you gave me
Oh you! ♡
W...WELL, I WOULD CHOOSE SOMETHING NICE FOR YOU...
REALLY, IT'S OKAY...
B...BUT ARE YOU GOING TO CELEBRATE WITH ANYONE ELSE...?
You don't have any other friends...
...MY LITTLE SISTER, MAYBE...
OH!
...ACTUALLY, SHE'S BEEN AVOIDING ME LATELY...
GASP!
ぶわっ
DON'T START CRYING!!

She Means, Him Getting Mad

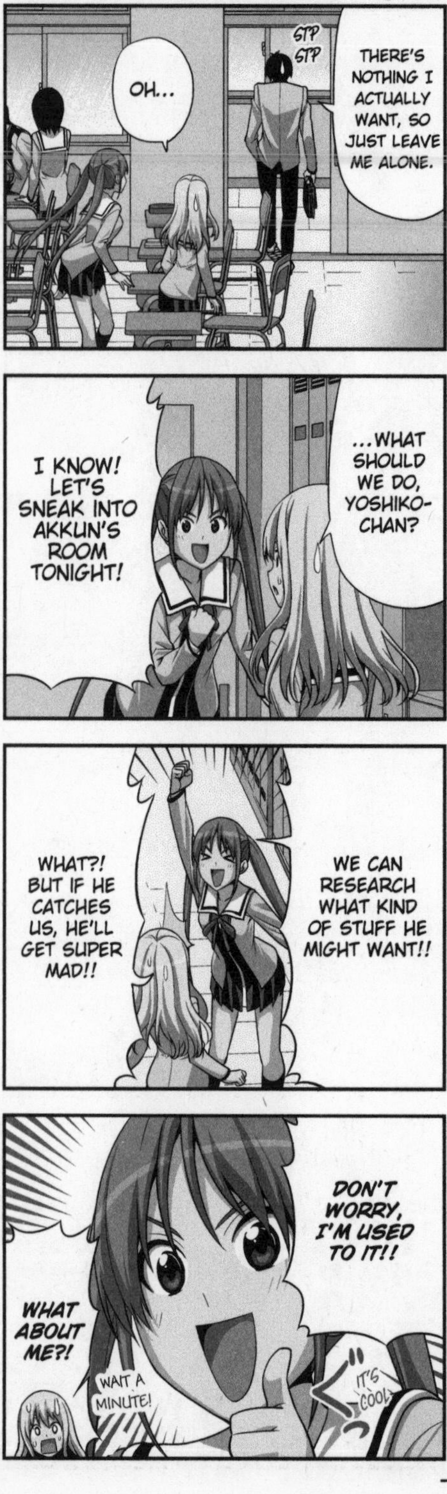
THERE'S NOTHING I ACTUALLY WANT, SO JUST LEAVE ME ALONE.
STP STP
OH...
...WHAT SHOULD WE DO, YOSHIKO-CHAN?
I KNOW! LET'S SNEAK INTO AKKUN'S ROOM TONIGHT!
WE CAN RESEARCH WHAT KIND OF STUFF HE MIGHT WANT!!
WHAT?! BUT IF HE CATCHES US, HE'LL GET SUPER MAD!!
DON'T WORRY, I'M USED TO IT!!
IT'S COOL
WHAT ABOUT ME?!
WAIT A MINUTE!

A Very Kibayashi-like Entrance

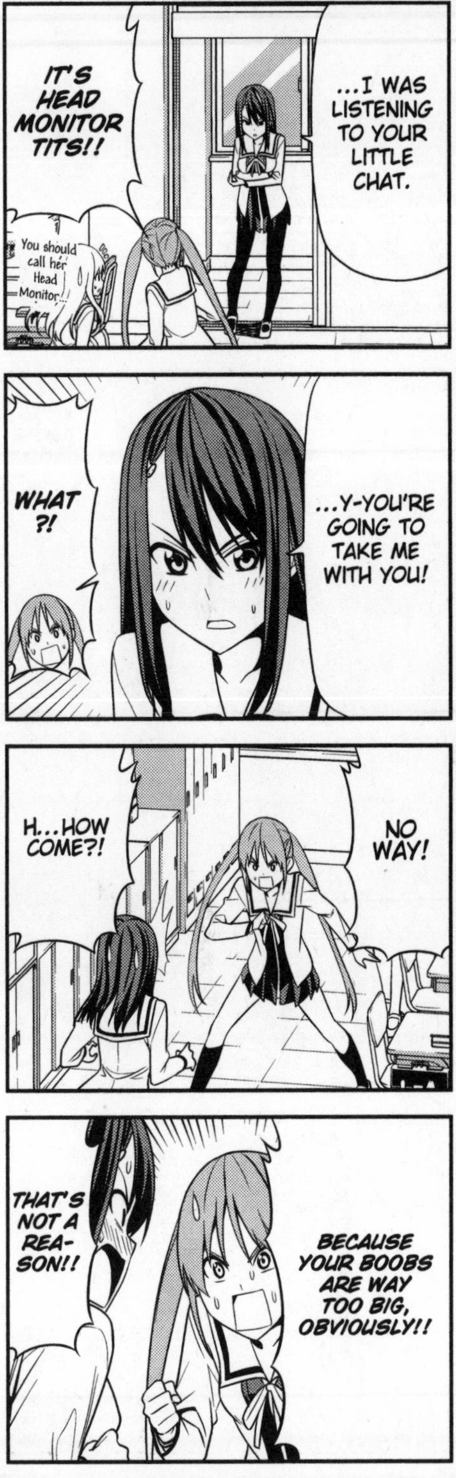

...I WAS LISTENING TO YOUR LITTLE CHAT.
IT'S HEAD MONITOR TITS!!
You should call her Head Monitor...
...Y-YOU'RE GOING TO TAKE ME WITH YOU!
WHAT?!
NO WAY!
H...HOW COME?!
BECAUSE YOUR BOOBS ARE WAY TOO BIG, OBVIOUSLY!!
THAT'S NOT A REA-SON!!

Snap Decision

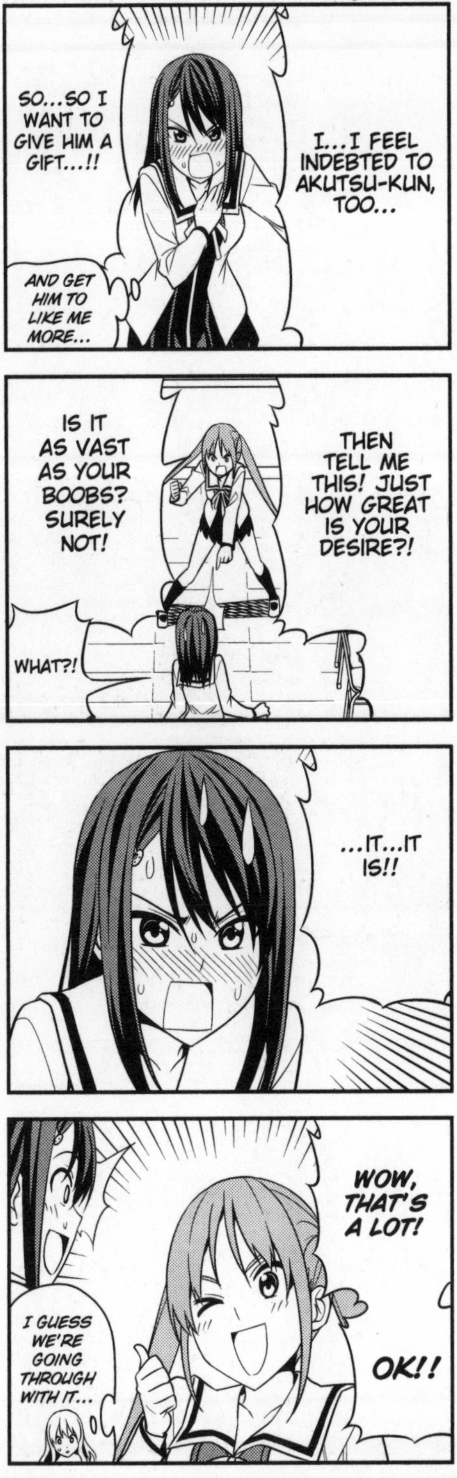

I...I FEEL INDEBTED TO AKUTSU-KUN, TOO...
SO...SO I WANT TO GIVE HIM A GIFT...!!
AND GET HIM TO LIKE ME MORE...
THEN TELL ME THIS! JUST HOW GREAT IS YOUR DESIRE?!
IS IT AS VAST AS YOUR BOOBS? SURELY NOT!
WHAT?!
...IT...IT IS!!
WOW, THAT'S A LOT!
OK!!
I GUESS WE'RE GOING THROUGH WITH IT...

Sayaka Jumps

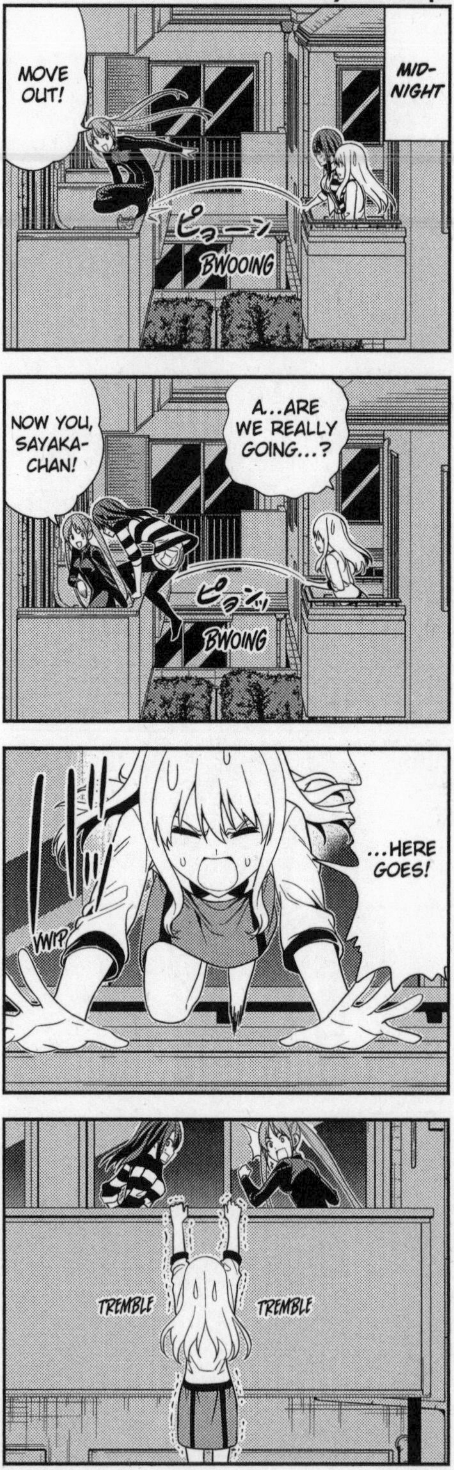
MID-NIGHT
MOVE OUT!
ピューン
BWOOING
A...ARE WE REALLY GOING...?
NOW YOU, SAYAKA-CHAN!
ピョンッ
BWOING
...HERE GOES!
VWIP
TREMBLE
TREMBLE

Crime Prevention

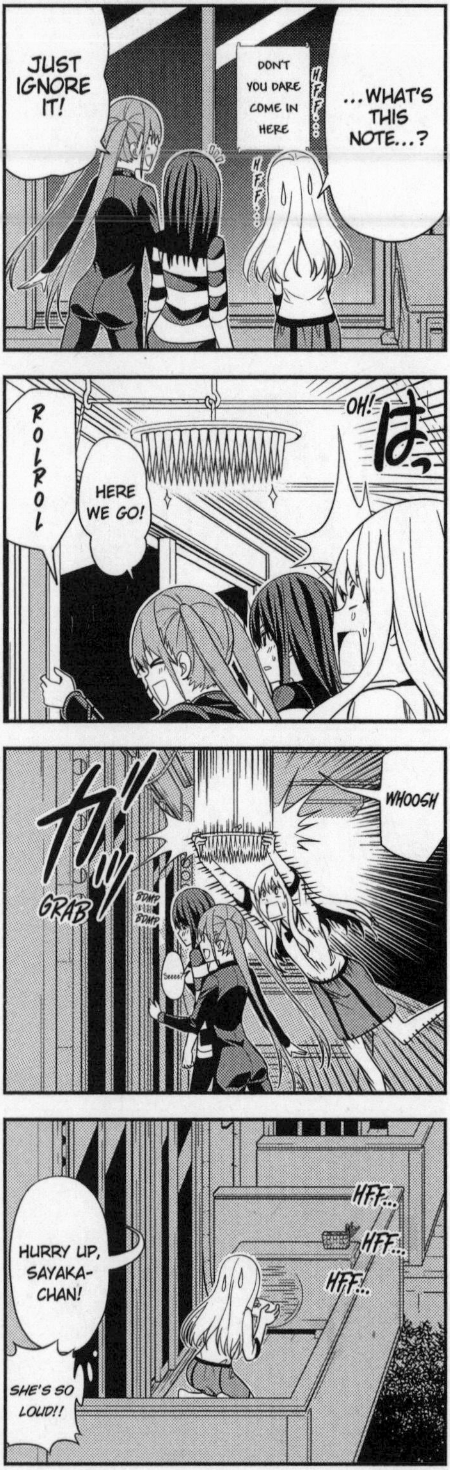
...WHAT'S THIS NOTE...?
DON'T YOU DARE COME IN HERE
HFF...
HFF...
JUST IGNORE IT!
OH!
は
HERE WE GO!
ROLROL
WHOOSH
ガッ
GRAB
BDMP BDMP
HFF...
HFF...
HFF...
HURRY UP, SAYAKA-CHAN!
SHE'S SO LOUD!!

This Is Happening

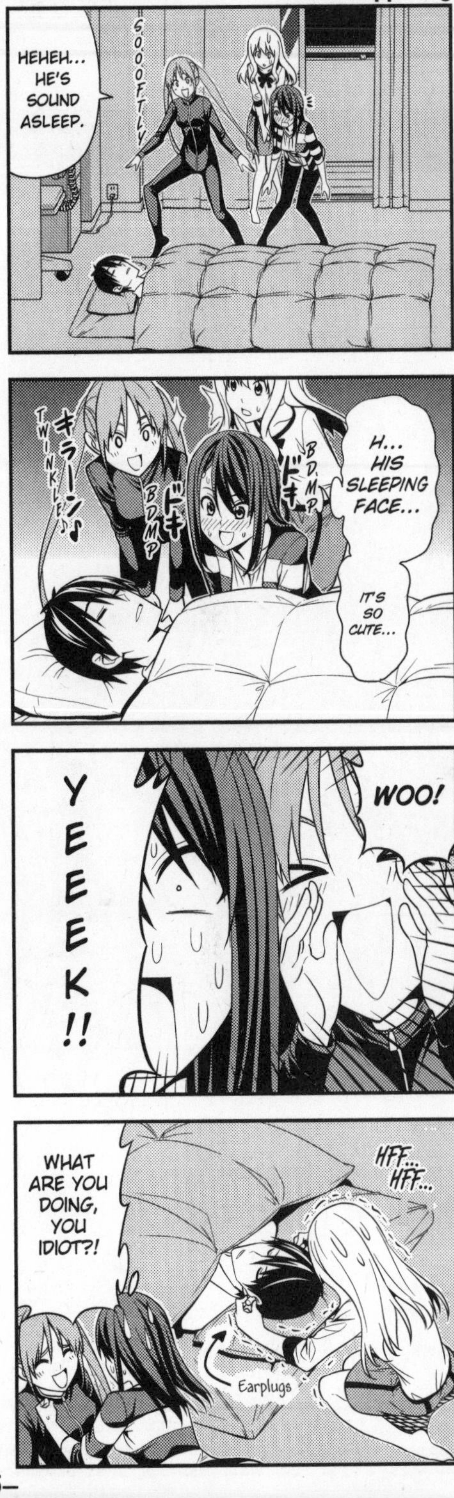
SOOOFTLY
HEHEH... HE'S SOUND ASLEEP.
H... HIS SLEEPING FACE...
IT'S SO CUTE...
ドキ BDMP
ドキ BDMP
キラーン♪ TWINKLE♪
WOO!
YEEEEK!!
HFF... HFF...
WHAT ARE YOU DOING, YOU IDIOT?!
Earplugs

Automatic Flash

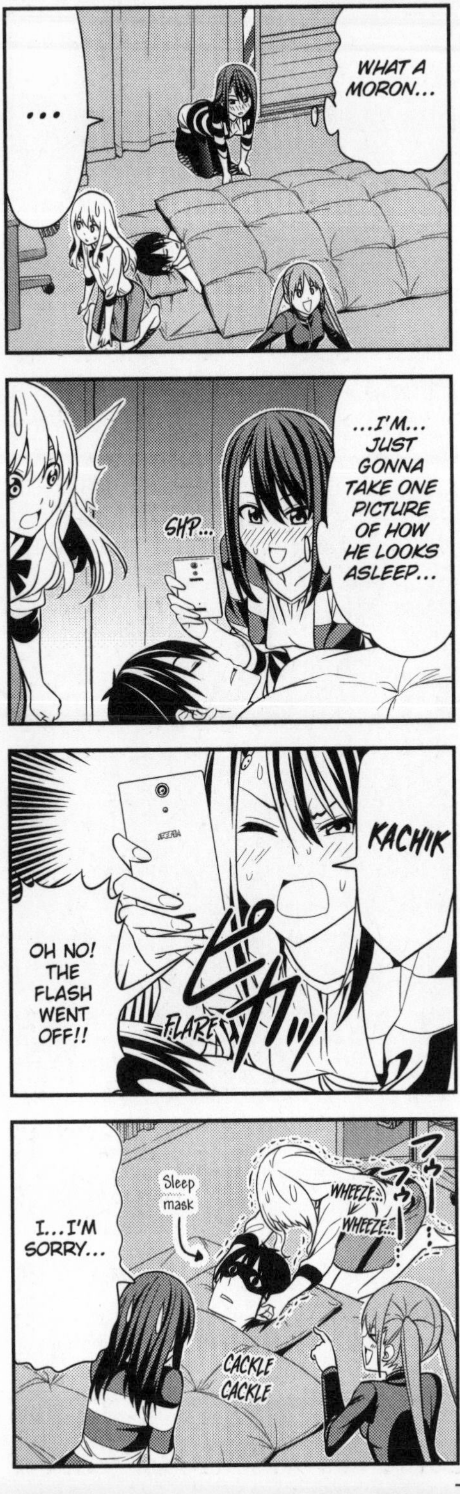
WHAT A MORON...
...
...I'M... JUST GONNA TAKE ONE PICTURE OF HOW HE LOOKS ASLEEP...
SHP...
KACHIK
ピカッ FLARE
OH NO! THE FLASH WENT OFF!!
フゥー フゥー
WHEEZE... WHEEZE...
Sleep mask
I...I'M SORRY...
CACKLE CACKLE

A Discovery!

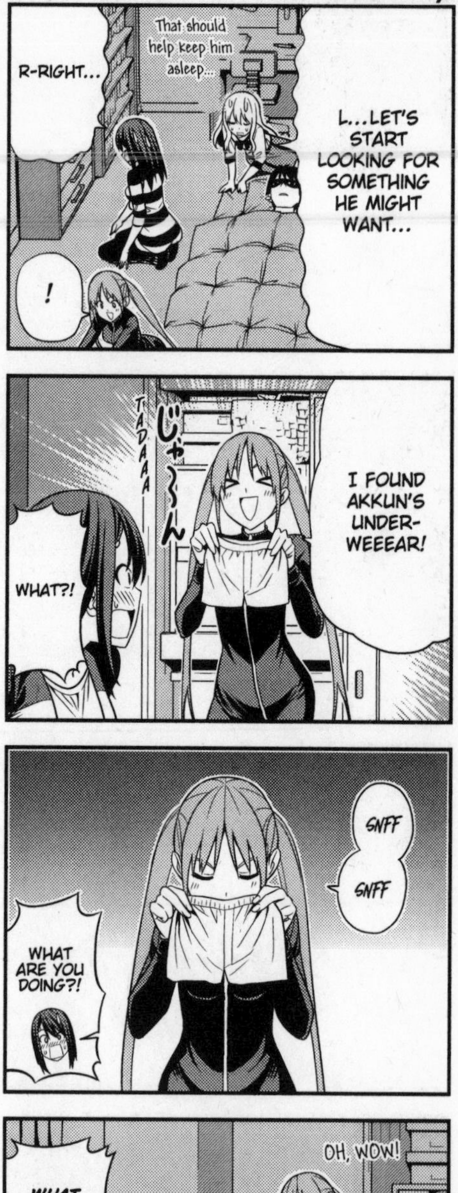
L...LET'S START LOOKING FOR SOMETHING HE MIGHT WANT...
That should help keep him asleep...
R-RIGHT...
!
I FOUND AKKUN'S UNDER-WEEEAR!
TADAAA
WHAT?!
SNFF
SNFF
WHAT ARE YOU DOING?!
OH, WOW!
WHAT DOES THAT MEAN?!
P... PLEASE BE QUIET-ER...

Cameo Over

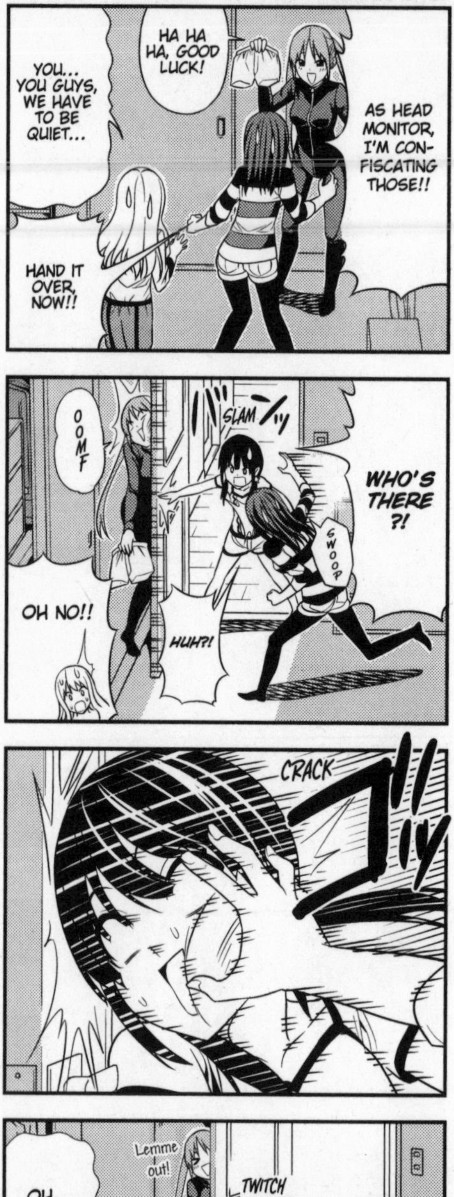
AS HEAD MONITOR, I'M CON-FISCATING THOSE!!
HA HA HA, GOOD LUCK!
YOU... YOU GUYS, WE HAVE TO BE QUIET...
HAND IT OVER, NOW!!
WHO'S THERE?!
SLAM
SWOOP
OOMF
HUH?!
OH NO!!
CRACK
OH NO!
TWITCH TWITCH
Lemme out!
OH... OH MY GOSH...

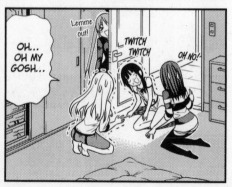

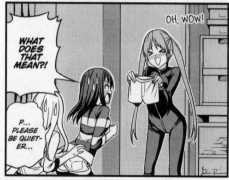

Single Bed

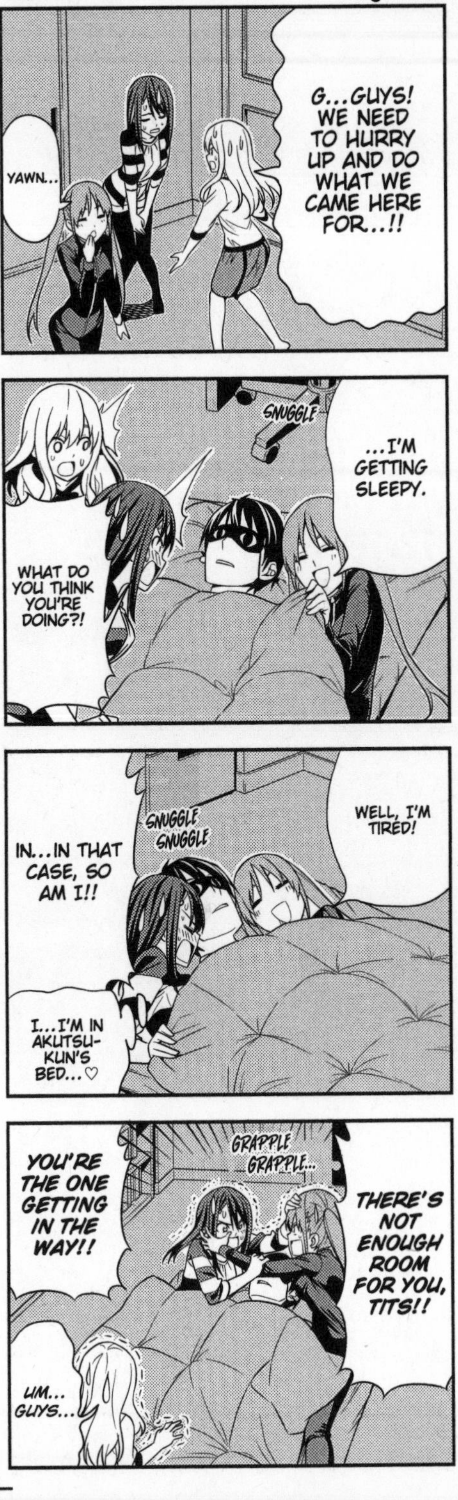
G...GUYS! WE NEED TO HURRY UP AND DO WHAT WE CAME HERE FOR...!!
YAWN...
...I'M GETTING SLEEPY.
SNUGGLE
WHAT DO YOU THINK YOU'RE DOING?!
WELL, I'M TIRED!
SNUGGLE SNUGGLE
IN...IN THAT CASE, SO AM I!!
I...I'M IN AKUTSU-KUN'S BED...♡
THERE'S NOT ENOUGH ROOM FOR YOU, TITS!!
GRAPPLE GRAPPLE...
YOU'RE THE ONE GETTING IN THE WAY!!
UM... GUYS...

Elbowing

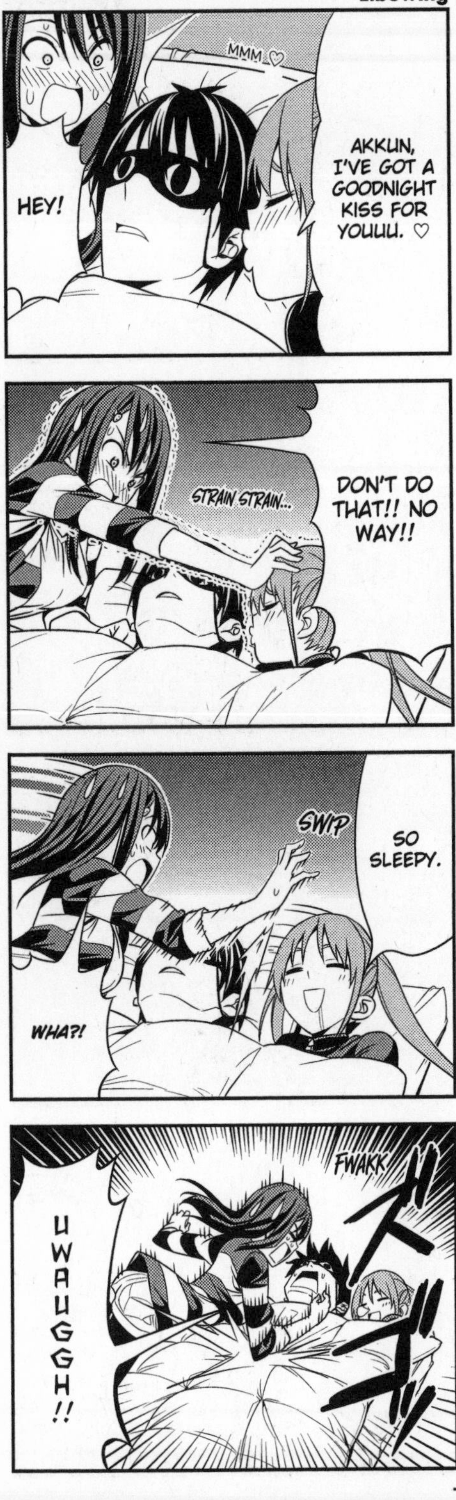
AKKUN, I'VE GOT A GOODNIGHT KISS FOR YOUUU. ♡
MMM ♡
HEY!
DON'T DO THAT!! NO WAY!!
STRAIN STRAIN...
SO SLEEPY.
SWIP
WHA?!
FWAKK
UWAUGGH!!

Sure, That Would Wake You Up

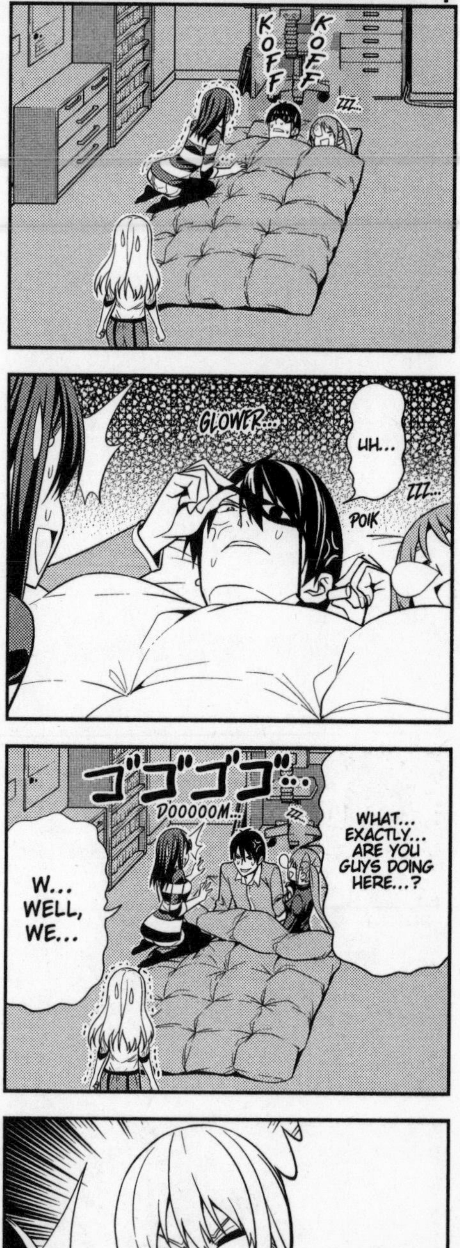
KOFF
KOFF
ZZZ...
GLOWER...
UH...
ZZZ...
POIK
ゴゴゴゴゴ...
DOOOOOM...
ZZZ...
WHAT... EXACTLY... ARE YOU GUYS DOING HERE...?
W... WELL, WE...
I COMPLETELY AGREE!!
WOAH-
ぎょっ

Sure, That Would Make You Mad

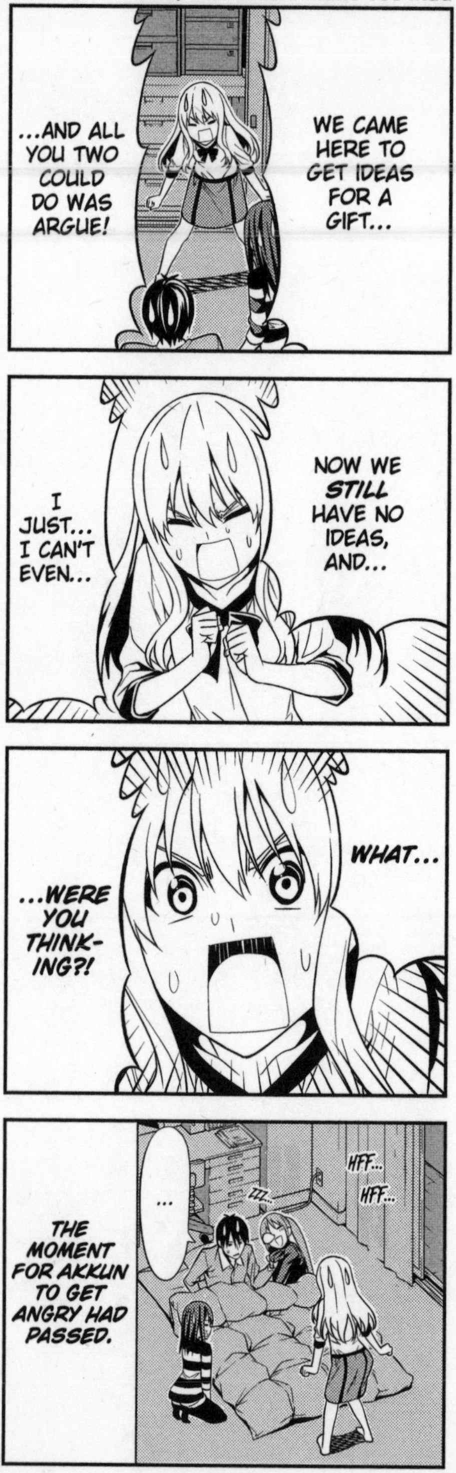
WE CAME HERE TO GET IDEAS FOR A GIFT...
...AND ALL YOU TWO COULD DO WAS ARGUE!
NOW WE STILL HAVE NO IDEAS, AND...
I JUST... I CAN'T EVEN...
WHAT...
...WERE YOU THINKING?!
HFF...
HFF...
ZZZ...
...
THE MOMENT FOR AKKUN TO GET ANGRY HAD PASSED.

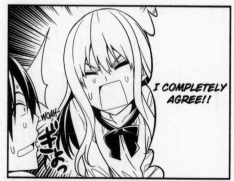

The Forgotten Baby Sister

GEEZ, WHAT WAS ALL THAT...?

...HM?

JOLT

(Please! Teach me,)

Aho-Girl

\ˈahôˌgərl\ *Japanese , noun.*
A clueless girl.

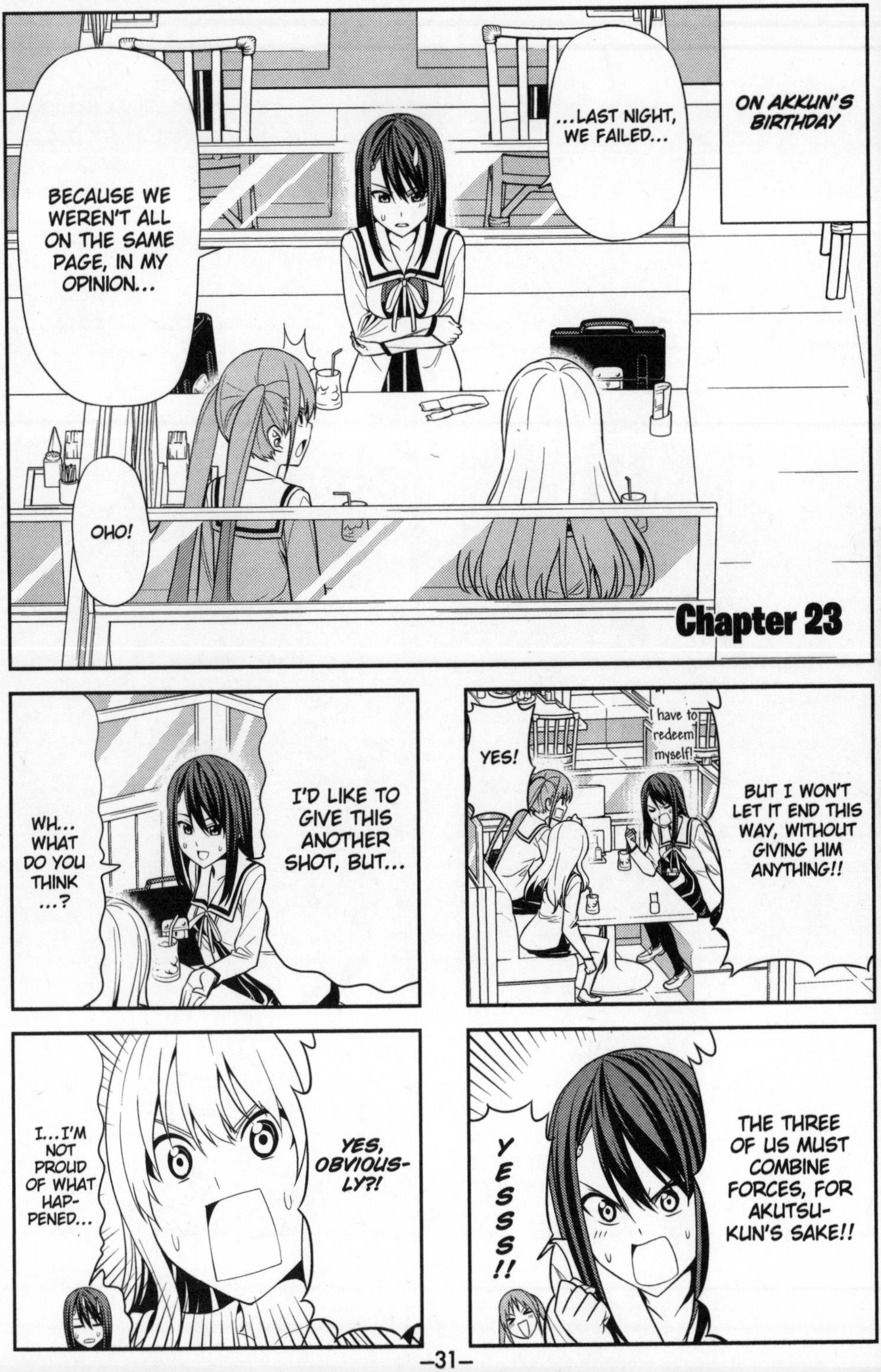
ON AKKUN'S BIRTHDAY
...LAST NIGHT, WE FAILED...
BECAUSE WE WEREN'T ALL ON THE SAME PAGE, IN MY OPINION...
OHO!
Chapter 23
I have to redeem myself!
BUT I WON'T LET IT END THIS WAY, WITHOUT GIVING HIM ANYTHING!!
YES!
I'D LIKE TO GIVE THIS ANOTHER SHOT, BUT...
WH... WHAT DO YOU THINK ...?
THE THREE OF US MUST COMBINE FORCES, FOR AKUTSU-KUN'S SAKE!!
YESSS!!
YES, OBVIOUSLY?!
I...I'M NOT PROUD OF WHAT HAPPENED...

Not Sure She Gives Great Advice

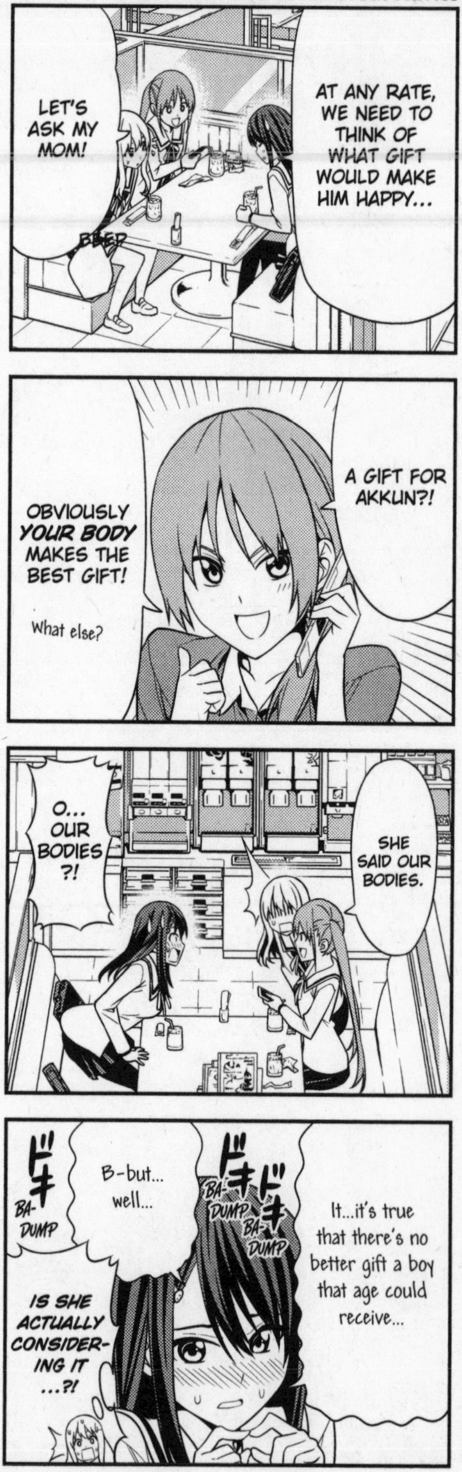
AT ANY RATE, WE NEED TO THINK OF WHAT GIFT WOULD MAKE HIM HAPPY...
LET'S ASK MY MOM!
BEEP
A GIFT FOR AKKUN?!
OBVIOUSLY *YOUR BODY* MAKES THE BEST GIFT!
What else?
SHE SAID OUR BODIES.
O... OUR BODIES?!
It...it's true that there's no better gift a boy that age could receive...
ドキドキ
BA-DUMP BA-DUMP
B-but... well...
ドキ
BA-DUMP
IS SHE ACTUALLY CONSIDERING IT...?!

Flash of Insight

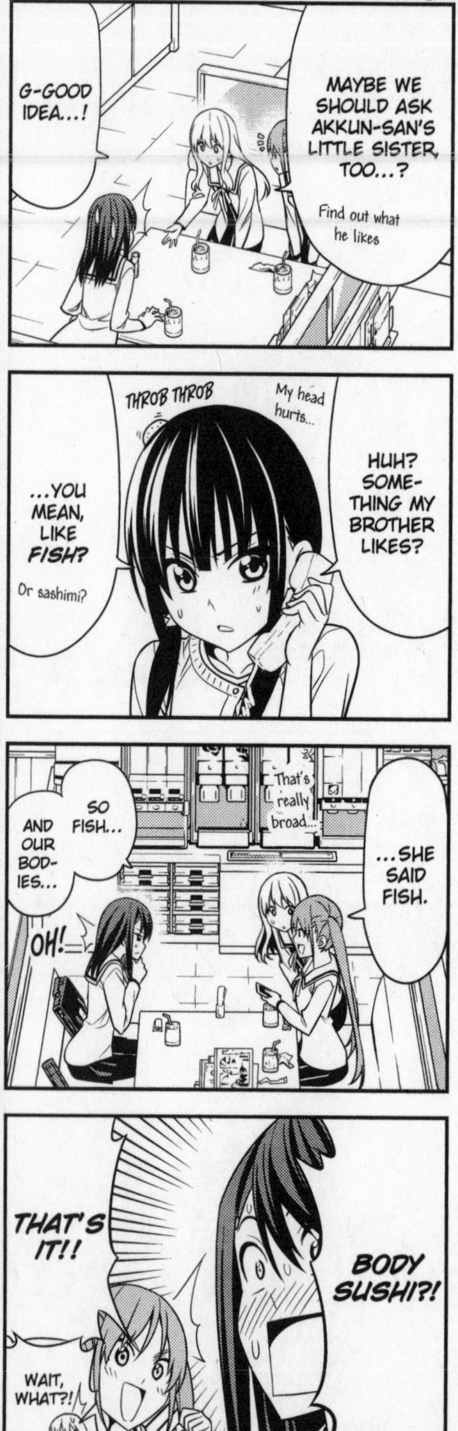
MAYBE WE SHOULD ASK AKKUN-SAN'S LITTLE SISTER, TOO...?
Find out what he likes
G-GOOD IDEA...!
HUH? SOMETHING MY BROTHER LIKES?
My head hurts...
THROB THROB
...YOU MEAN, LIKE *FISH?*
Or sashimi?
...SHE SAID FISH.
That's really broad...
SO FISH...
AND OUR BODIES...
OH!
BODY SUSHI?!
THAT'S IT!!
WAIT, WHAT?!

Immediate Action

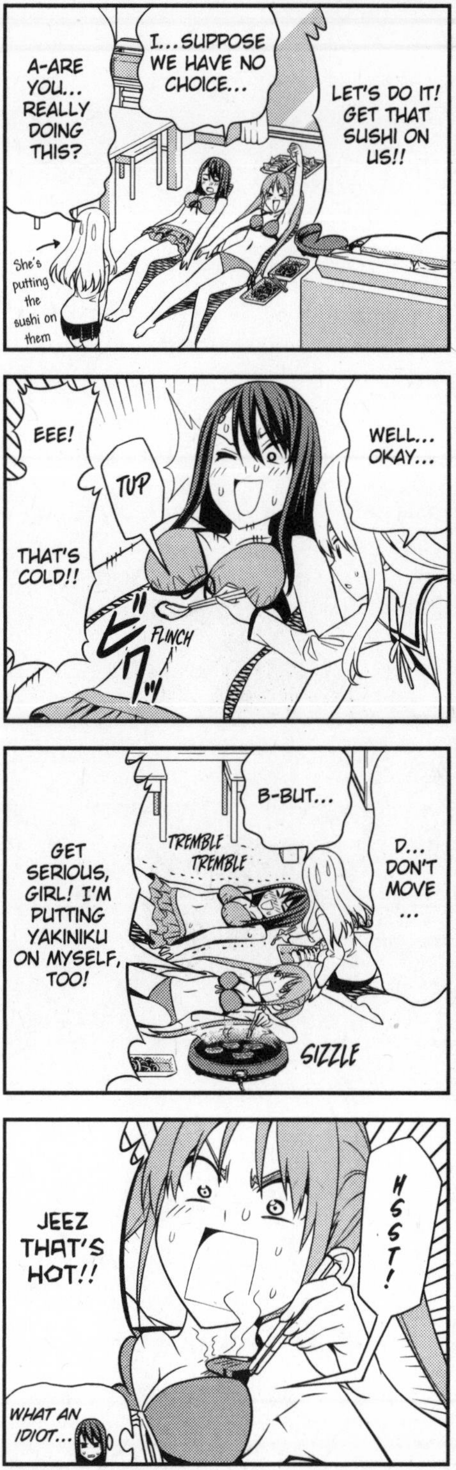
LET'S DO IT! GET THAT SUSHI ON US!!
I... SUPPOSE WE HAVE NO CHOICE...
A-ARE YOU... REALLY DOING THIS?
She's putting the sushi on them
WELL... OKAY...
EEE!
TUP
THAT'S COLD!!
FLINCH
B-BUT...
D... DON'T MOVE ...
TREMBLE TREMBLE
GET SERIOUS, GIRL! I'M PUTTING YAKINIKU ON MYSELF, TOO!
SIZZLE
HSST!
JEEZ THAT'S HOT!!
WHAT AN IDIOT...

Guts

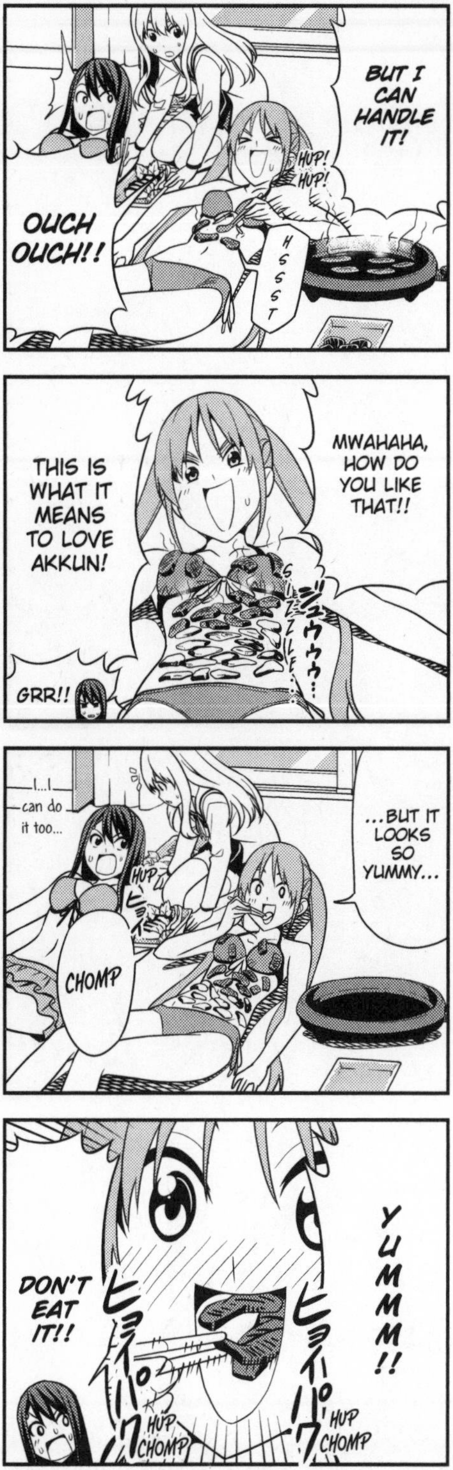
BUT I CAN HANDLE IT!
HUP! HUP!
HSSST
OUCH OUCH!!
MWAHAHA, HOW DO YOU LIKE THAT!!
THIS IS WHAT IT MEANS TO LOVE AKKUN!
SIZZLE
GRR!!
...BUT IT LOOKS SO YUMMY...
HUP
CHOMP
I...I can do it too...
YUMMMM!!
DON'T EAT IT!!
HUP CHOMP
HUP CHOMP

Hunger

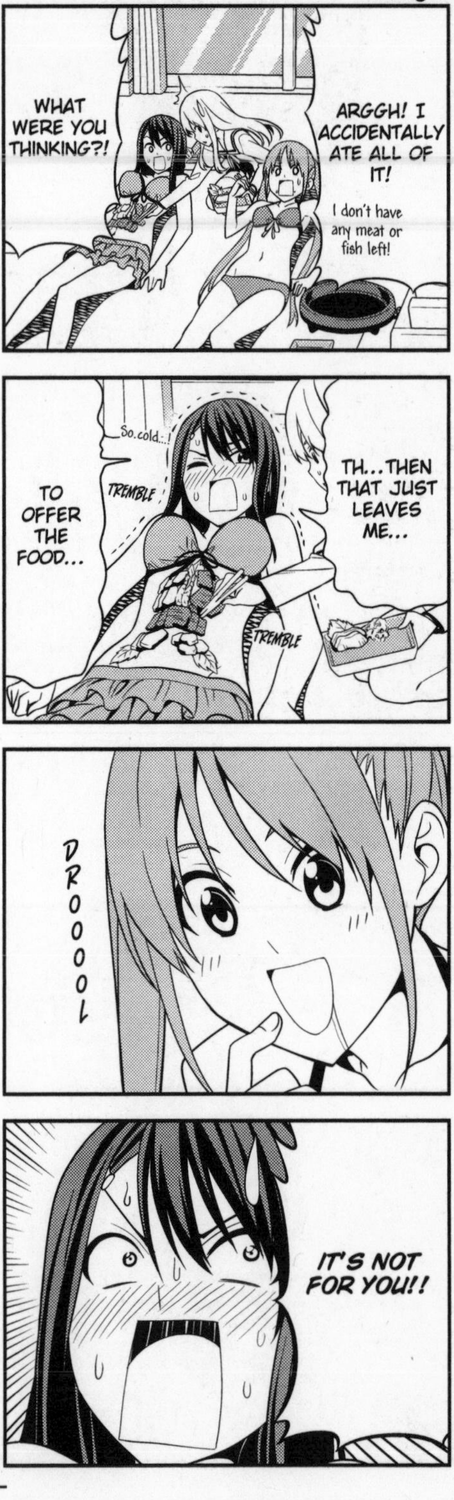
ARGGH! I ACCIDENTALLY ATE ALL OF IT!
I don't have any meat or fish left!
WHAT WERE YOU THINKING?!
TH...THEN THAT JUST LEAVES ME...
So.cold...!
TREMBLE
TO OFFER THE FOOD...
TREMBLE
DROOOOOL
IT'S NOT FOR YOU!!

It's the Boobs

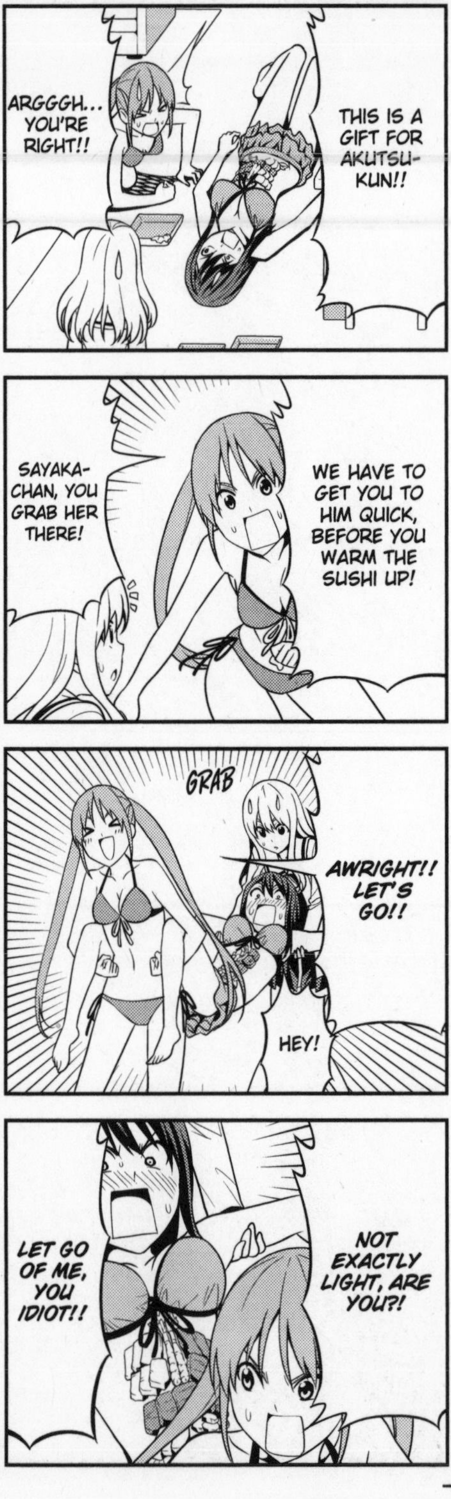
THIS IS A GIFT FOR AKUTSU-KUN!!
ARGGGH... YOU'RE RIGHT!!
WE HAVE TO GET YOU TO HIM QUICK, BEFORE YOU WARM THE SUSHI UP!
SAYAKA-CHAN, YOU GRAB HER THERE!
AWRIGHT!! LET'S GO!!
GRAB
HEY!
NOT EXACTLY LIGHT, ARE YOU?!
LET GO OF ME, YOU IDIOT!!

It's May in the Story

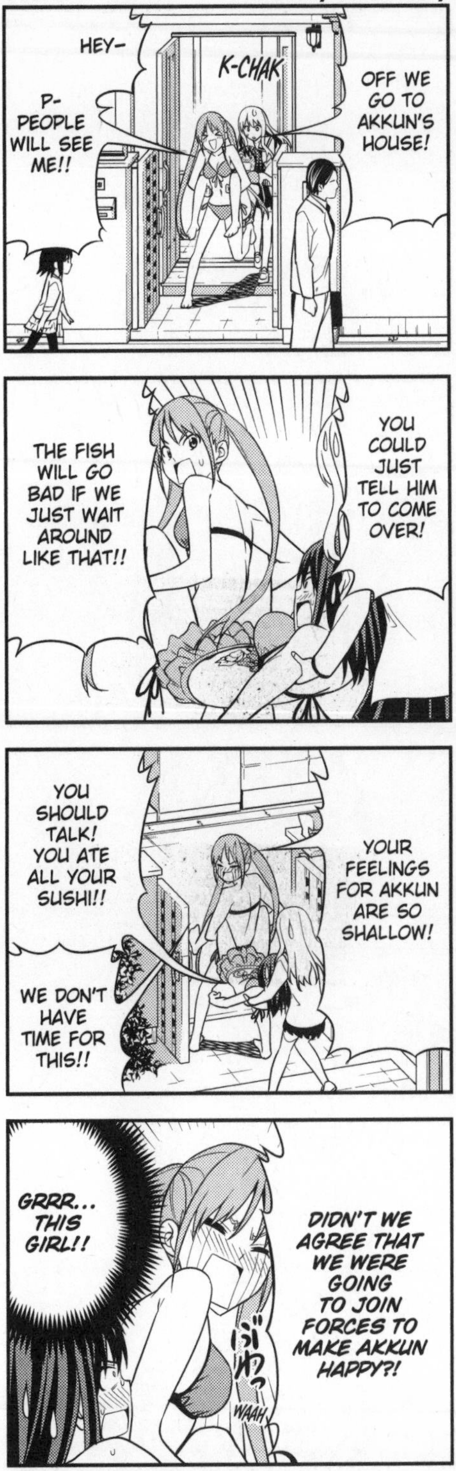
OFF WE GO TO AKKUN'S HOUSE!
K-CHAK
HEY–
P-PEOPLE WILL SEE ME!!
YOU COULD JUST TELL HIM TO COME OVER!
THE FISH WILL GO BAD IF WE JUST WAIT AROUND LIKE THAT!!
YOUR FEELINGS FOR AKKUN ARE SO SHALLOW!
YOU SHOULD TALK! YOU ATE ALL YOUR SUSHI!!
WE DON'T HAVE TIME FOR THIS!!
DIDN'T WE AGREE THAT WE WERE GOING TO JOIN FORCES TO MAKE AKKUN HAPPY?!
ぶわっ
WAAH
GRRR... THIS GIRL!!

Resolve

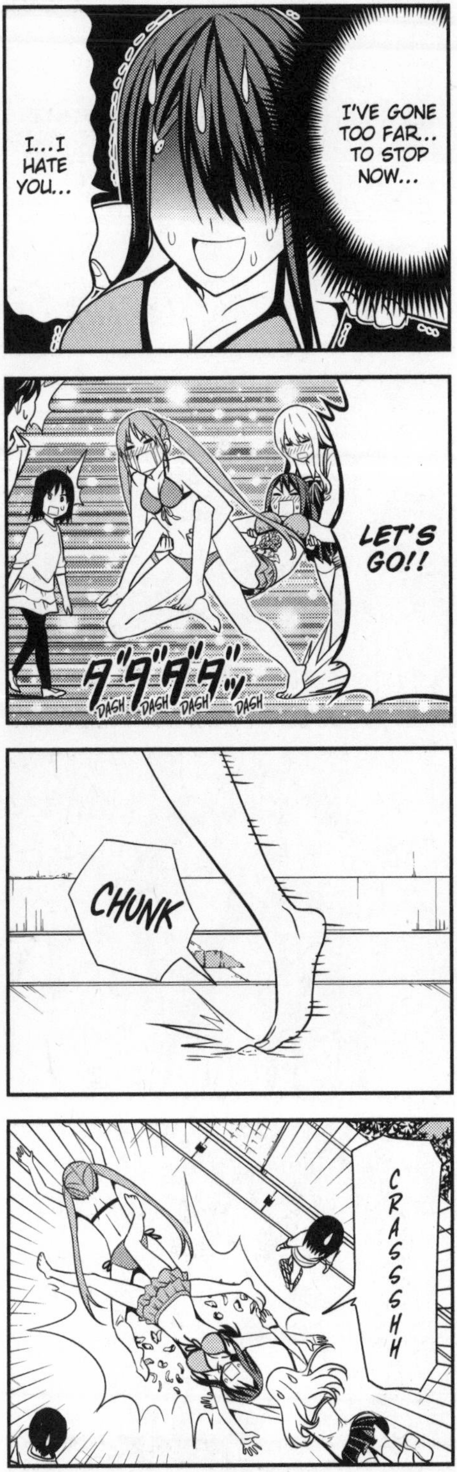
I'VE GONE TOO FAR... TO STOP NOW...
I...I HATE YOU...
LET'S GO!!
ダダダダッ
DASH DASH DASH DASH
CHUNK
CRASSSHH

Predictable Reaction

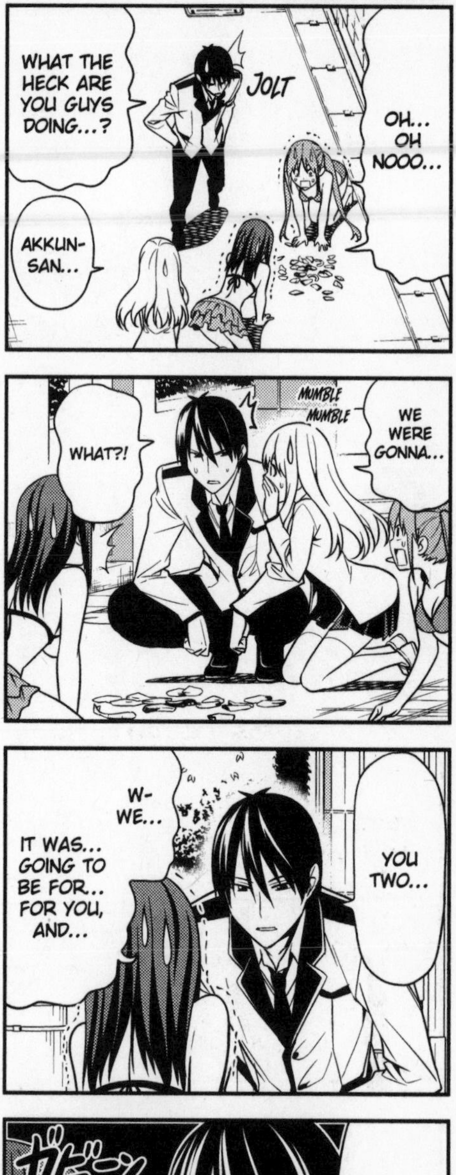
JOLT
WHAT THE HECK ARE YOU GUYS DOING...?
OH... OH NOOO...
AKKUN-SAN...
MUMBLE MUMBLE
WE WERE GONNA...
WHAT?!
YOU TWO...
W- WE...
IT WAS... GOING TO BE FOR... FOR YOU, AND...
ARE YOU STUPID?
ガビーン
SHAAME

That's Unexpected

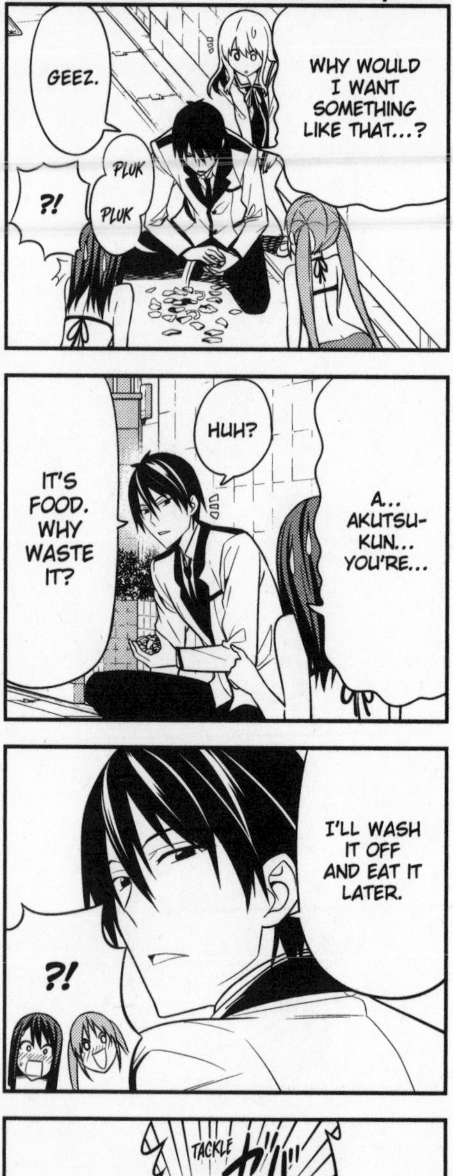
WHY WOULD I WANT SOMETHING LIKE THAT...?
GEEZ.
PLUK
PLUK
?!
A... AKUTSU-KUN... YOU'RE...
HUH?
IT'S FOOD. WHY WASTE IT?
I'LL WASH IT OFF AND EAT IT LATER.
?!
I LOVE YOU! ♡
TACKLE
DON'T TOUCH ME! YOU REEK!!

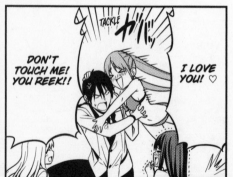

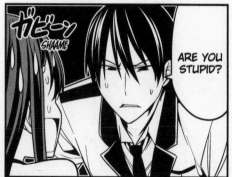

Why Don't You Get Dressed First

IS EVERY-THING READY, AKKUN?!
WE'RE GOOD HERE!!
GO AHEAD!!
I'M NOT PUTTING IT ON YOU.

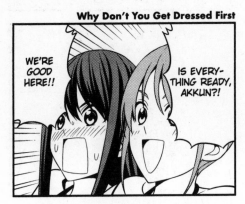

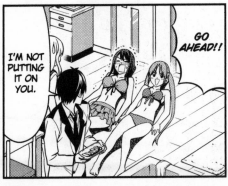

(She brings the city to life)

Aho-Girl

\'ahô,gərl\ *Japanese , noun*.

A clueless girl.

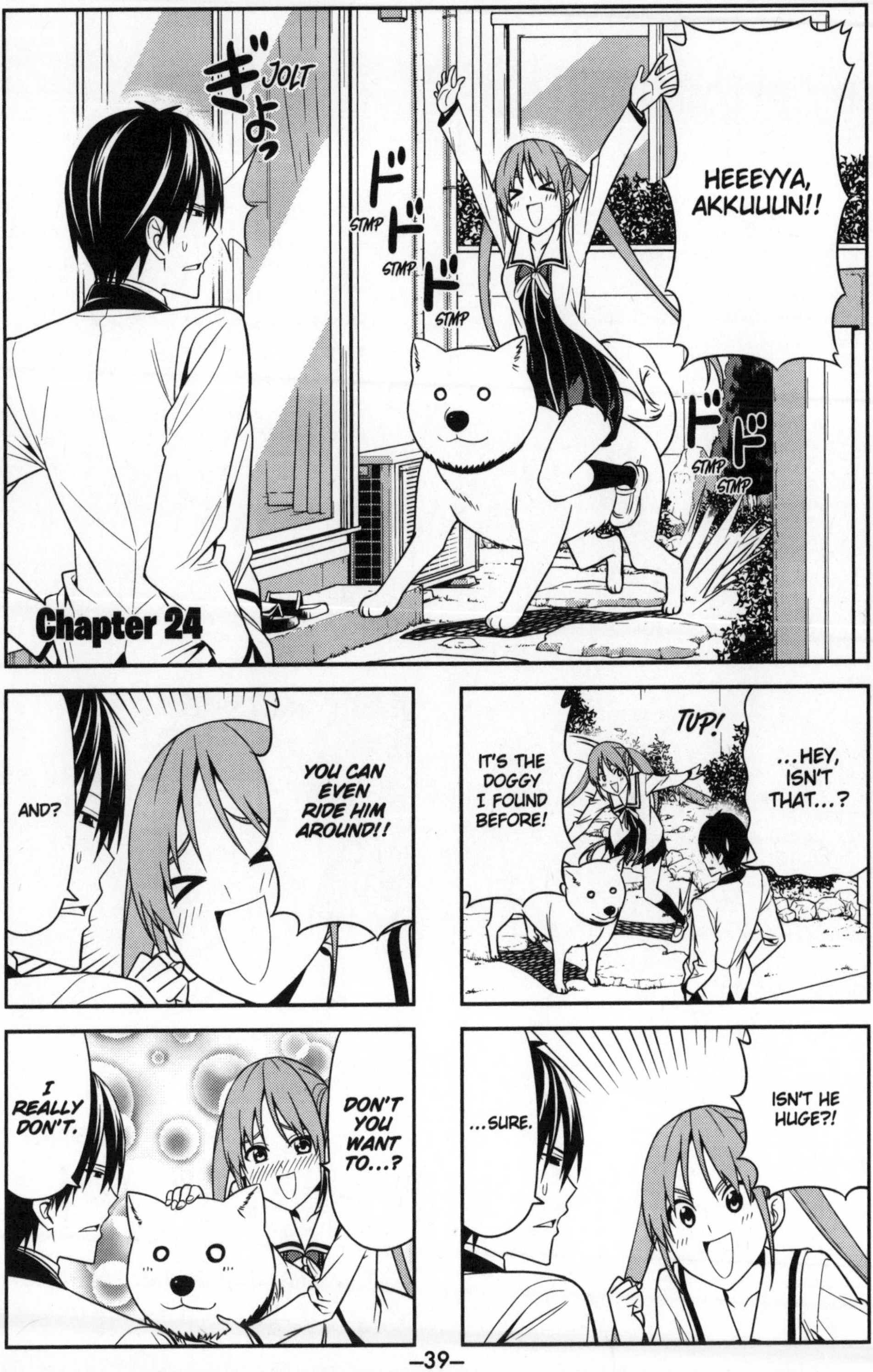
HEEEYYA, AKKUUUN!!
ドド
STMP STMP
ドドド
STMP STMP STMP
ぎょっ
JOLT
Chapter 24
...HEY, ISN'T THAT...?
TUP!
IT'S THE DOGGY I FOUND BEFORE!
YOU CAN EVEN RIDE HIM AROUND!!
AND?
ISN'T HE HUGE?!
...SURE.
DON'T YOU WANT TO...?
I REALLY DON'T.

Didn't Even Notice

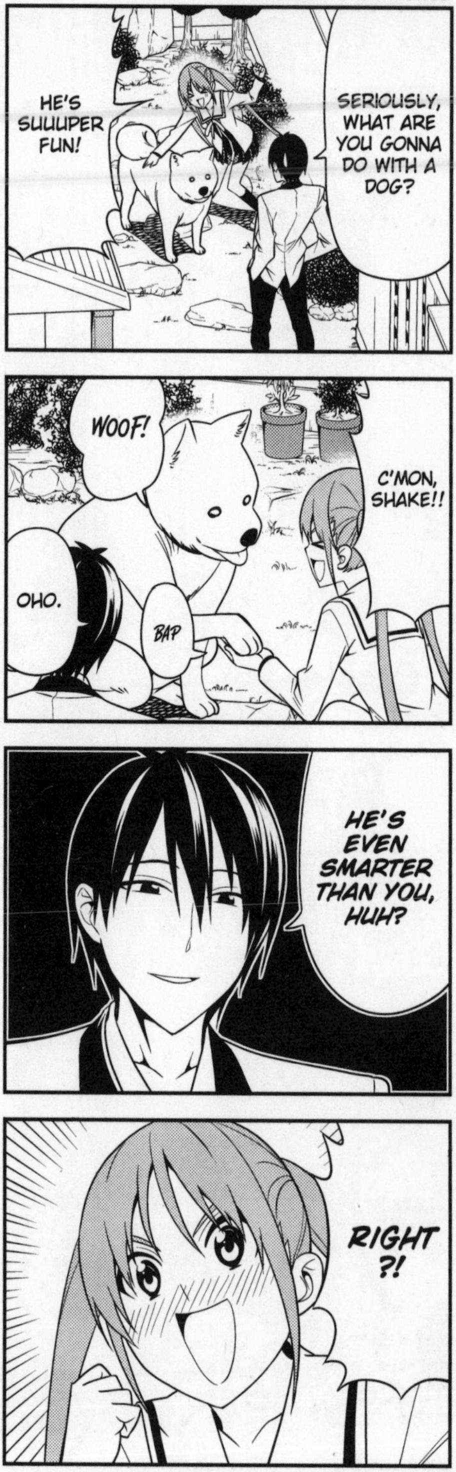
SERIOUSLY, WHAT ARE YOU GONNA DO WITH A DOG?
HE'S SUUUPER FUN!
C'MON, SHAKE!!
WOOF!
BAP
OHO.
HE'S EVEN SMARTER THAN YOU, HUH?
RIGHT ?!

Mom's More Worried about the Money

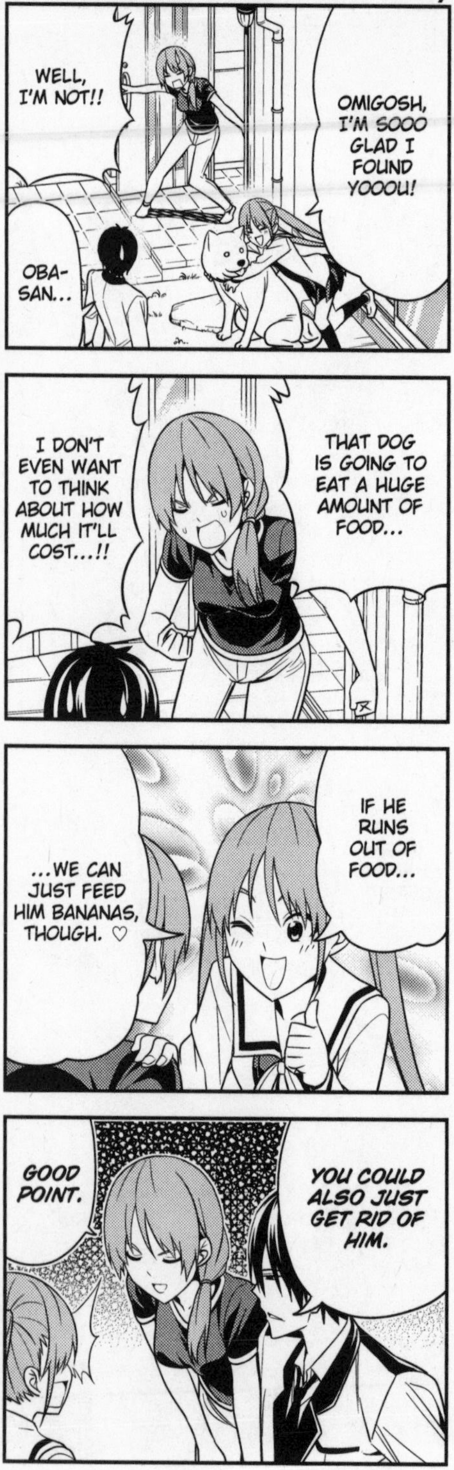
OMIGOSH, I'M SOOO GLAD I FOUND YOOOU!
WELL, I'M NOT!!
OBA-SAN...
THAT DOG IS GOING TO EAT A HUGE AMOUNT OF FOOD...
I DON'T EVEN WANT TO THINK ABOUT HOW MUCH IT'LL COST...!!
IF HE RUNS OUT OF FOOD...
...WE CAN JUST FEED HIM BANANAS, THOUGH. ♡
YOU COULD ALSO JUST GET RID OF HIM.
GOOD POINT.

Pushing It

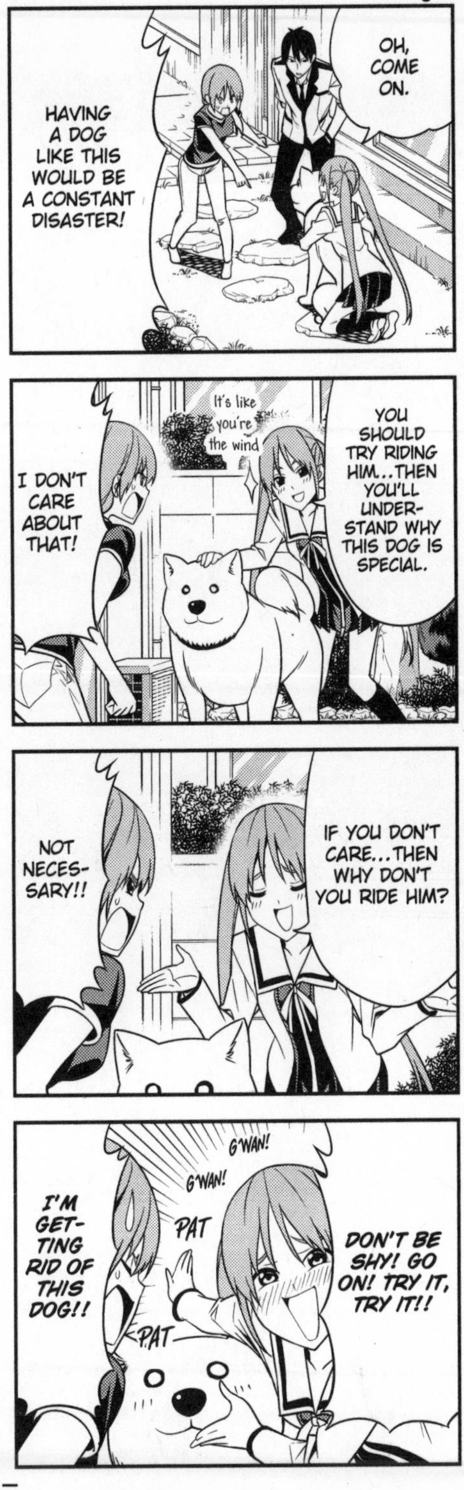
OH, COME ON.
HAVING A DOG LIKE THIS WOULD BE A CONSTANT DISASTER!
YOU SHOULD TRY RIDING HIM...THEN YOU'LL UNDER-STAND WHY THIS DOG IS SPECIAL.
It's like you're the wind
I DON'T CARE ABOUT THAT!
IF YOU DON'T CARE...THEN WHY DON'T YOU RIDE HIM?
NOT NECES-SARY!!
G'WAN!
G'WAN!
DON'T BE SHY! GO ON! TRY IT, TRY IT!!
PAT
PAT
I'M GET-TING RID OF THIS DOG!!

The Quest Begins

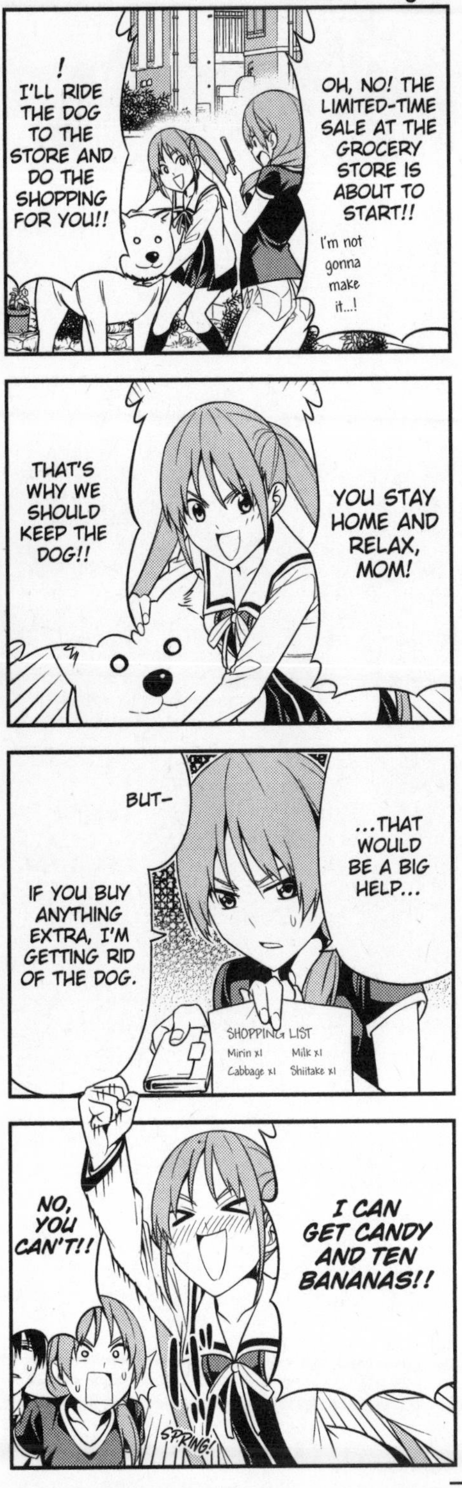
OH, NO! THE LIMITED-TIME SALE AT THE GROCERY STORE IS ABOUT TO START!!
I'm not gonna make it...!
!
I'LL RIDE THE DOG TO THE STORE AND DO THE SHOPPING FOR YOU!!
YOU STAY HOME AND RELAX, MOM!
THAT'S WHY WE SHOULD KEEP THE DOG!!
...THAT WOULD BE A BIG HELP...
BUT–
IF YOU BUY ANYTHING EXTRA, I'M GETTING RID OF THE DOG.
SHOPPING LIST
Mirin x1
Milk x1
Cabbage x1
Shiitake x1
I CAN GET CANDY AND TEN BANANAS!!
NO, YOU CAN'T!!
SPRING!

Limited Edition

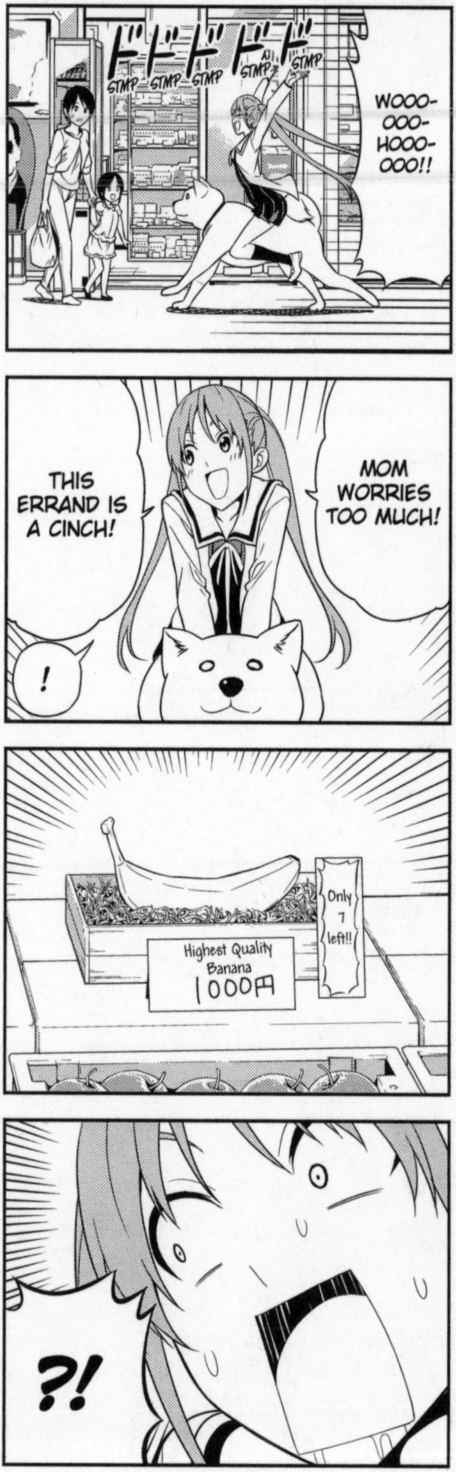
ドドドドド
STMP STMP STMP STMP STMP
WOOO-OOO-HOOO-OOO!!
MOM WORRIES TOO MUCH!
THIS ERRAND IS A CINCH!
!
Only 7 left!!
Highest Quality Banana 1000円
?!

Conflicted

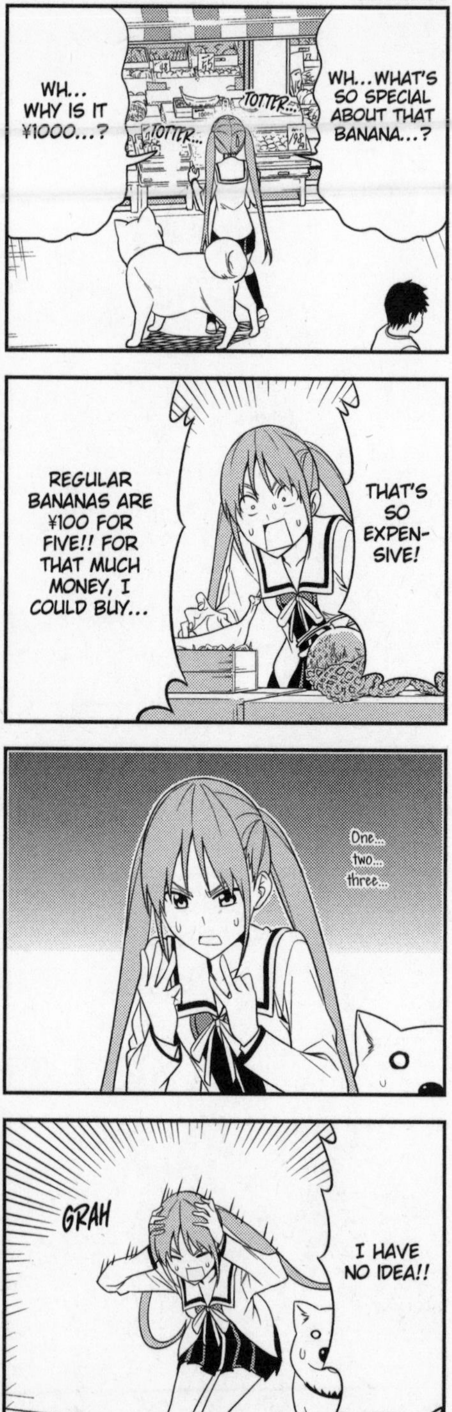
WH...WHAT'S SO SPECIAL ABOUT THAT BANANA...?
WH... WHY IS IT ¥1000...?
TOTTER...
TOTTER...
THAT'S SO EXPEN-SIVE!
REGULAR BANANAS ARE ¥100 FOR FIVE!! FOR THAT MUCH MONEY, I COULD BUY...
One... two... three...
I HAVE NO IDEA!!
GRAH

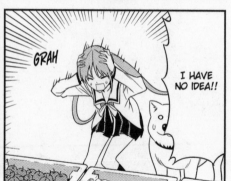

The Word on the Street

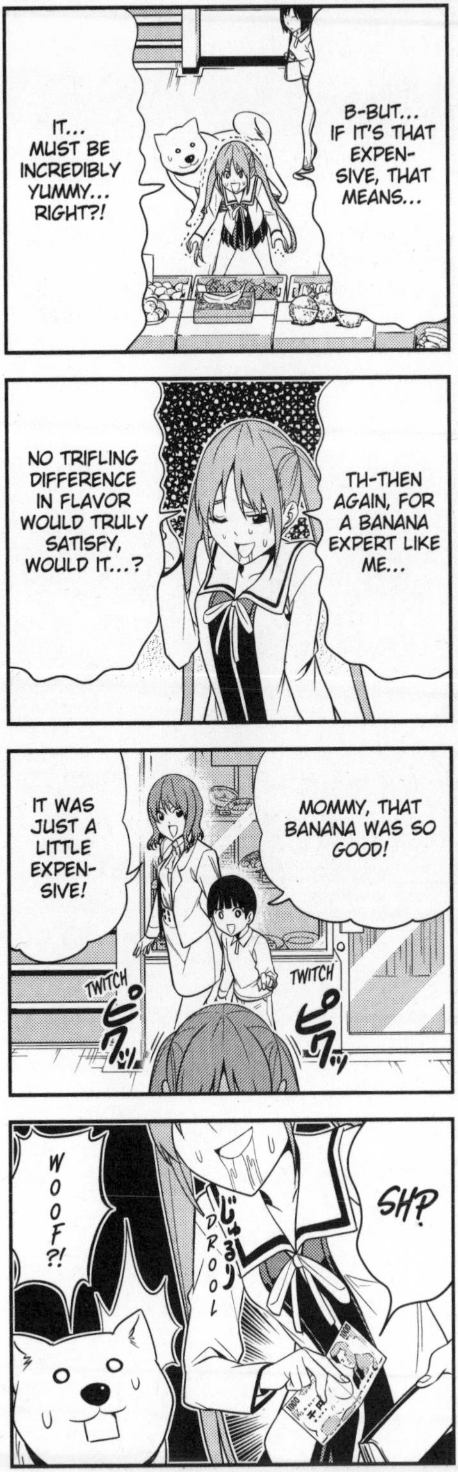
B-BUT... IF IT'S THAT EXPEN-SIVE, THAT MEANS...
IT... MUST BE INCREDIBLY YUMMY... RIGHT?!
TH-THEN AGAIN, FOR A BANANA EXPERT LIKE ME...
NO TRIFLING DIFFERENCE IN FLAVOR WOULD TRULY SATISFY, WOULD IT...?
MOMMY, THAT BANANA WAS SO GOOD!
IT WAS JUST A LITTLE EXPEN-SIVE!
TWITCH
TWITCH
SHP
DROOL
WOOOF?!

The Dog's Persuasive

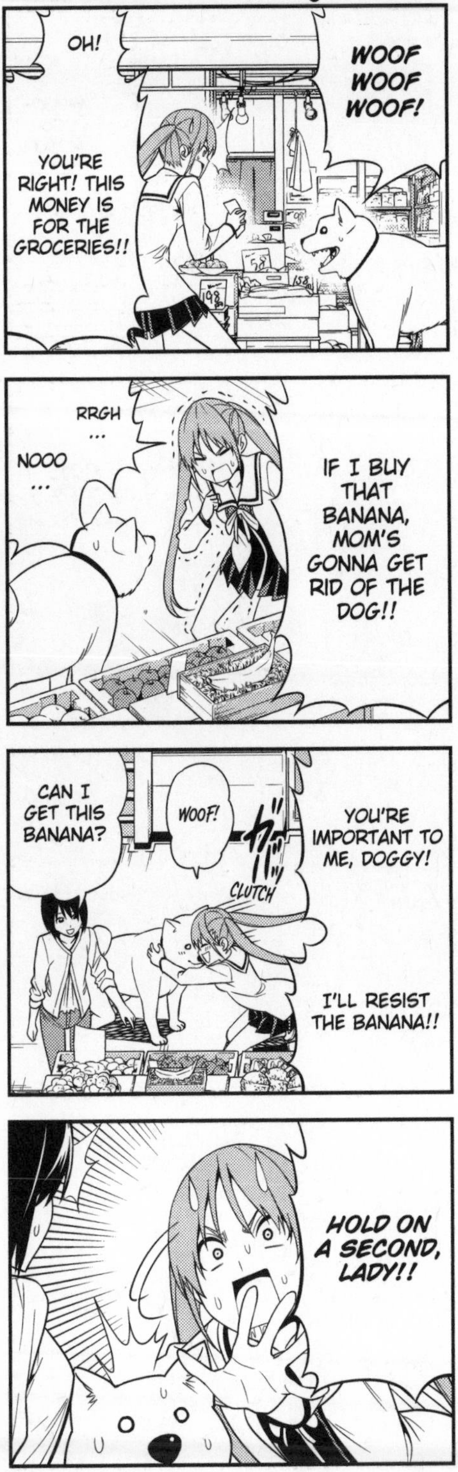
WOOF WOOF WOOF!
OH!
YOU'RE RIGHT! THIS MONEY IS FOR THE GROCERIES!!
IF I BUY THAT BANANA, MOM'S GONNA GET RID OF THE DOG!!
RRGH ...
NOOO ...
YOU'RE IMPORTANT TO ME, DOGGY!
WOOF!
CAN I GET THIS BANANA?
CLUTCH
I'LL RESIST THE BANANA!!
HOLD ON A SECOND, LADY!!

Temptation

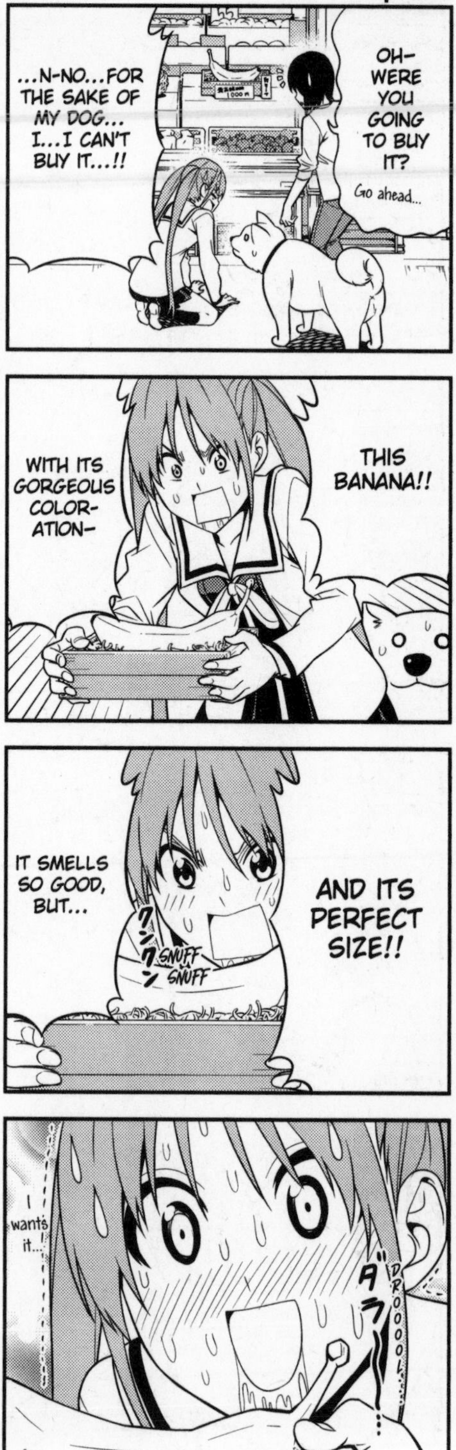
OH— WERE YOU GOING TO BUY IT?
Go ahead...
...N-NO...FOR THE SAKE OF MY DOG... I...I CAN'T BUY IT...!!
THIS BANANA!!
WITH ITS GORGEOUS COLOR-ATION—
AND ITS PERFECT SIZE!!
IT SMELLS SO GOOD, BUT...
クンクン
SNUFF SNUFF
I wants it...
ダラ~
DROOOOOL...

All in a Flash

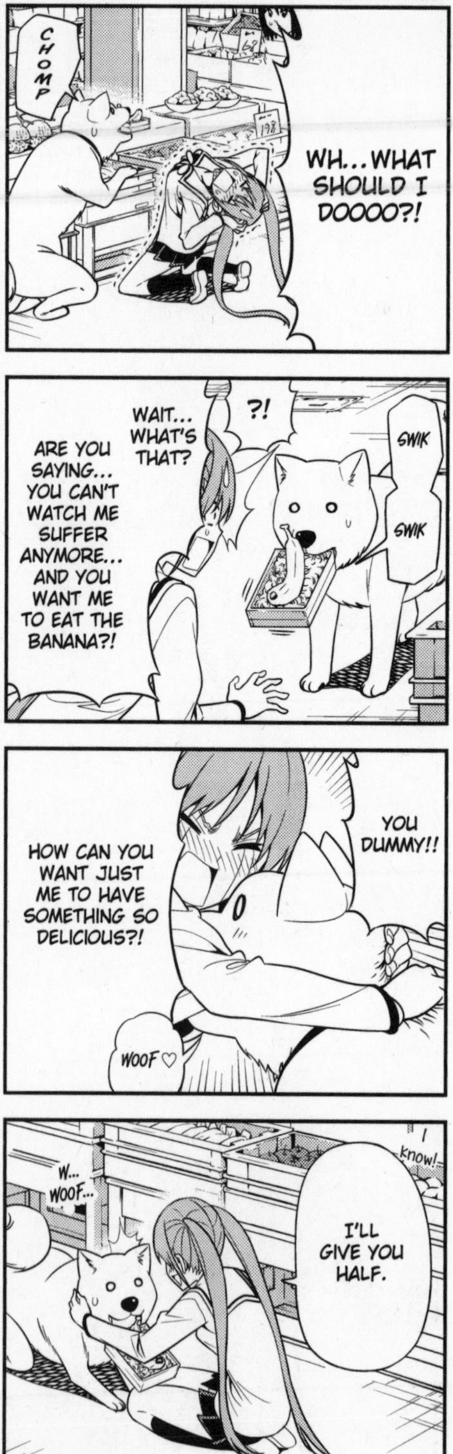
WH...WHAT SHOULD I DOOOO?!
CHOMP
SWIK
SWIK
?!
WAIT... WHAT'S THAT?
ARE YOU SAYING... YOU CAN'T WATCH ME SUFFER ANYMORE... AND YOU WANT ME TO EAT THE BANANA?!
YOU DUMMY!!
HOW CAN YOU WANT JUST ME TO HAVE SOMETHING SO DELICIOUS?!
WOOF ♡
I know!
I'LL GIVE YOU HALF.
W... WOOF...

Impact

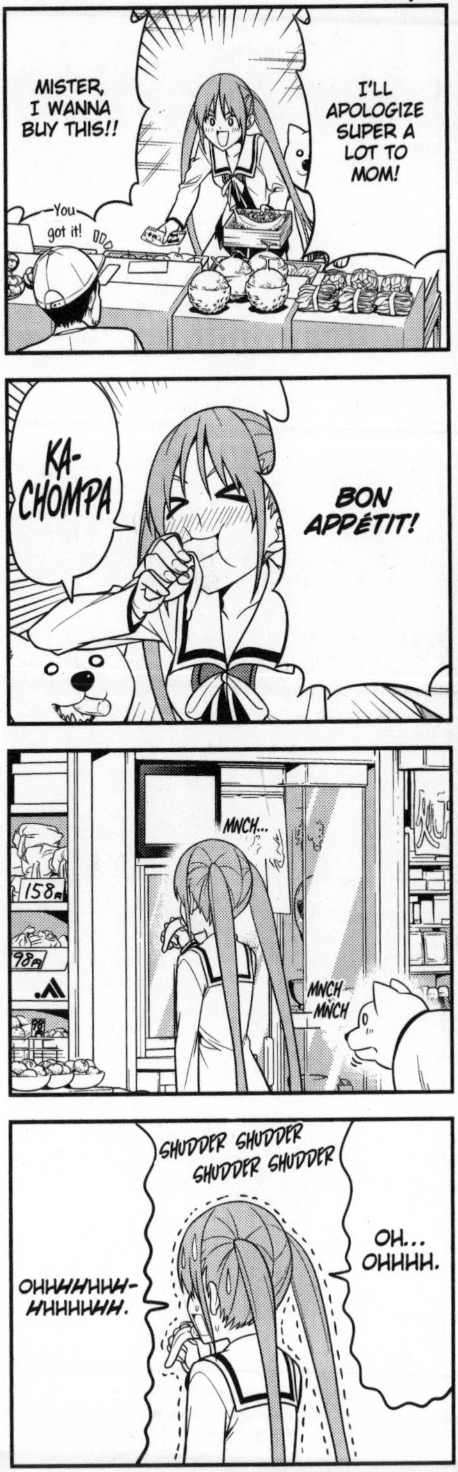
I'LL APOLOGIZE SUPER A LOT TO MOM!
MISTER, I WANNA BUY THIS!!
You got it!
BON APPÉTIT!
KA-CHOMPA
MNCH...
MNCH MNCH
SHUDDER SHUDDER SHUDDER SHUDDER
OH... OHHHH.
OHHHHHHHH-HHHHHHH.

Joy

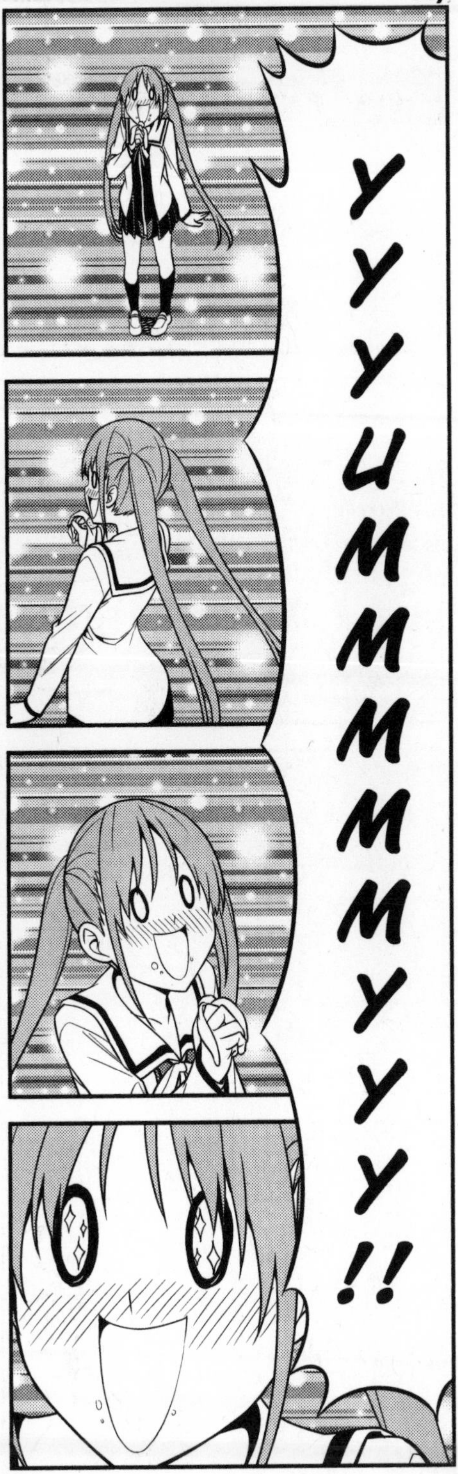
YYYUMMMMMYYY!!

No Words for It

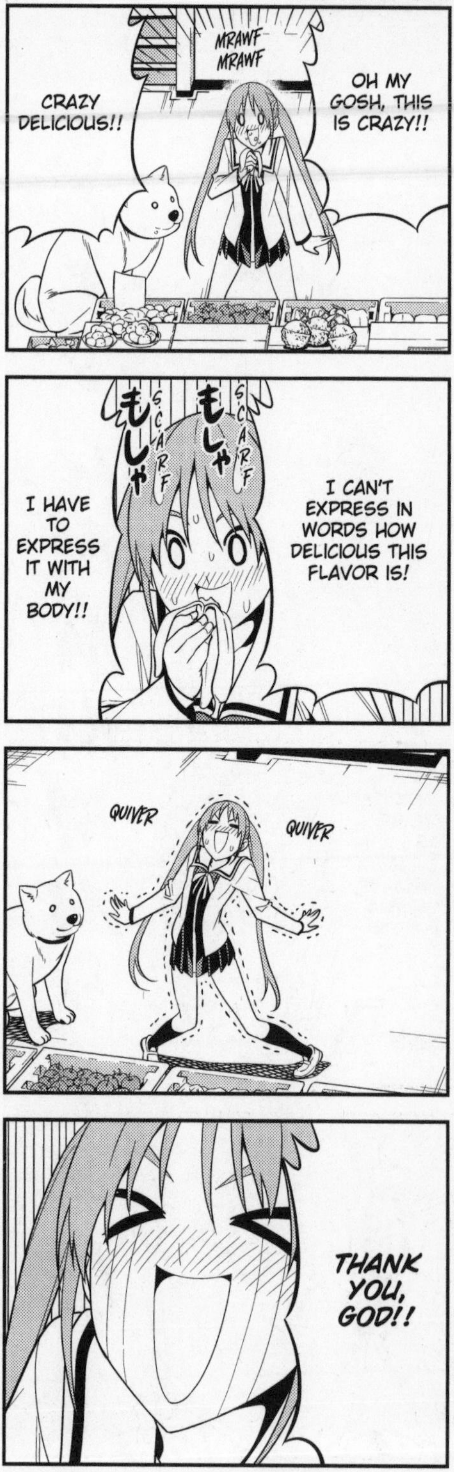
MRAWF MRAWF
OH MY GOSH, THIS IS CRAZY!!
CRAZY DELICIOUS!!
SCARF SCARF
I CAN'T EXPRESS IN WORDS HOW DELICIOUS THIS FLAVOR IS!
I HAVE TO EXPRESS IT WITH MY BODY!!
QUIVER
QUIVER
THANK YOU, GOD!!

Predictable Result

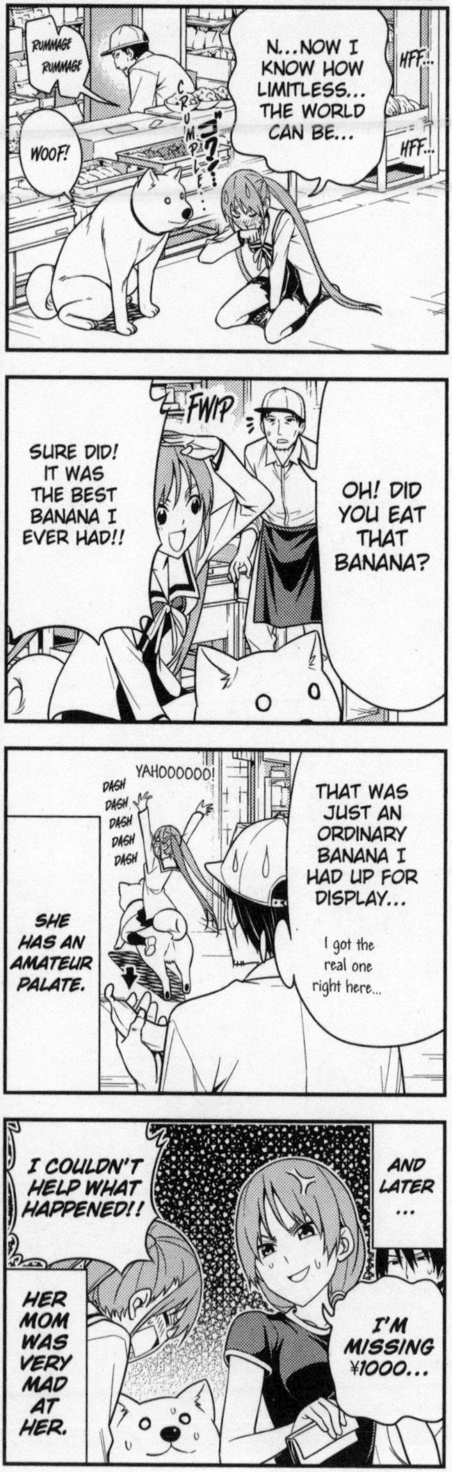
HFF... HFF...
N...NOW I KNOW HOW LIMITLESS... THE WORLD CAN BE...
CRUMPLE
RUMMAGE RUMMAGE
WOOF!
OH! DID YOU EAT THAT BANANA?
FWIP
SURE DID! IT WAS THE BEST BANANA I EVER HAD!!
THAT WAS JUST AN ORDINARY BANANA I HAD UP FOR DISPLAY...
I got the real one right here...
YAHOOOOOO!
DASH DASH DASH DASH DASH
SHE HAS AN AMATEUR PALATE.
AND LATER...
I'M MISSING ¥1000...
I COULDN'T HELP WHAT HAPPENED!!
HER MOM WAS VERY MAD AT HER.

Back to Square One

NOW THAT I'VE EXPERIENCED THAT INCREDIBLE TASTE...

I SUPPOSE... REGULAR BANANAS WILL BE RUINED FOR ME...

CHOMP

OH MY GOD, THAT'S YUMMY!!

(Dig here,)

Aho-Girl

\ˈahôˌgərl\ *Japanese , noun*.
A clueless girl.

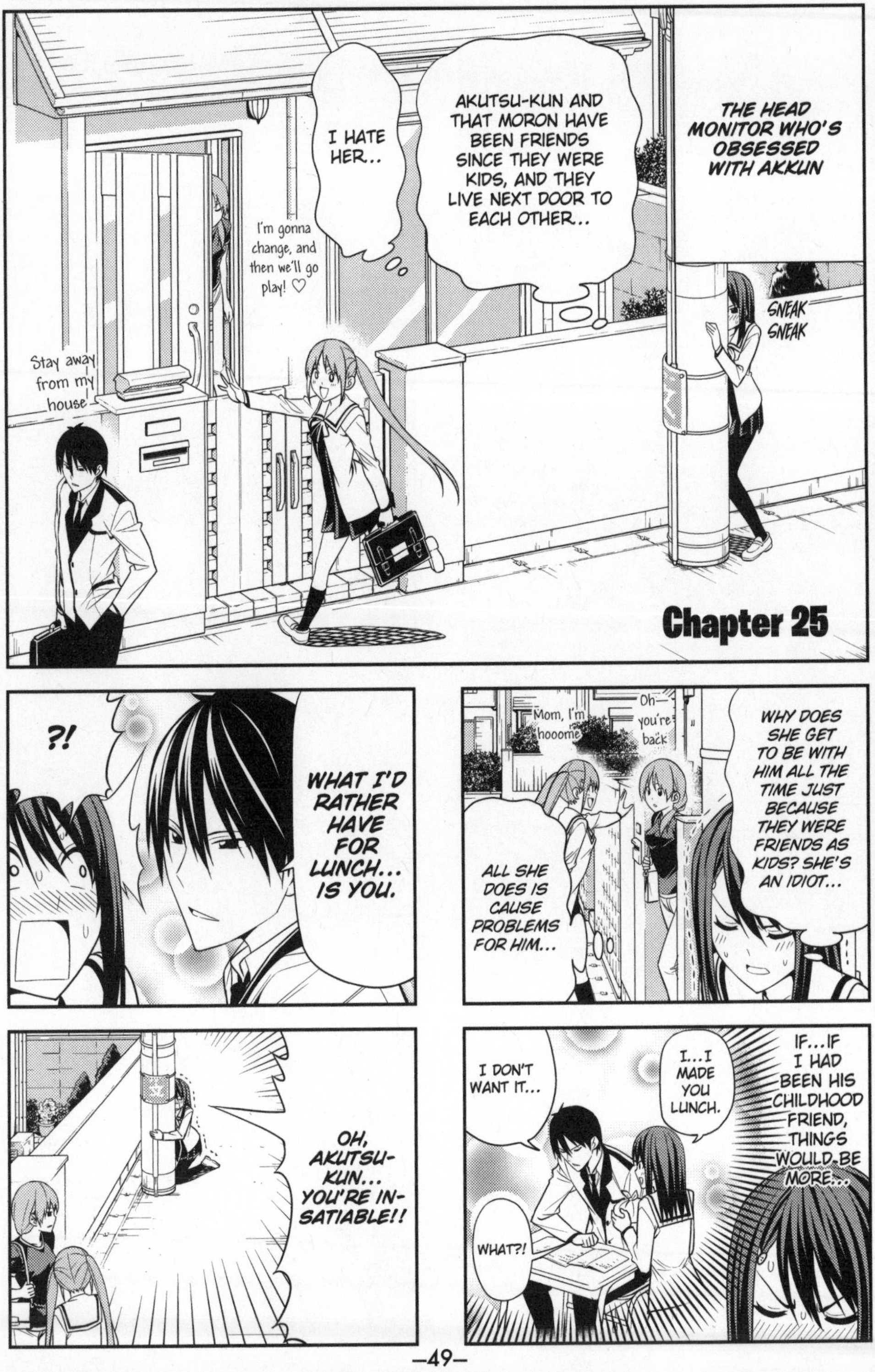
THE HEAD MONITOR WHO'S OBSESSED WITH AKKUN
SNEAK SNEAK
AKUTSU-KUN AND THAT MORON HAVE BEEN FRIENDS SINCE THEY WERE KIDS, AND THEY LIVE NEXT DOOR TO EACH OTHER...
I HATE HER...
I'm gonna change, and then we'll go play! ♡
Stay away from my house
Chapter 25
WHY DOES SHE GET TO BE WITH HIM ALL THE TIME JUST BECAUSE THEY WERE FRIENDS AS KIDS? SHE'S AN IDIOT...
Oh— you're back
Mom, I'm hooome
ALL SHE DOES IS CAUSE PROBLEMS FOR HIM...
WHAT I'D RATHER HAVE FOR LUNCH... IS YOU.
?!
IF...IF I HAD BEEN HIS CHILDHOOD FRIEND, THINGS WOULD BE MORE...
I...I MADE YOU LUNCH.
I DON'T WANT IT...
WHAT?!
OH, AKUTSU-KUN... YOU'RE INSATIABLE!!

No Mercy

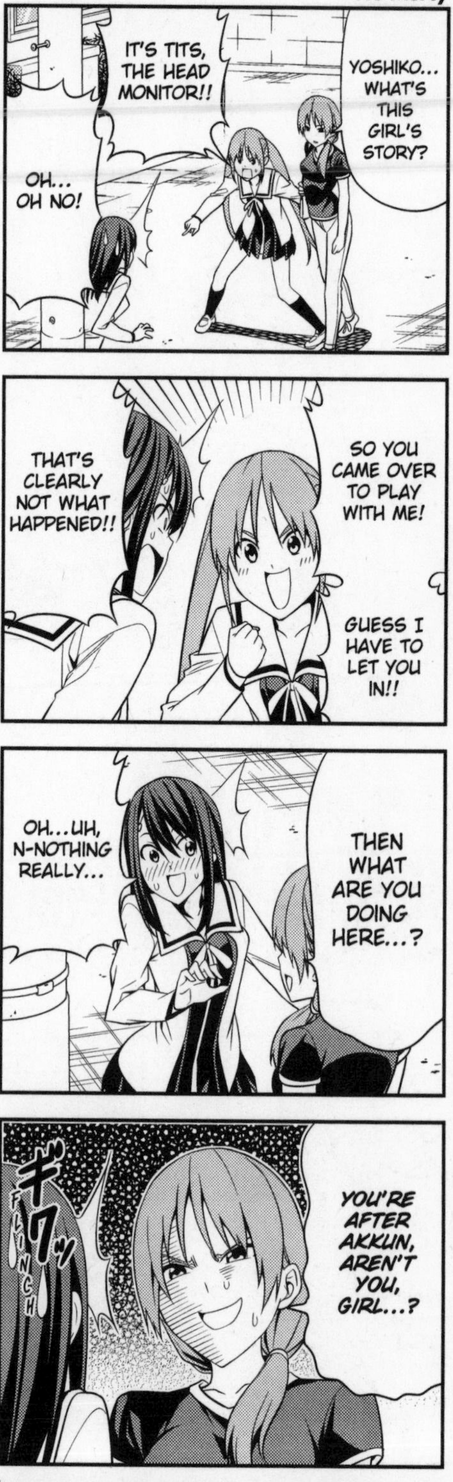
YOSHIKO... WHAT'S THIS GIRL'S STORY?
IT'S TITS, THE HEAD MONITOR!!
OH... OH NO!
SO YOU CAME OVER TO PLAY WITH ME!
THAT'S CLEARLY NOT WHAT HAPPENED!!
GUESS I HAVE TO LET YOU IN!!
THEN WHAT ARE YOU DOING HERE...?
OH...UH, N-NOTHING REALLY...
YOU'RE AFTER AKKUN, AREN'T YOU, GIRL...?
ギクッ
FLINCH

Check Volume 1 Chapter 14

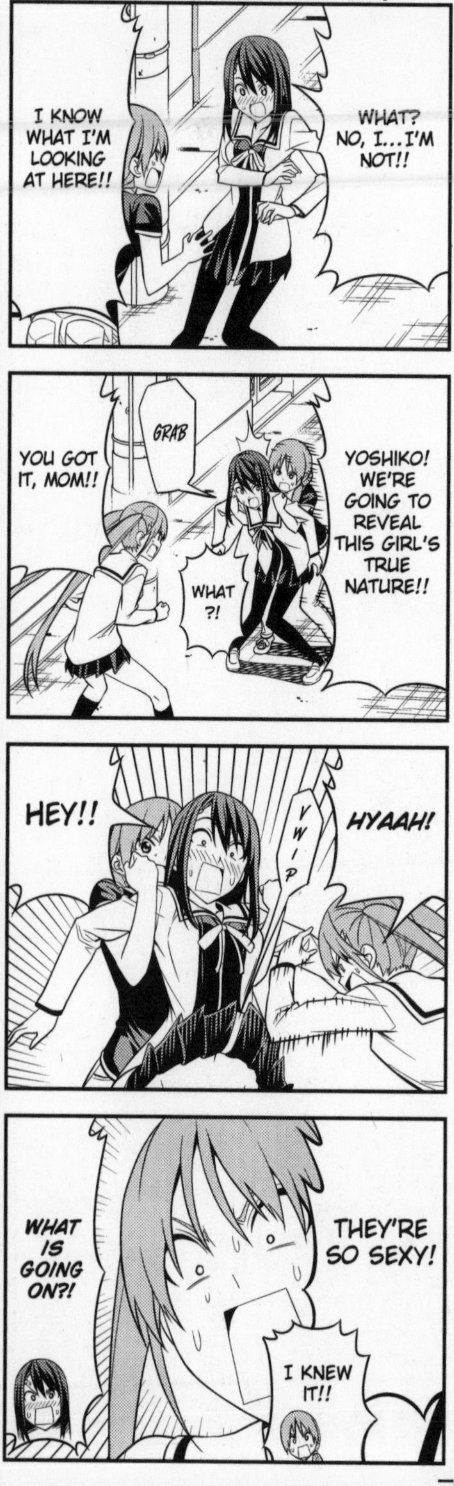
WHAT? NO, I...I'M NOT!!
I KNOW WHAT I'M LOOKING AT HERE!!
YOSHIKO! WE'RE GOING TO REVEAL THIS GIRL'S TRUE NATURE!!
GRAB
YOU GOT IT, MOM!!
WHAT ?!
HYAAH!
VWIP
HEY!!
THEY'RE SO SEXY!
WHAT IS GOING ON?!
I KNEW IT!!

Forced Logic

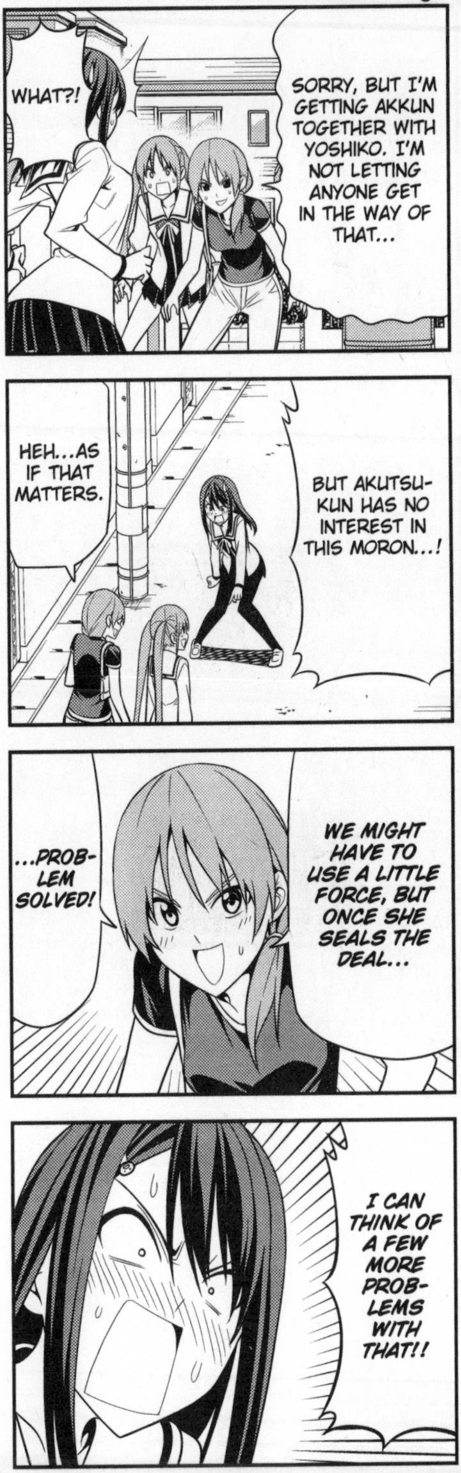
SORRY, BUT I'M GETTING AKKUN TOGETHER WITH YOSHIKO. I'M NOT LETTING ANYONE GET IN THE WAY OF THAT...
WHAT?!
BUT AKUTSU-KUN HAS NO INTEREST IN THIS MORON...!
HEH...AS IF THAT MATTERS.
WE MIGHT HAVE TO USE A LITTLE FORCE, BUT ONCE SHE SEALS THE DEAL...
...PROBLEM SOLVED!
I CAN THINK OF A FEW MORE PROBLEMS WITH THAT!!

A Rich Vocabulary Isn't Always a Plus

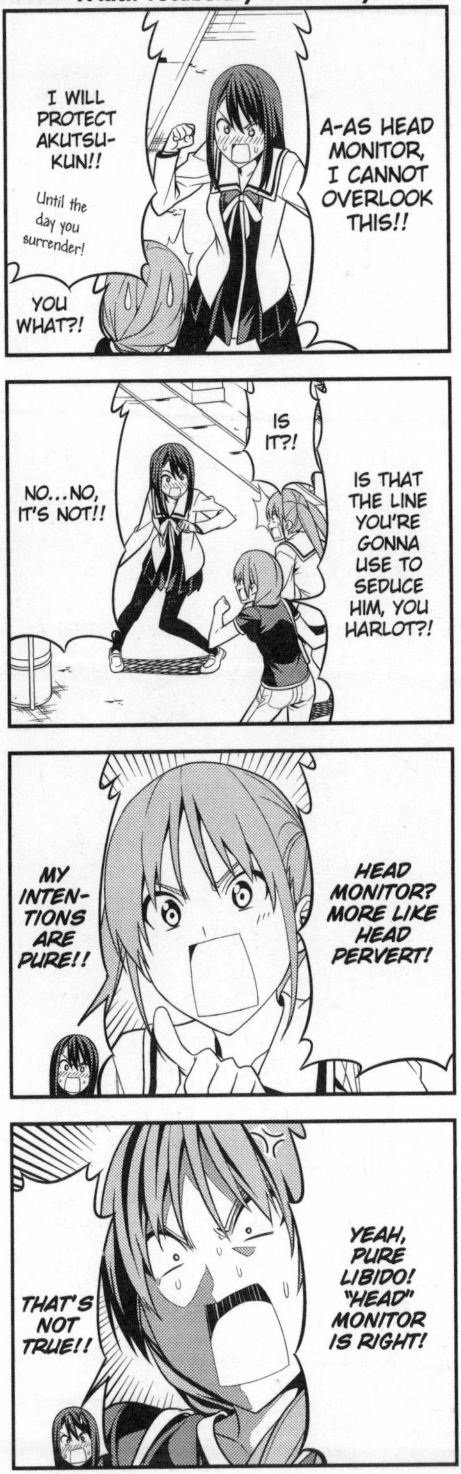
A-AS HEAD MONITOR, I CANNOT OVERLOOK THIS!!
I WILL PROTECT AKUTSU-KUN!!
Until the day you surrender!
YOU WHAT?!
IS THAT THE LINE YOU'RE GONNA USE TO SEDUCE HIM, YOU HARLOT?!
IS IT?!
NO...NO, IT'S NOT!!
HEAD MONITOR? MORE LIKE HEAD PERVERT!
MY INTENTIONS ARE PURE!!
YEAH, PURE LIBIDO! "HEAD" MONITOR IS RIGHT!
THAT'S NOT TRUE!!

Yoshie (the Mother)'s Contract

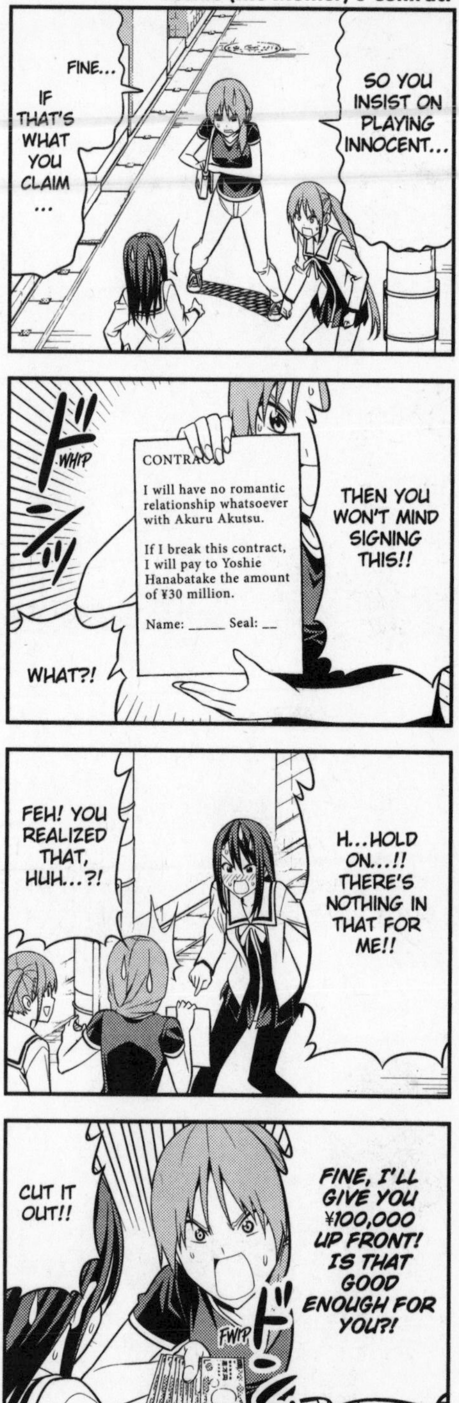
SO YOU INSIST ON PLAYING INNOCENT...
FINE... IF THAT'S WHAT YOU CLAIM ...
THEN YOU WON'T MIND SIGNING THIS!!
WHIP
CONTRACT
I will have no romantic relationship whatsoever with Akuru Akutsu.
If I break this contract, I will pay to Yoshie Hanabatake the amount of ¥30 million.
Name: _____ Seal: __
WHAT?!
H...HOLD ON...!! THERE'S NOTHING IN THAT FOR ME!!
FEH! YOU REALIZED THAT, HUH...?!
FINE, I'LL GIVE YOU ¥100,000 UP FRONT! IS THAT GOOD ENOUGH FOR YOU?!
FWIP
CUT IT OUT!!

Special Move

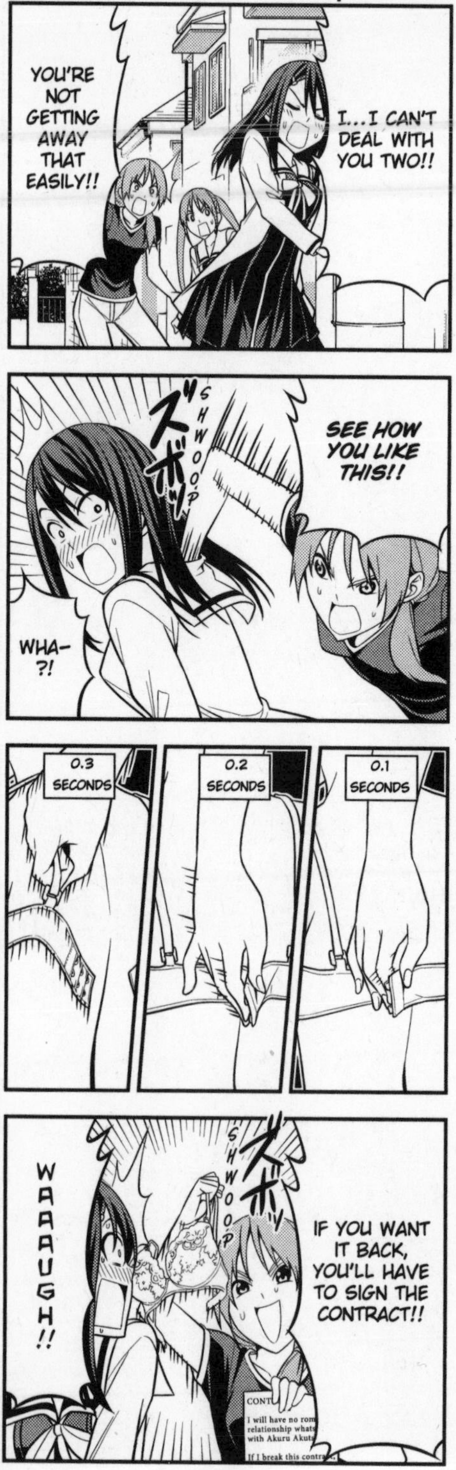
I...I CAN'T DEAL WITH YOU TWO!!
YOU'RE NOT GETTING AWAY THAT EASILY!!
SEE HOW YOU LIKE THIS!!
SHWOOOP
WHA-?!
0.1 SECONDS
0.2 SECONDS
0.3 SECONDS
IF YOU WANT IT BACK, YOU'LL HAVE TO SIGN THE CONTRACT!!
SHWOOP
WAAAUGH!!

Return Fire

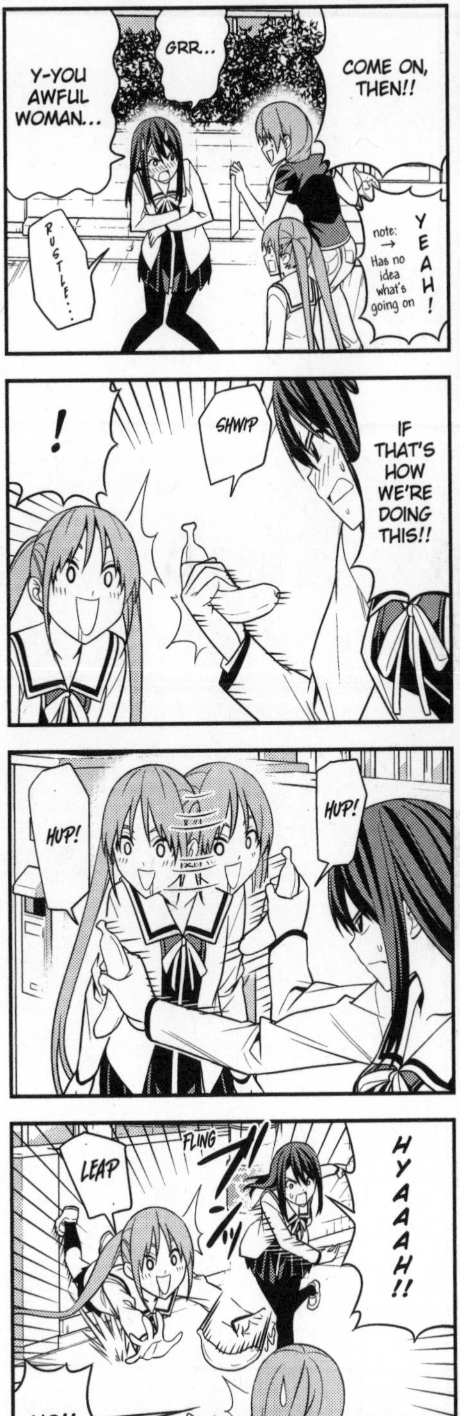
COME ON, THEN!!
GRR...
Y-YOU AWFUL WOMAN...
YEAH!
note: → Has no idea what's going on
RUSTLE...
IF THAT'S HOW WE'RE DOING THIS!!
SHWIP
!
HUP!
HUP!
HYAAAAH!!
FLING
LEAP
NO!!

Awakening

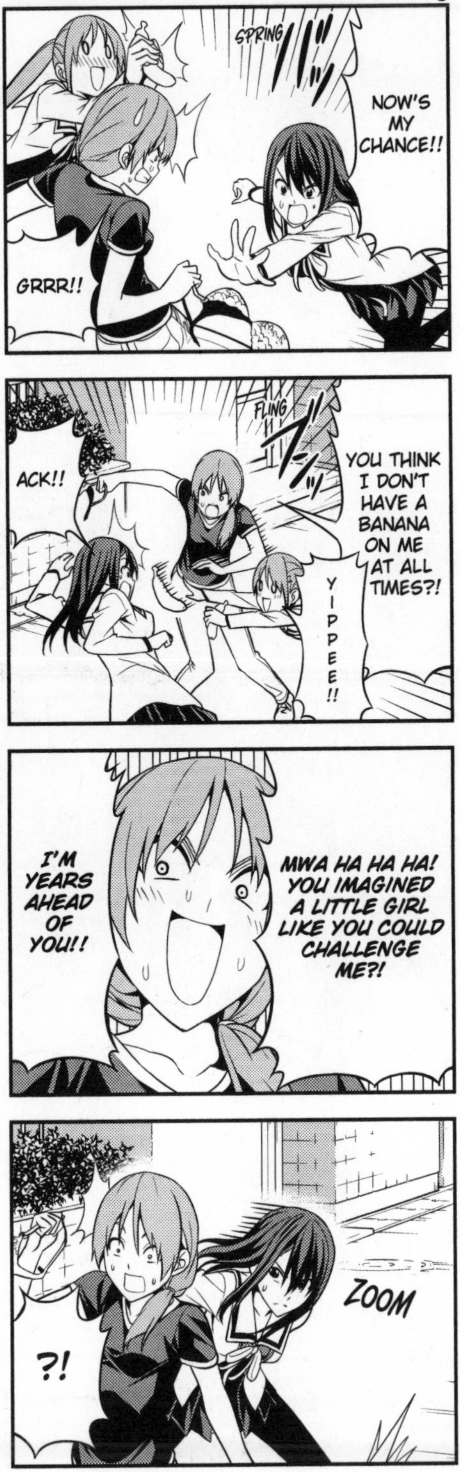
NOW'S MY CHANCE!!
SPRING
GRRR!!
YOU THINK I DON'T HAVE A BANANA ON ME AT ALL TIMES?!
YIPPEE!!
FLING
ACK!!
MWA HA HA HA! YOU IMAGINED A LITTLE GIRL LIKE YOU COULD CHALLENGE ME?!
I'M YEARS AHEAD OF YOU!!
ZOOM
?!

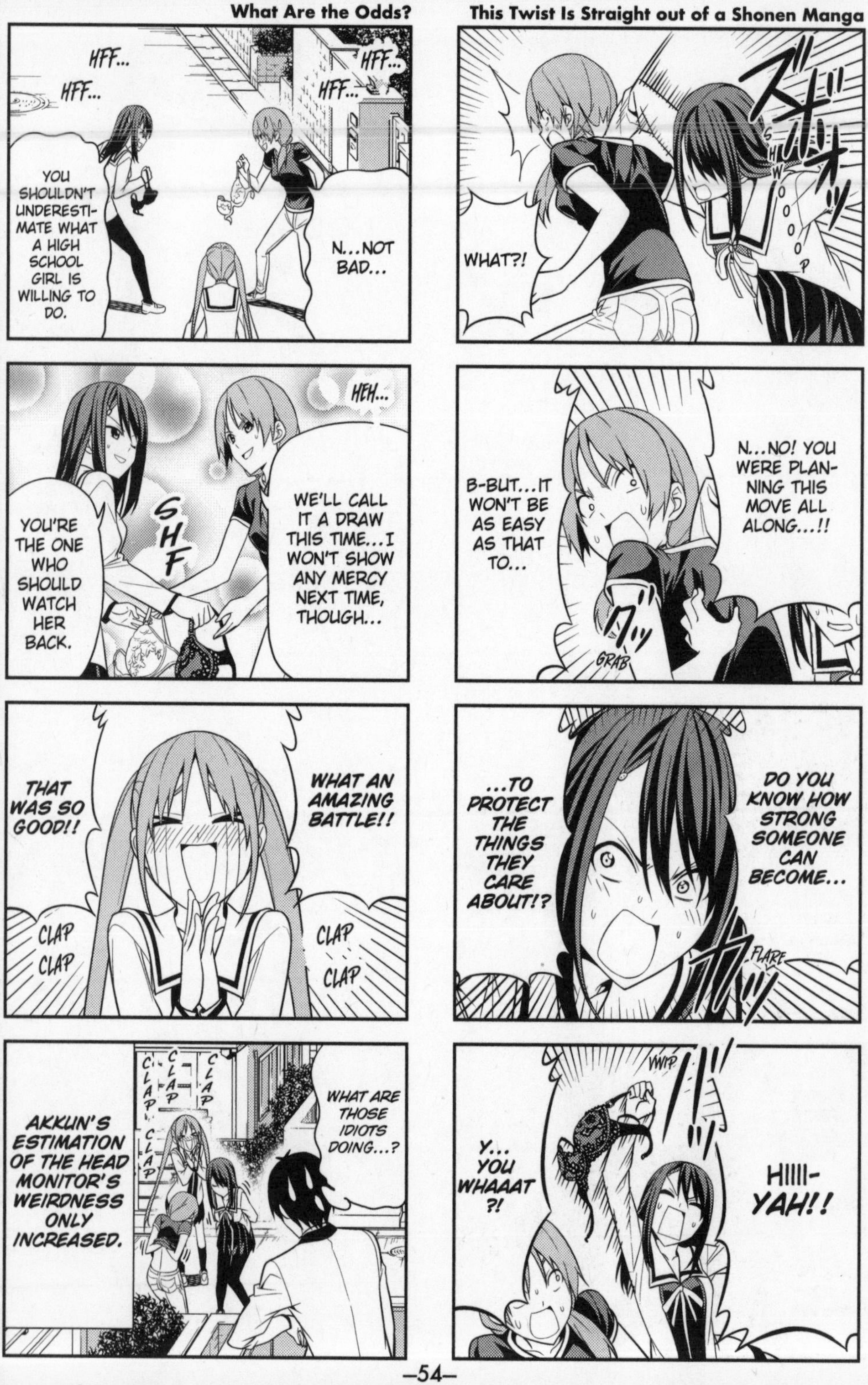
This Twist Is Straight out of a Shonen Manga
ズボッ
SHWOOOOP
WHAT?!
N...NO! YOU WERE PLANNING THIS MOVE ALL ALONG...!!
B-BUT...IT WON'T BE AS EASY AS THAT TO...
グッ
GRAB
DO YOU KNOW HOW STRONG SOMEONE CAN BECOME...
...TO PROTECT THE THINGS THEY CARE ABOUT!?
FLARE
HIIII-YAH!!
VWIP
Y... YOU WHAAAT ?!
What Are the Odds?
HFF... HFF...
HFF... HFF...
N...NOT BAD...
YOU SHOULDN'T UNDERESTIMATE WHAT A HIGH SCHOOL GIRL IS WILLING TO DO.
HEH...
WE'LL CALL IT A DRAW THIS TIME...I WON'T SHOW ANY MERCY NEXT TIME, THOUGH...
SHF
YOU'RE THE ONE WHO SHOULD WATCH HER BACK.
WHAT AN AMAZING BATTLE!!
THAT WAS SO GOOD!!
CLAP CLAP
CLAP CLAP
WHAT ARE THOSE IDIOTS DOING...?
CLAP CLAP CLAP CLAP CLAP
AKKUN'S ESTIMATION OF THE HEAD MONITOR'S WEIRDNESS ONLY INCREASED.

No Time for Remorse

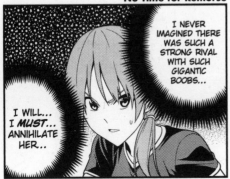

I NEVER IMAGINED THERE WAS SUCH A STRONG RIVAL WITH SUCH GIGANTIC BOOBS...
I WILL... I *MUST*... ANNIHILATE HER...
WHAT A DEGENER-ATE OLD LADY...
I HAVE TO PROTECT AKUTSU-KUN...!!
THEIR BATTLE CON-TINUES...

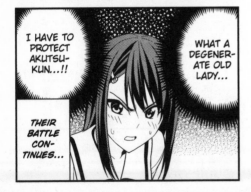

Aho-Girl

\\'ahô͵gərl\\ *Japanese , noun.*
A clueless girl.

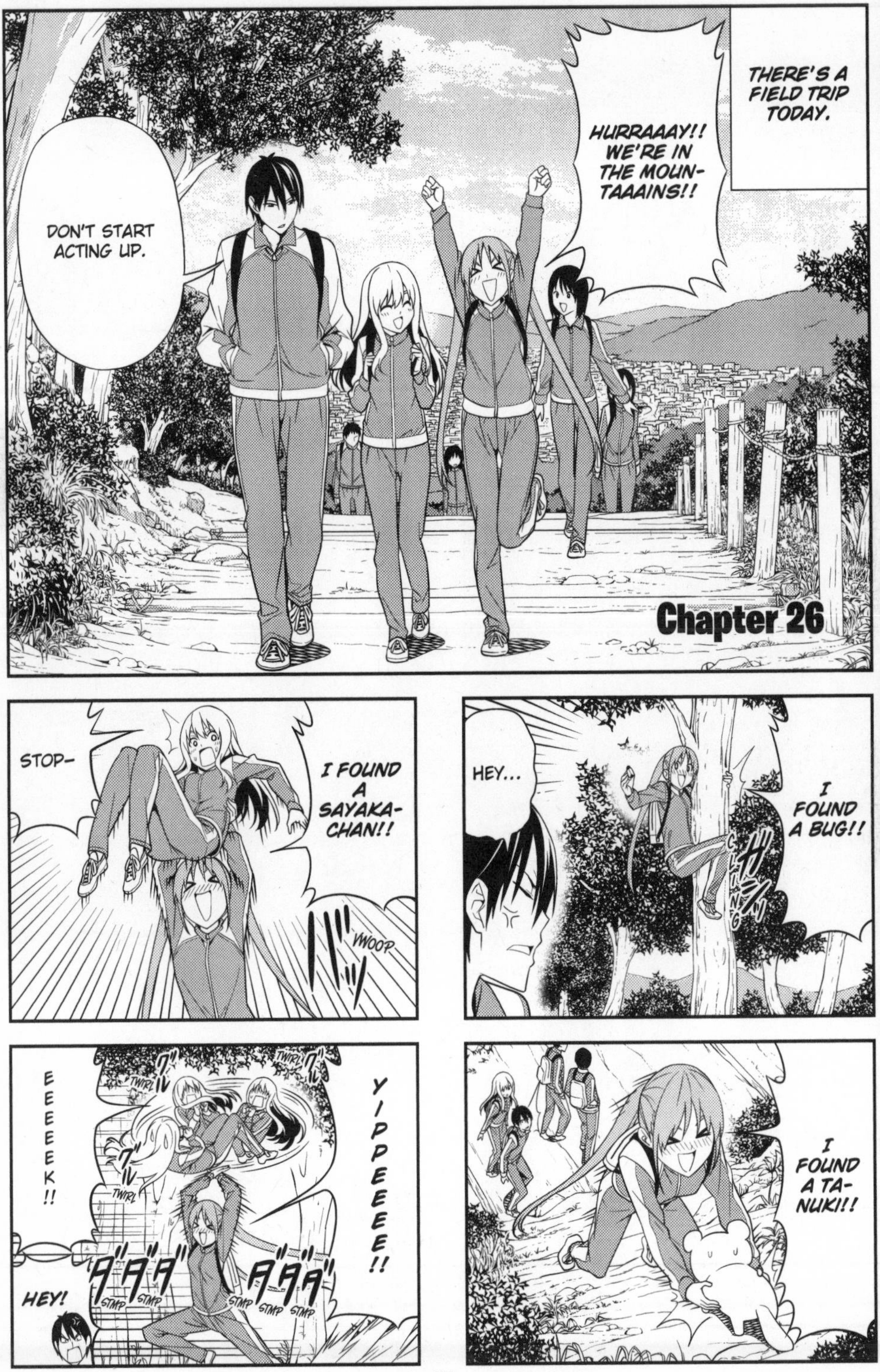
THERE'S A FIELD TRIP TODAY.
HURRAAAY!! WE'RE IN THE MOUN-TAAAINS!!
DON'T START ACTING UP.
Chapter 26
I FOUND A BUG!!
CLING
HEY...
I FOUND A SAYAKA-CHAN!!
STOP-
VWOOP
I FOUND A TA-NUKI!!
YIPPEEEEE!!
TWIRL
TWIRL
TWIRL
EEEEEEK!!
STMP STMP STMP
STMP STMP STMP
HEY!

Wild Child

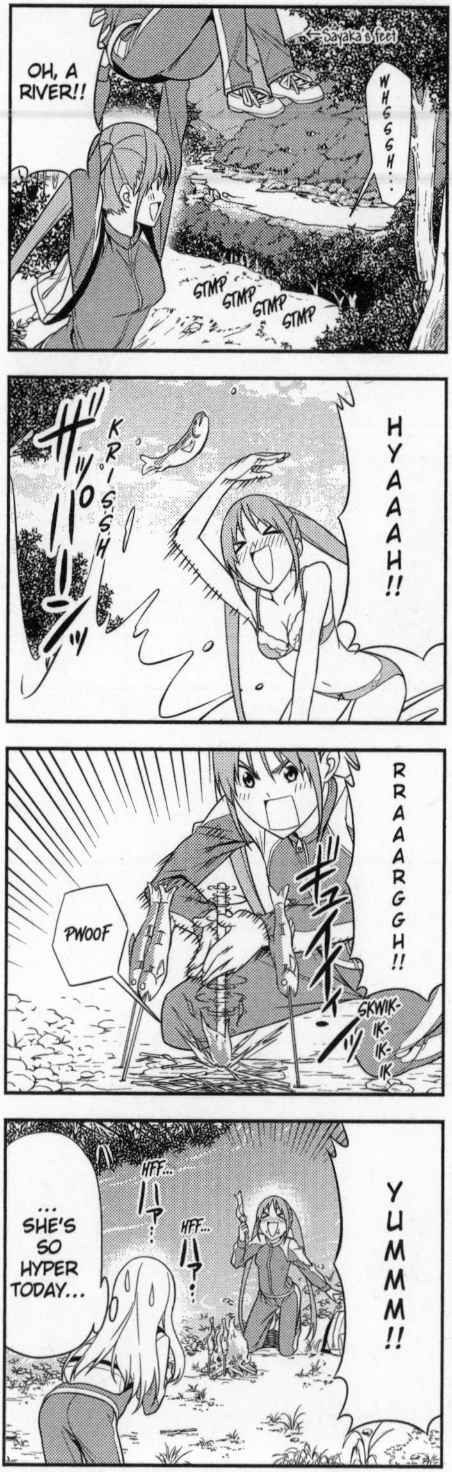
←Sayaka's feet
WHSSSH...
OH, A RIVER!!
STMP STMP STMP STMP
HYAAAAH!!
KRISSH
ザッパーンッ
RRAAAARGGH!!
ギュイイーンッ
SKWIK-IK-IK-IK
PWOOF
YUMMMM!!
HFF... ハァ...
HFF... ハァ...
...SHE'S SO HYPER TODAY...

She'll Probably Survive

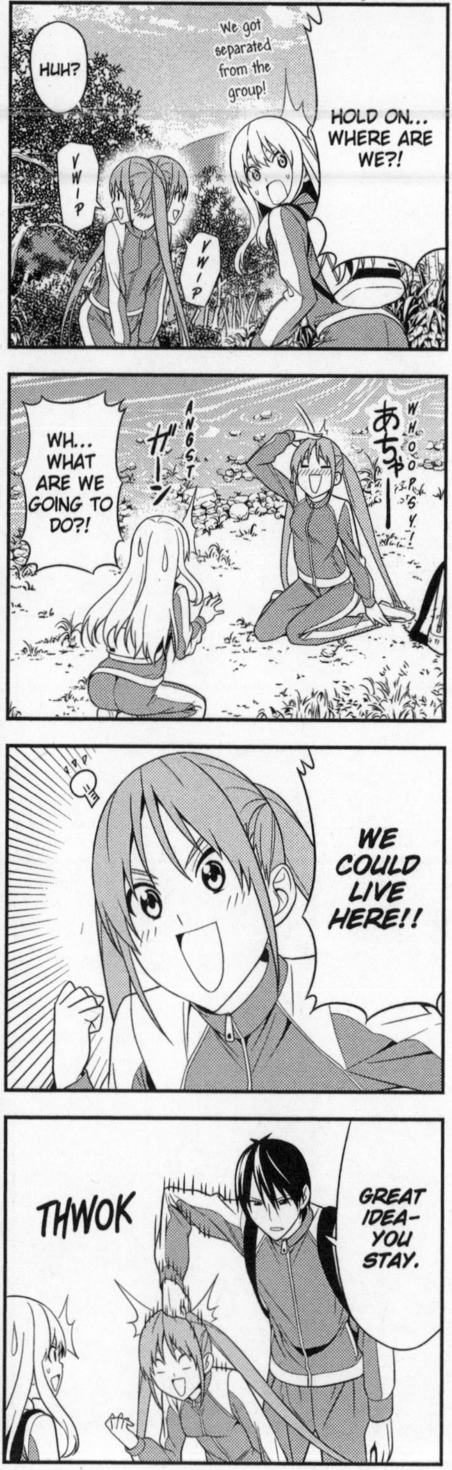
We got separated from the group!
HOLD ON... WHERE ARE WE?!
HUH?
VWIP
VWIP
あちゃー
WHOOPSY!
ANGST
ガーン
WH... WHAT ARE WE GOING TO DO?!
WE COULD LIVE HERE!!
GREAT IDEA-YOU STAY.
THWOK

The Appearance of Kindness

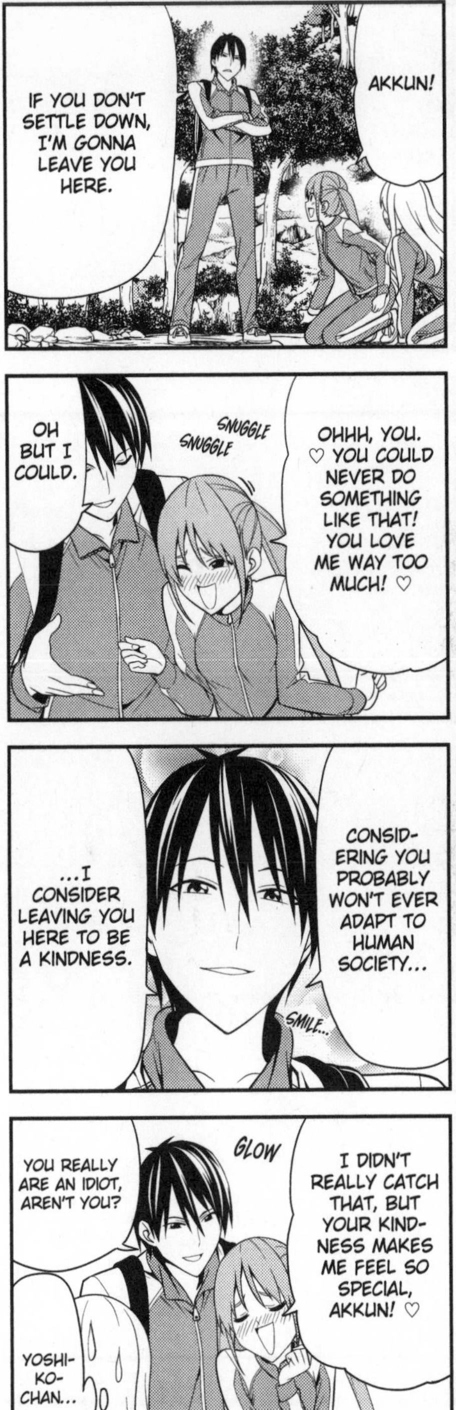
AKKUN!
IF YOU DON'T SETTLE DOWN, I'M GONNA LEAVE YOU HERE.
OHHH, YOU. ♡ YOU COULD NEVER DO SOMETHING LIKE THAT! YOU LOVE ME WAY TOO MUCH! ♡
SNUGGLE SNUGGLE
OH BUT I COULD.
CONSID-ERING YOU PROBABLY WON'T EVER ADAPT TO HUMAN SOCIETY...
...I CONSIDER LEAVING YOU HERE TO BE A KINDNESS.
SMILE...
I DIDN'T REALLY CATCH THAT, BUT YOUR KIND-NESS MAKES ME FEEL SO SPECIAL, AKKUN! ♡
GLOW
YOU REALLY ARE AN IDIOT, AREN'T YOU?
YOSHI-KO-CHAN...

Red Flag

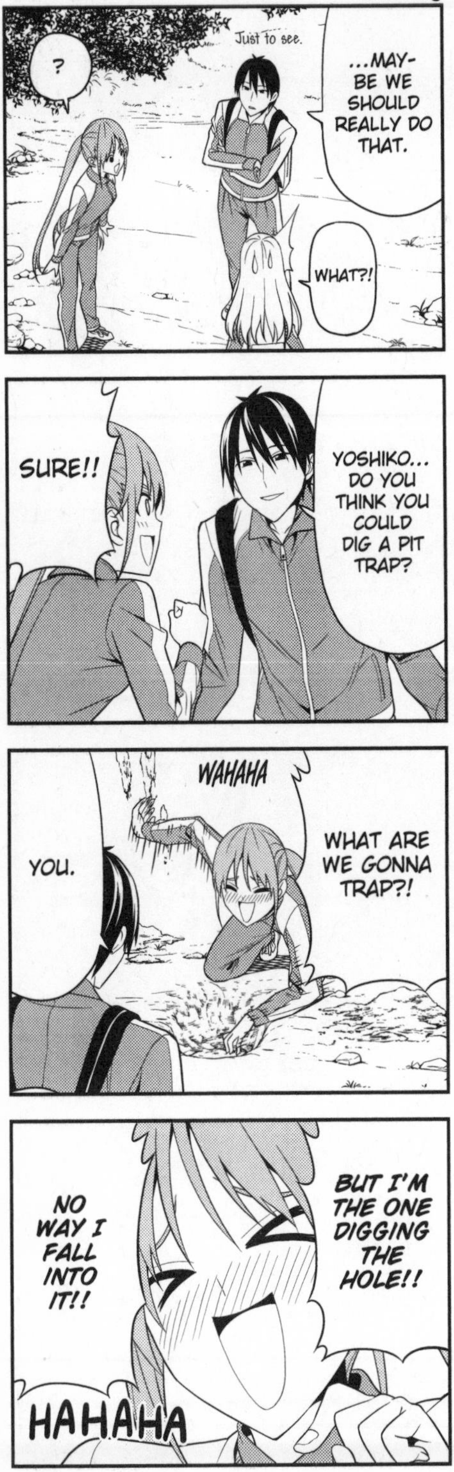
...MAY-BE WE SHOULD REALLY DO THAT.
Just to see.
WHAT?!
?
YOSHIKO... DO YOU THINK YOU COULD DIG A PIT TRAP?
SURE!!
WAHAHA
WHAT ARE WE GONNA TRAP?!
YOU.
BUT I'M THE ONE DIGGING THE HOLE!!
NO WAY I FALL INTO IT!!
HAHAHA

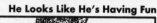

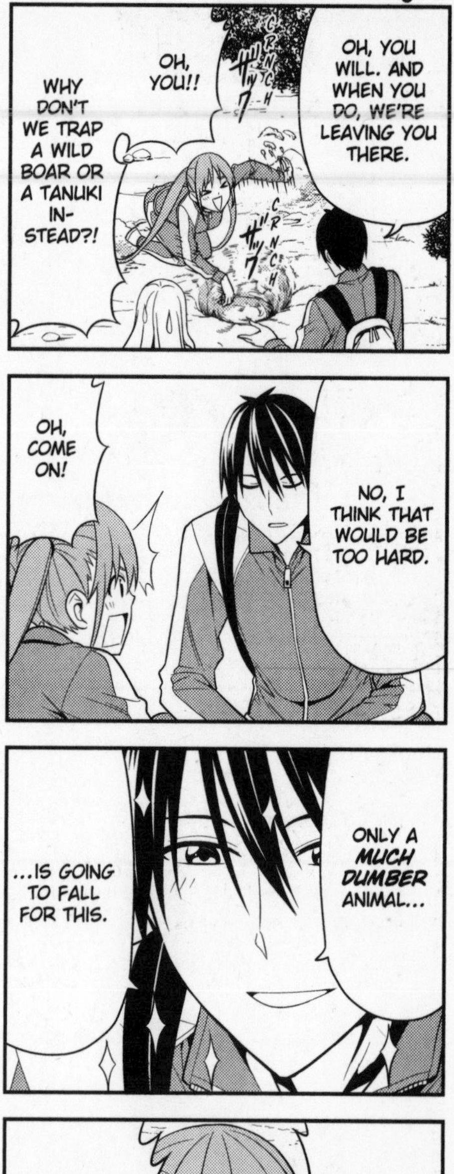
OH, YOU WILL. AND WHEN YOU DO, WE'RE LEAVING YOU THERE.
CRNCH
OH, YOU!!
WHY DON'T WE TRAP A WILD BOAR OR A TANUKI IN-STEAD?!
CRNCH
NO, I THINK THAT WOULD BE TOO HARD.
OH, COME ON!
ONLY A *MUCH DUMBER* ANIMAL...
...IS GOING TO FALL FOR THIS.
WHAT KIND OF ANIMAL IS THAT?!
I CAN'T WAIT TO SEE!!
I ALREADY TOLD YOU. IT'S YOU.

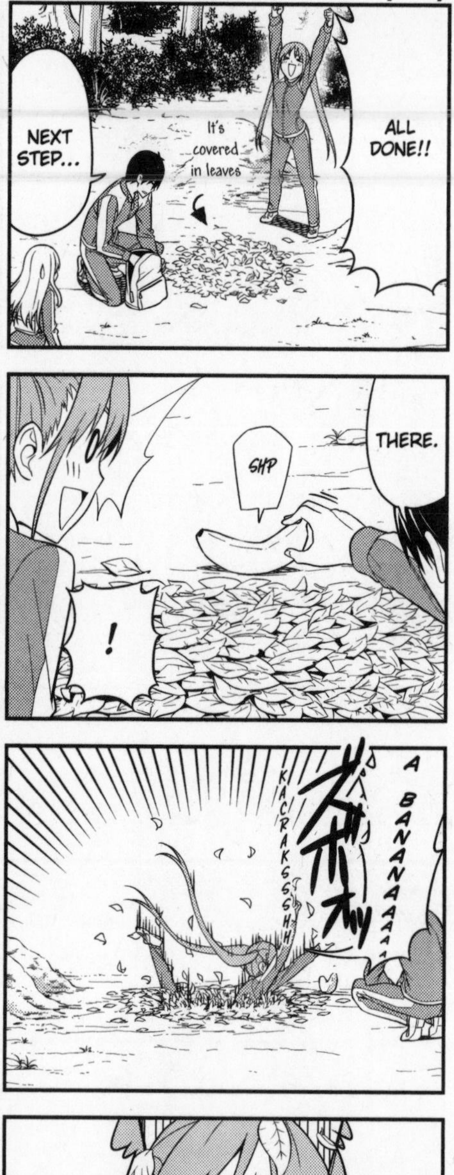
ALL DONE!!
It's covered in leaves
NEXT STEP...
THERE.
SHP
!
A BANANAAAAA
KACRAKSSSHH
I...
I FELL FOR IT!!

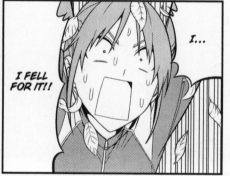

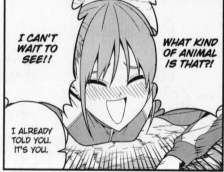

Triggering the Trap

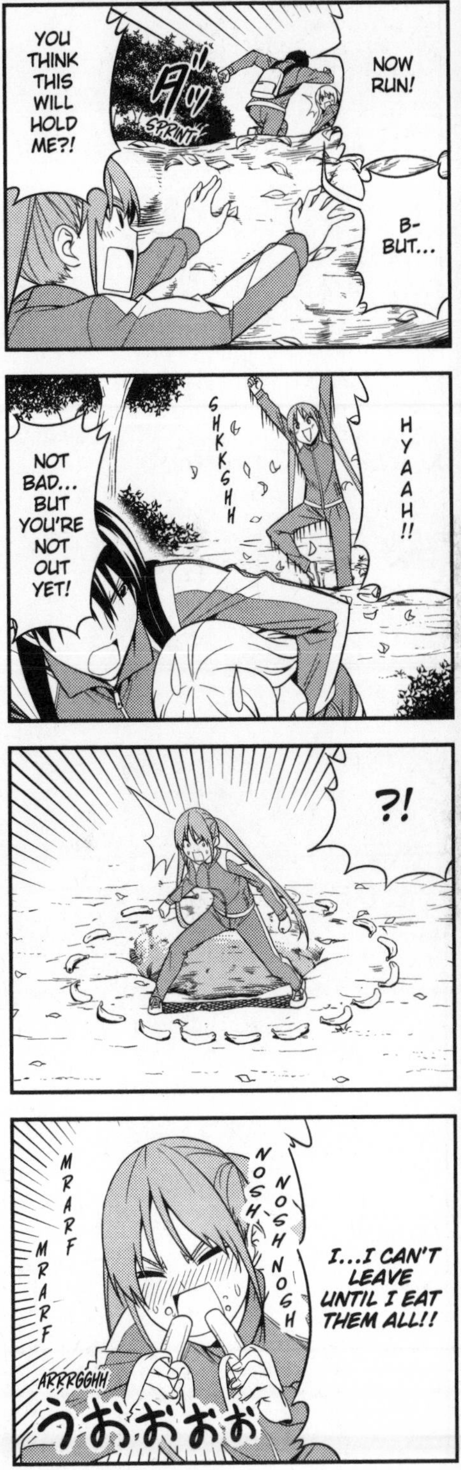
NOW RUN!
B-BUT...
ダッ
SPRINT
YOU THINK THIS WILL HOLD ME?!
HYAAAH!!
SHKKSHH
NOT BAD... BUT YOU'RE NOT OUT YET!
?!
I...I CAN'T LEAVE UNTIL I EAT THEM ALL!!
NOSH NOSH
NOSH NOSH
MRARF
MRARF
ARRRGGHH
うおおおぉ

Banana Machine Gun

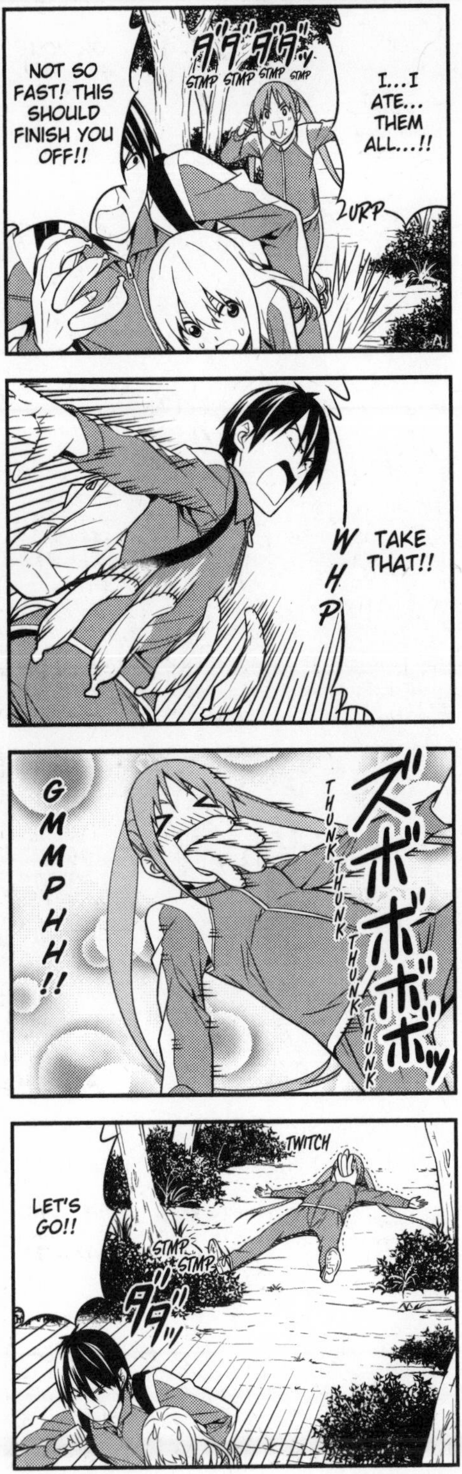
I...I ATE... THEM ALL...!!
ZURP
ダダダダッ
STMP STMP STMP STMP
NOT SO FAST! THIS SHOULD FINISH YOU OFF!!
TAKE THAT!!
WHP
ズボボボボッ
THUNK THUNK THUNK THUNK
GMMPHH!!
TWITCH
LET'S GO!!
STMP STMP
ダダッ

Optimism

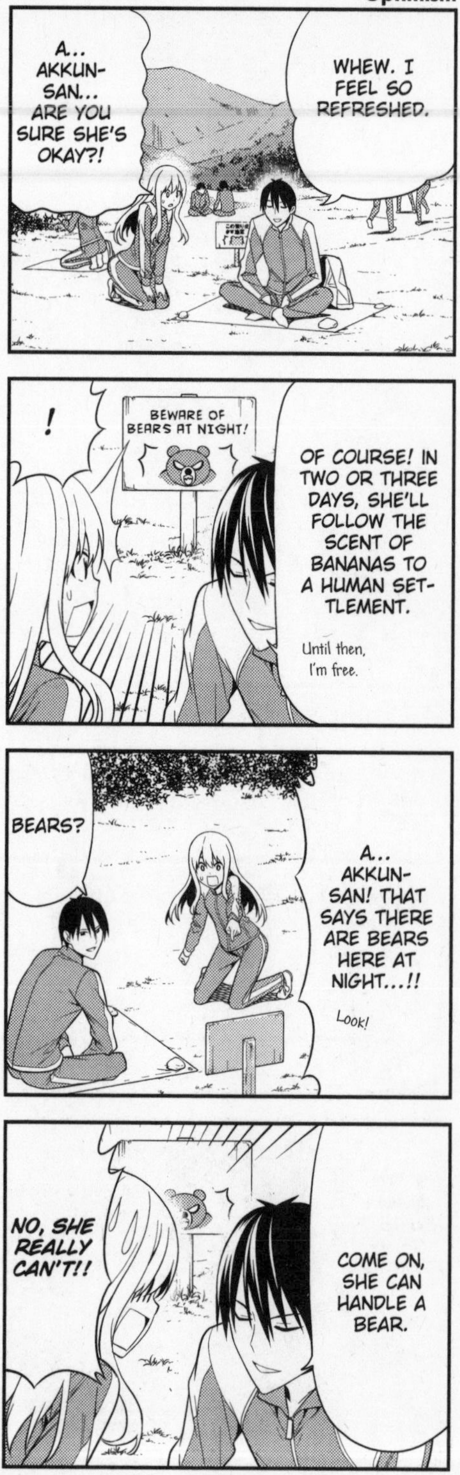
WHEW. I FEEL SO REFRESHED.
A... AKKUN-SAN... ARE YOU SURE SHE'S OKAY?!
OF COURSE! IN TWO OR THREE DAYS, SHE'LL FOLLOW THE SCENT OF BANANAS TO A HUMAN SET-TLEMENT.
Until then, I'm free.
BEWARE OF BEARS AT NIGHT!
!
A... AKKUN-SAN! THAT SAYS THERE ARE BEARS HERE AT NIGHT...!!
Look!
BEARS?
COME ON, SHE CAN HANDLE A BEAR.
NO, SHE REALLY CAN'T!!

Going Fishing

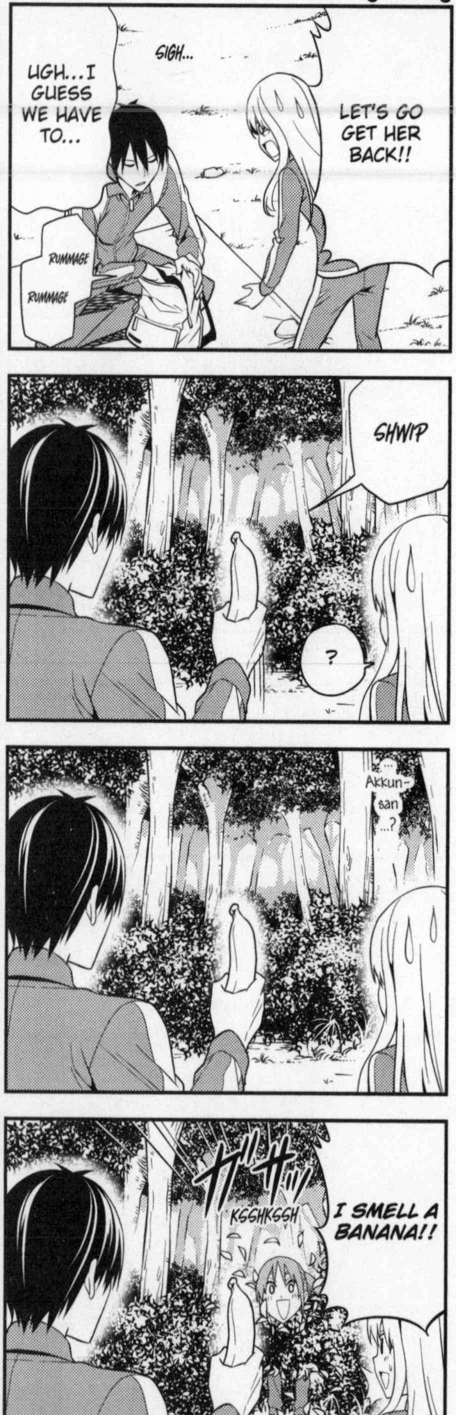
LET'S GO GET HER BACK!!
SIGH...
UGH...I GUESS WE HAVE TO...
RUMMAGE
RUMMAGE
SHWIP
?
... Akkun-san ...?
I SMELL A BANANA!!
KSSHKSSH

The Master

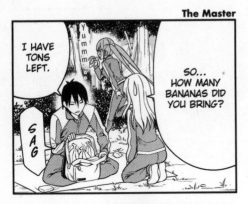

SO... HOW MANY BANANAS DID YOU BRING?
Yummm
I HAVE TONS LEFT.
SAG
WHEN WE GO ON TRIPS, SHE TENDS TO GO A LITTLE CRAZY.
SO I HAVE TO PREP A LOT MORE OF THEM THAN USUAL IN ORDER TO CONTROL HER.
IS THIS AN EX-PRESSION OF HIS AFFECTION ...?

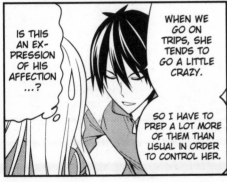

Aho-Girl

\ˈahôˌgərl\ *Japanese , noun.*
A clueless girl.

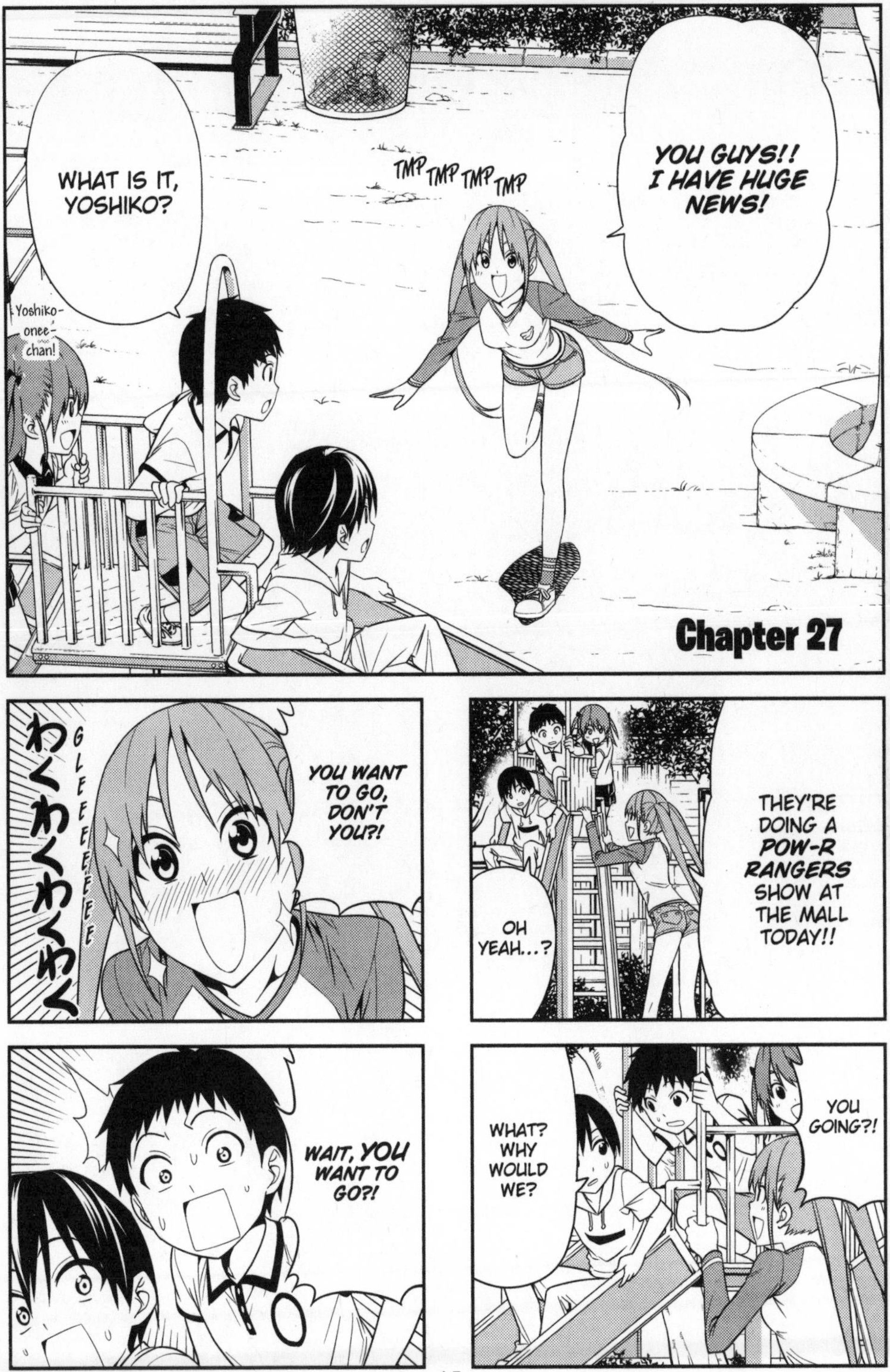
YOU GUYS!! I HAVE HUGE NEWS!
TMP TMP TMP TMP
WHAT IS IT, YOSHIKO?
Yoshiko-onee-chan!
Chapter 27
THEY'RE DOING A POW-R RANGERS SHOW AT THE MALL TODAY!!
OH YEAH...?
YOU WANT TO GO, DON'T YOU?!
わくわくわくわく
GLEEEEEEE
YOU GOING?!
WHAT? WHY WOULD WE?
WAIT, YOU WANT TO GO?!

In Full Costume

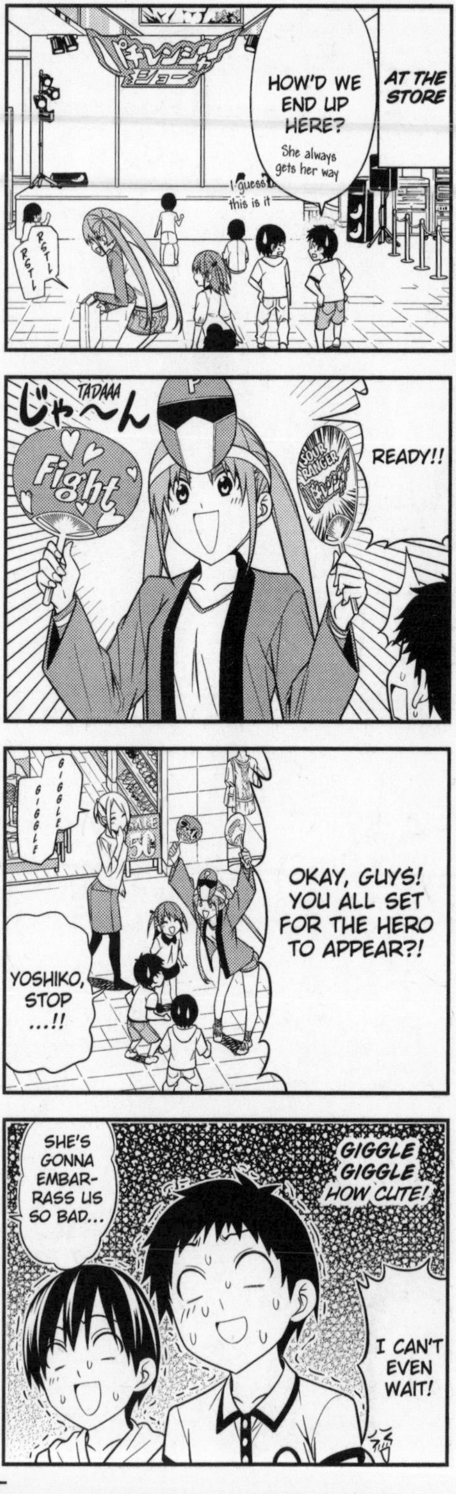
AT THE STORE
HOW'D WE END UP HERE?
She always gets her way
I guess this is it
RSTL RSTL
じゃ〜ん
TADAAA
READY!!
SOUR RANGER
Fight
OKAY, GUYS! YOU ALL SET FOR THE HERO TO APPEAR?!
GIGGLE GIGGLE
YOSHIKO, STOP ...!!
GIGGLE GIGGLE HOW CUTE!
SHE'S GONNA EMBARRASS US SO BAD...
I CAN'T EVEN WAIT!

100% Effort

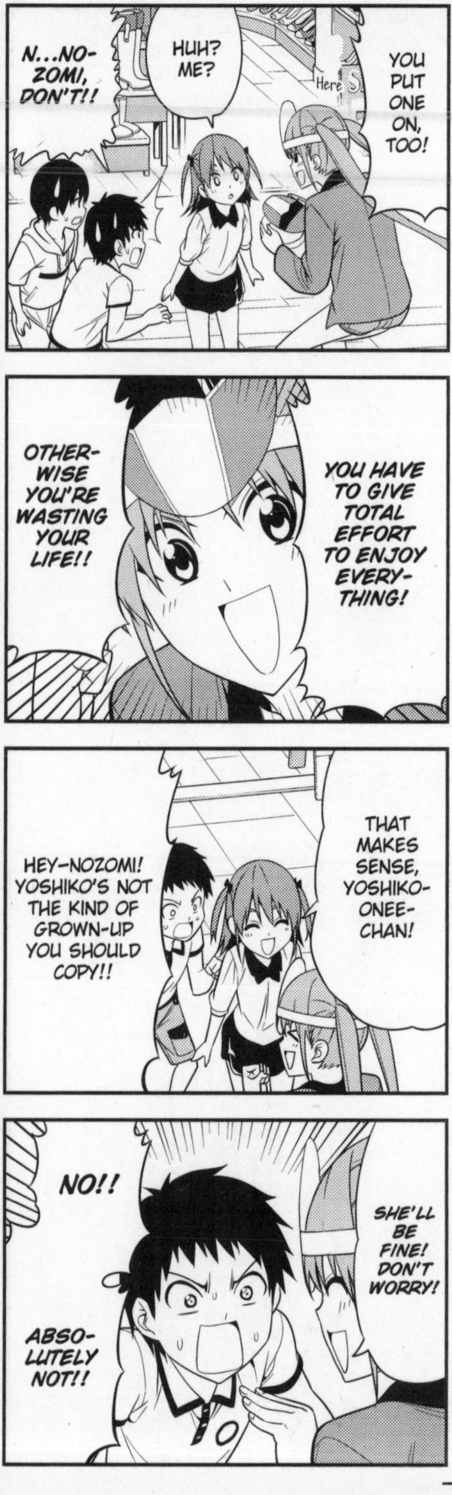
YOU PUT ONE ON, TOO!
Here
HUH? ME?
N...NO-ZOMI, DON'T!!
YOU HAVE TO GIVE TOTAL EFFORT TO ENJOY EVERYTHING!
OTHER-WISE YOU'RE WASTING YOUR LIFE!!
THAT MAKES SENSE, YOSHIKO-ONEE-CHAN!
HEY—NOZOMI! YOSHIKO'S NOT THE KIND OF GROWN-UP YOU SHOULD COPY!!
SHE'LL BE FINE! DON'T WORRY!
NO!!
ABSO-LUTELY NOT!!

Plant the Flag

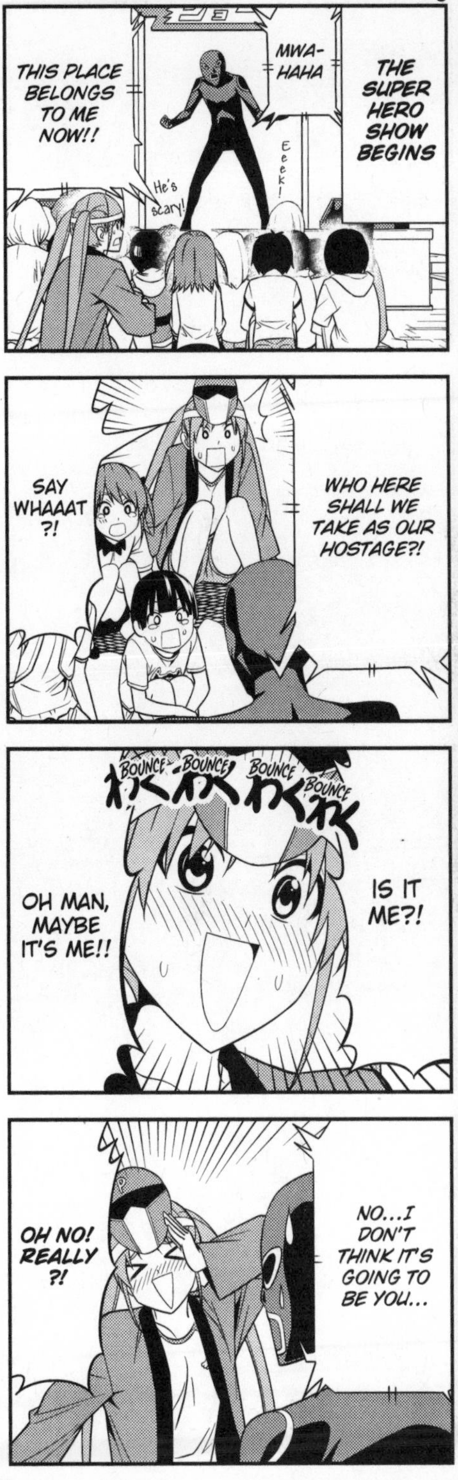
THE SUPER HERO SHOW BEGINS
MWA-HAHA
THIS PLACE BELONGS TO ME NOW!!
Eeeek!
He's scary!
WHO HERE SHALL WE TAKE AS OUR HOSTAGE?!
SAY WHAAAT?!
BOUNCE BOUNCE BOUNCE BOUNCE
IS IT ME?!
OH MAN, MAYBE IT'S ME!!
NO...I DON'T THINK IT'S GOING TO BE YOU...
OH NO! REALLY?!

Determination

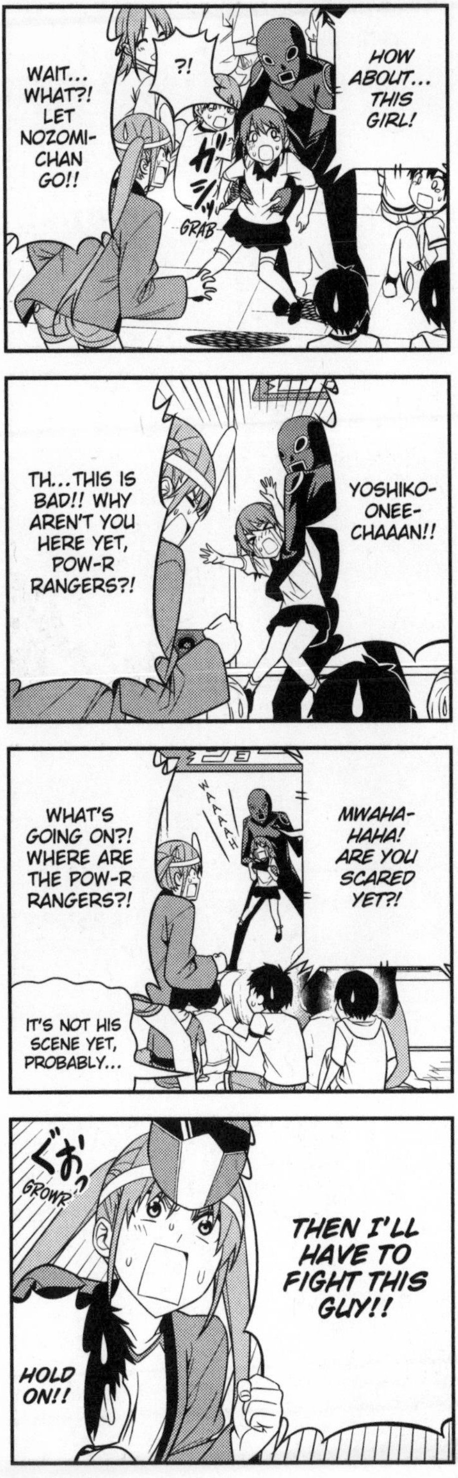
HOW ABOUT... THIS GIRL!
?!
WAIT... WHAT?! LET NOZOMI-CHAN GO!!
GRAB
YOSHIKO-ONEE-CHAAAN!!
TH...THIS IS BAD!! WHY AREN'T YOU HERE YET, POW-R RANGERS?!
WAAAAH
MWAHA-HAHA! ARE YOU SCARED YET?!
WHAT'S GOING ON?! WHERE ARE THE POW-R RANGERS?!
IT'S NOT HIS SCENE YET, PROBABLY...
THEN I'LL HAVE TO FIGHT THIS GUY!!
GROWR
HOLD ON!!

Kind of, Yeah

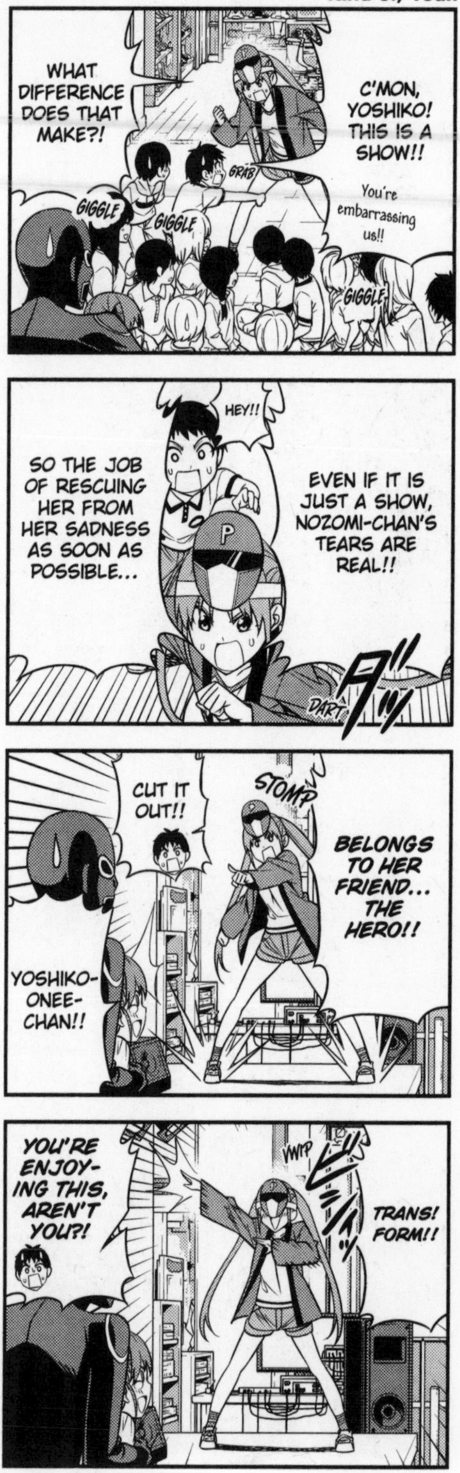

C'MON, YOSHIKO! THIS IS A SHOW!!
You're embarrassing us!!
GRAB
GIGGLE
GIGGLE
GIGGLE
WHAT DIFFERENCE DOES THAT MAKE?!
EVEN IF IT IS JUST A SHOW, NOZOMI-CHAN'S TEARS ARE REAL!!
HEY!!
SO THE JOB OF RESCUING HER FROM HER SADNESS AS SOON AS POSSIBLE...
DART
STOMP
BELONGS TO HER FRIEND... THE HERO!!
CUT IT OUT!!
YOSHIKO-ONEE-CHAN!!
VWIP
TRANS! FORM!!
YOU'RE ENJOY-ING THIS, AREN'T YOU?!

This Is How They See Yoshiko

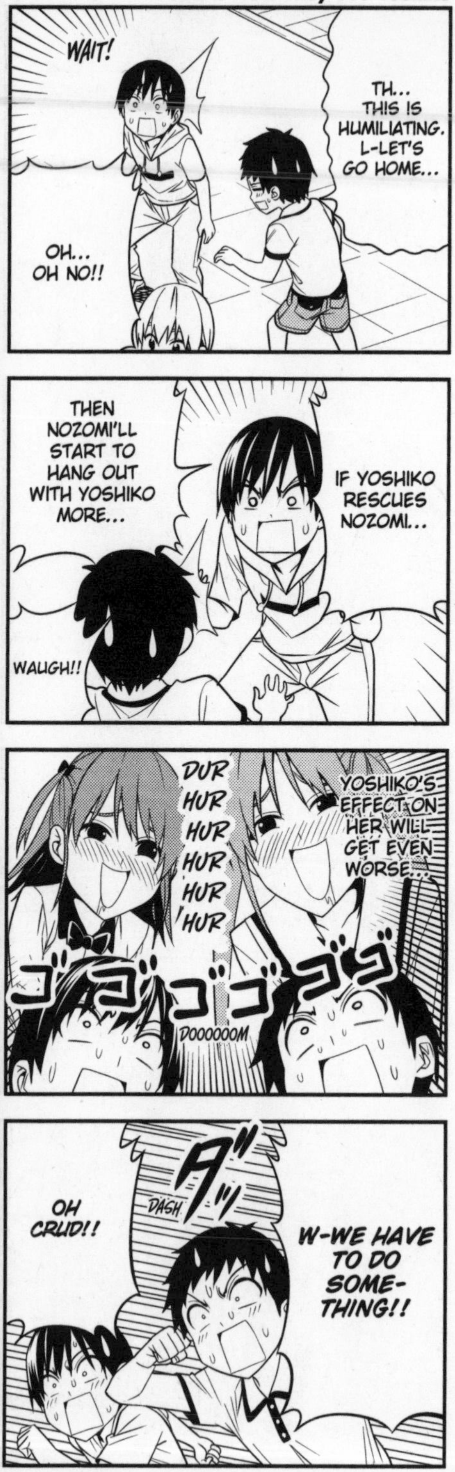

TH... THIS IS HUMILIATING. L-LET'S GO HOME...
WAIT!
OH... OH NO!!
IF YOSHIKO RESCUES NOZOMI...
THEN NOZOMI'LL START TO HANG OUT WITH YOSHIKO MORE...
WAUGH!!
YOSHIKO'S EFFECT ON HER WILL GET EVEN WORSE...
DUR HUR HUR HUR HUR HUR
ゴゴゴゴゴゴ
DOOOOOOM
W-WE HAVE TO DO SOME-THING!!
DASH
OH CRUD!!

Stop Right There

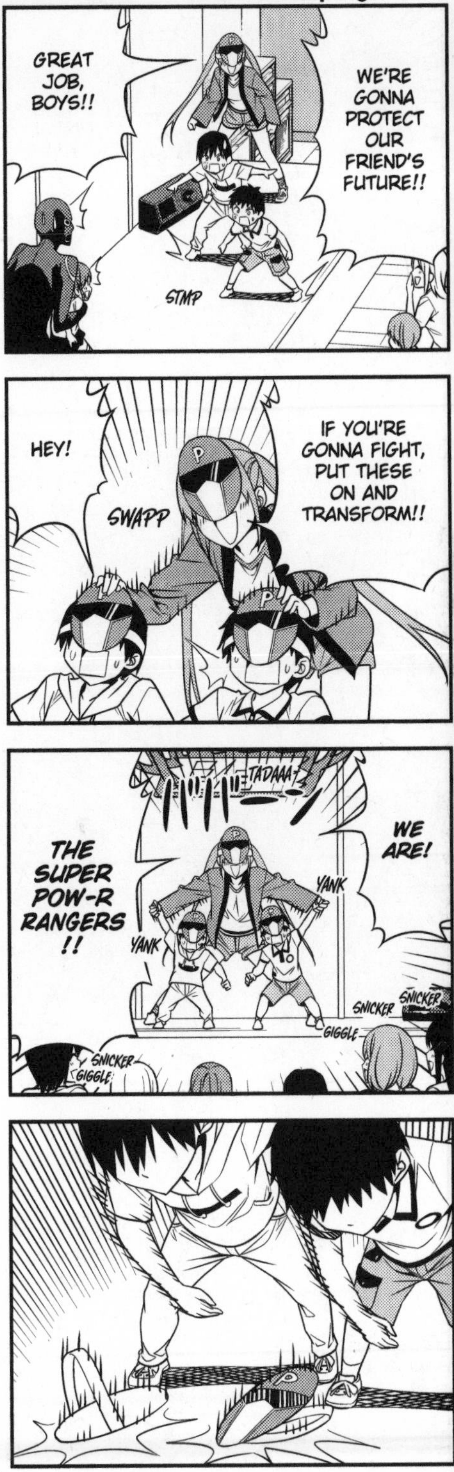
WE'RE GONNA PROTECT OUR FRIEND'S FUTURE!!
GREAT JOB, BOYS!!
STMP
IF YOU'RE GONNA FIGHT, PUT THESE ON AND TRANSFORM!!
HEY!
SWAPP
TADAAA
WE ARE!
THE SUPER POW-R RANGERS!!
YANK
YANK
SNICKER
SNICKER
GIGGLE
SNICKER
GIGGLE

A Single Strike to the Sagittal

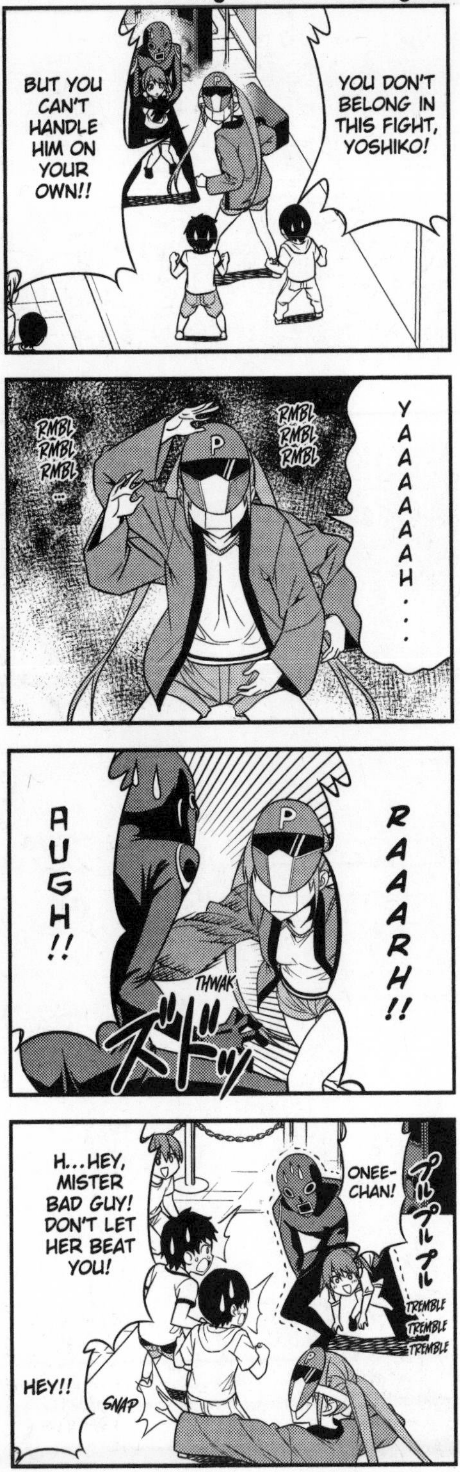
YOU DON'T BELONG IN THIS FIGHT, YOSHIKO!
BUT YOU CAN'T HANDLE HIM ON YOUR OWN!!
YAAAAAAAH...
RMBL RMBL RMBL
RMBL RMBL RMBL ...
RAAAARH!!
AUGH!!
THWAK
ズドッ
ONEE-CHAN!
H...HEY, MISTER BAD GUY! DON'T LET HER BEAT YOU!
プルプル
TREMBLE TREMBLE TREMBLE
HEY!!
SNAP

Grown-ups Just Don't Understand

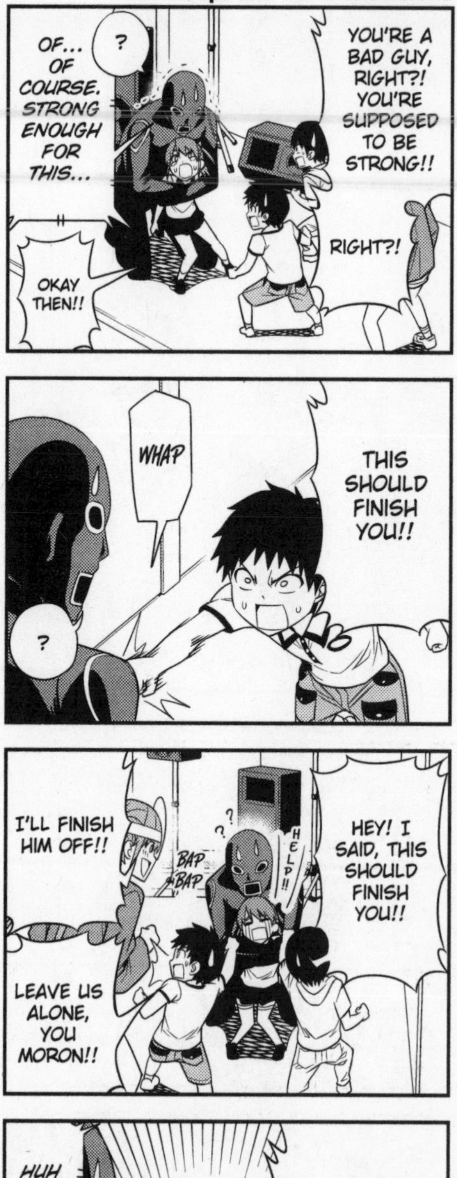
YOU'RE A BAD GUY, RIGHT?! YOU'RE SUPPOSED TO BE STRONG!!
?
OF... OF COURSE. STRONG ENOUGH FOR THIS...
RIGHT?!
OKAY THEN!!
THIS SHOULD FINISH YOU!!
WHAP
?
HEY! I SAID, THIS SHOULD FINISH YOU!!
HELP!!
? ?
BAP BAP
I'LL FINISH HIM OFF!!
LEAVE US ALONE, YOU MORON!!
CAN'T YOU FOLLOW A CUE?!
WHAP THWAK
HUH ?!
WHAT ?!

So What If It's a Lie!

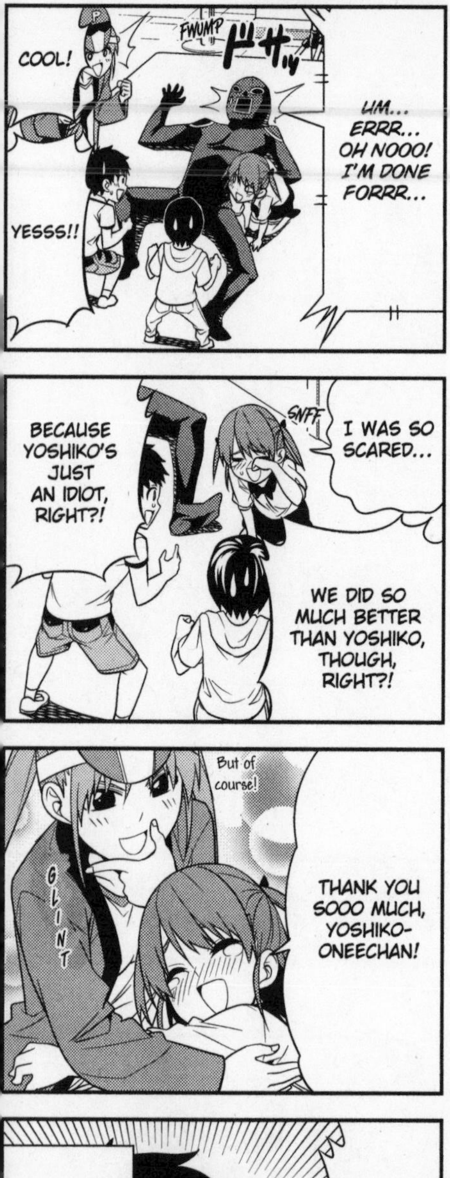
UM... ERRR... OH NOOO! I'M DONE FORRR...
FWUMP ドサッ
COOL!
YESSS!!
I WAS SO SCARED...
SNFF
WE DID SO MUCH BETTER THAN YOSHIKO, THOUGH, RIGHT?!
BECAUSE YOSHIKO'S JUST AN IDIOT, RIGHT?!
THANK YOU SOOO MUCH, YOSHIKO-ONEECHAN!
But of course!
GLINT
ARE YOU SERIOUS?!
YOU'LL HAVE TO KEEP FIGHTING TO PROTECT HER FUTURE, BOYS.

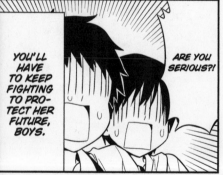

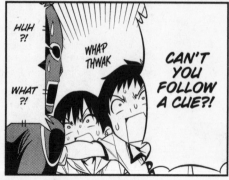

The Strongest Challenger Appears

WHAT DO YOU THINK YOU'RE DOING...?
WHAT!
A NEW BAD GUY!!
YOU IDIOT!!
SHWAKK!
UWAUGH!!

He was just passing by ↲

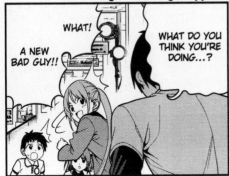

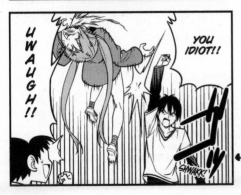

(Five stars, shining in the heavens! Five-Star Squadron!!)

Aho-Girl

\ˈahôˌɡərl\ *Japanese , noun.*
A clueless girl.

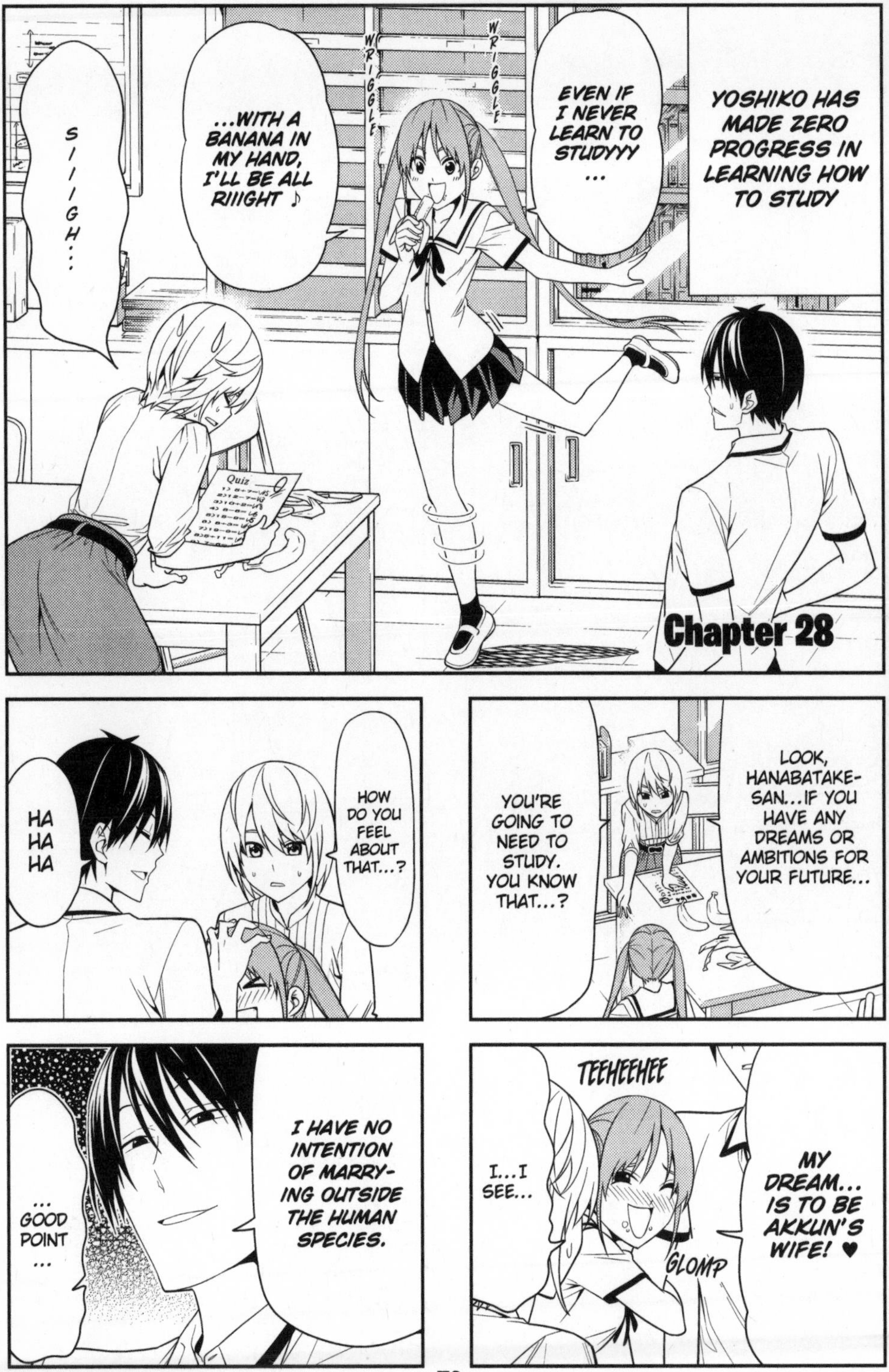
YOSHIKO HAS MADE ZERO PROGRESS IN LEARNING HOW TO STUDY
Chapter 28
EVEN IF I NEVER LEARN TO STUDYYY ...
WRIGGLE
WRIGGLE
...WITH A BANANA IN MY HAND, I'LL BE ALL RIIIGHT ♪
SIIIGH...
LOOK, HANABATAKE-SAN...IF YOU HAVE ANY DREAMS OR AMBITIONS FOR YOUR FUTURE...
YOU'RE GOING TO NEED TO STUDY. YOU KNOW THAT...?
HOW DO YOU FEEL ABOUT THAT...?
HA HA HA
TEEHEEHEE
MY DREAM... IS TO BE AKKUN'S WIFE! ♥
GLOMP
I...I SEE...
I HAVE NO INTENTION OF MARRY-ING OUTSIDE THE HUMAN SPECIES.
...GOOD POINT...

Smile of an Angel

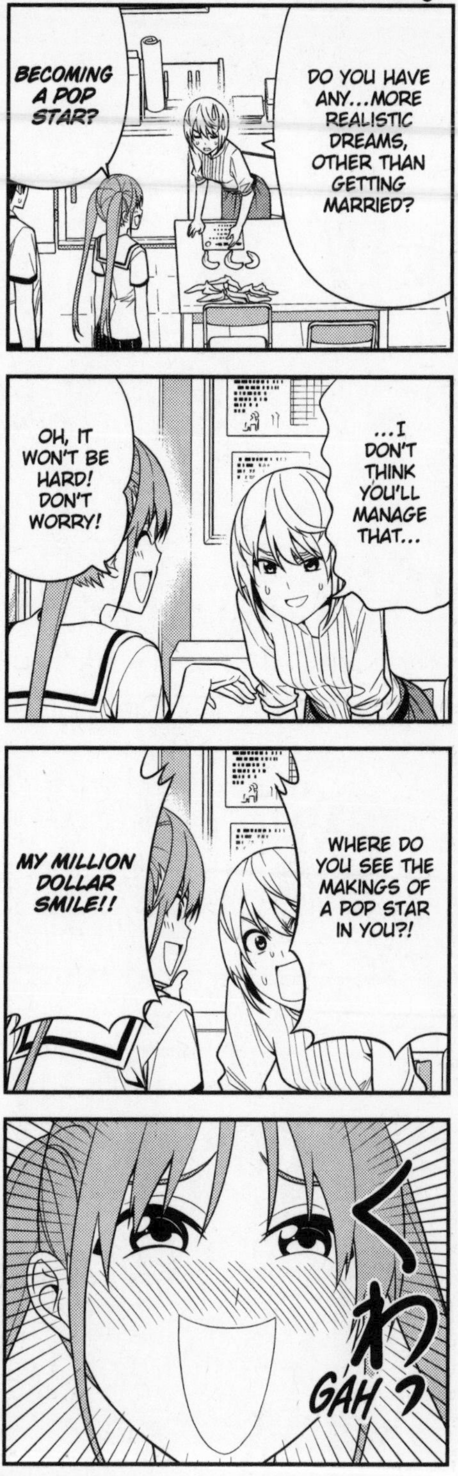
DO YOU HAVE ANY…MORE REALISTIC DREAMS, OTHER THAN GETTING MARRIED?
BECOMING A POP STAR?
…I DON'T THINK YOU'LL MANAGE THAT…
OH, IT WON'T BE HARD! DON'T WORRY!
WHERE DO YOU SEE THE MAKINGS OF A POP STAR IN YOU?!
MY MILLION DOLLAR SMILE!!
くわっ
GAH

I Told You So

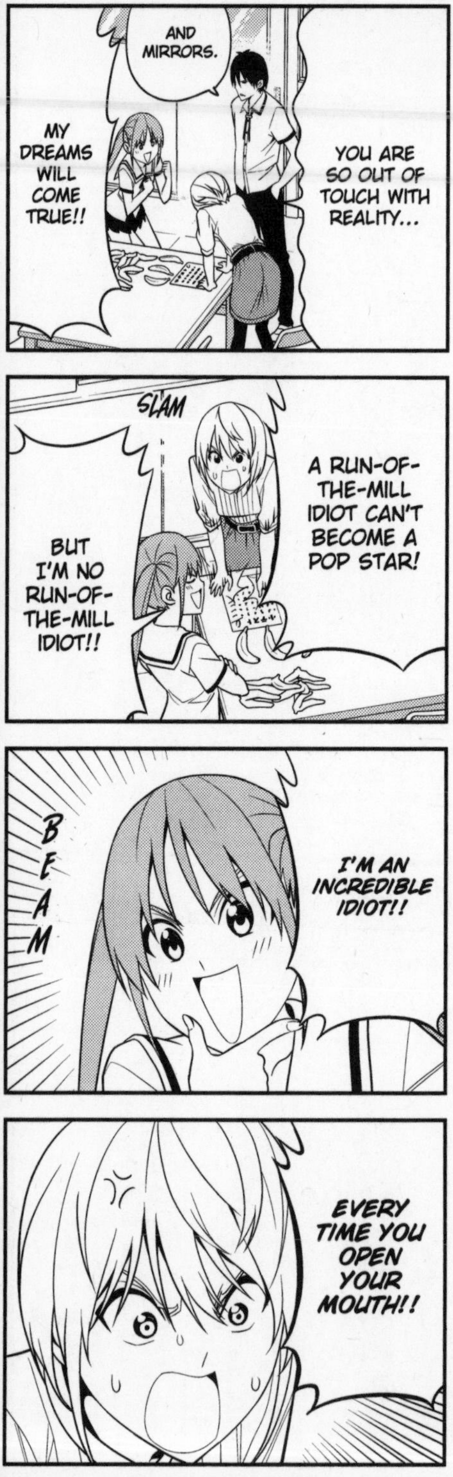
AND MIRRORS.
YOU ARE SO OUT OF TOUCH WITH REALITY…
MY DREAMS WILL COME TRUE!!
SLAM
A RUN-OF-THE-MILL IDIOT CAN'T BECOME A POP STAR!
BUT I'M NO RUN-OF-THE-MILL IDIOT!!
I'M AN INCREDIBLE IDIOT!!
BEAM
EVERY TIME YOU OPEN YOUR MOUTH!!

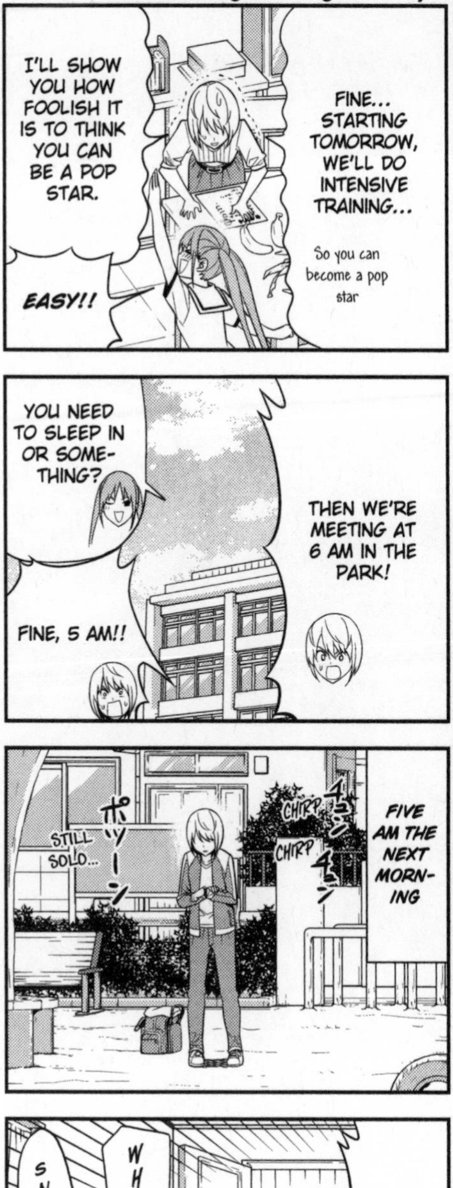
FINE... STARTING TOMORROW, WE'LL DO INTENSIVE TRAINING...
So you can become a pop star
I'LL SHOW YOU HOW FOOLISH IT IS TO THINK YOU CAN BE A POP STAR.
EASY!!
THEN WE'RE MEETING AT 6 AM IN THE PARK!
FINE, 5 AM!!
YOU NEED TO SLEEP IN OR SOME-THING?
FIVE AM THE NEXT MORN-ING
CHIRP
CHIRP
ポツーン
STILL SOLO...
HANA-BATAKE-SAN!!
WHAM
SNRK...

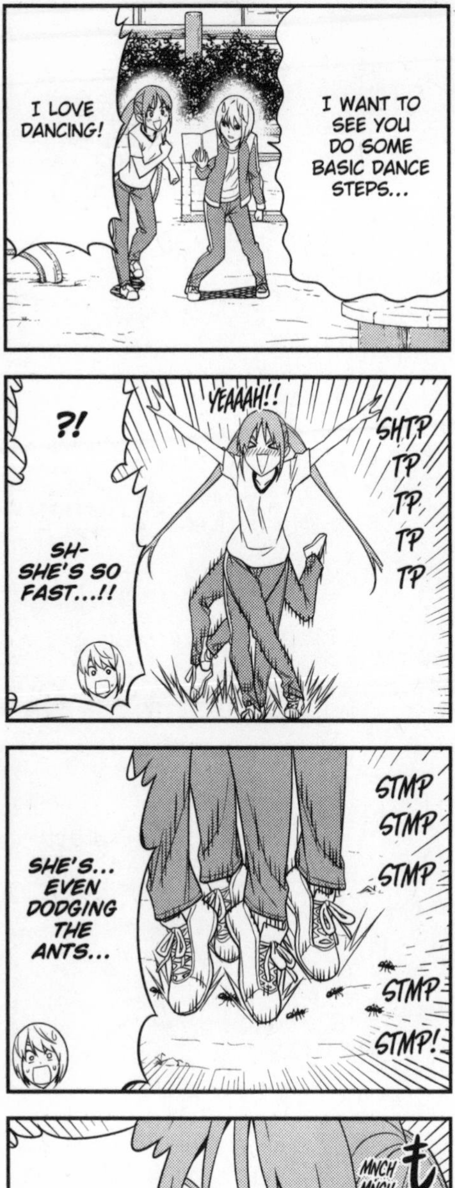
I WANT TO SEE YOU DO SOME BASIC DANCE STEPS...
I LOVE DANCING!
SHTP TP TP TP TP
YEAAAH!!
?!
SH- SHE'S SO FAST...!!
STMP STMP STMP
STMP
STMP!
SHE'S... EVEN DODGING THE ANTS...
もしゃもしゃもしゃもしゃ
MNCH MNCH MNCH MNCH
AND EATING A BANANA!!

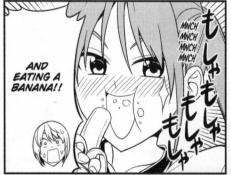

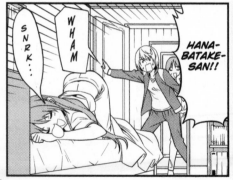

Natural Gifts

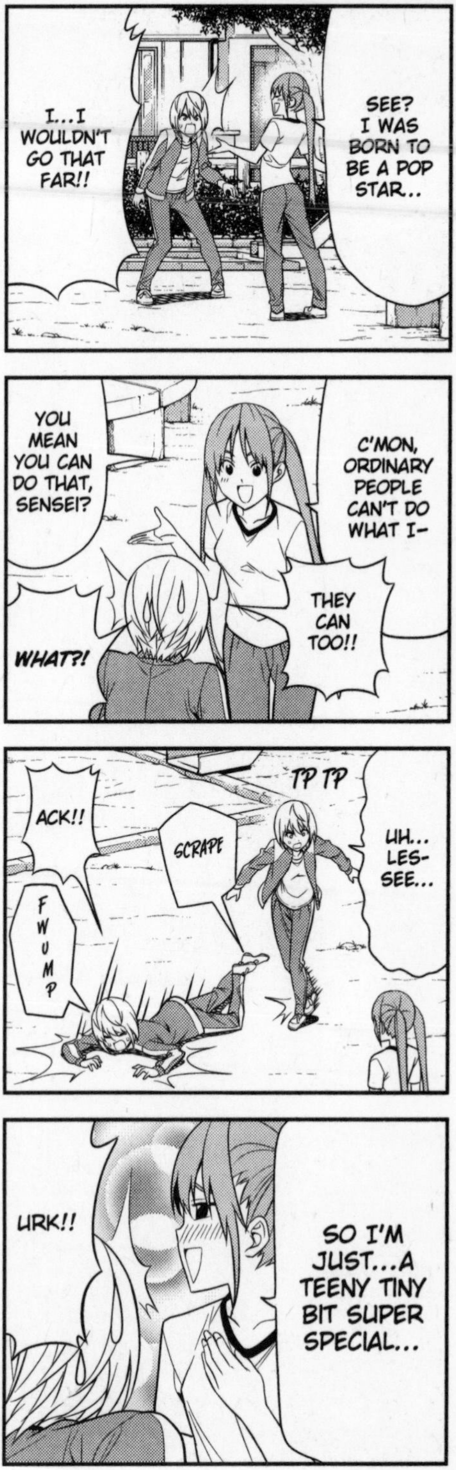
SEE? I WAS BORN TO BE A POP STAR...
I...I WOULDN'T GO THAT FAR!!
C'MON, ORDINARY PEOPLE CAN'T DO WHAT I-
YOU MEAN YOU CAN DO THAT, SENSEI?
THEY CAN TOO!!
WHAT?!
TP TP
UH... LES-SEE...
ACK!!
SCRAPE
FWUMP
SO I'M JUST...A TEENY TINY BIT SUPER SPECIAL...
URK!!

Athletic Ability: Same

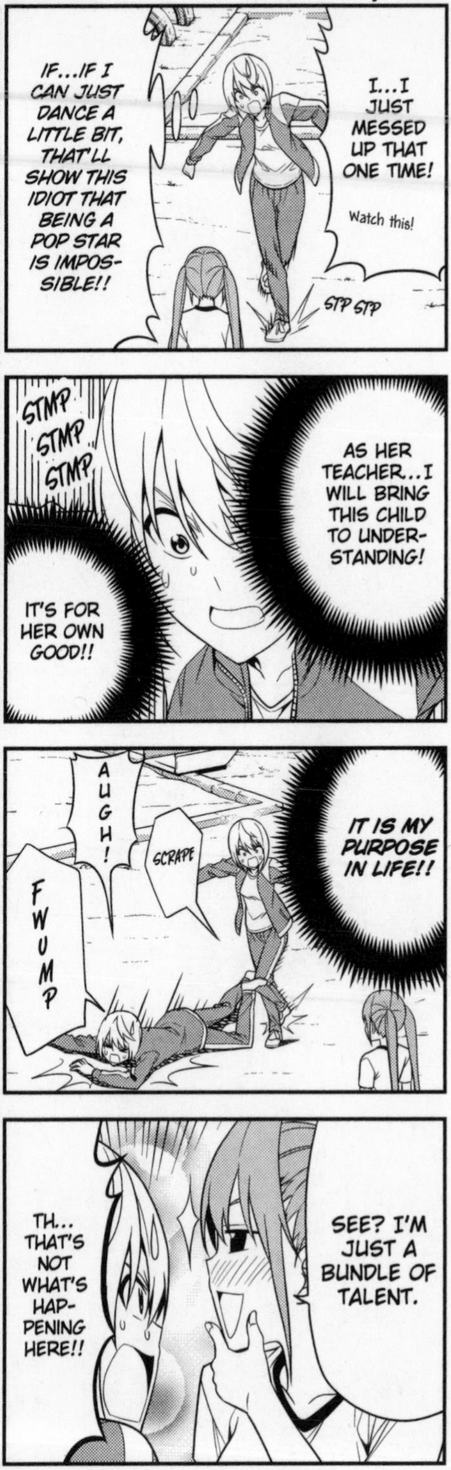
I...I JUST MESSED UP THAT ONE TIME!
Watch this!
IF...IF I CAN JUST DANCE A LITTLE BIT, THAT'LL SHOW THIS IDIOT THAT BEING A POP STAR IS IMPOSSIBLE!!
STP STP
AS HER TEACHER...I WILL BRING THIS CHILD TO UNDERSTANDING!
STMP STMP STMP
IT'S FOR HER OWN GOOD!!
IT IS MY PURPOSE IN LIFE!!
AUGH!
SCRAPE
FWUMP
SEE? I'M JUST A BUNDLE OF TALENT.
TH... THAT'S NOT WHAT'S HAPPENING HERE!!

I Won't Give Up!

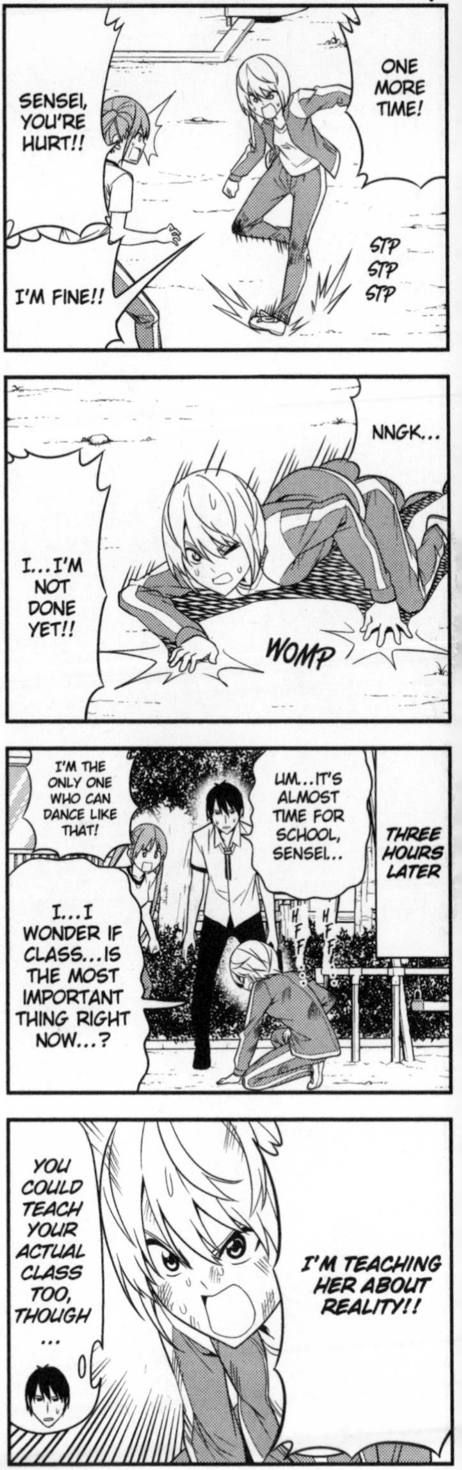
ONE MORE TIME!
SENSEI, YOU'RE HURT!!
STP STP STP
I'M FINE!!
NNGK...
I...I'M NOT DONE YET!!
WOMP
THREE HOURS LATER
UM...IT'S ALMOST TIME FOR SCHOOL, SENSEI...
I'M THE ONLY ONE WHO CAN DANCE LIKE THAT!
HFF HFF
I...I WONDER IF CLASS...IS THE MOST IMPORTANT THING RIGHT NOW...?
I'M TEACHING HER ABOUT REALITY!!
YOU COULD TEACH YOUR ACTUAL CLASS TOO, THOUGH...

Stubborn Teacher

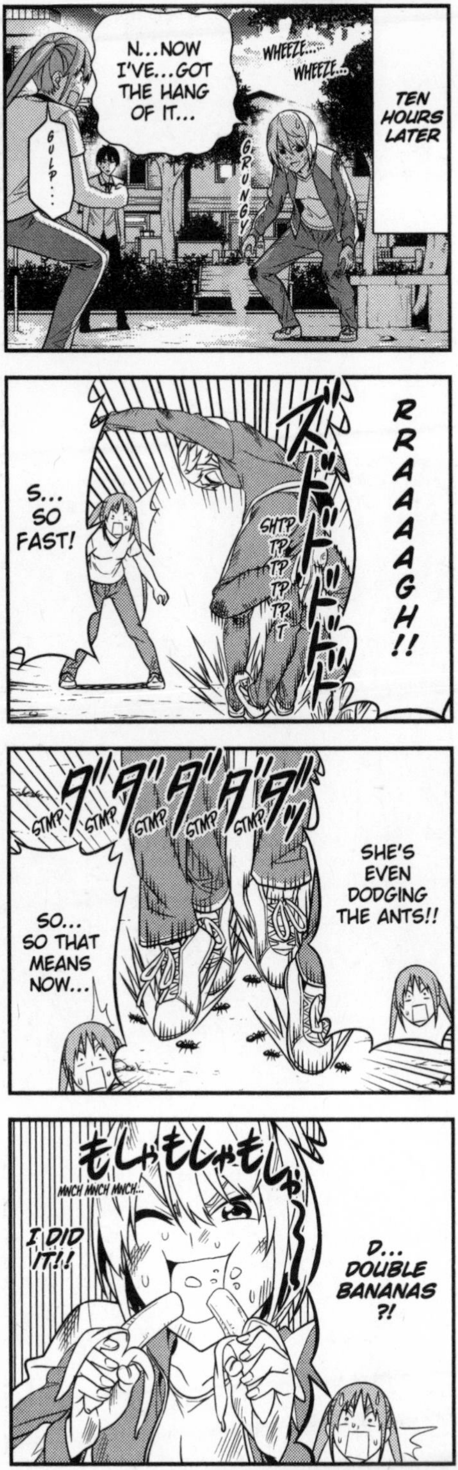
TEN HOURS LATER
WHEEZE... WHEEZE...
N...NOW I'VE...GOT THE HANG OF IT...
GRUNGY
GULP...
RRAAAAAGH!!
ズドドドドド
SHTP TP TP TP TP T
S... SO FAST!
ダダダダダッ
STMP STMP STMP STMP STMP
SHE'S EVEN DODGING THE ANTS!!
SO... SO THAT MEANS NOW...
もしゃもしゃもしゃ～
MNCH MNCH MNCH...
D... DOUBLE BANANAS?!
I DID IT!!

Pinnacle of Effort

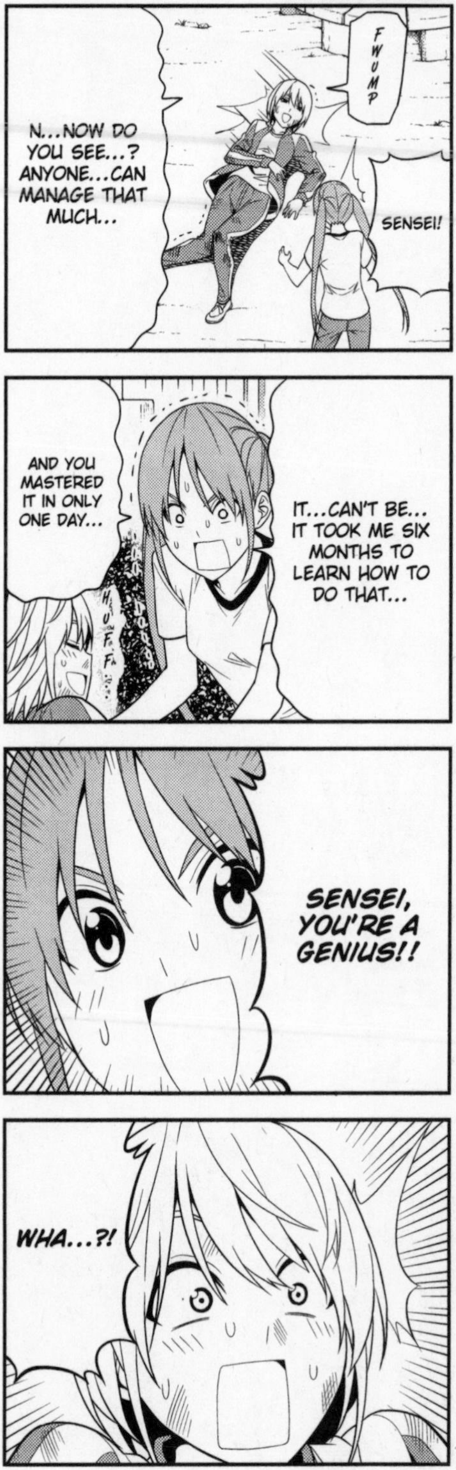
FWUMP
N...NOW DO YOU SEE...? ANYONE...CAN MANAGE THAT MUCH...
SENSEI!
IT...CAN'T BE... IT TOOK ME SIX MONTHS TO LEARN HOW TO DO THAT...
AND YOU MASTERED IT IN ONLY ONE DAY...
HUFF
SENSEI, YOU'RE A GENIUS!!
WHA...?!

The Corrupted Mentor

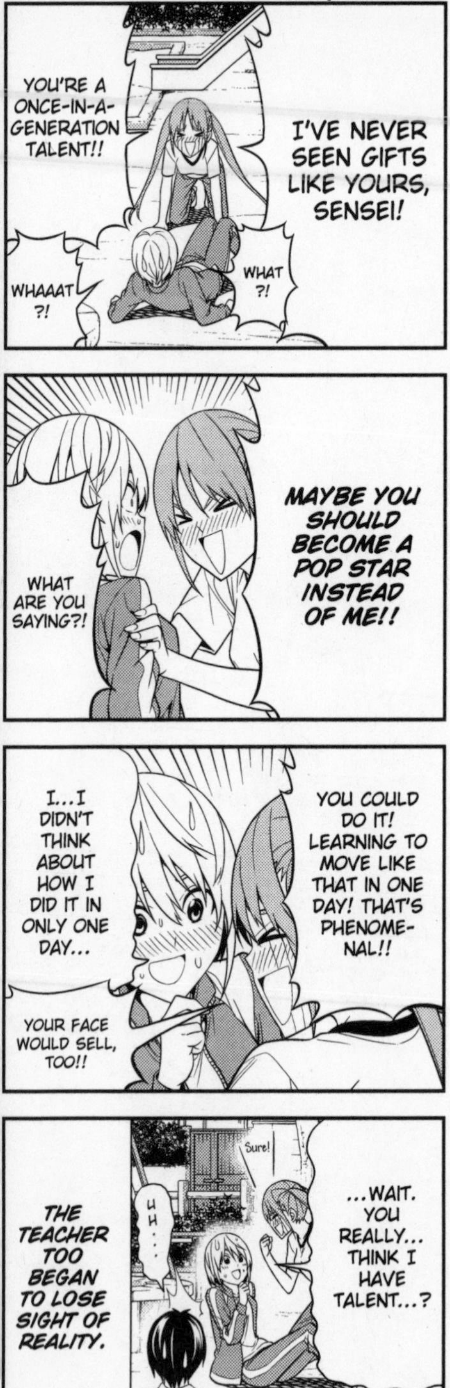
I'VE NEVER SEEN GIFTS LIKE YOURS, SENSEI!
YOU'RE A ONCE-IN-A-GENERATION TALENT!!
WHAT ?!
WHAAAT ?!
MAYBE YOU SHOULD BECOME A POP STAR INSTEAD OF ME!!
WHAT ARE YOU SAYING?!
YOU COULD DO IT! LEARNING TO MOVE LIKE THAT IN ONE DAY! THAT'S PHENOME-NAL!!
I...I DIDN'T THINK ABOUT HOW I DID IT IN ONLY ONE DAY...
YOUR FACE WOULD SELL, TOO!!
...WAIT. YOU REALLY... THINK I HAVE TALENT...?
Sure!
UH...
THE TEACHER TOO BEGAN TO LOSE SIGHT OF REALITY.

A Frank Argument

I CAN'T LEAVE THINGS LIKE THIS...!!
You could totally do it!
I...I NEVER THOUGHT OF BEING A POP STAR..
TREMBLE TREMBLE
W-WHAT DO YOU THINK, AKUTSU-KUN...?
REMEMBER HOW OLD YOU ARE?!

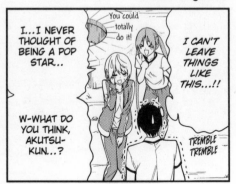

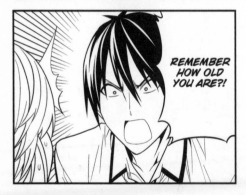

Aho-Girl

\'ahô͵gərl\ *Japanese , noun*.
A clueless girl.

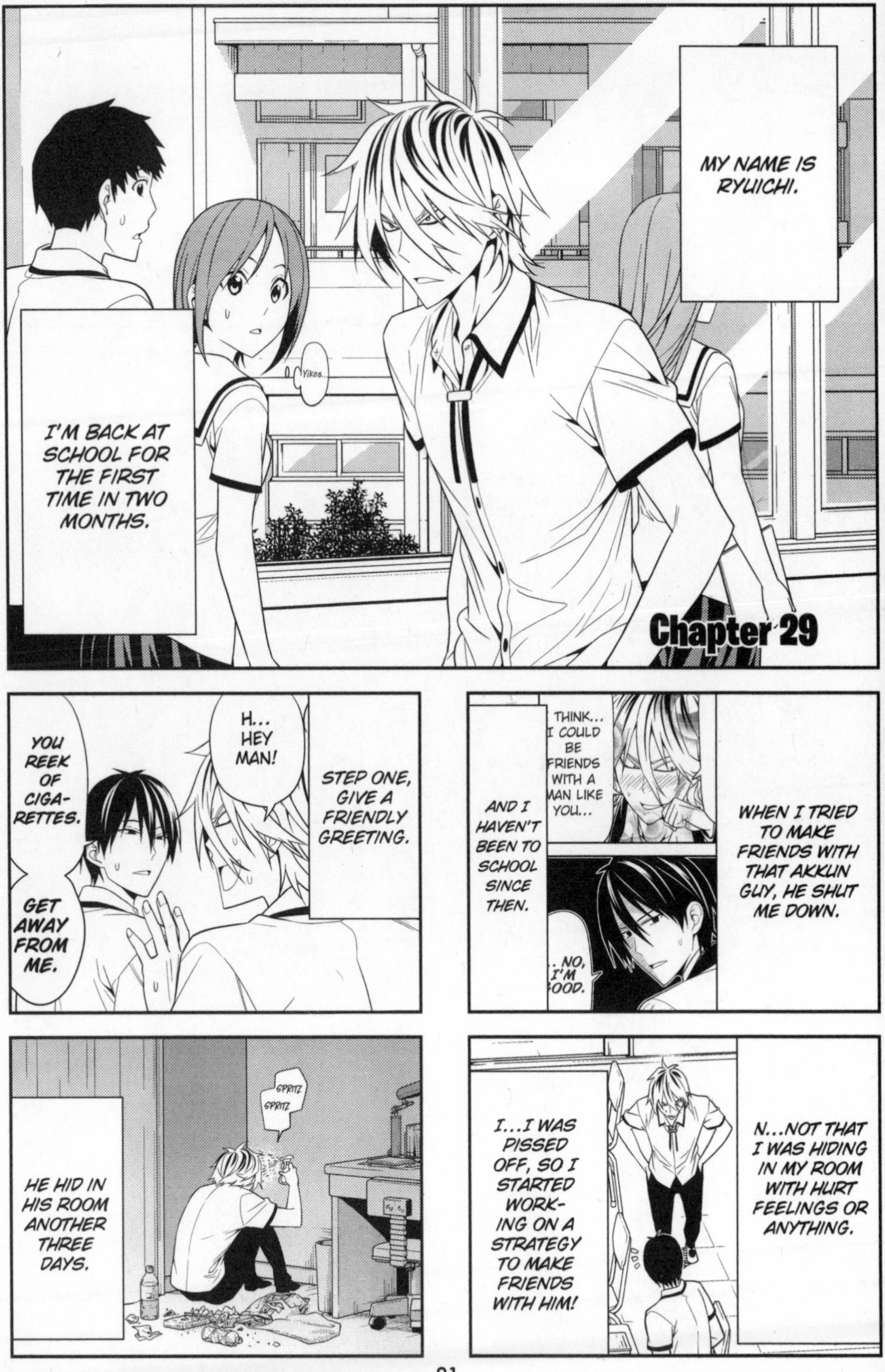
MY NAME IS RYUICHI.
Yikes...
I'M BACK AT SCHOOL FOR THE FIRST TIME IN TWO MONTHS.
Chapter 29
WHEN I TRIED TO MAKE FRIENDS WITH THAT AKKUN GUY, HE SHUT ME DOWN.
I THINK... I COULD BE FRIENDS WITH A MAN LIKE YOU...
AND I HAVEN'T BEEN TO SCHOOL SINCE THEN.
...NO, I'M GOOD.
STEP ONE, GIVE A FRIENDLY GREETING.
H... HEY MAN!
YOU REEK OF CIGARETTES.
GET AWAY FROM ME.
N...NOT THAT I WAS HIDING IN MY ROOM WITH HURT FEELINGS OR ANYTHING.
I...I WAS PISSED OFF, SO I STARTED WORKING ON A STRATEGY TO MAKE FRIENDS WITH HIM!
SPRITZ
SPRITZ
HE HID IN HIS ROOM ANOTHER THREE DAYS.

When You Haven't Seen Them for Two Months

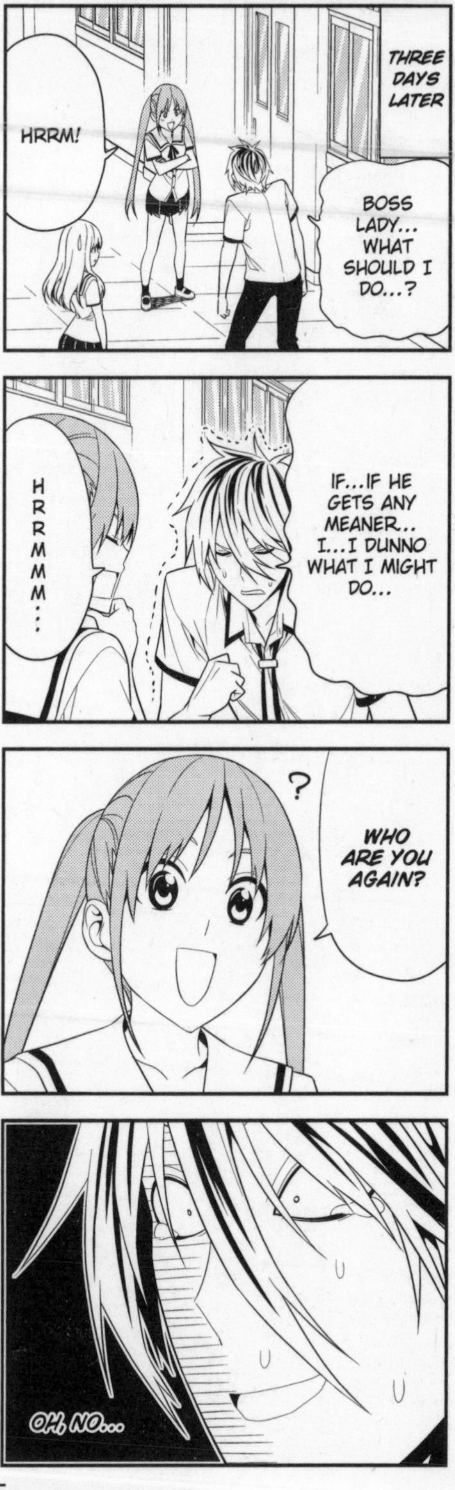

THREE DAYS LATER
BOSS LADY... WHAT SHOULD I DO...?
HRRM!
IF...IF HE GETS ANY MEANER... I...I DUNNO WHAT I MIGHT DO...
HRRMMM...
WHO ARE YOU AGAIN?
?
OH, NO...

Naïveté

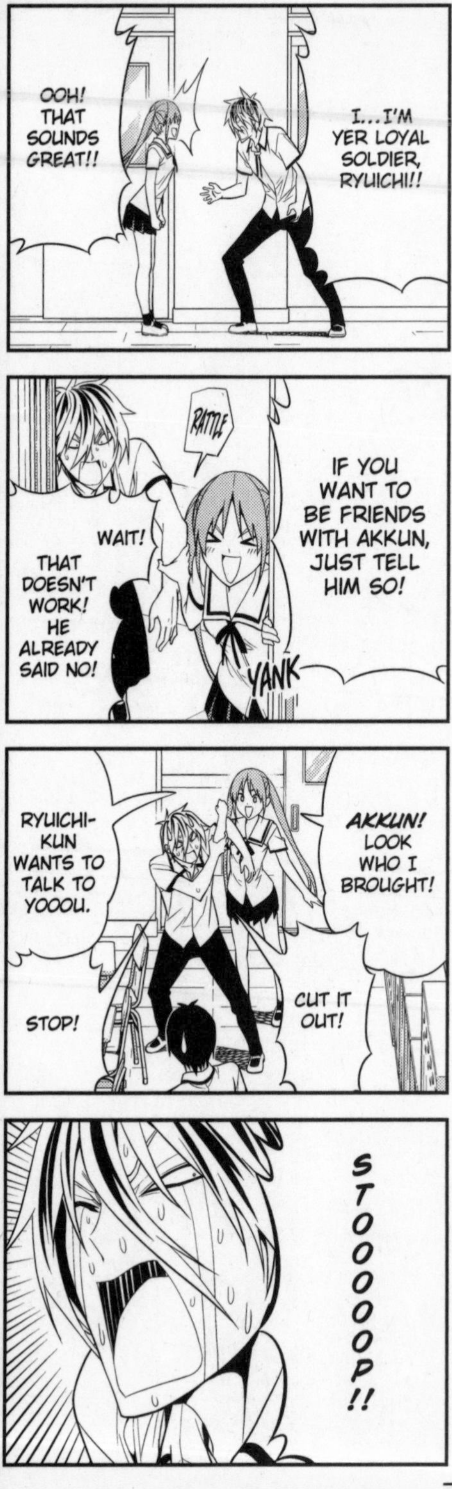

I...I'M YER LOYAL SOLDIER, RYUICHI!!
OOH! THAT SOUNDS GREAT!!
IF YOU WANT TO BE FRIENDS WITH AKKUN, JUST TELL HIM SO!
RATTLE
WAIT!
THAT DOESN'T WORK! HE ALREADY SAID NO!
YANK
AKKUN! LOOK WHO I BROUGHT!
RYUICHI-KUN WANTS TO TALK TO YOOOU.
CUT IT OUT!
STOP!
STOOOOOOP!!

Somewhat Eccentric

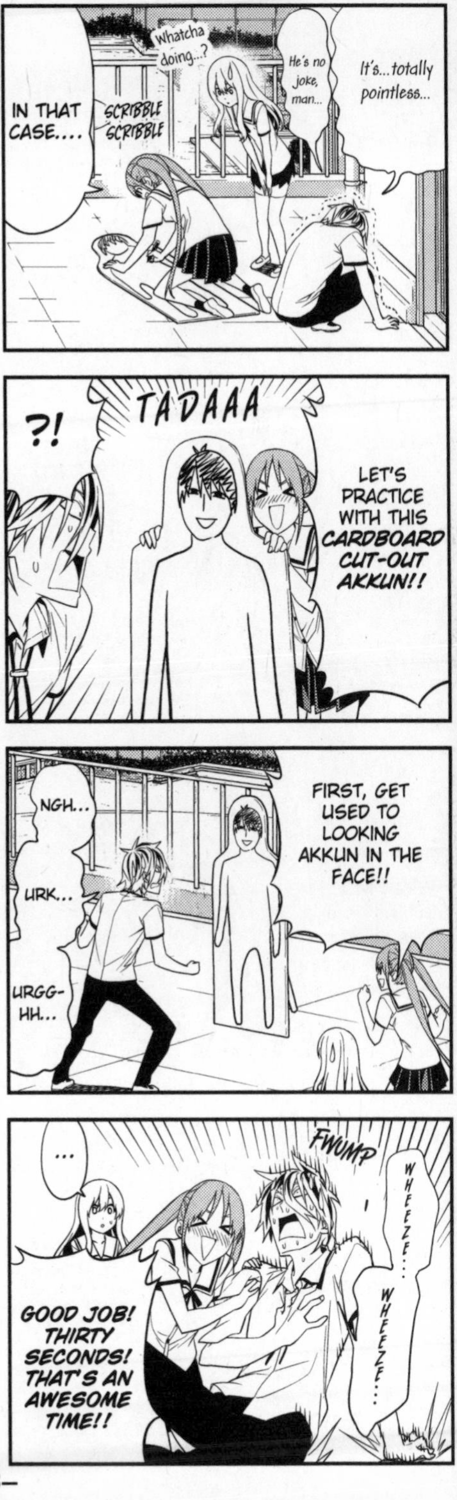
It's...totally pointless...
He's no joke, man...
Whatcha doing...?
SCRIBBLE SCRIBBLE
IN THAT CASE....
TADAAA
LET'S PRACTICE WITH THIS CARDBOARD CUT-OUT AKKUN!!
?!
FIRST, GET USED TO LOOKING AKKUN IN THE FACE!!
NGH...
URK...
URGG-HH...
WHEEZE... WHEEZE...
FWUMP
...
GOOD JOB! THIRTY SECONDS! THAT'S AN AWESOME TIME!!

Lesson in Love

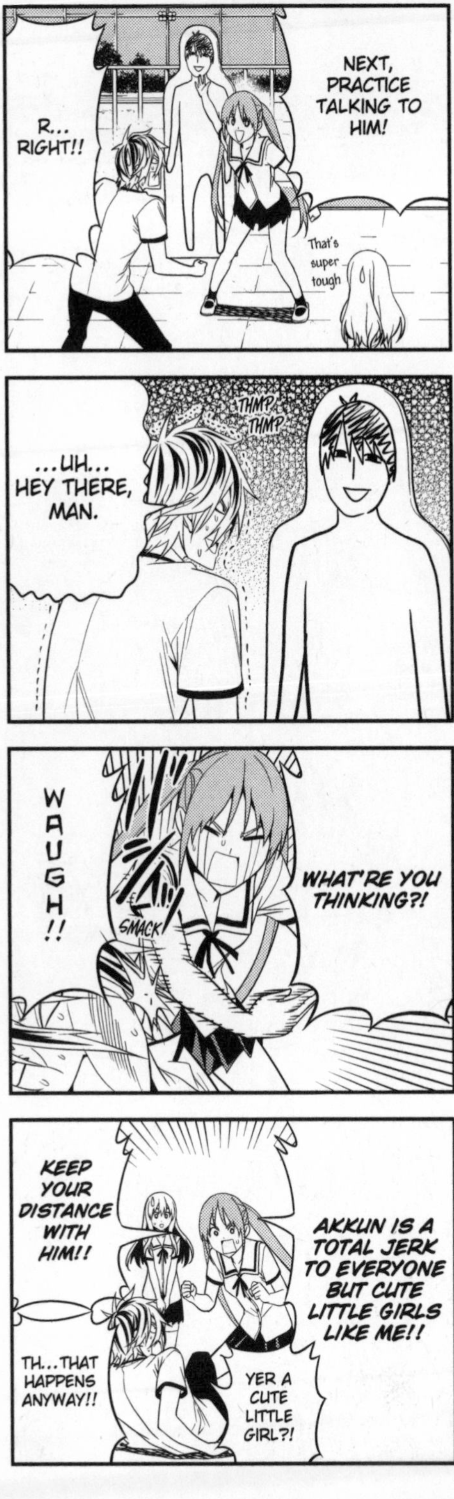
NEXT, PRACTICE TALKING TO HIM!
R... RIGHT!!
That's super tough
THMP THMP
...UH... HEY THERE, MAN.
WHAT'RE YOU THINKING?!
SMACK
WAUGH!!
AKKUN IS A TOTAL JERK TO EVERYONE BUT CUTE LITTLE GIRLS LIKE ME!!
YER A CUTE LITTLE GIRL?!
KEEP YOUR DISTANCE WITH HIM!!
TH...THAT HAPPENS ANYWAY!!

That Wasn't the Plan

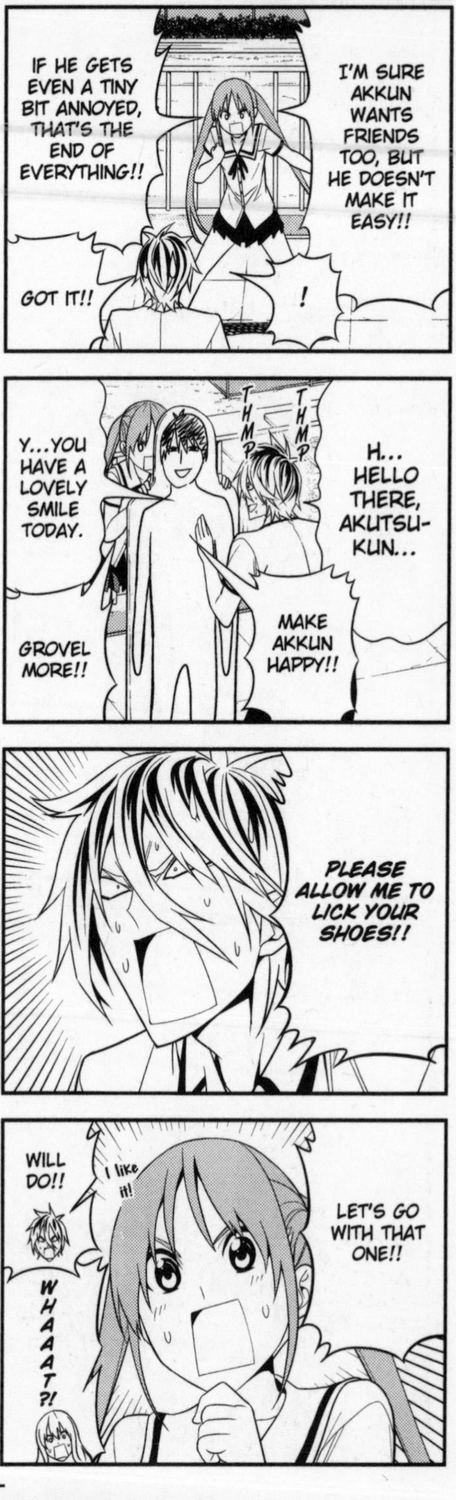
I'M SURE AKKUN WANTS FRIENDS TOO, BUT HE DOESN'T MAKE IT EASY!!
IF HE GETS EVEN A TINY BIT ANNOYED, THAT'S THE END OF EVERYTHING!!
!
GOT IT!!
H... HELLO THERE, AKUTSU-KUN...
THMP
THMP
Y...YOU HAVE A LOVELY SMILE TODAY.
MAKE AKKUN HAPPY!!
GROVEL MORE!!
PLEASE ALLOW ME TO LICK YOUR SHOES!!
LET'S GO WITH THAT ONE!!
I like it!
WILL DO!!
WHAAAAT?!

You Have to Stop Them, Sayaka

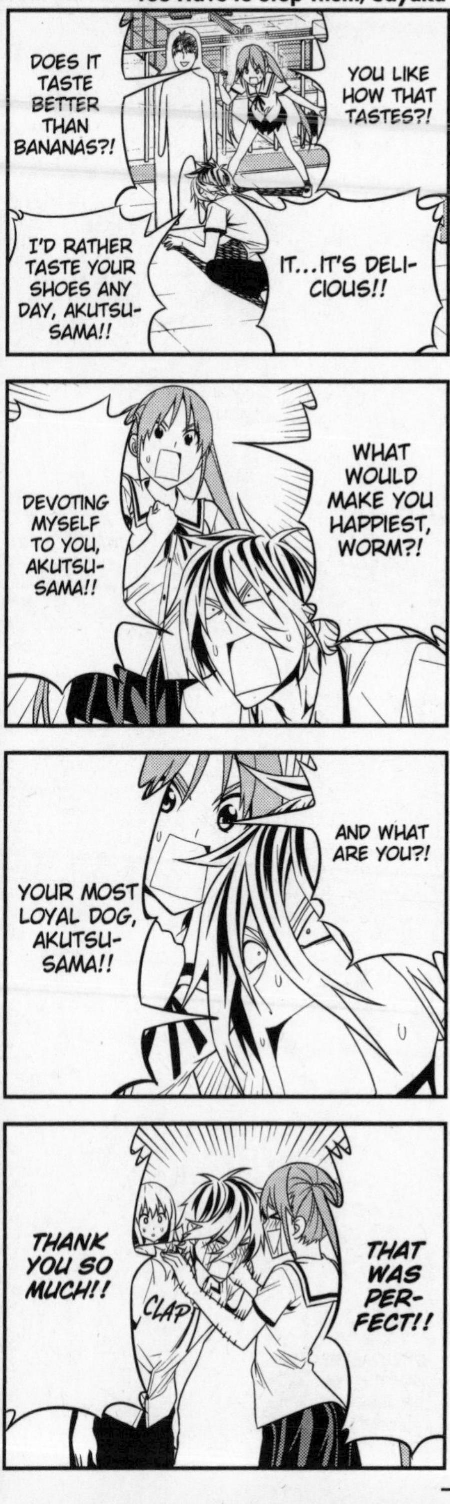
YOU LIKE HOW THAT TASTES?!
DOES IT TASTE BETTER THAN BANANAS?!
IT...IT'S DELICIOUS!!
I'D RATHER TASTE YOUR SHOES ANY DAY, AKUTSU-SAMA!!
WHAT WOULD MAKE YOU HAPPIEST, WORM?!
DEVOTING MYSELF TO YOU, AKUTSU-SAMA!!
AND WHAT ARE YOU?!
YOUR MOST LOYAL DOG, AKUTSU-SAMA!!
THAT WAS PERFECT!!
CLAP
THANK YOU SO MUCH!!

Devastating Opening Move

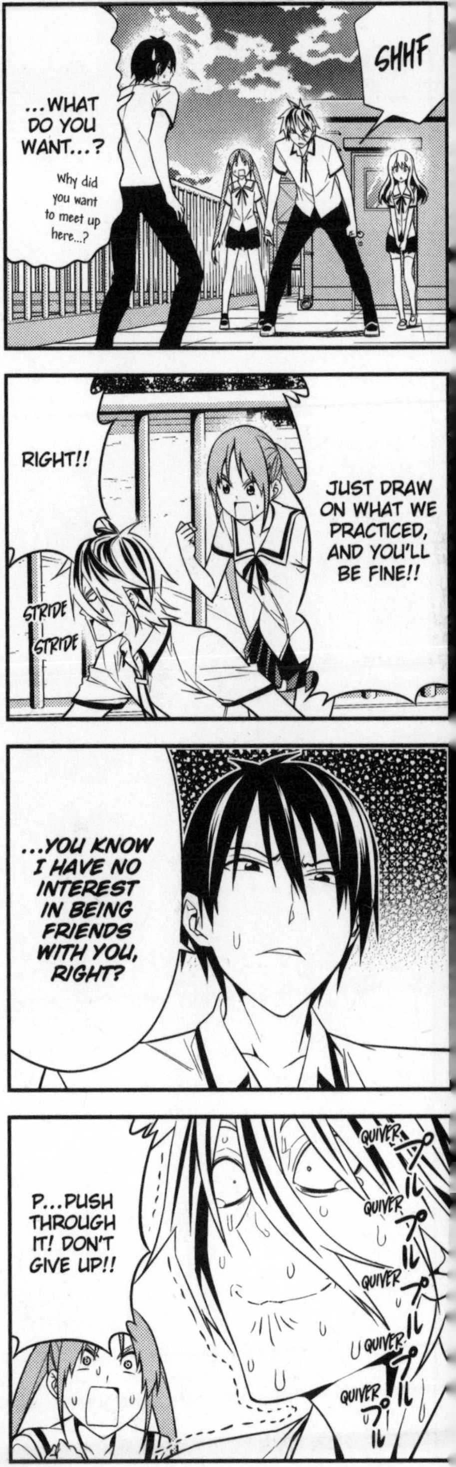
SHHF
...WHAT DO YOU WANT...?
Why did you want to meet up here...?
JUST DRAW ON WHAT WE PRACTICED, AND YOU'LL BE FINE!!
RIGHT!!
STRIDE
STRIDE
...YOU KNOW I HAVE NO INTEREST IN BEING FRIENDS WITH YOU, RIGHT?
QUIVER
QUIVER
QUIVER
QUIVER
QUIVER
P...PUSH THROUGH IT! DON'T GIVE UP!!

You Trying to Sell Something?

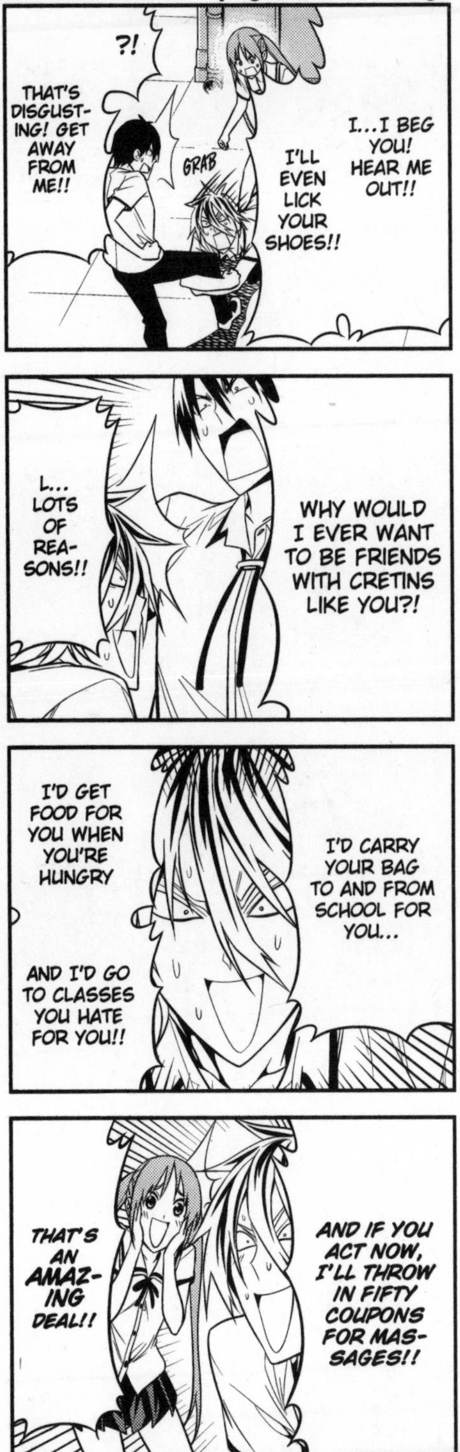
I...I BEG YOU! HEAR ME OUT!!
I'LL EVEN LICK YOUR SHOES!!
GRAB
?!
THAT'S DISGUST-ING! GET AWAY FROM ME!!
WHY WOULD I EVER WANT TO BE FRIENDS WITH CRETINS LIKE YOU?!
L... LOTS OF REA-SONS!!
I'D CARRY YOUR BAG TO AND FROM SCHOOL FOR YOU...
I'D GET FOOD FOR YOU WHEN YOU'RE HUNGRY
AND I'D GO TO CLASSES YOU HATE FOR YOU!!
AND IF YOU ACT NOW, I'LL THROW IN FIFTY COUPONS FOR MAS-SAGES!!
THAT'S AN AMAZ-ING DEAL!!

Servile Character

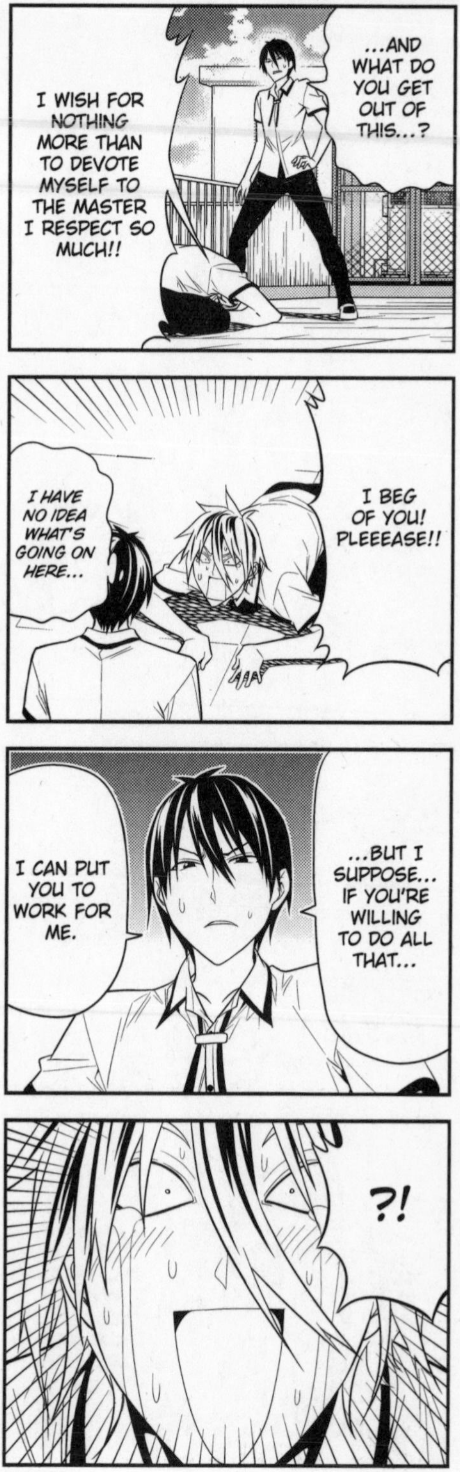
...AND WHAT DO YOU GET OUT OF THIS...?
I WISH FOR NOTHING MORE THAN TO DEVOTE MYSELF TO THE MASTER I RESPECT SO MUCH!!
I BEG OF YOU! PLEEEASE!!
I HAVE NO IDEA WHAT'S GOING ON HERE...
...BUT I SUPPOSE... IF YOU'RE WILLING TO DO ALL THAT...
I CAN PUT YOU TO WORK FOR ME.
?!

He Finally Noticed

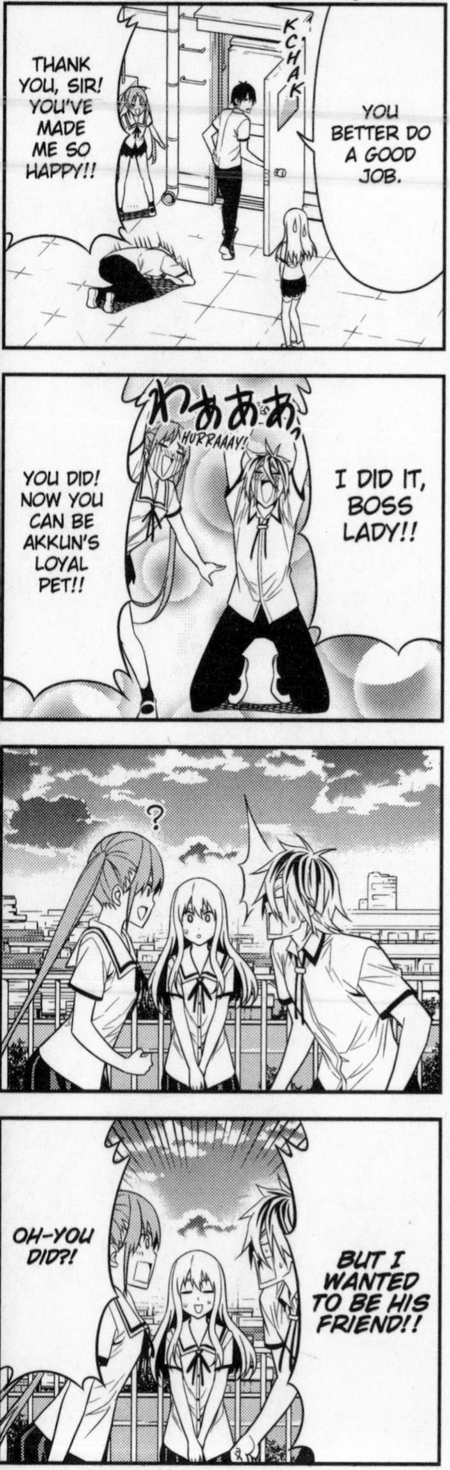
KCHAK
YOU BETTER DO A GOOD JOB.
THANK YOU, SIR! YOU'VE MADE ME SO HAPPY!!
わぁあぁあっ
HURRAAAY!
I DID IT, BOSS LADY!!
YOU DID! NOW YOU CAN BE AKKUN'S LOYAL PET!!
?
BUT I WANTED TO BE HIS FRIEND!!
OH-YOU DID?!

Surrogate Akkun

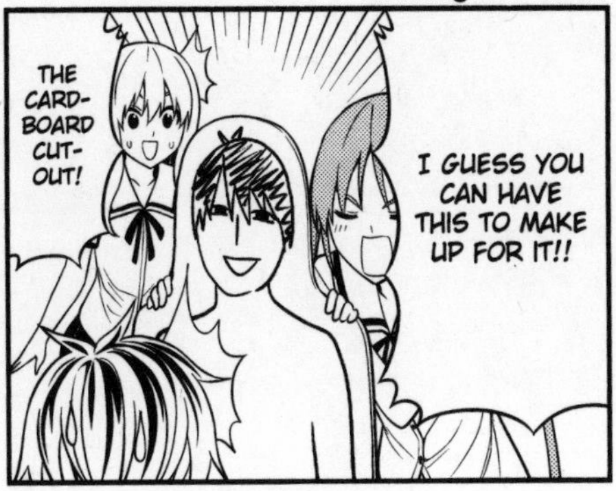
I GUESS YOU CAN HAVE THIS TO MAKE UP FOR IT!!
THE CARD-BOARD CUT-OUT!

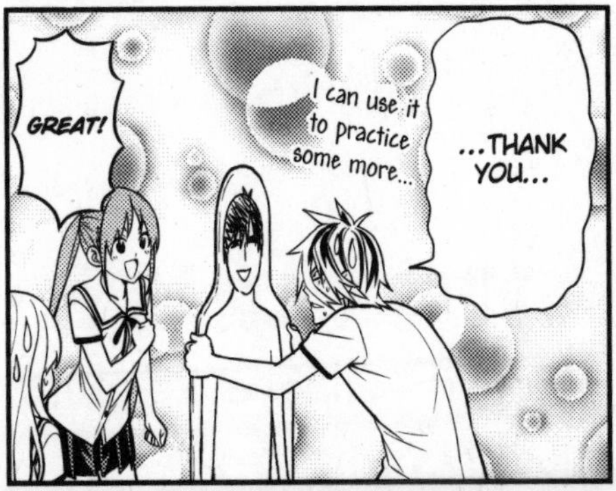
...THANK YOU...
I can use it to practice some more...
GREAT!

(Be-Bop High)

Aho-Girl

\ˈahô͵gərl\ *Japanese , noun.*
A clueless girl.

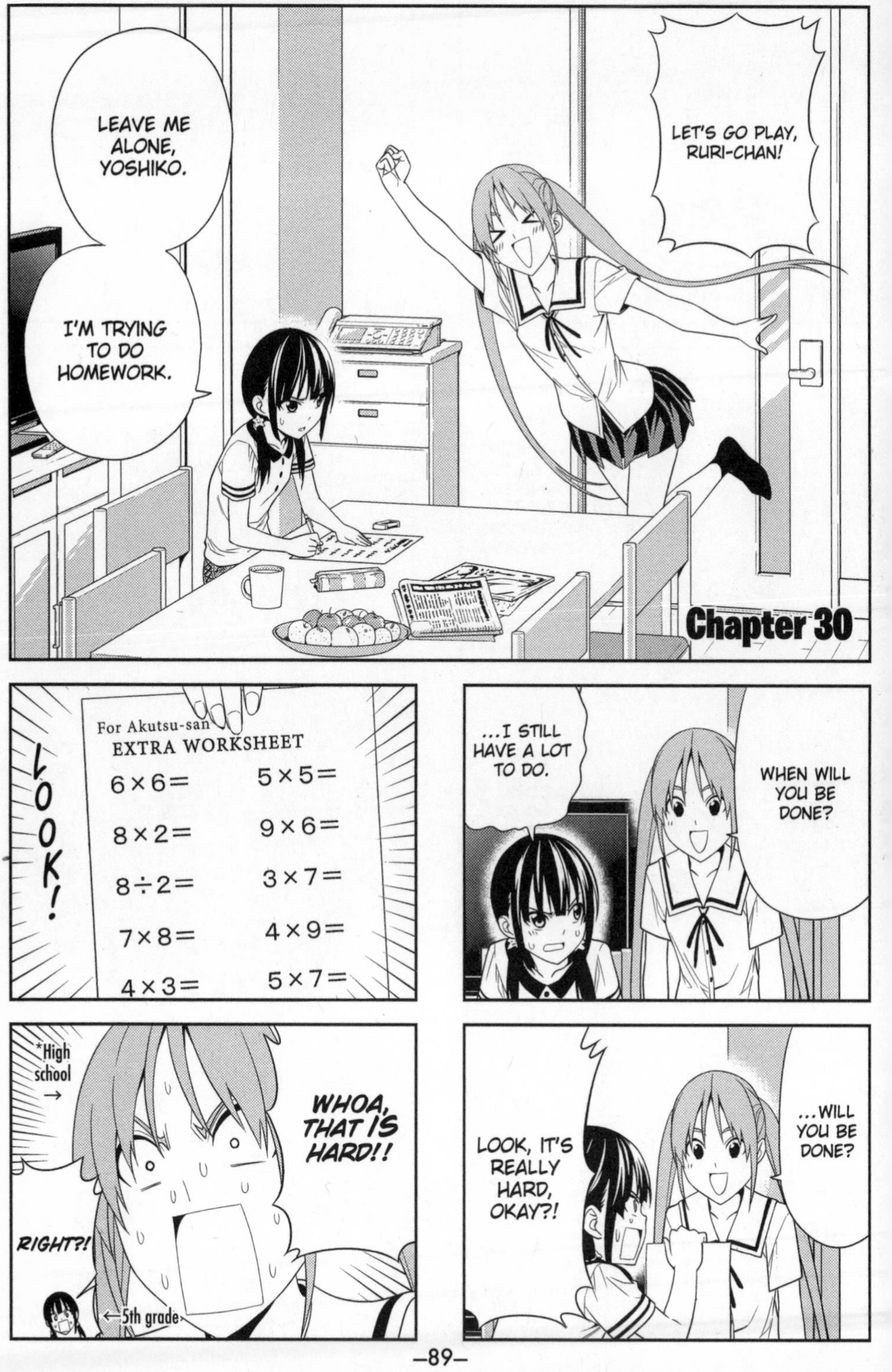
LET'S GO PLAY, RURI-CHAN!
LEAVE ME ALONE, YOSHIKO.
I'M TRYING TO DO HOMEWORK.
Chapter 30
WHEN WILL YOU BE DONE?
...I STILL HAVE A LOT TO DO.
For Akutsu-san
EXTRA WORKSHEET
6×6= 5×5=
8×2= 9×6=
8÷2= 3×7=
7×8= 4×9=
4×3= 5×7=
LOOK!
...WILL YOU BE DONE?
LOOK, IT'S REALLY HARD, OKAY?!
WHOA, THAT IS HARD!!
*High school →
RIGHT?!
←5th grade

That's Enough!

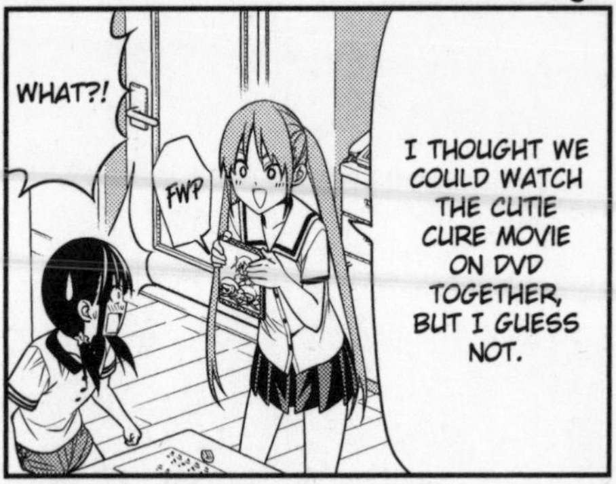
I THOUGHT WE COULD WATCH THE CUTIE CURE MOVIE ON DVD TOGETHER, BUT I GUESS NOT.
FWP
WHAT?!

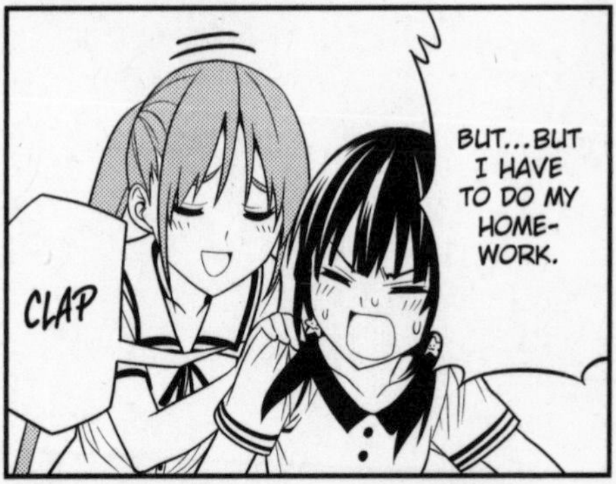
BUT...BUT I HAVE TO DO MY HOME-WORK.
CLAP

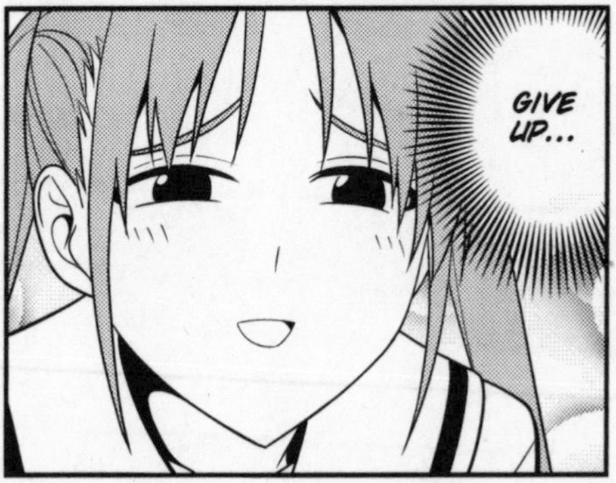
GIVE UP...

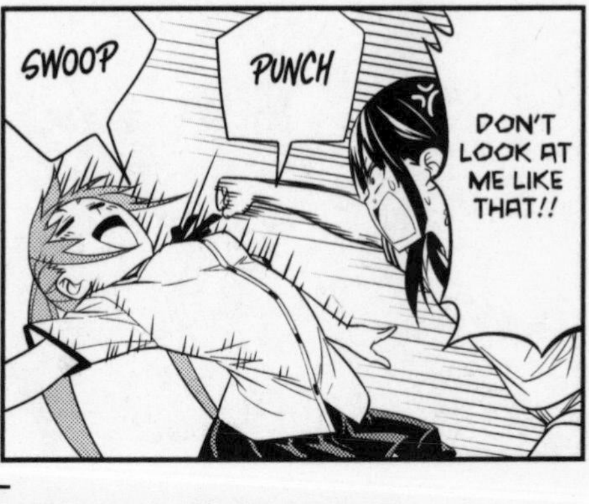
PUNCH
DON'T LOOK AT ME LIKE THAT!!
SWOOP

I Get 60%

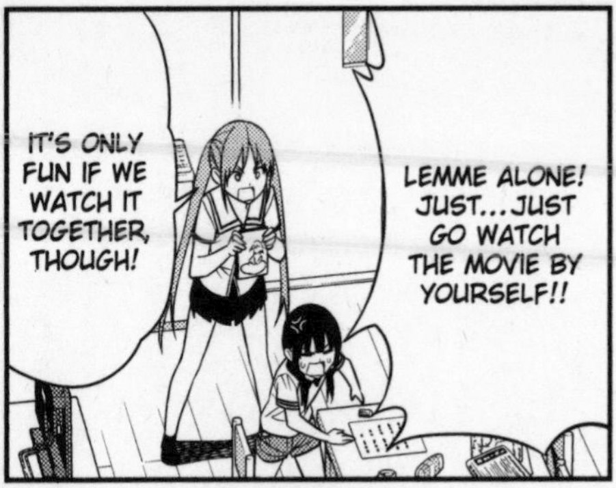
LEMME ALONE! JUST...JUST GO WATCH THE MOVIE BY YOURSELF!!
IT'S ONLY FUN IF WE WATCH IT TOGETHER, THOUGH!

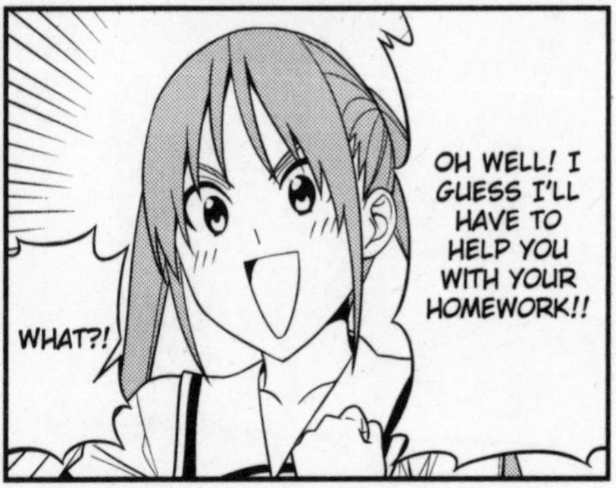
OH WELL! I GUESS I'LL HAVE TO HELP YOU WITH YOUR HOMEWORK!!
WHAT?!

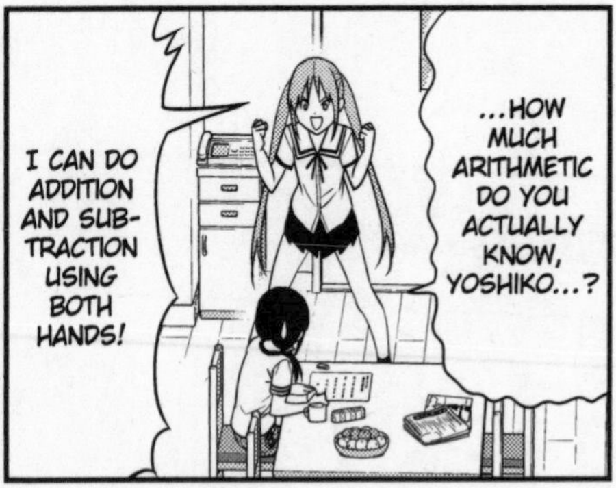
...HOW MUCH ARITHMETIC DO YOU ACTUALLY KNOW, YOSHIKO...?
I CAN DO ADDITION AND SUB-TRACTION USING BOTH HANDS!

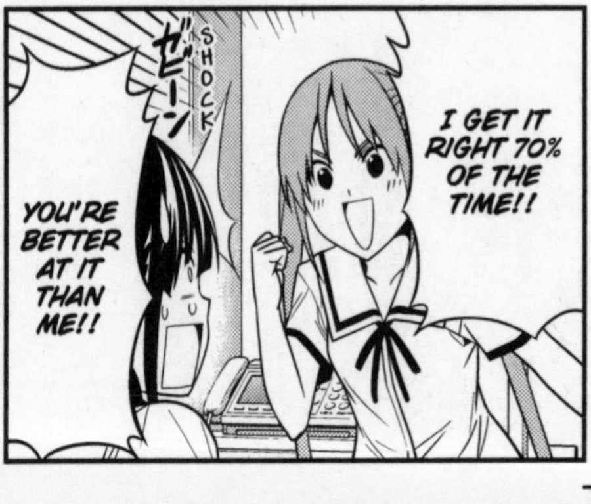
I GET IT RIGHT 70% OF THE TIME!!
SHOCK
ゼーン
YOU'RE BETTER AT IT THAN ME!!

The Menace of Yoshiko

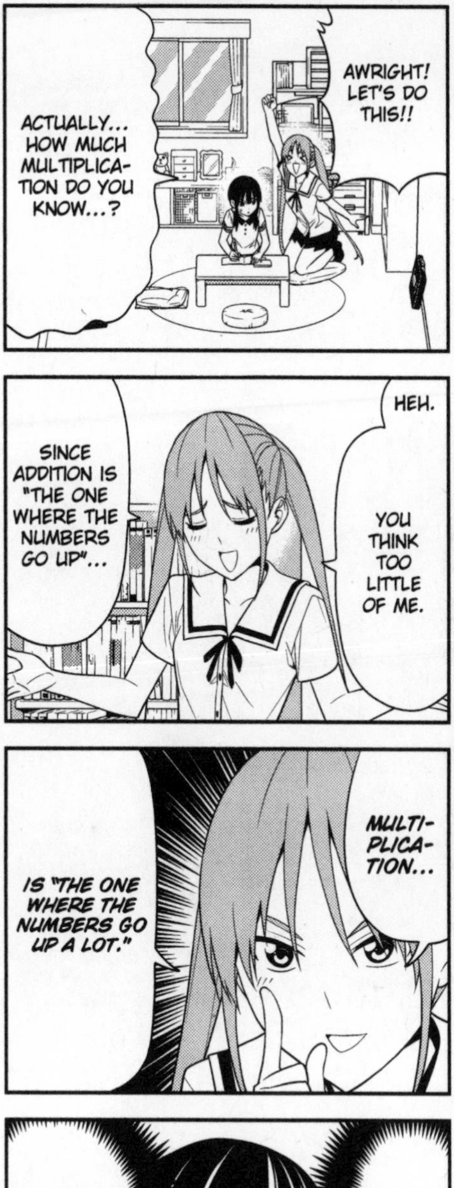

AWRIGHT! LET'S DO THIS!!
ACTUALLY... HOW MUCH MULTIPLICATION DO YOU KNOW...?
HEH.
YOU THINK TOO LITTLE OF ME.
SINCE ADDITION IS "THE ONE WHERE THE NUMBERS GO UP"...
MULTIPLICATION...
IS "THE ONE WHERE THE NUMBERS GO UP A LOT."
WOW...
SHE'S WAY BETTER AT IT THAN I EVER THOUGHT ...!!
GLP...

That's Not All!

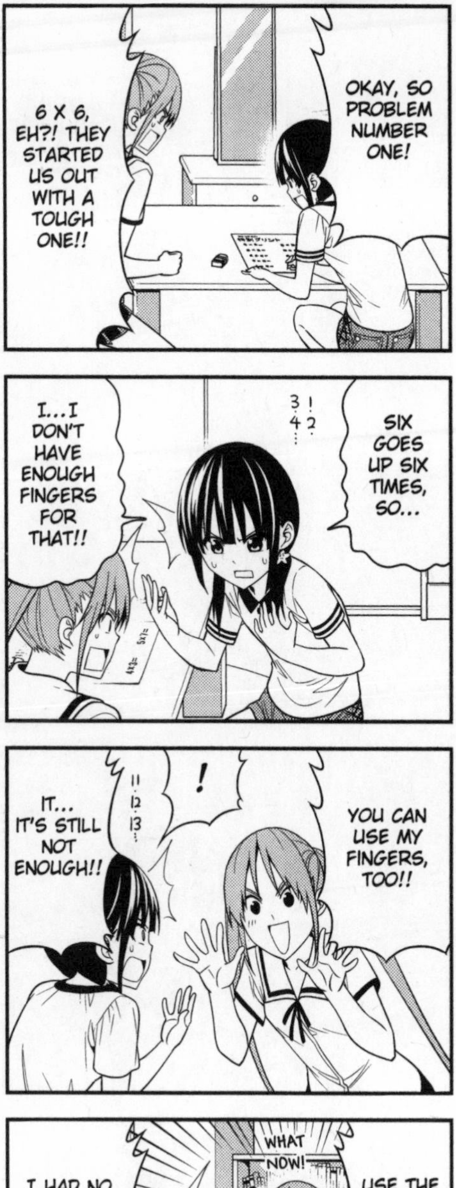

OKAY, SO PROBLEM NUMBER ONE!
6 X 6, EH?! THEY STARTED US OUT WITH A TOUGH ONE!!
SIX GOES UP SIX TIMES, SO...
1 2 3 4...
I...I DON'T HAVE ENOUGH FINGERS FOR THAT!!
YOU CAN USE MY FINGERS, TOO!!
!
11 12 13...
IT... IT'S STILL NOT ENOUGH!!
USE THE TOES, TOO!!
WHAT NOW!
I HAD NO IDEA YOU WERE THIS SMART, YOSHIKO!!

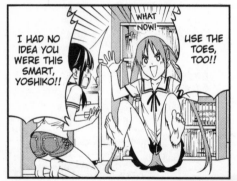

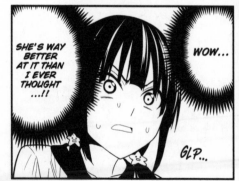

Sacrificial Lamb

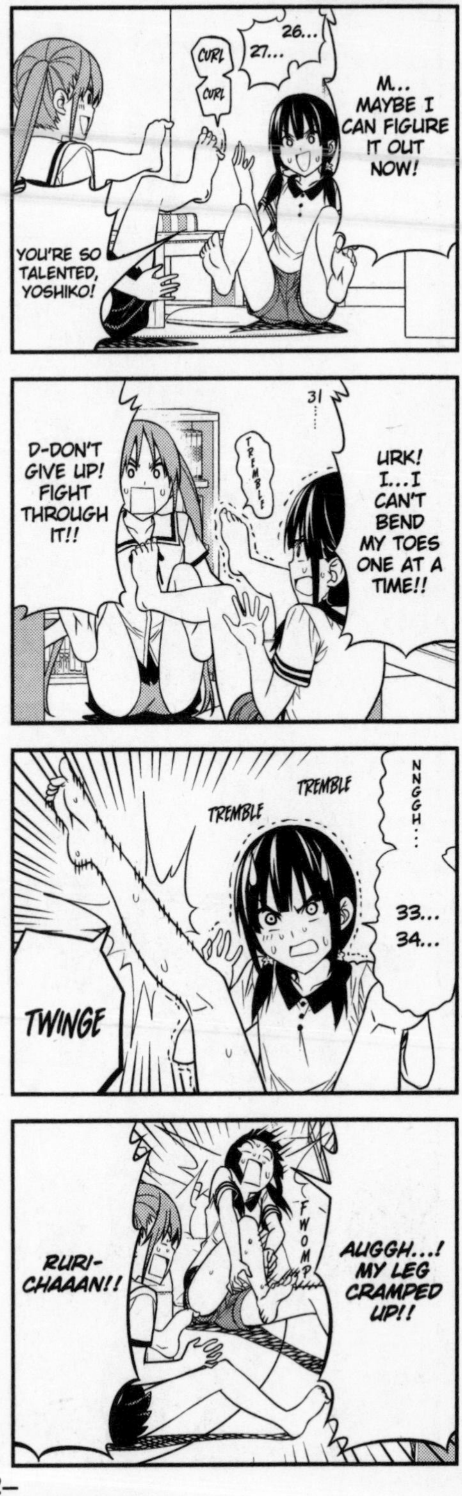
26...
27...
M...
MAYBE I
CAN FIGURE
IT OUT
NOW!
CURL
CURL
YOU'RE SO
TALENTED,
YOSHIKO!
31...
URK!
I...I
CAN'T
BEND
MY TOES
ONE AT A
TIME!!
TREMBLE
D-DON'T
GIVE UP!
FIGHT
THROUGH
IT!!
NNGGH...
33...
34...
TREMBLE
TREMBLE
TWINGE
AUGGH...!
MY LEG
CRAMPED
UP!!
FWOMP
RURI-
CHAAAN!!

A Criminal Act

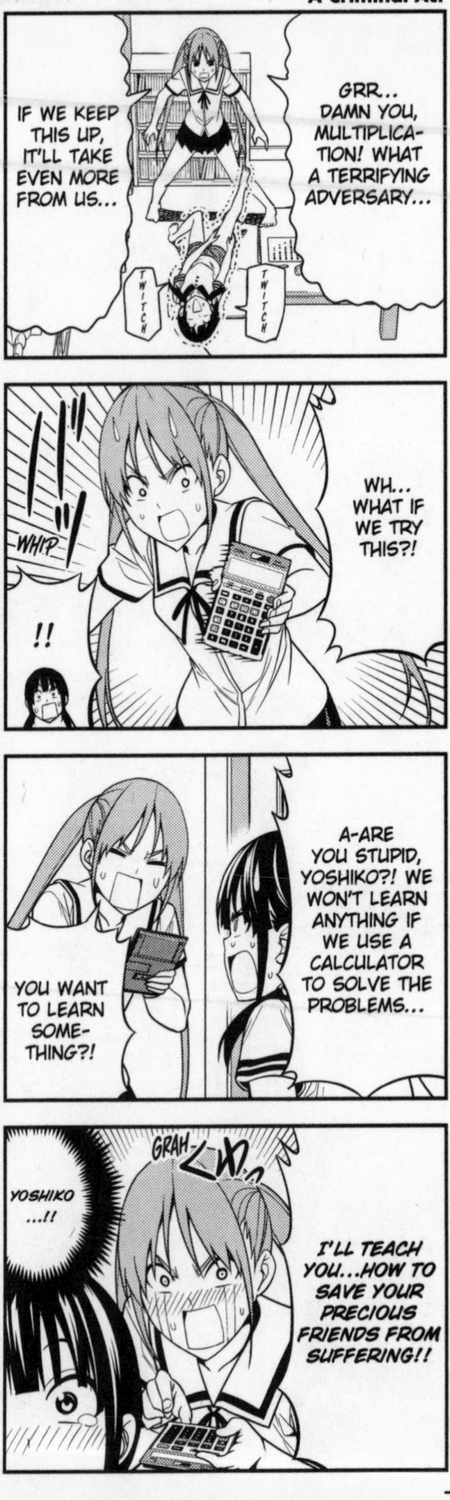
GRR...
DAMN YOU,
MULTIPLICA-
TION! WHAT
A TERRIFYING
ADVERSARY...
IF WE KEEP
THIS UP,
IT'LL TAKE
EVEN MORE
FROM US...
TWITCH
TWITCH
WH...
WHAT IF
WE TRY
THIS?!
!!
WHIP
!!
A-ARE
YOU STUPID,
YOSHIKO?! WE
WON'T LEARN
ANYTHING IF
WE USE A
CALCULATOR
TO SOLVE THE
PROBLEMS...
YOU WANT
TO LEARN
SOME-
THING?!
I'LL TEACH
YOU...HOW TO
SAVE YOUR
PRECIOUS
FRIENDS FROM
SUFFERING!!
GRAH-
YOSHIKO
...!!

Together

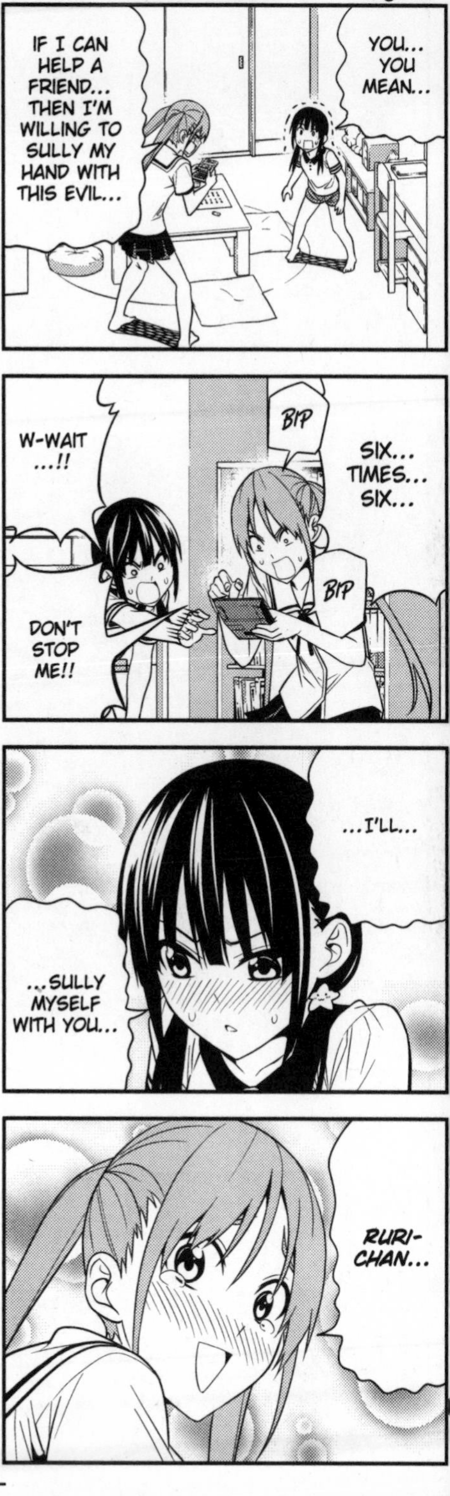
YOU... YOU MEAN...
IF I CAN HELP A FRIEND... THEN I'M WILLING TO SULLY MY HAND WITH THIS EVIL...
BIP
SIX... TIMES... SIX...
BIP
W-WAIT ...!!
DON'T STOP ME!!
...I'LL...
...SULLY MYSELF WITH YOU...
RURI-CHAN...

A Dubious Conclusion

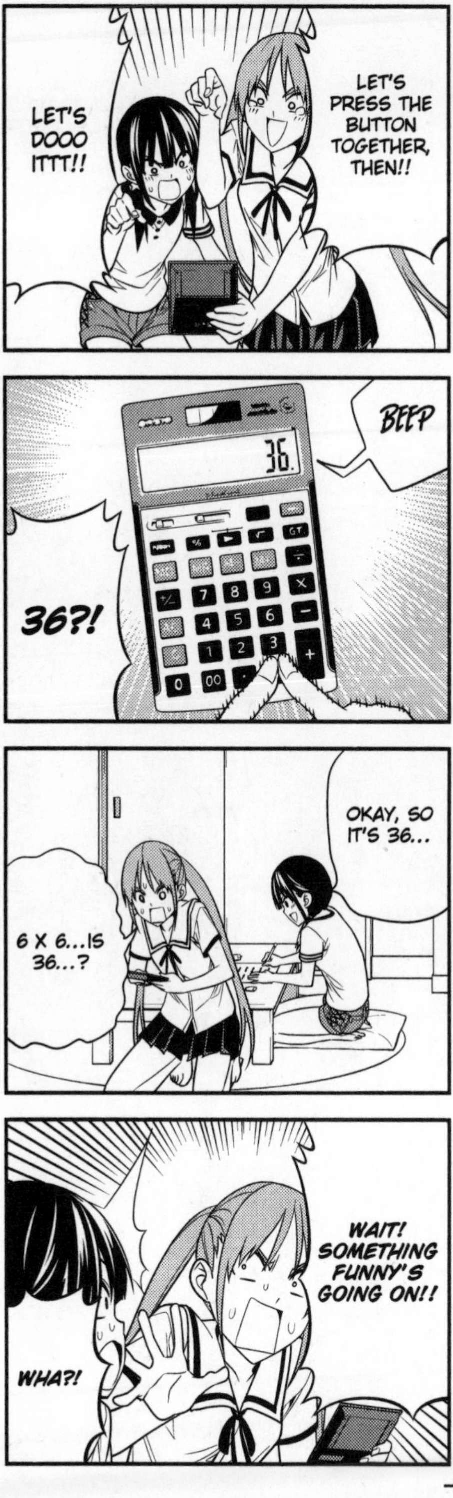
LET'S PRESS THE BUTTON TOGETHER, THEN!!
LET'S DOOO ITTT!!
BEEP
36.
36?!
OKAY, SO IT'S 36...
6 X 6...IS 36...?
WAIT! SOMETHING FUNNY'S GOING ON!!
WHA?!

A Deft Trick

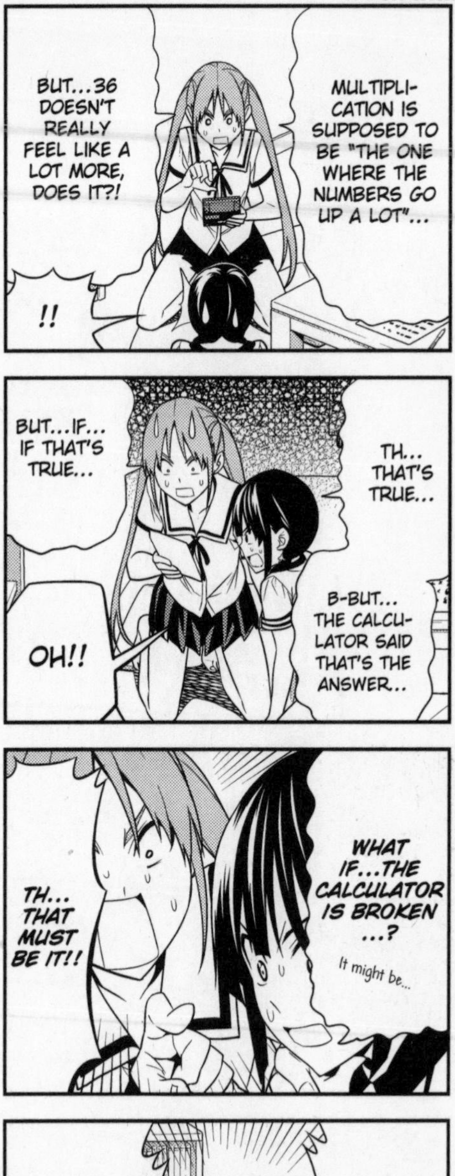

MULTIPLICATION IS SUPPOSED TO BE "THE ONE WHERE THE NUMBERS GO UP A LOT"...
BUT...36 DOESN'T REALLY FEEL LIKE A LOT MORE, DOES IT?!
!!
TH... THAT'S TRUE...
BUT...IF... IF THAT'S TRUE...
B-BUT... THE CALCULATOR SAID THAT'S THE ANSWER...
OH!!
WHAT IF...THE CALCULATOR IS BROKEN...?
It might be...
TH... THAT MUST BE IT!!
WHEW... THAT WAS A CLOSE ONE!!
WE NEVER WOULD HAVE FIGURED THAT OUT IF WE WEREN'T HELPING EACH OTHER!!

Into the Labyrinth

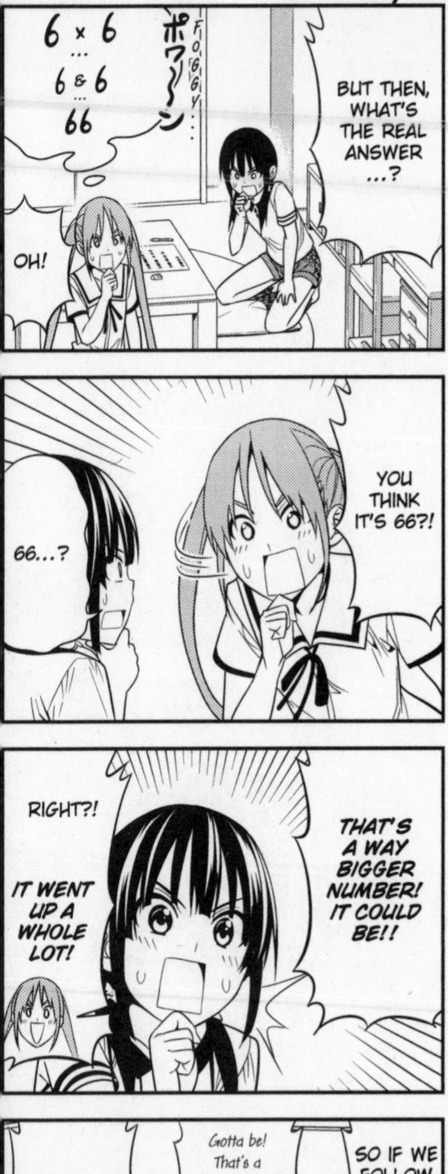

BUT THEN, WHAT'S THE REAL ANSWER...?
ポワ~ン FOGGY...
6 × 6 ... 6 & 6 ... 66
OH!
YOU THINK IT'S 66?!
66...?
THAT'S A WAY BIGGER NUMBER! IT COULD BE!!
RIGHT?!
IT WENT UP A WHOLE LOT!
SO IF WE FOLLOW THAT RULE, THEN 8 X 2...
IS 82!!
Gotta be! That's a way higher number!
You got it! You can do this!!
THIS IS HORRIBLE...
SLUMP...

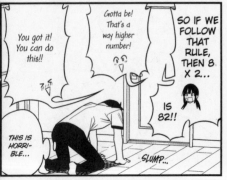

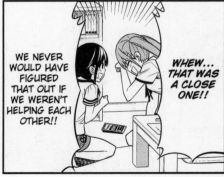

The Shame

THE NEXT DAY
AKUTSU-SAN... THIS... IS NOT CORRECT...
*Teacher
GIGGLE GIGGLE
?!
YOSHIKOOOO!!
PUNCH
SWOOP
WELL, IT HAPPENS.

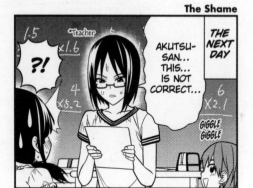

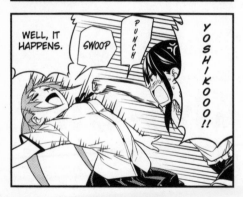

(We're messing around too much; we're children of summer)

Aho-Girl

\'ahô,gərl\ *Japanese , noun*.

A clueless girl.

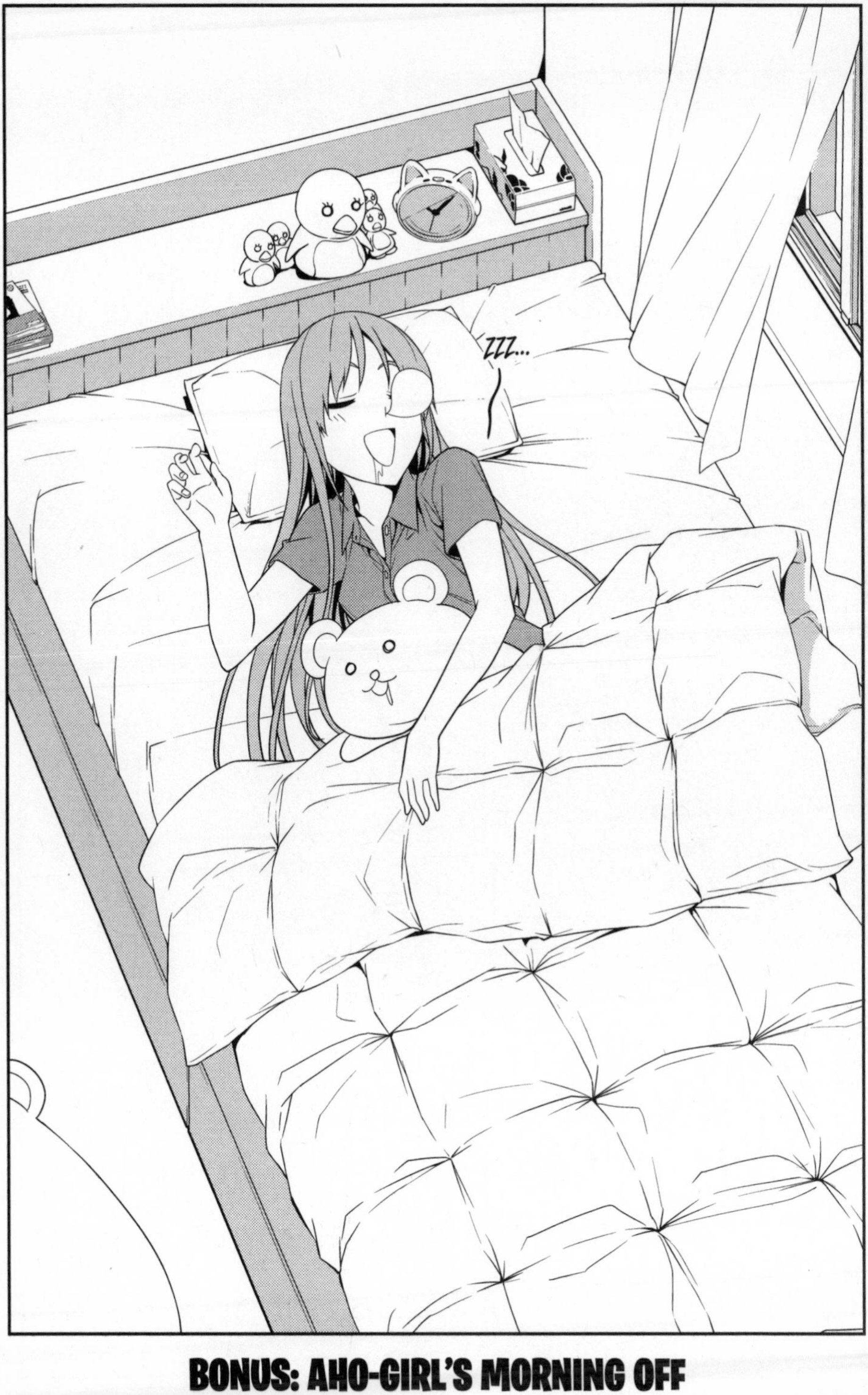
ZZZ...

BONUS: AHO-GIRL'S MORNING OFF

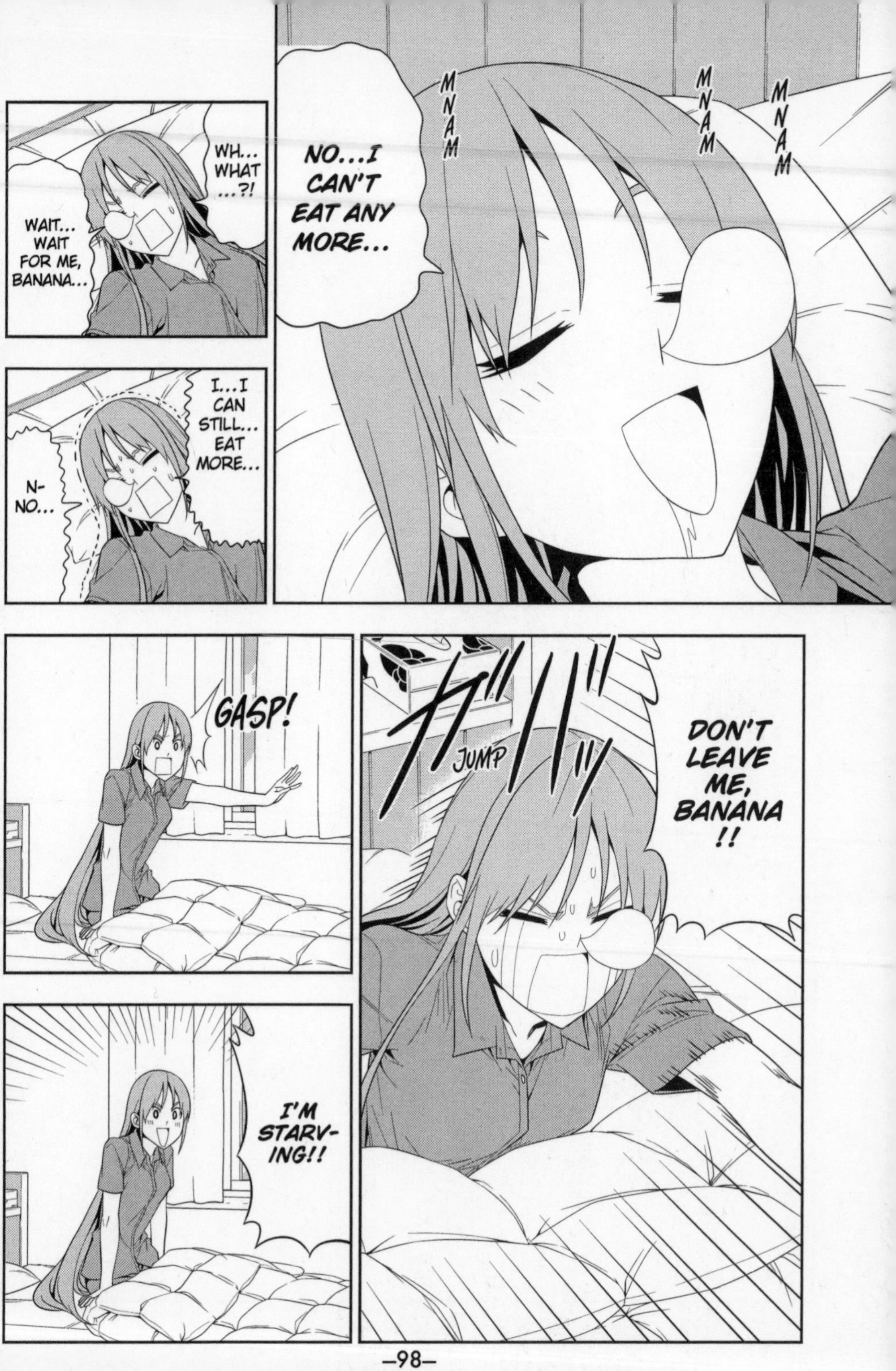

MNAM
MNAM
MNAM
NO...I CAN'T EAT ANY MORE...
WH... WHAT ...?!
WAIT... WAIT FOR ME, BANANA...
I...I CAN STILL... EAT MORE...
N-NO...
JUMP
DON'T LEAVE ME, BANANA !!
GASP!
I'M STARV-ING!!

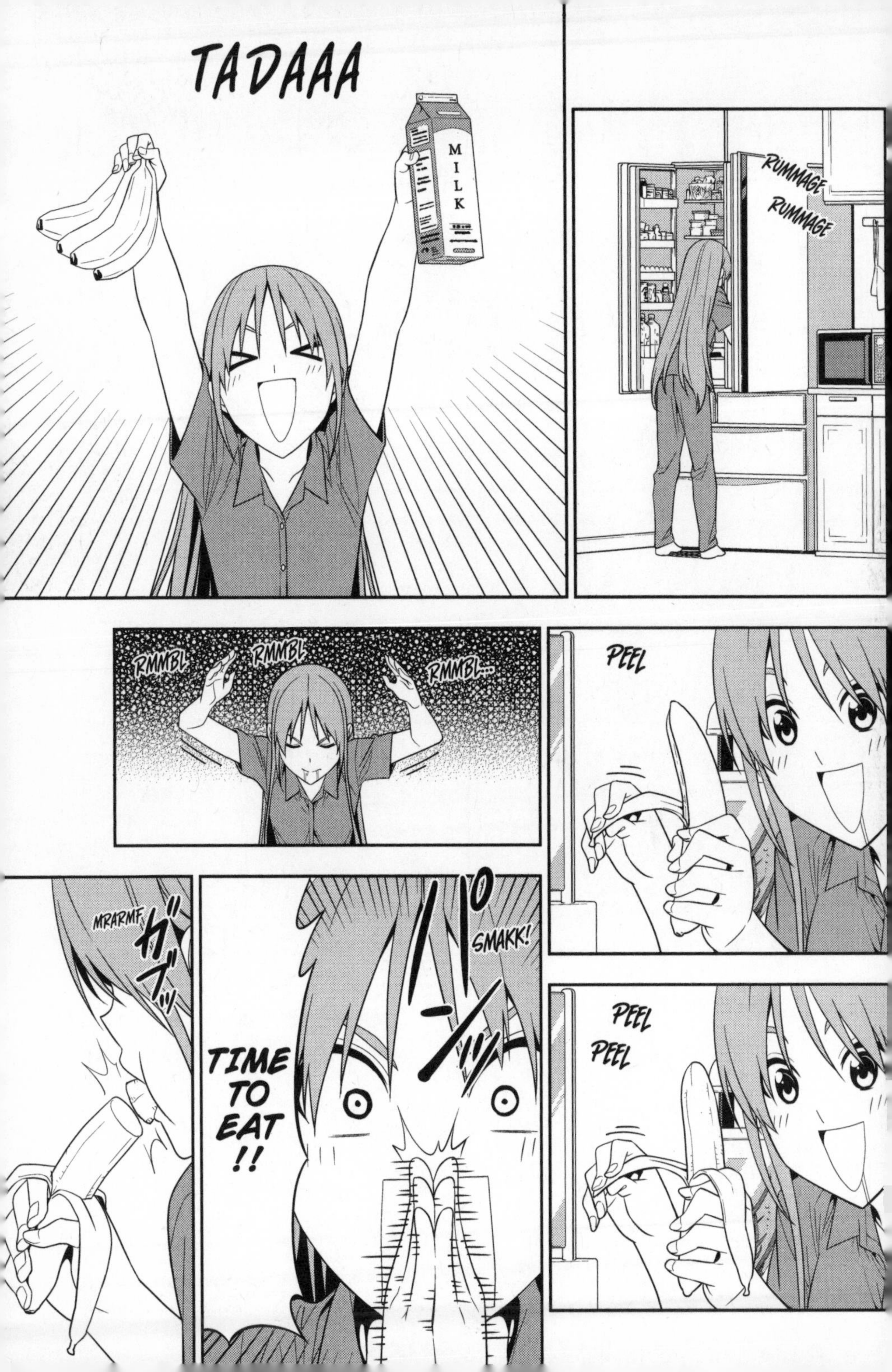
RUMMAGE
RUMMAGE
TADAAA
MILK
RMMBL
RMMBL
RMMBL...
PEEL
PEEL
PEEL
SMAKK!
TIME TO EAT !!
MRARMF
ガブッ

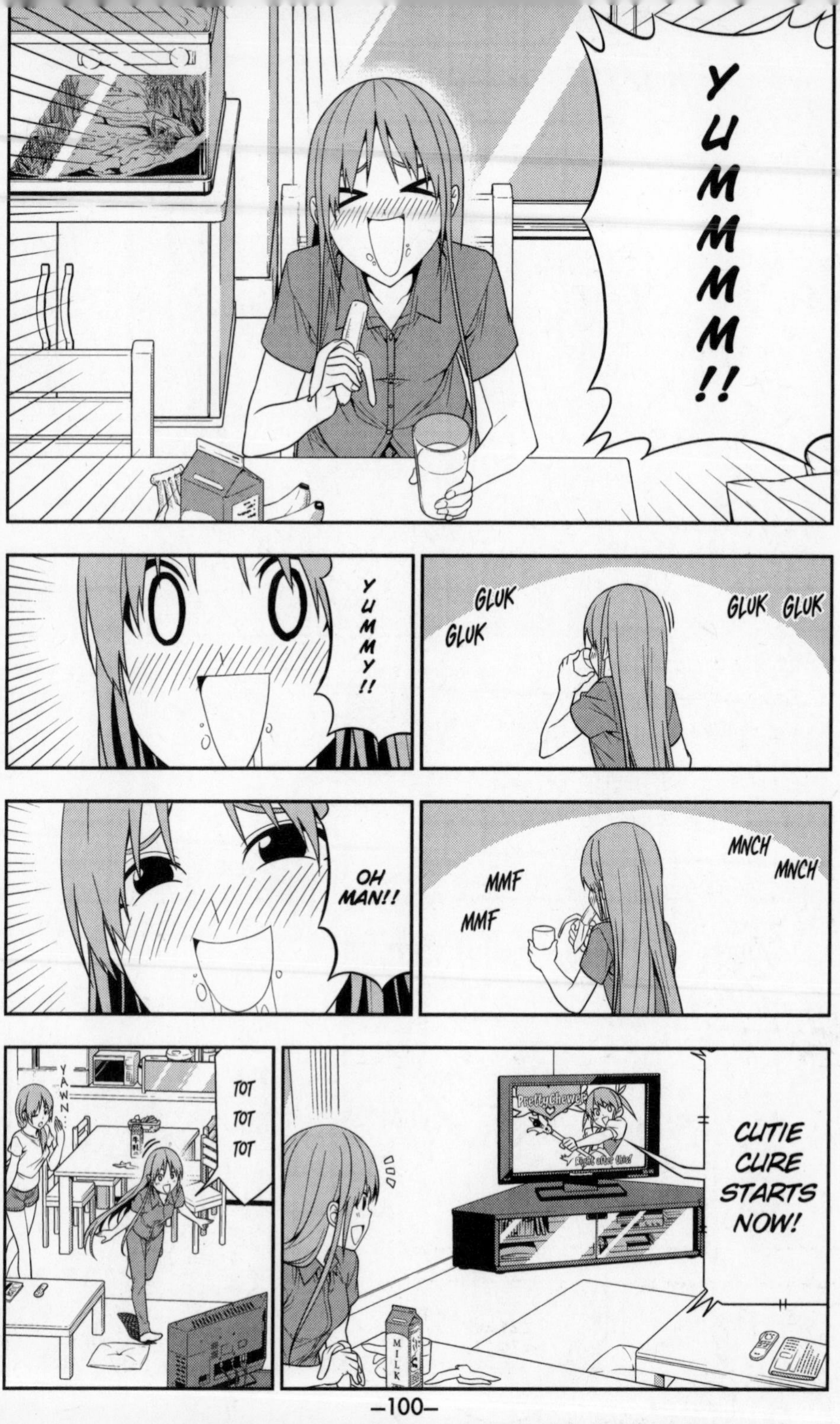
YUMMMMM!!
GLUK GLUK
GLUK
GLUK
YUMMY!!
MNCH
MNCH
MMF
MMF
OH MAN!!
CUTIE CURE STARTS NOW!
Pretty Chewer
TOT
TOT
TOT
YAWN...

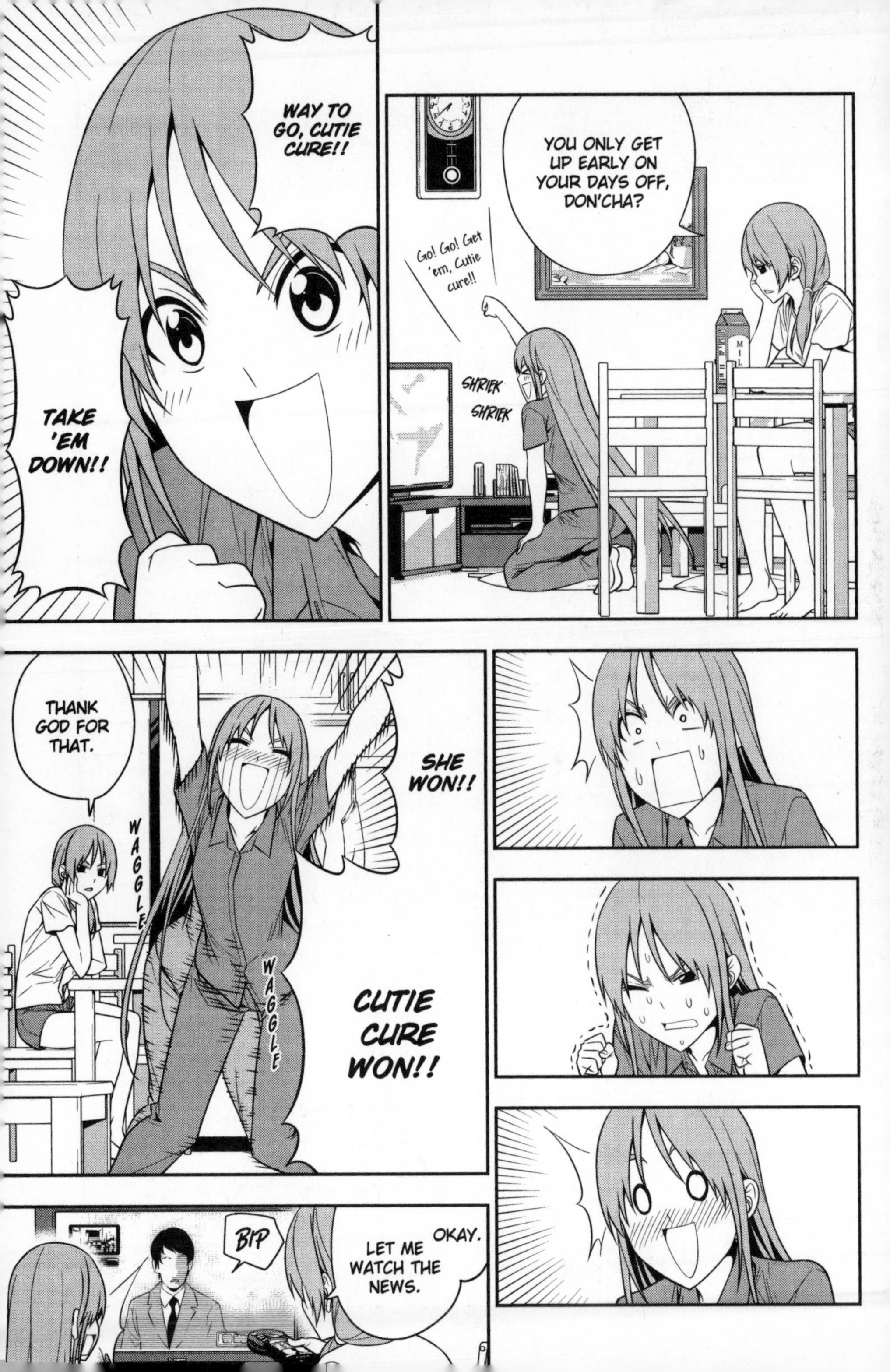
YOU ONLY GET UP EARLY ON YOUR DAYS OFF, DON'CHA?
Go! Go! Get 'em, Cutie cure!!
SHRIEK
SHRIEK
WAY TO GO, CUTIE CURE!!
TAKE 'EM DOWN!!
SHE WON!!
THANK GOD FOR THAT.
CUTIE CURE WON!!
WAGGLE
WAGGLE
OKAY.
LET ME WATCH THE NEWS.
BIP

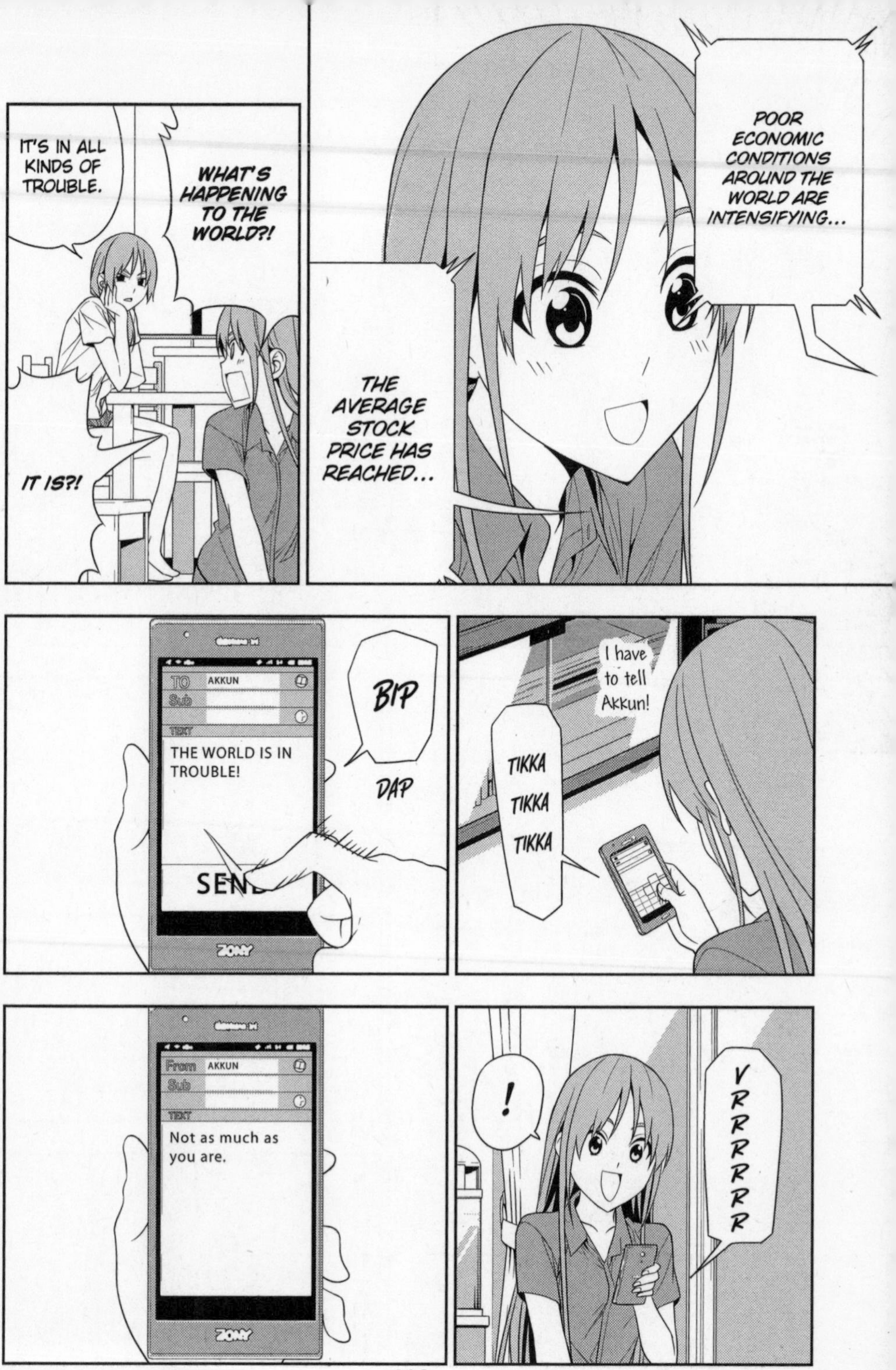
POOR ECONOMIC CONDITIONS AROUND THE WORLD ARE INTENSIFYING...
THE AVERAGE STOCK PRICE HAS REACHED...
WHAT'S HAPPENING TO THE WORLD?!
IT'S IN ALL KINDS OF TROUBLE.
IT IS?!
I have to tell Akkun!
TIKKA TIKKA TIKKA
BIP
DAP
TO AKKUN
Sub
TEXT
THE WORLD IS IN TROUBLE!
SEND
ZONY
!
VRRRRRR
From AKKUN
Sub
TEXT
Not as much as you are.
ZONY

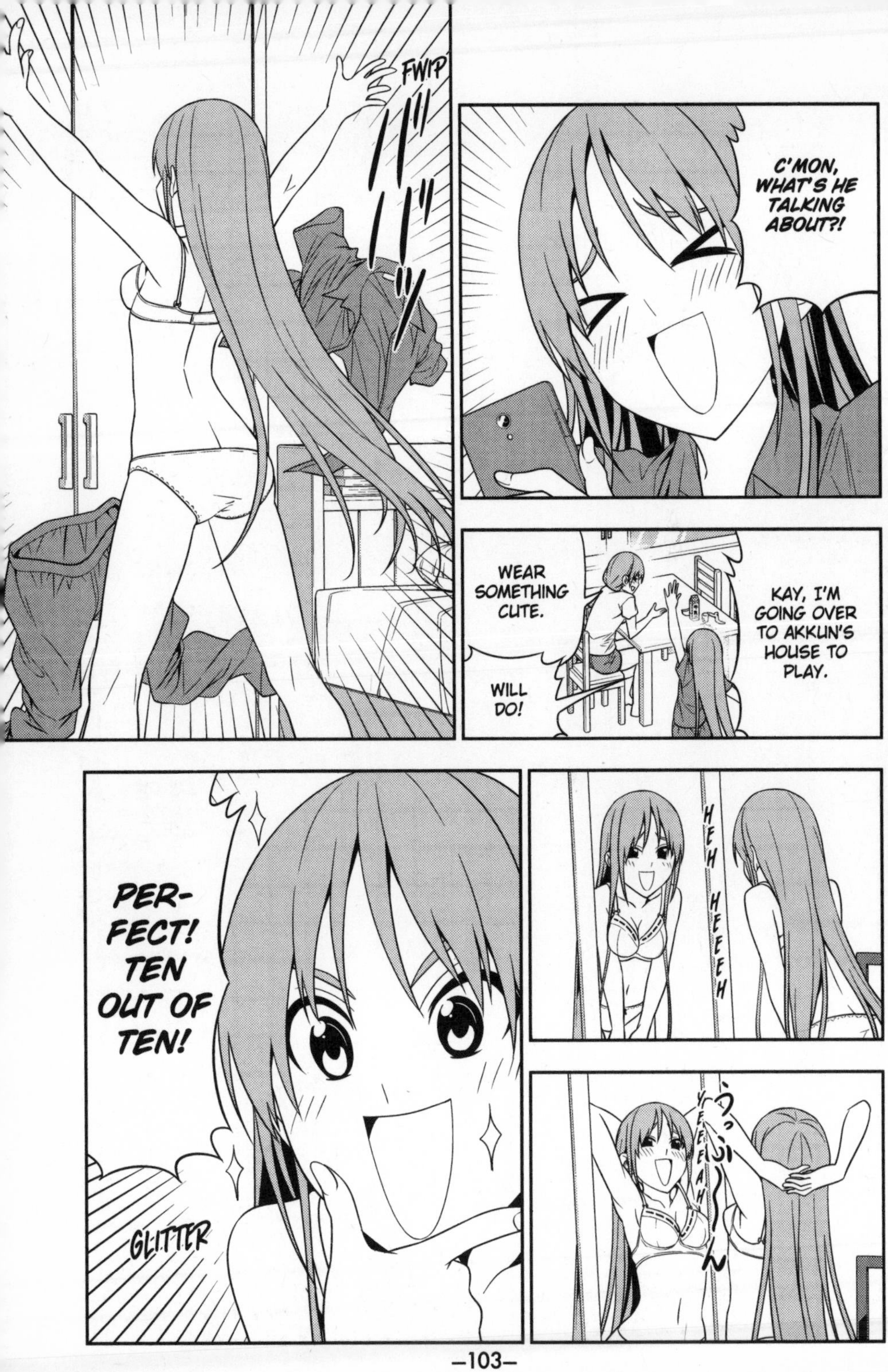
C'MON, WHAT'S HE TALKING ABOUT?!
KAY, I'M GOING OVER TO AKKUN'S HOUSE TO PLAY.
WEAR SOMETHING CUTE.
WILL DO!
FWIP
HEH HEEEH
YEEEAH
うっふ〜ん
PER-FECT! TEN OUT OF TEN!
GLITTER

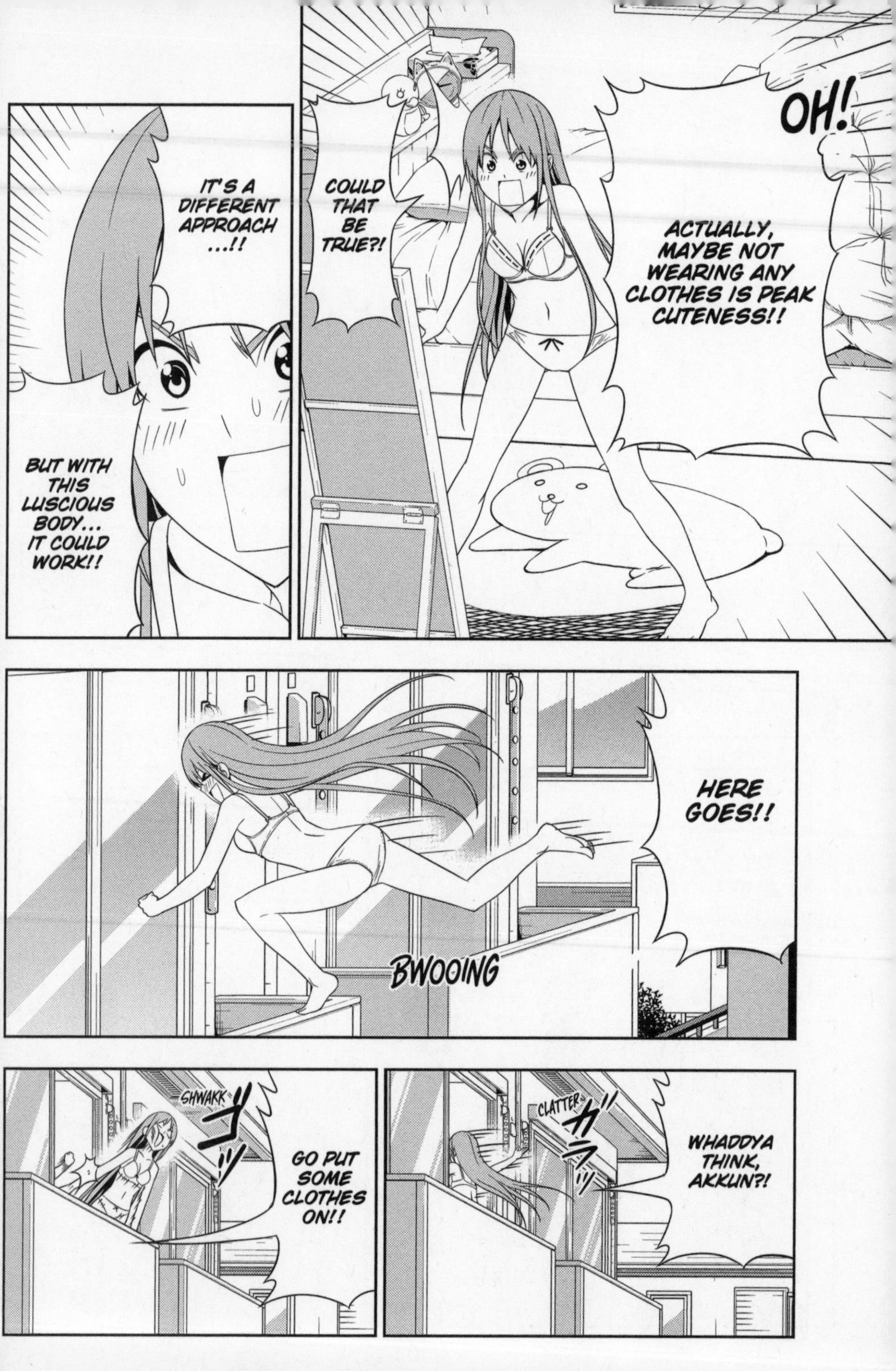
OH!
ACTUALLY, MAYBE NOT WEARING ANY CLOTHES IS PEAK CUTENESS!!
COULD THAT BE TRUE?!
IT'S A DIFFERENT APPROACH ...!!
BUT WITH THIS LUSCIOUS BODY... IT COULD WORK!!
HERE GOES!!
BWOOING
CLATTER
WHADDYA THINK, AKKUN?!
SHWAKK
GO PUT SOME CLOTHES ON!!

Of Course

CLATTER
ガラッ
OH COME ON, DON'T BE SHY!!
SHWAKK
ゴッ
GO PUT SOME CLOTHES ON!!

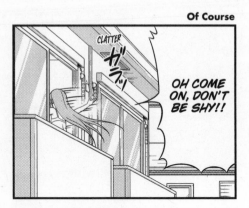

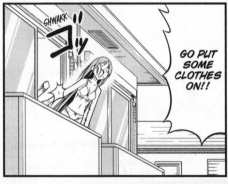

(When I'm eating—how should I put it? I'm)

Aho-Girl

\'ahô,gərl\ *Japanese , noun*.

A clueless girl.

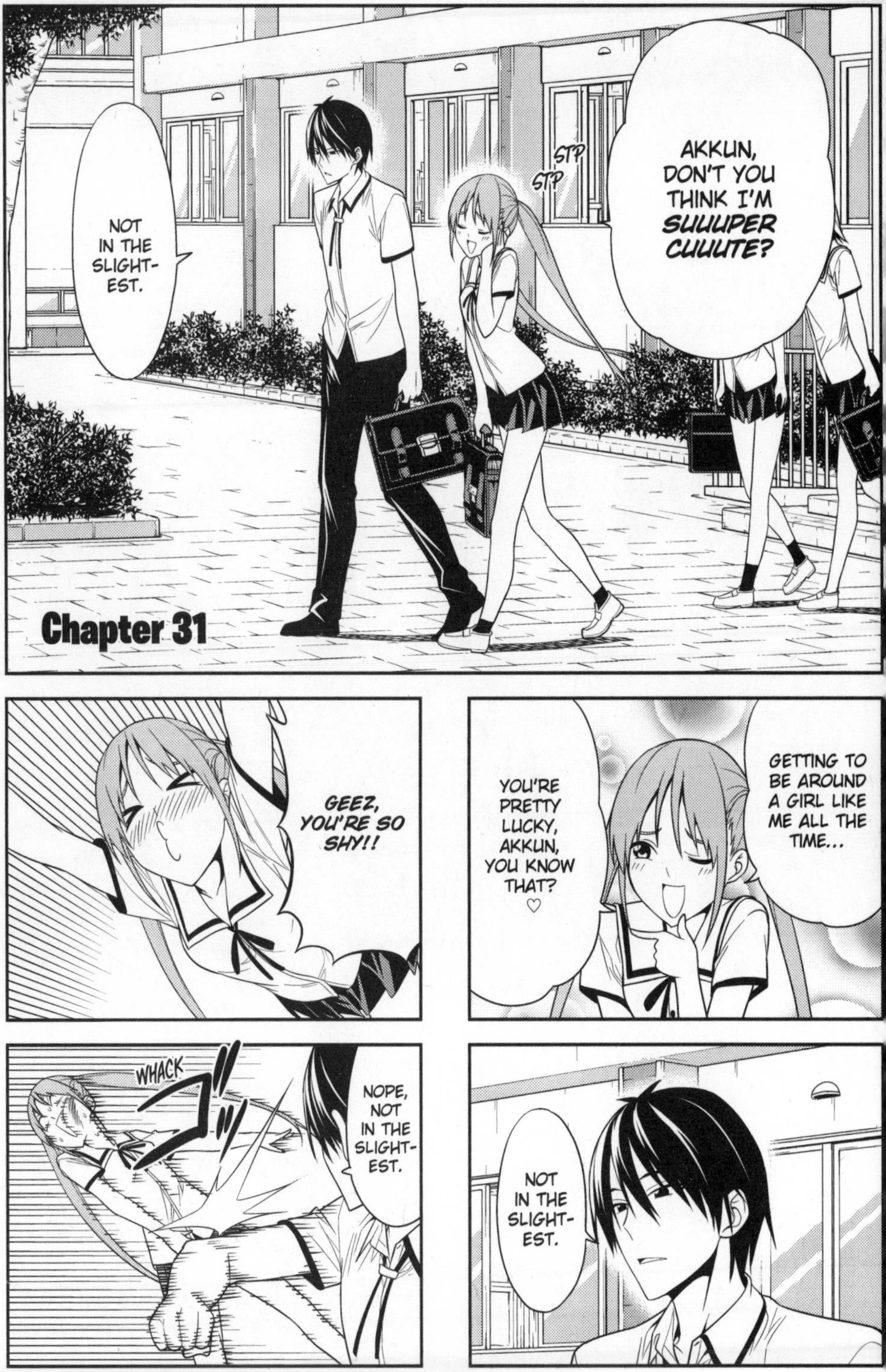
AKKUN, DON'T YOU THINK I'M SUUUPER CUUUTE?
STP STP
NOT IN THE SLIGHT-EST.
Chapter 31
GETTING TO BE AROUND A GIRL LIKE ME ALL THE TIME...
YOU'RE PRETTY LUCKY, AKKUN, YOU KNOW THAT? ♡
GEEZ, YOU'RE SO SHY!!
NOT IN THE SLIGHT-EST.
NOPE, NOT IN THE SLIGHT-EST.
WHACK

A Chance Meeting

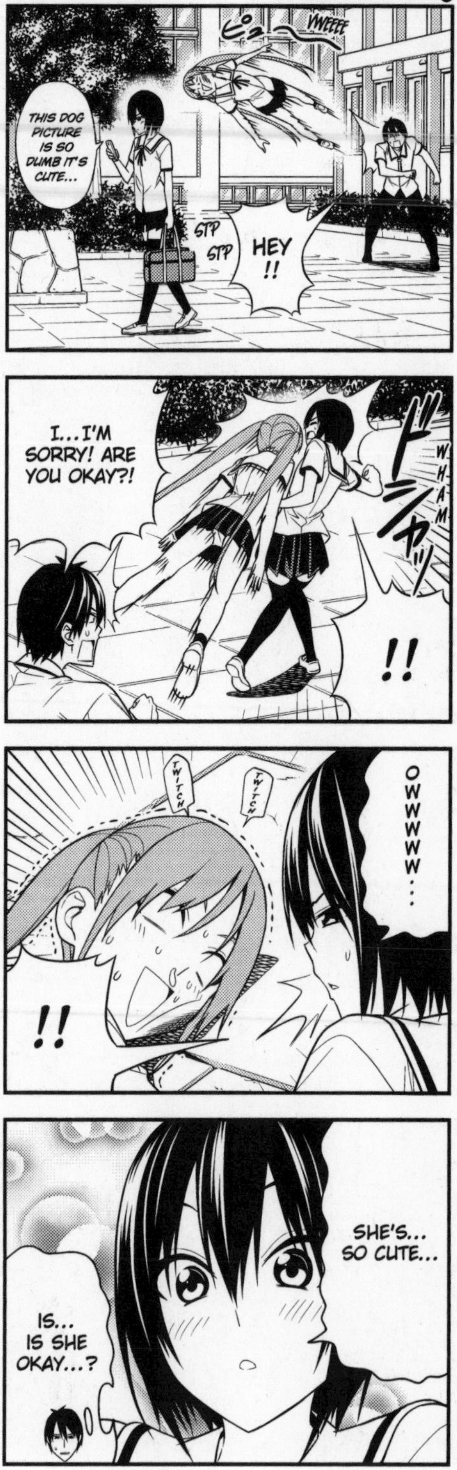
VWEEEE
HEY !!
STP STP
THIS DOG PICTURE IS SO DUMB IT'S CUTE...
WHAM
I...I'M SORRY! ARE YOU OKAY?!
!!
OWWWWW...
TWITCH
TWITCH
!!
SHE'S... SO CUTE...
IS... IS SHE OKAY...?

Victory Dance

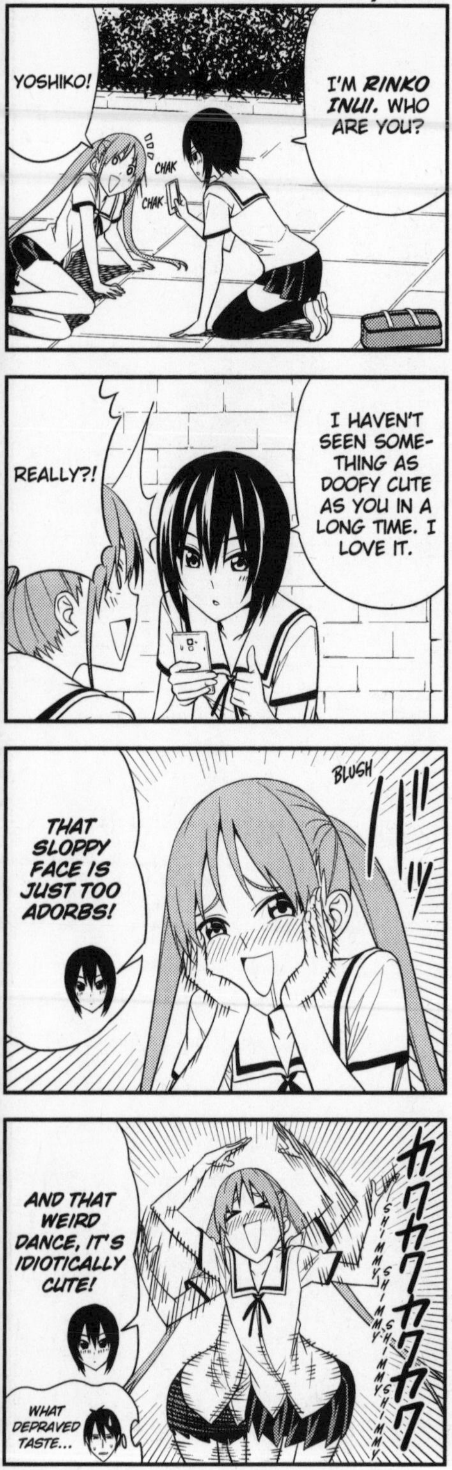
I'M RINKO INUI. WHO ARE YOU?
CHAK
CHAK
YOSHIKO!
I HAVEN'T SEEN SOMETHING AS DOOFY CUTE AS YOU IN A LONG TIME. I LOVE IT.
REALLY?!
BLUSH
THAT SLOPPY FACE IS JUST TOO ADORBS!
SHIMMY SHIMMY SHIMMY SHIMMY
AND THAT WEIRD DANCE, IT'S IDIOTICALLY CUTE!
WHAT DEPRAVED TASTE...

Training

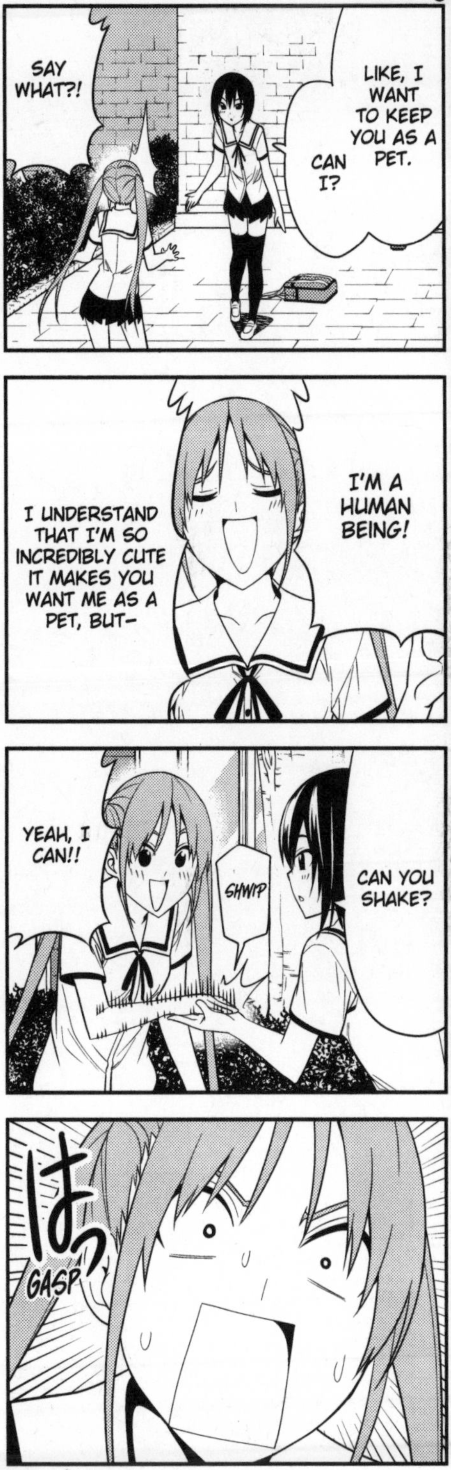
LIKE, I WANT TO KEEP YOU AS A PET.
CAN I?
SAY WHAT?!
I'M A HUMAN BEING!
I UNDERSTAND THAT I'M SO INCREDIBLY CUTE IT MAKES YOU WANT ME AS A PET, BUT-
CAN YOU SHAKE?
SHWIP
YEAH, I CAN!!
はっ
GASP

Training 2

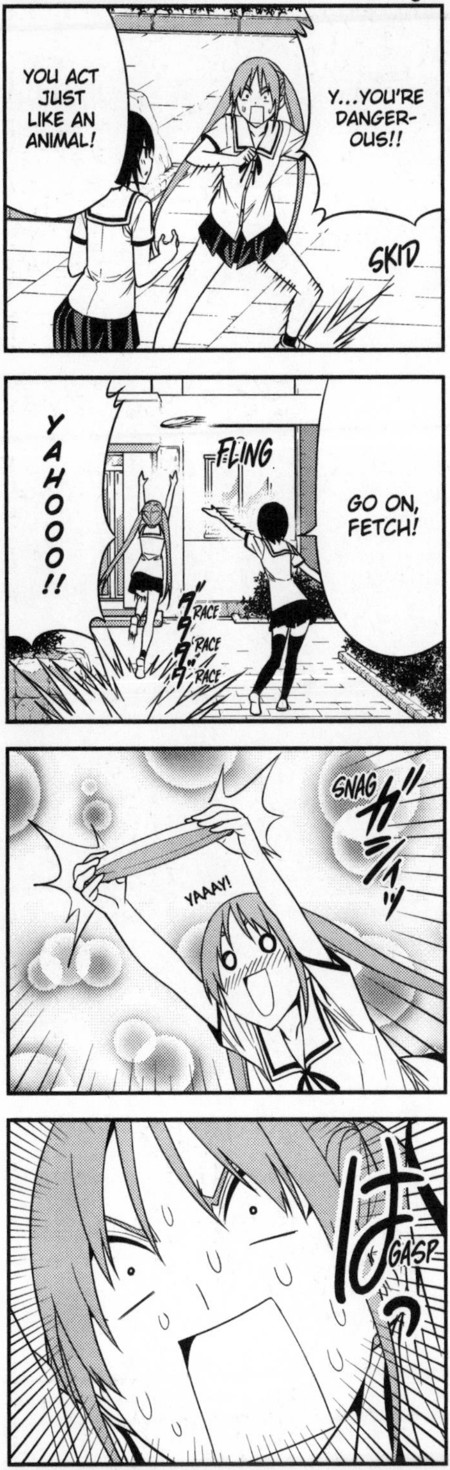
Y...YOU'RE DANGER-OUS!!
YOU ACT JUST LIKE AN ANIMAL!
SKID
GO ON, FETCH!
FLING
YAHOOOO!!
RACE RACE RACE
SNAG
YAAAY!
はっ
GASP

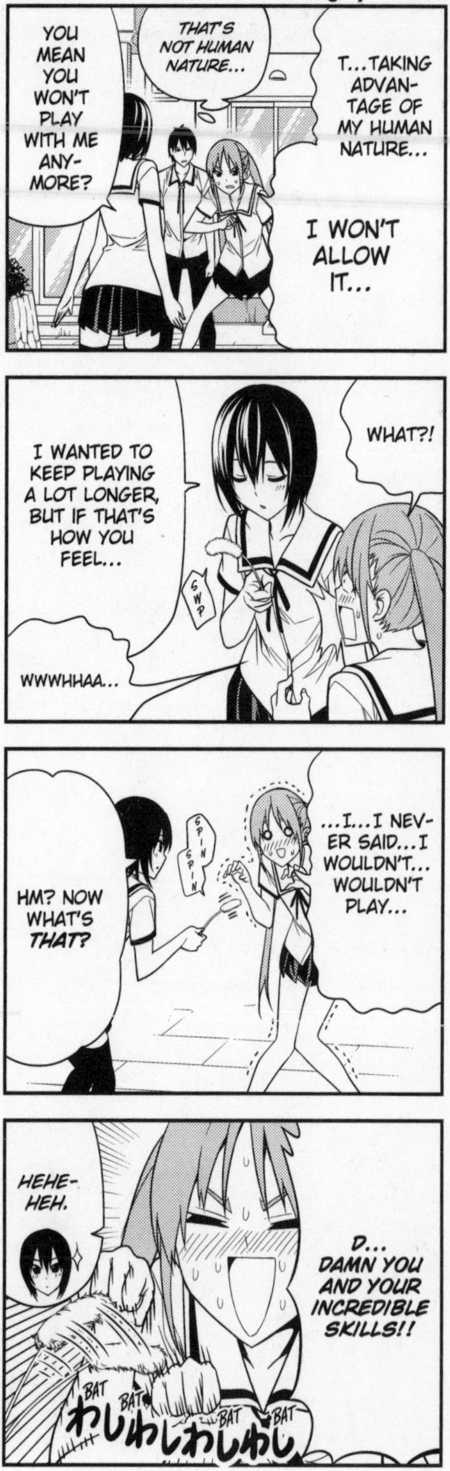
T...TAKING ADVAN-TAGE OF MY HUMAN NATURE...
I WON'T ALLOW IT...
THAT'S NOT HUMAN NATURE...
YOU MEAN YOU WON'T PLAY WITH ME ANY-MORE?
WHAT?!
I WANTED TO KEEP PLAYING A LOT LONGER, BUT IF THAT'S HOW YOU FEEL...
SWP
WWWHHAA...
...I...I NEV-ER SAID...I WOULDN'T... WOULDN'T PLAY...
SPIN SPIN
HM? NOW WHAT'S THAT?
D... DAMN YOU AND YOUR INCREDIBLE SKILLS!!
BAT BAT BAT BAT
わしわしわしわし
HEHE-HEH.

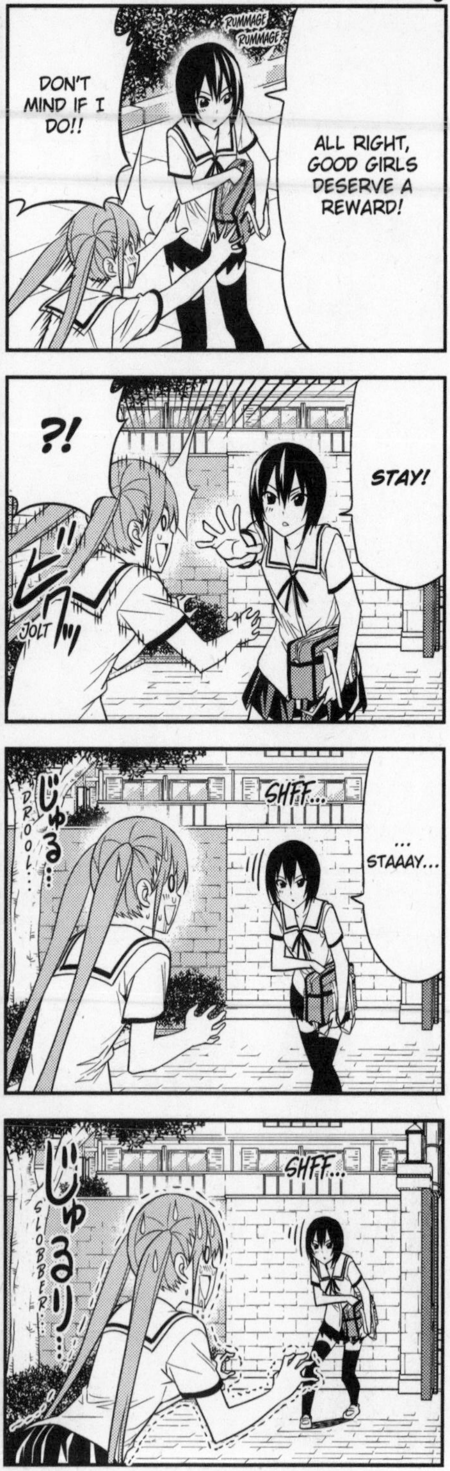
RUMMAGE RUMMAGE
ALL RIGHT, GOOD GIRLS DESERVE A REWARD!
DON'T MIND IF I DO!!
STAY!
?!
ビクッ
JOLT
... STAAAY...
SHFF...
じゅる...
DROOL...
SHFF...
じゅるり...
SLOBBER...

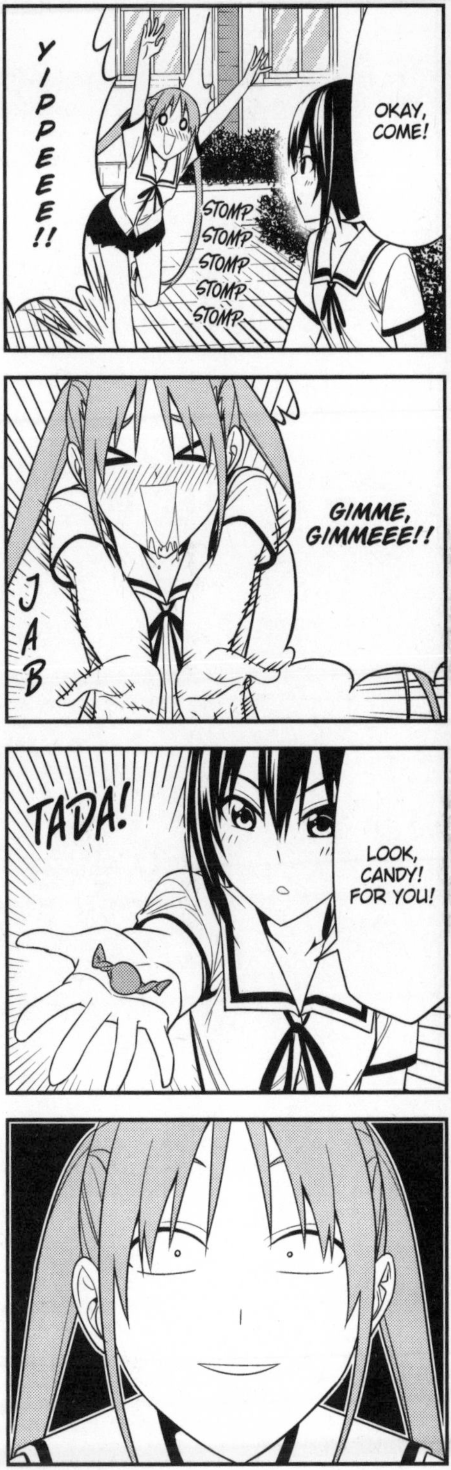
OKAY, COME!
YIPPEEE!!
STOMP STOMP STOMP STOMP STOMP
GIMME, GIMMEEE!!
JAB
TADA!
LOOK, CANDY! FOR YOU!

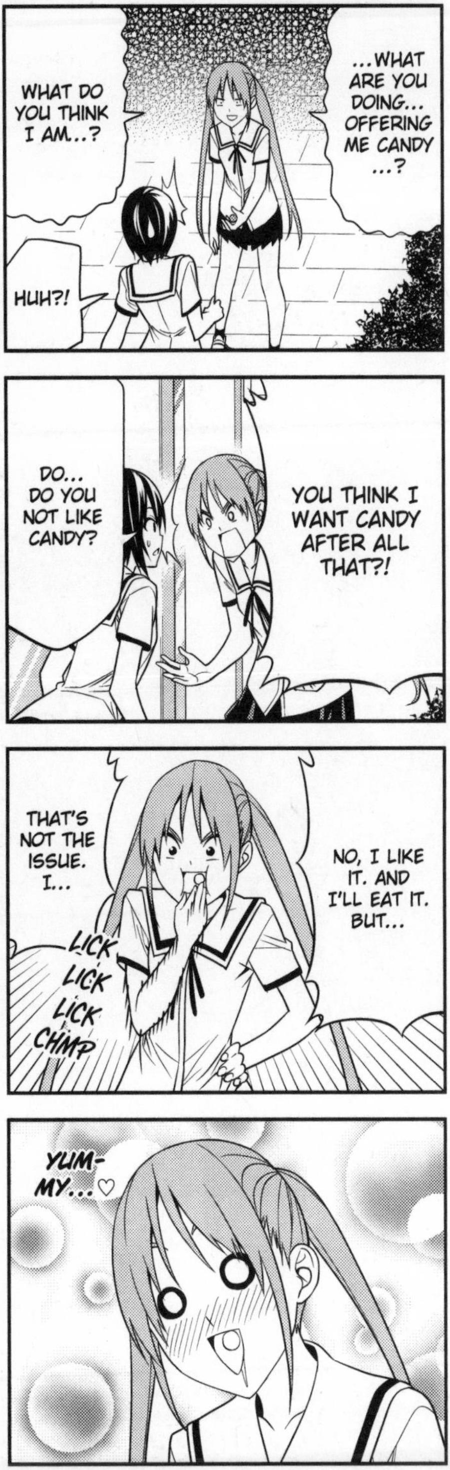
...WHAT ARE YOU DOING... OFFERING ME CANDY ...?
WHAT DO YOU THINK I AM...?
HUH?!
YOU THINK I WANT CANDY AFTER ALL THAT?!
DO... DO YOU NOT LIKE CANDY?
NO, I LIKE IT. AND I'LL EAT IT. BUT...
THAT'S NOT THE ISSUE. I...
LICK LICK LICK CHMP
YUM-MY...♡

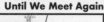

The Taste of Defeat

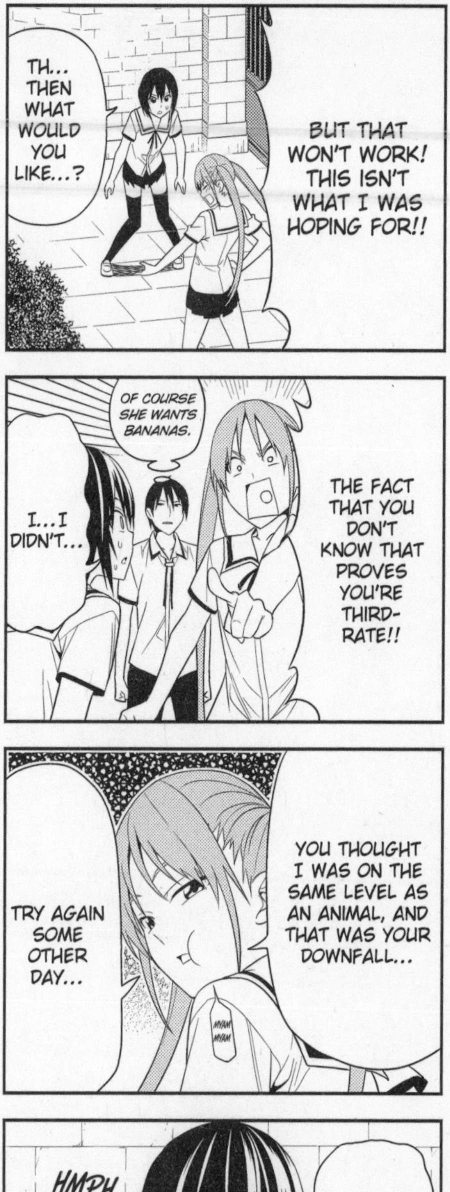
BUT THAT WON'T WORK! THIS ISN'T WHAT I WAS HOPING FOR!!
TH... THEN WHAT WOULD YOU LIKE...?
THE FACT THAT YOU DON'T KNOW THAT PROVES YOU'RE THIRD-RATE!!
OF COURSE SHE WANTS BANANAS.
I...I DIDN'T...
YOU THOUGHT I WAS ON THE SAME LEVEL AS AN ANIMAL, AND THAT WAS YOUR DOWNFALL...
TRY AGAIN SOME OTHER DAY...
MYAM MYAM
...I CAN'T DENY IT...
HMPH...
BECAUSE SHE IS ON THE SAME LEVEL.

Until We Meet Again

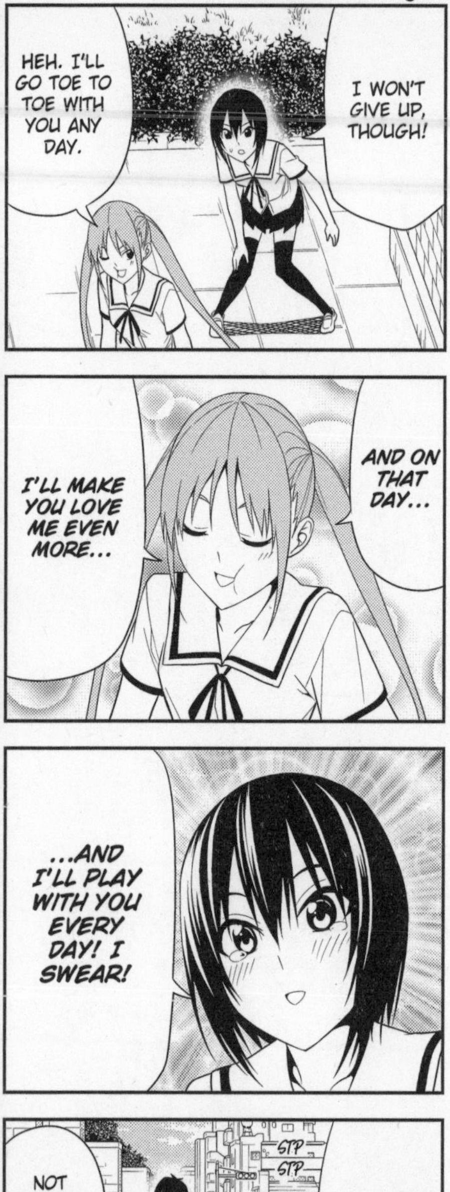
I WON'T GIVE UP, THOUGH!
HEH. I'LL GO TOE TO TOE WITH YOU ANY DAY.
AND ON THAT DAY...
I'LL MAKE YOU LOVE ME EVEN MORE...
...AND I'LL PLAY WITH YOU EVERY DAY! I SWEAR!
STP STP
THAT GIRL SEEMS PRETTY PROMISING—
DOESN'T SHE?
NOT IN THE SLIGHTEST.
Not like I care

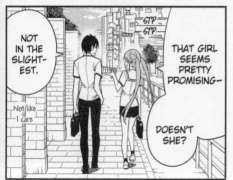

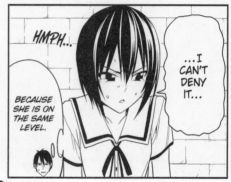

An Ordinary Sensation

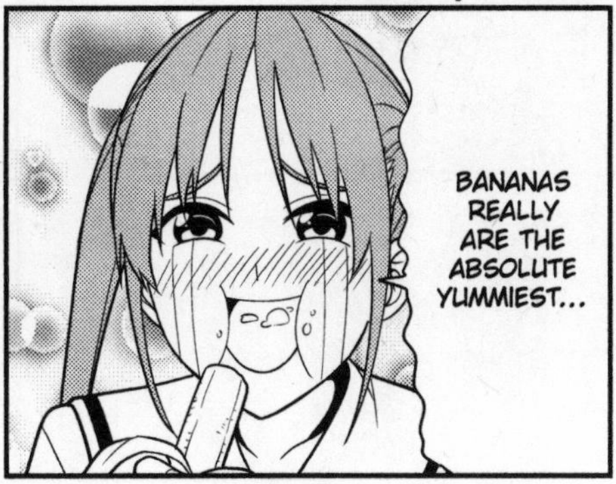
BANANAS REALLY ARE THE ABSOLUTE YUMMIEST...

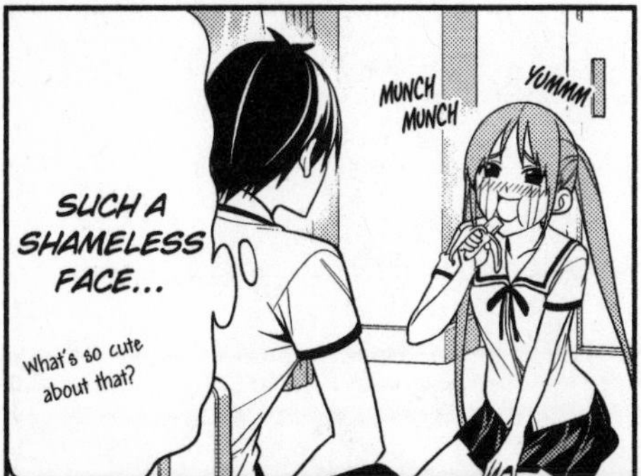
YUMMM
MUNCH MUNCH
SUCH A SHAMELESS FACE...
What's so cute about that?

Name **Rinko Inui**

Sex

Height **162cm**

Weight **48kg**

Blood type **B**

Birthday **06/14**

Memo

A girl with depraved tastes. Second-year student in high school.

She's so aloof, we don't really know what she's thinking at this point.

Becomes obsessed with things that snag her interest, but is otherwise a normal person.

Was raised with a great deal of freedom.

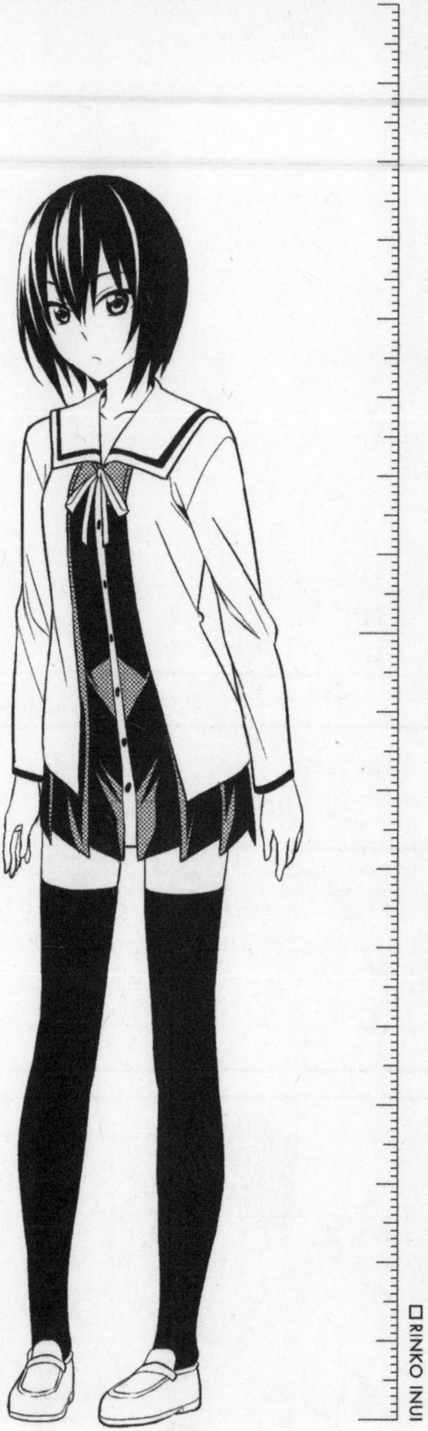
RINKO INUI

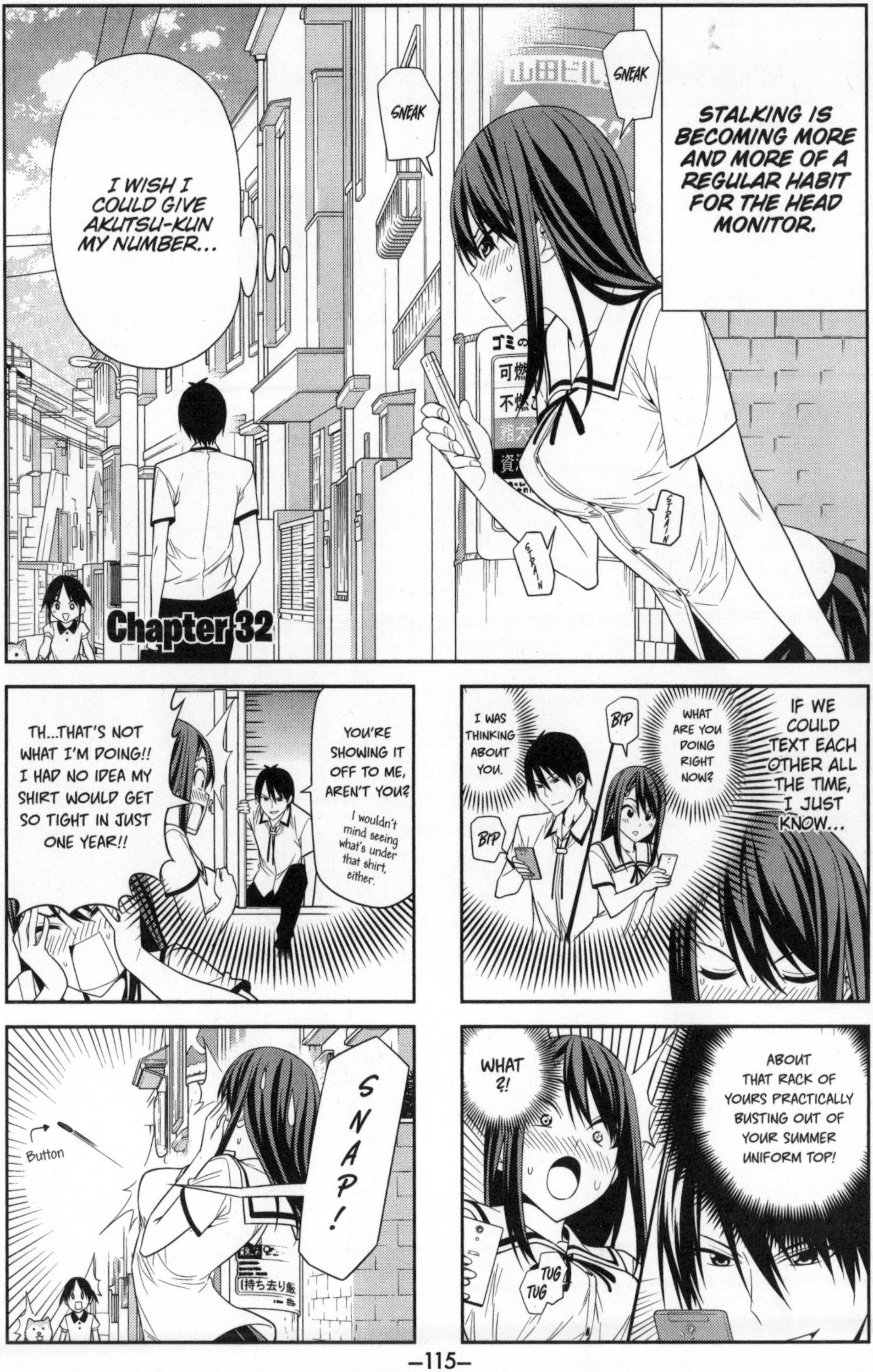
STALKING IS BECOMING MORE AND MORE OF A REGULAR HABIT FOR THE HEAD MONITOR.
SNEAK
SNEAK
STRAIN
STRAIN
I WISH I COULD GIVE AKUTSU-KUN MY NUMBER...
Chapter 32
IF WE COULD TEXT EACH OTHER ALL THE TIME, I JUST KNOW...
WHAT ARE YOU DOING RIGHT NOW?
BIP
I WAS THINKING ABOUT YOU.
BIP
YOU'RE SHOWING IT OFF TO ME, AREN'T YOU?
I wouldn't mind seeing what's under that shirt, either.
TH...THAT'S NOT WHAT I'M DOING!! I HAD NO IDEA MY SHIRT WOULD GET SO TIGHT IN JUST ONE YEAR!!
ABOUT THAT RACK OF YOURS PRACTICALLY BUSTING OUT OF YOUR SUMMER UNIFORM TOP!
WHAT?!
TUG TUG
SNAP!
Button

Lousy Negotiator

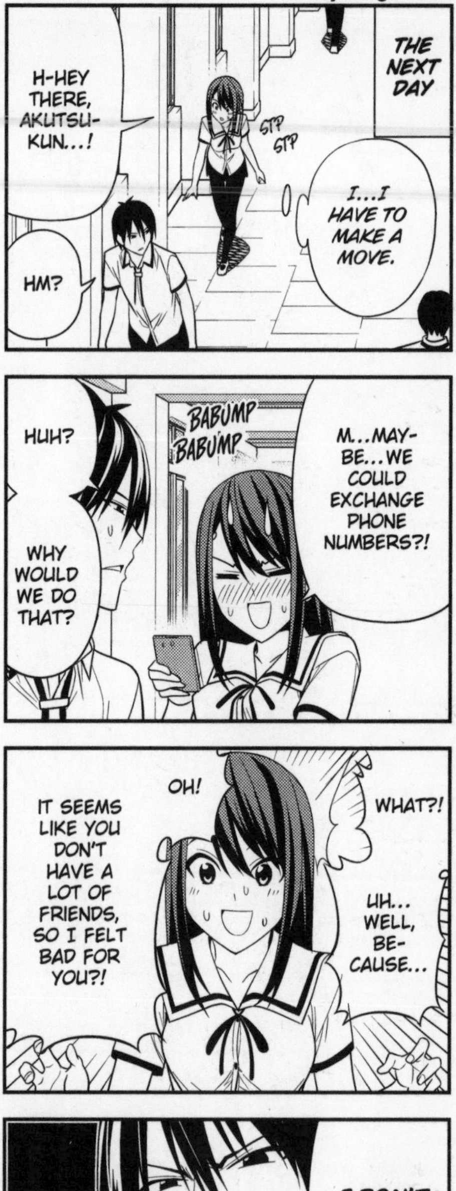
THE NEXT DAY
I...I HAVE TO MAKE A MOVE.
STP STP
H-HEY THERE, AKUTSU-KUN...!
HM?
M...MAY-BE...WE COULD EXCHANGE PHONE NUMBERS?!
BABUMP BABUMP
HUH?
WHY WOULD WE DO THAT?
WHAT?!
UH... WELL, BE-CAUSE...
OH!
IT SEEMS LIKE YOU DON'T HAVE A LOT OF FRIENDS, SO I FELT BAD FOR YOU?!
I DON'T WANT YOUR HELP.
WHAAAAT?!

Deleted and Forgotten

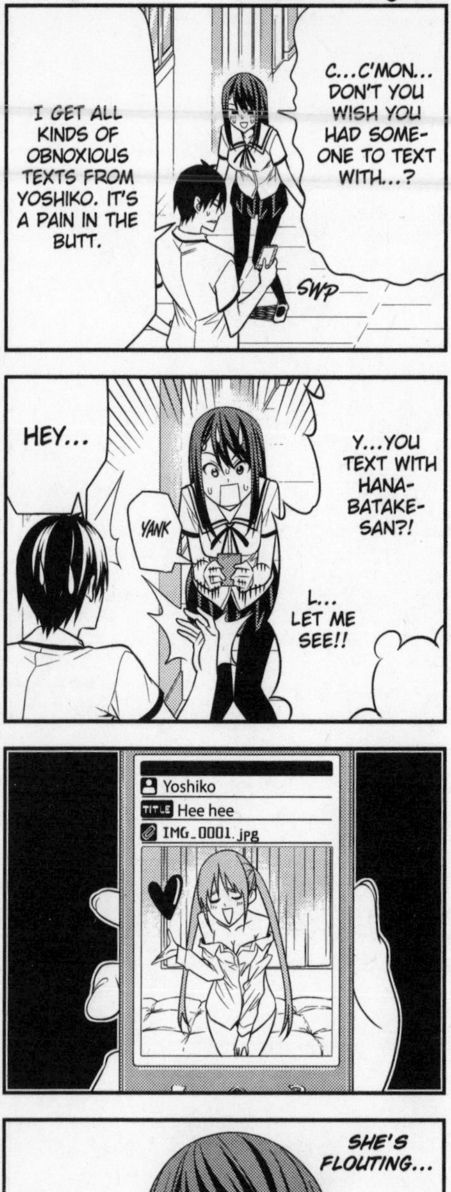
C...C'MON... DON'T YOU WISH YOU HAD SOME-ONE TO TEXT WITH...?
SWP
I GET ALL KINDS OF OBNOXIOUS TEXTS FROM YOSHIKO. IT'S A PAIN IN THE BUTT.
Y...YOU TEXT WITH HANA-BATAKE-SAN?!
HEY...
YANK
L... LET ME SEE!!
Yoshiko
TITLE Hee hee
IMG_0001.jpg
SHE'S FLOUTING...
...ALL SEMBLANCE OF DECENCY AND MORALITY...

Attacking Drive

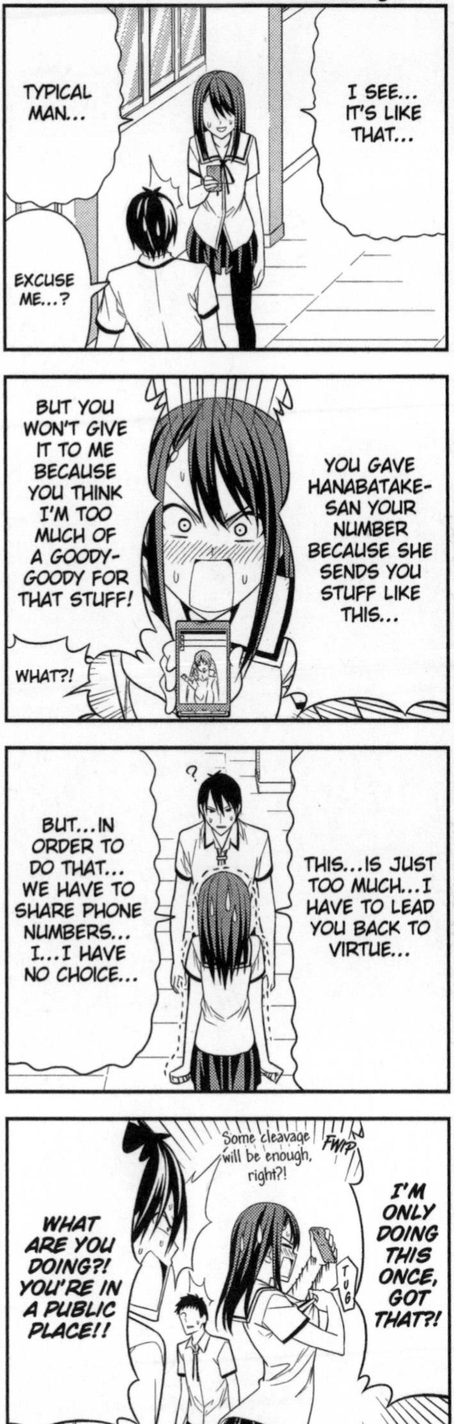
I SEE... IT'S LIKE THAT...
TYPICAL MAN...
EXCUSE ME...?
YOU GAVE HANABATAKE-SAN YOUR NUMBER BECAUSE SHE SENDS YOU STUFF LIKE THIS...
BUT YOU WON'T GIVE IT TO ME BECAUSE YOU THINK I'M TOO MUCH OF A GOODY-GOODY FOR THAT STUFF!
WHAT?!
THIS...IS JUST TOO MUCH...I HAVE TO LEAD YOU BACK TO VIRTUE...
BUT...IN ORDER TO DO THAT... WE HAVE TO SHARE PHONE NUMBERS... I...I HAVE NO CHOICE...
I'M ONLY DOING THIS ONCE, GOT THAT?!
FWIP
Some cleavage will be enough, right?!
TUG
WHAT ARE YOU DOING?! YOU'RE IN A PUBLIC PLACE!!

A Dangerous Situation

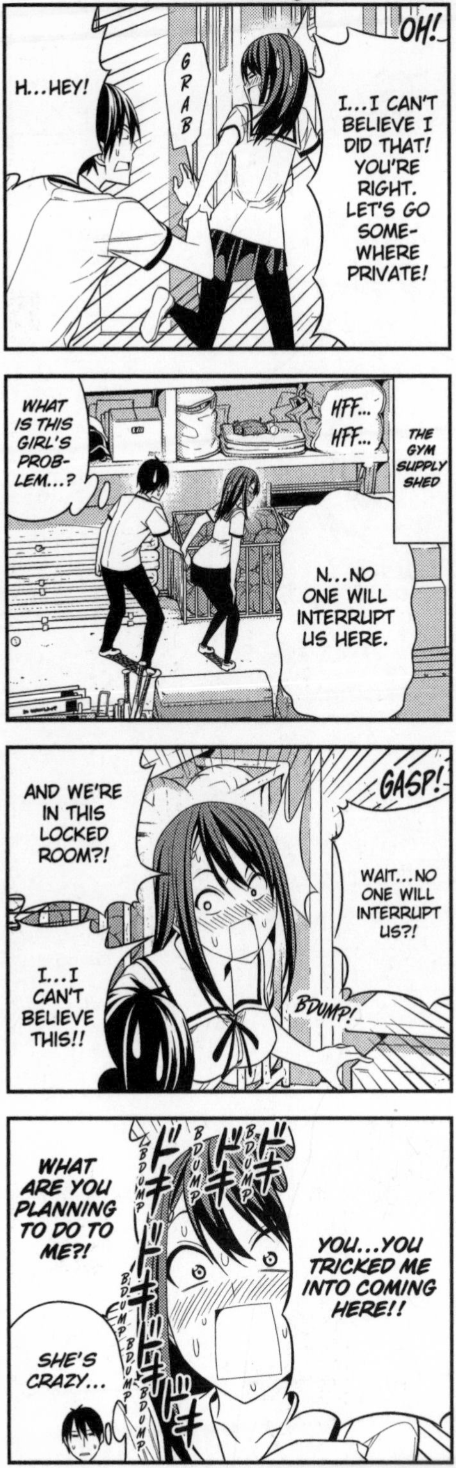
OH!
I...I CAN'T BELIEVE I DID THAT! YOU'RE RIGHT. LET'S GO SOME-WHERE PRIVATE!
GRAB
H...HEY!
THE GYM SUPPLY SHED
HFF... HFF...
N...NO ONE WILL INTERRUPT US HERE.
WHAT IS THIS GIRL'S PROB-LEM...?
GASP!
WAIT...NO ONE WILL INTERRUPT US?!
AND WE'RE IN THIS LOCKED ROOM?!
BDUMP!
I...I CAN'T BELIEVE THIS!!
YOU...YOU TRICKED ME INTO COMING HERE!!
ドキドキ
BDUMP BDUMP
ドキドキドキドキ
BDUMP BDUMP BDUMP BDUMP
WHAT ARE YOU PLANNING TO DO TO ME?!
SHE'S CRAZY...

She's the Type to Do Things in Order

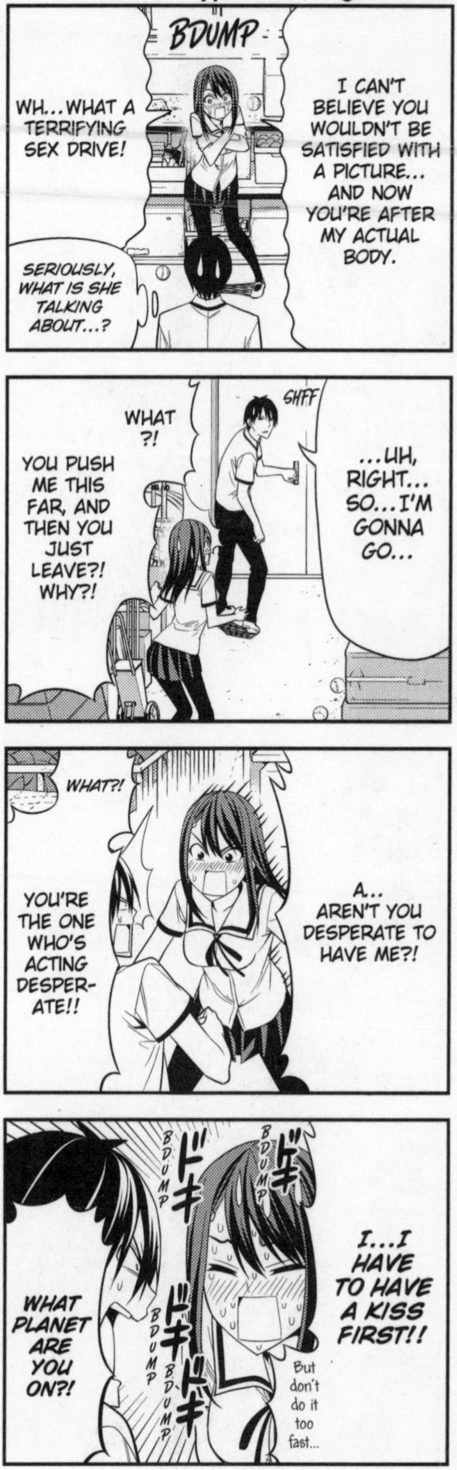
BDUMP
I CAN'T BELIEVE YOU WOULDN'T BE SATISFIED WITH A PICTURE... AND NOW YOU'RE AFTER MY ACTUAL BODY.
WH...WHAT A TERRIFYING SEX DRIVE!
SERIOUSLY, WHAT IS SHE TALKING ABOUT...?
SHFF
...UH, RIGHT... SO...I'M GONNA GO...
WHAT ?!
YOU PUSH ME THIS FAR, AND THEN YOU JUST LEAVE?! WHY?!
A... AREN'T YOU DESPERATE TO HAVE ME?!
WHAT?!
YOU'RE THE ONE WHO'S ACTING DESPERATE!!
BDUMP
BDUMP
I...I HAVE TO HAVE A KISS FIRST!!
But don't do it too fast...
WHAT PLANET ARE YOU ON?!
BDUMP
BDUMP

Fear of Death

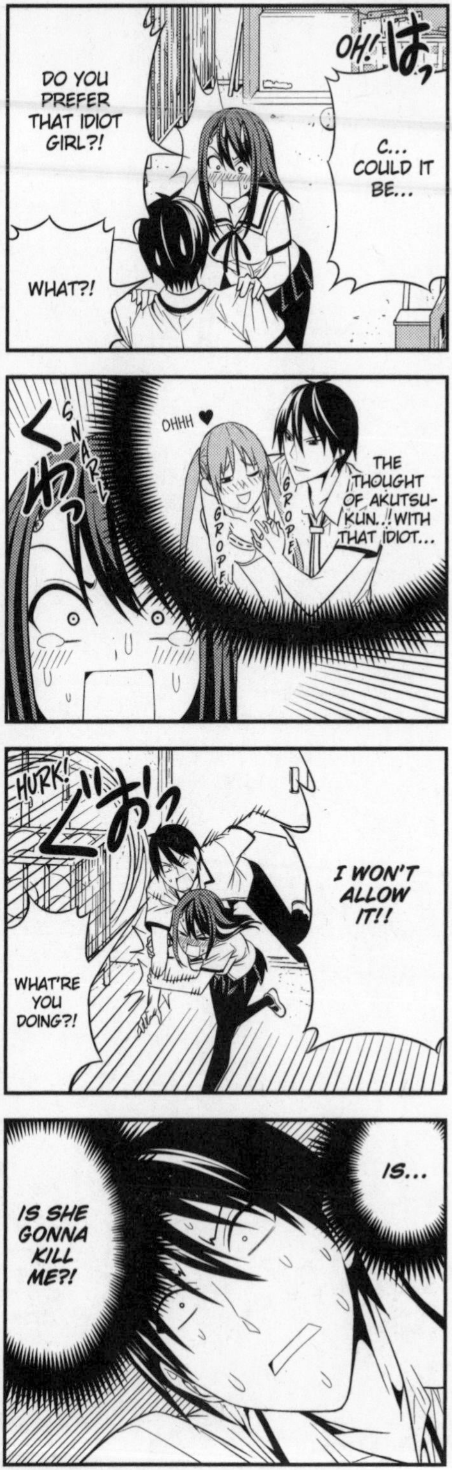
OH! はっ
C... COULD IT BE...
DO YOU PREFER THAT IDIOT GIRL?!
WHAT?!
THE THOUGHT OF AKUTSU-KUN...WITH THAT IDIOT...
OHHH ♥
GROPE
GROPE
くわっ SNARL
I WON'T ALLOW IT!!
HURK! ぐおっ
WHAT'RE YOU DOING?!
IS...
IS SHE GONNA KILL ME?!

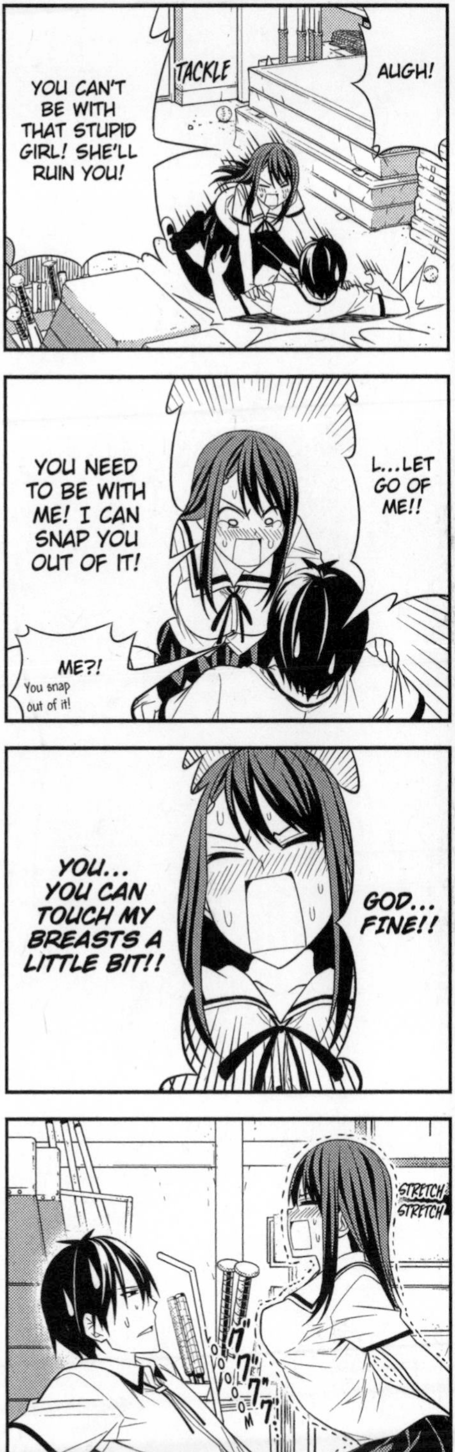
AUGH!
TACKLE
YOU CAN'T BE WITH THAT STUPID GIRL! SHE'LL RUIN YOU!
L...LET GO OF ME!!
YOU NEED TO BE WITH ME! I CAN SNAP YOU OUT OF IT!
ME?!
You snap out of it!
GOD... FINE!!
YOU... YOU CAN TOUCH MY BREASTS A LITTLE BIT!!
STRETCH STRETCH

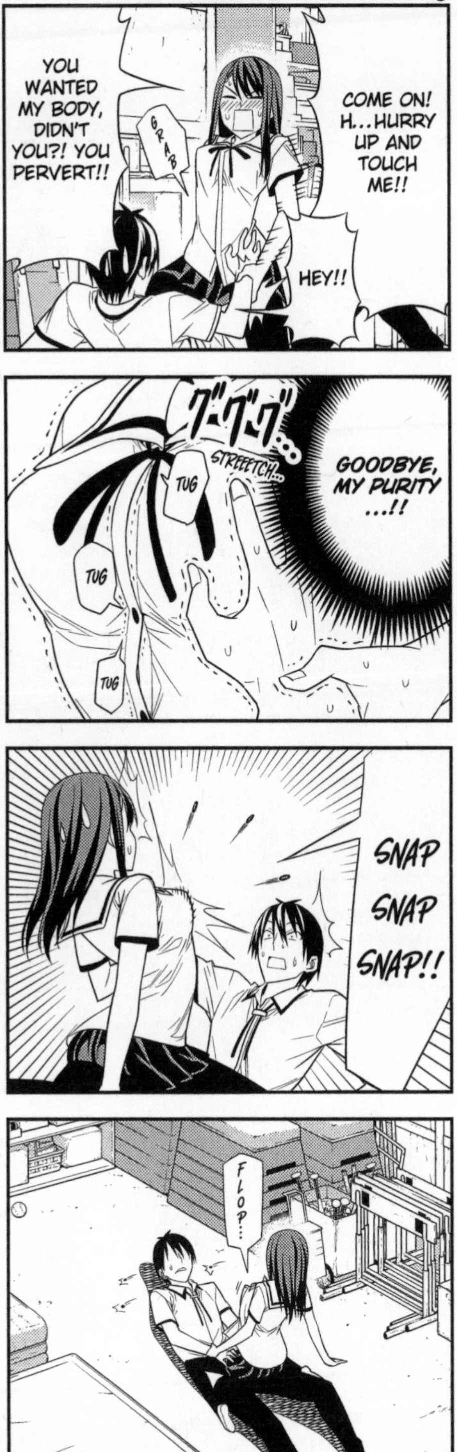
COME ON! H...HURRY UP AND TOUCH ME!!
YOU WANTED MY BODY, DIDN'T YOU?! YOU PERVERT!!
GRAB
HEY!!
GOODBYE, MY PURITY ...!!
STREEETCH...
TUG
TUG
TUG
SNAP
SNAP
SNAP!!
FLOP...

Chaos

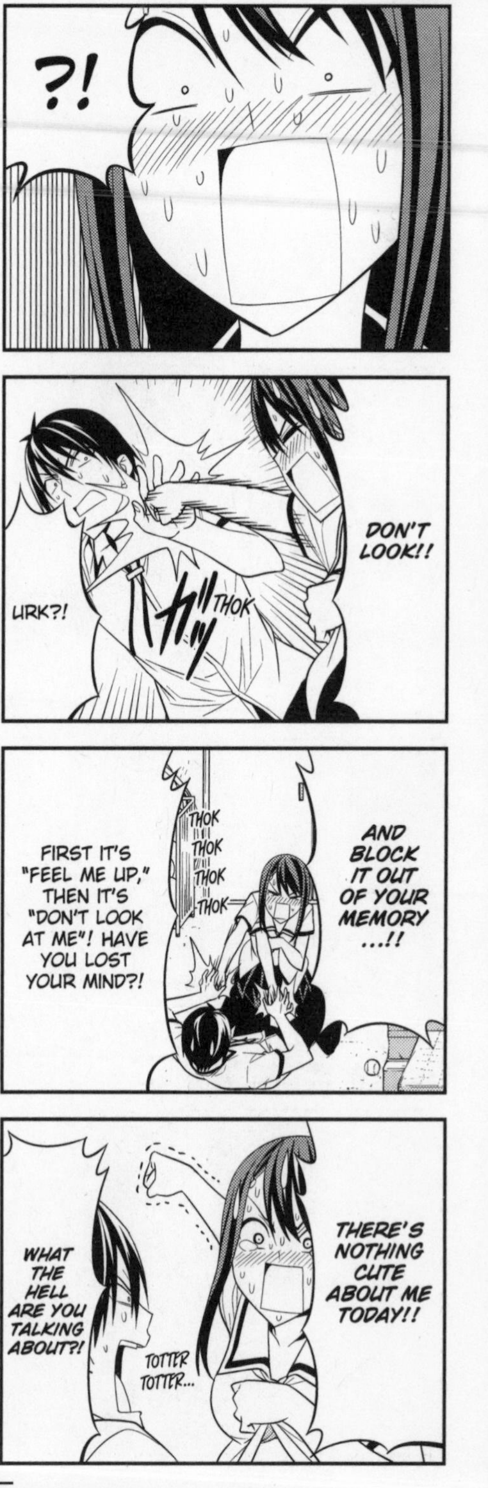
?!
DON'T LOOK!!
THOK
URK?!
AND BLOCK IT OUT OF YOUR MEMORY ...!!
THOK THOK THOK THOK
FIRST IT'S "FEEL ME UP," THEN IT'S "DON'T LOOK AT ME"! HAVE YOU LOST YOUR MIND?!
THERE'S NOTHING CUTE ABOUT ME TODAY!!
TOTTER TOTTER...
WHAT THE HELL ARE YOU TALKING ABOUT?!

Force Shut Down

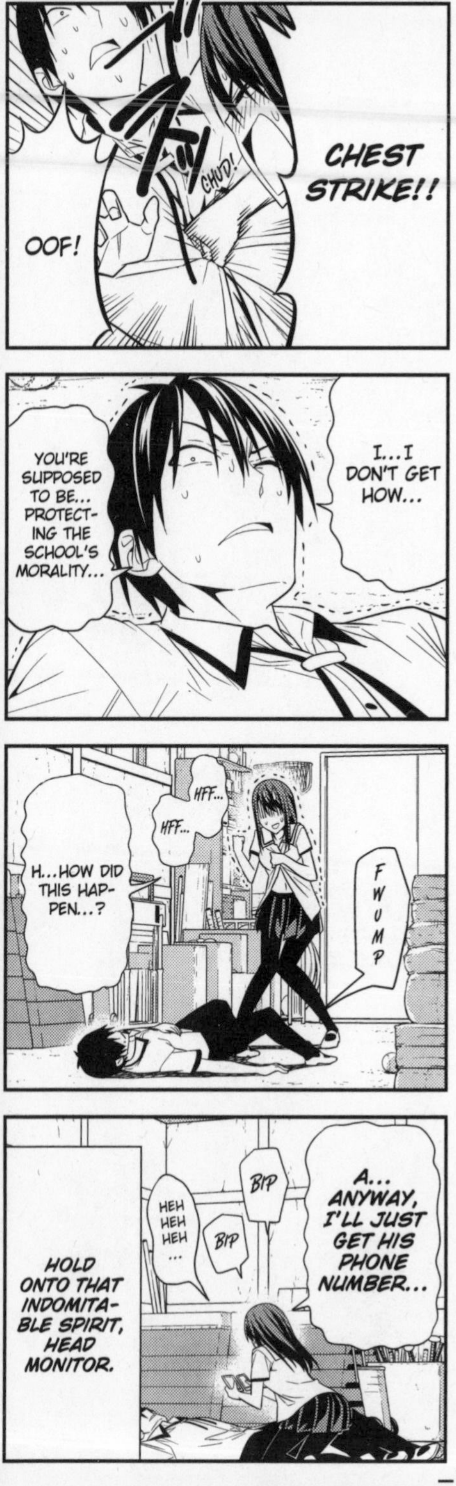
CHEST STRIKE!!
CHUD!
OOF!
I...I DON'T GET HOW...
YOU'RE SUPPOSED TO BE... PROTECT-ING THE SCHOOL'S MORALITY...
FWUMP
HFF...
HFF...
H...HOW DID THIS HAP-PEN...?
A... ANYWAY, I'LL JUST GET HIS PHONE NUMBER...
BIP
BIP
HEH HEH HEH ...
HOLD ONTO THAT INDOMITA-BLE SPIRIT, HEAD MONITOR.

Growth Chart

TWO
YEARS
AGO

ONE
YEAR
AGO

THIS
YEAR

(The Threat from Zeon is)

Aho-Girl

\\'ahô͵gərl\\ *Japanese , noun.*
A clueless girl.

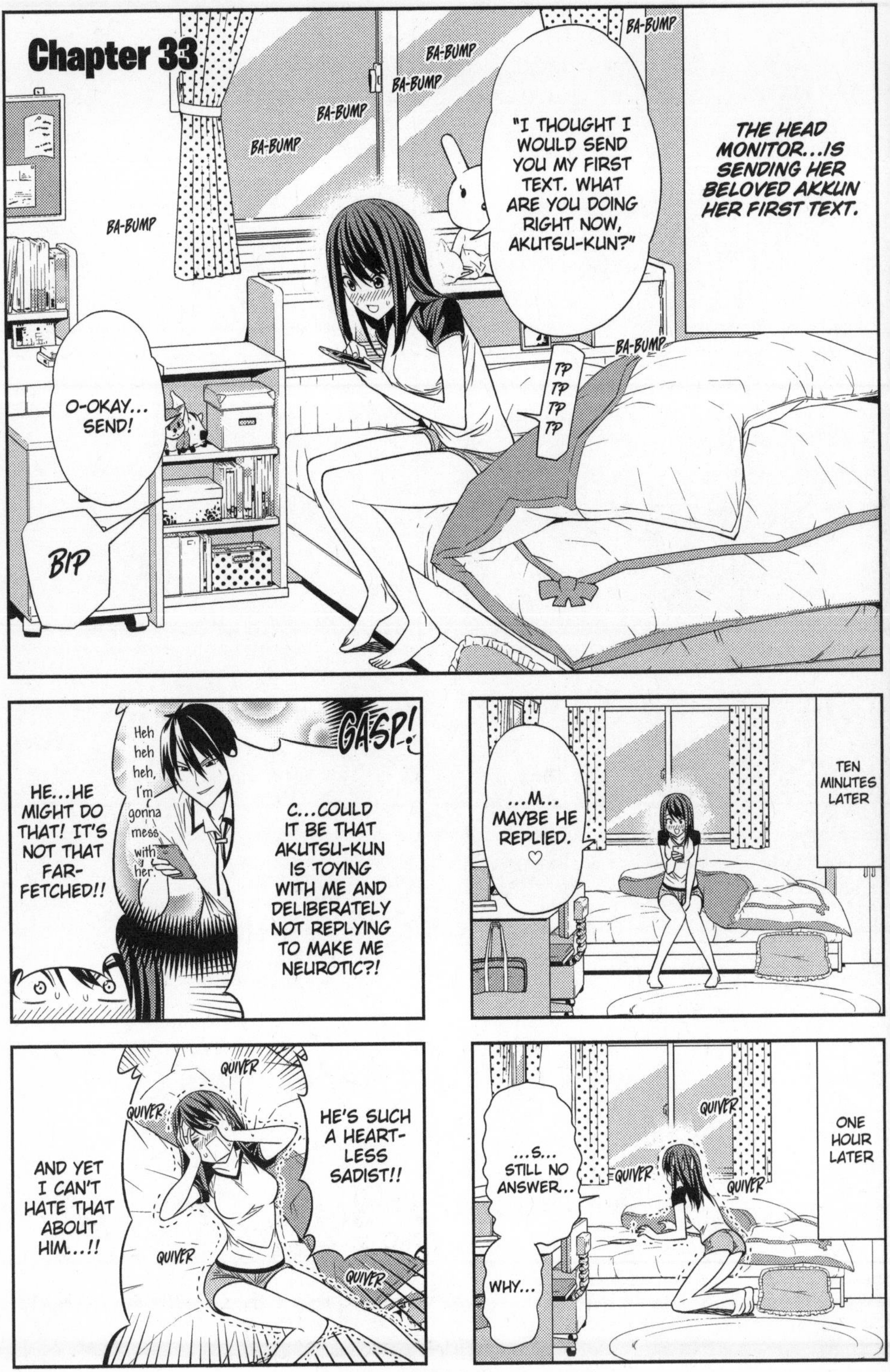
Chapter 33
THE HEAD MONITOR...IS SENDING HER BELOVED AKKUN HER FIRST TEXT.
BA-BUMP
"I THOUGHT I WOULD SEND YOU MY FIRST TEXT. WHAT ARE YOU DOING RIGHT NOW, AKUTSU-KUN?"
BA-BUMP
BA-BUMP
BA-BUMP
BA-BUMP
BA-BUMP
BA-BUMP
TP TP TP TP
O-OKAY... SEND!
BIP
TEN MINUTES LATER
...M... MAYBE HE REPLIED. ♡
GASP!
C...COULD IT BE THAT AKUTSU-KUN IS TOYING WITH ME AND DELIBERATELY NOT REPLYING TO MAKE ME NEUROTIC?!
Heh heh heh, I'm gonna mess with her.
HE...HE MIGHT DO THAT! IT'S NOT THAT FAR-FETCHED!!
ONE HOUR LATER
QUIVER
QUIVER
QUIVER
...S... STILL NO ANSWER...
WHY...
HE'S SUCH A HEART-LESS SADIST!!
QUIVER
QUIVER
AND YET I CAN'T HATE THAT ABOUT HIM...!!
QUIVER
QUIVER

Like "Trifle," "Swine," and "Appreciate"

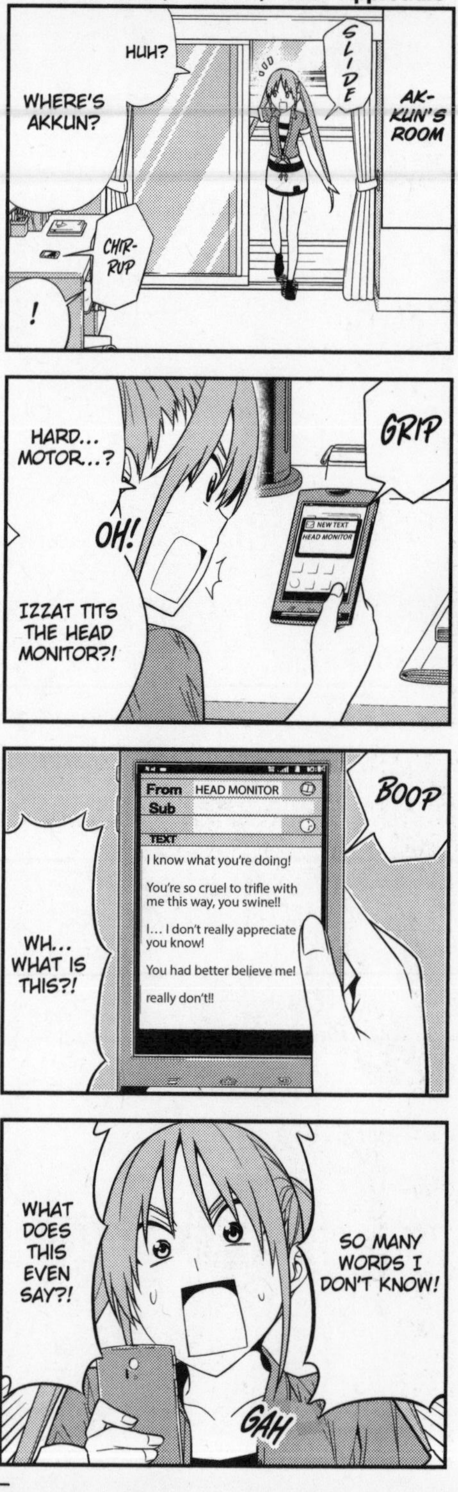
AK-KUN'S ROOM
SLIDE
HUH?
WHERE'S AKKUN?
CHIR-RUP
!
GRIP
HARD... MOTOR...?
NEW TEXT
HEAD MONITOR
OH!
IZZAT TITS THE HEAD MONITOR?!
BOOP
From HEAD MONITOR
Sub
TEXT
I know what you're doing!
You're so cruel to trifle with me this way, you swine!!
I... I don't really appreciate you know!
You had better believe me!
really don't!!
WH... WHAT IS THIS?!
SO MANY WORDS I DON'T KNOW!
WHAT DOES THIS EVEN SAY?!
GAH

A Touching Love Text

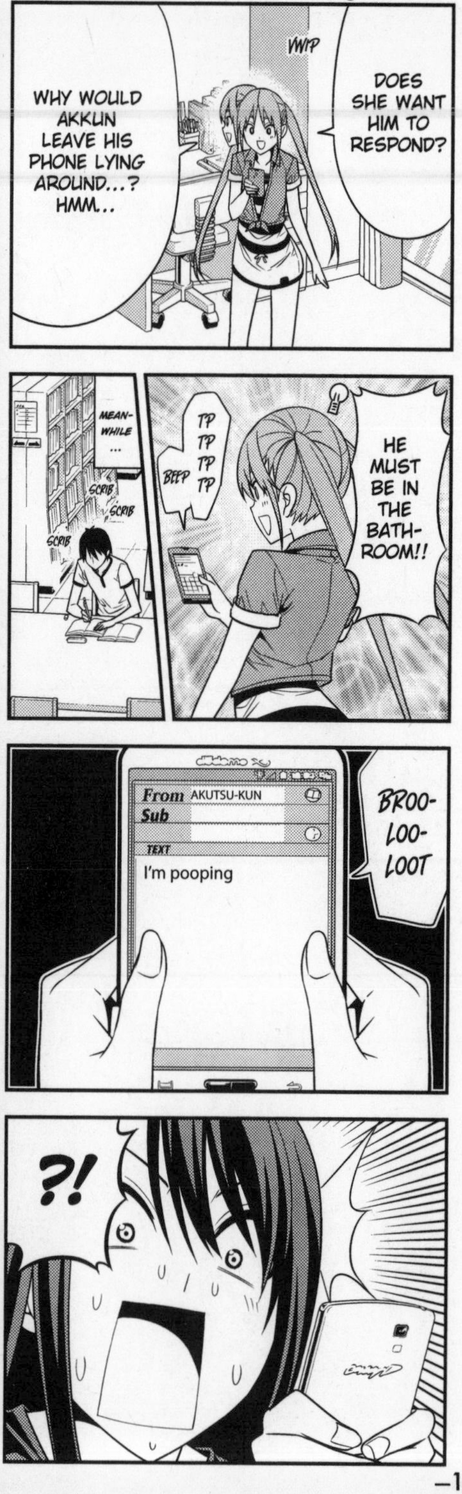
DOES SHE WANT HIM TO RESPOND?
VWIP
WHY WOULD AKKUN LEAVE HIS PHONE LYING AROUND...? HMM...
HE MUST BE IN THE BATH-ROOM!!
TP TP TP TP
BEEP
MEAN-WHILE...
SCRIB
SCRIB
SCRIB
BROO-LOO-LOOT
From AKUTSU-KUN
Sub
TEXT
I'm pooping
?!

Misunderstanding

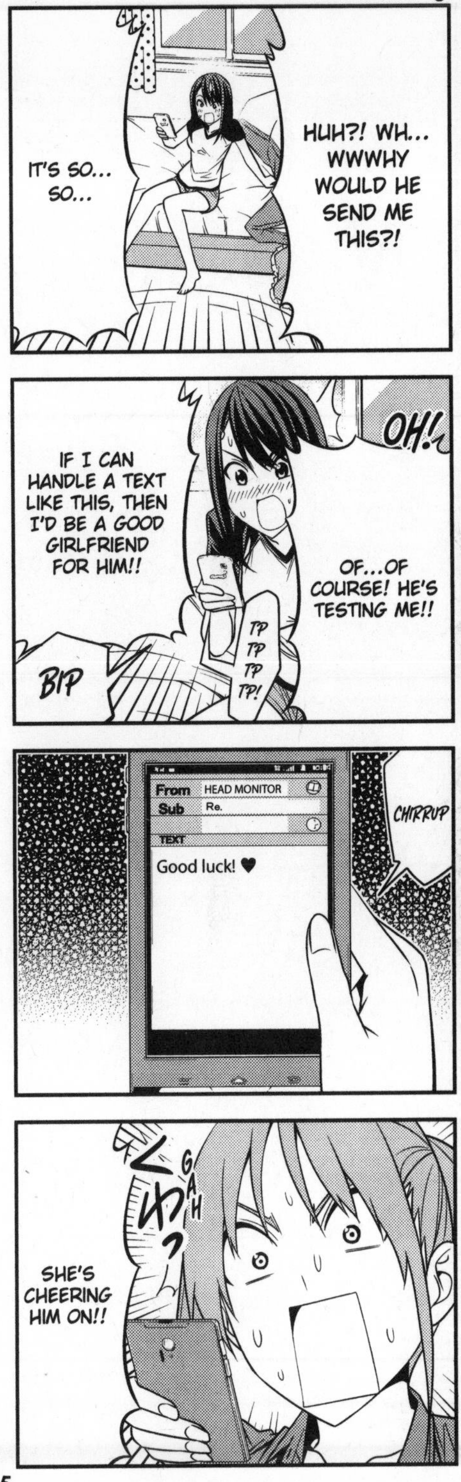
HUH?! WH... WWWHY WOULD HE SEND ME THIS?!
IT'S SO... SO...
OH!
OF...OF COURSE! HE'S TESTING ME!!
IF I CAN HANDLE A TEXT LIKE THIS, THEN I'D BE A GOOD GIRLFRIEND FOR HIM!!
TP TP TP TP!
BIP
CHIRRUP
From HEAD MONITOR
Sub Re.
TEXT
Good luck! ♥
くわっ
GAH
SHE'S CHEERING HIM ON!!

It Might Actually Be Okay to Give Up

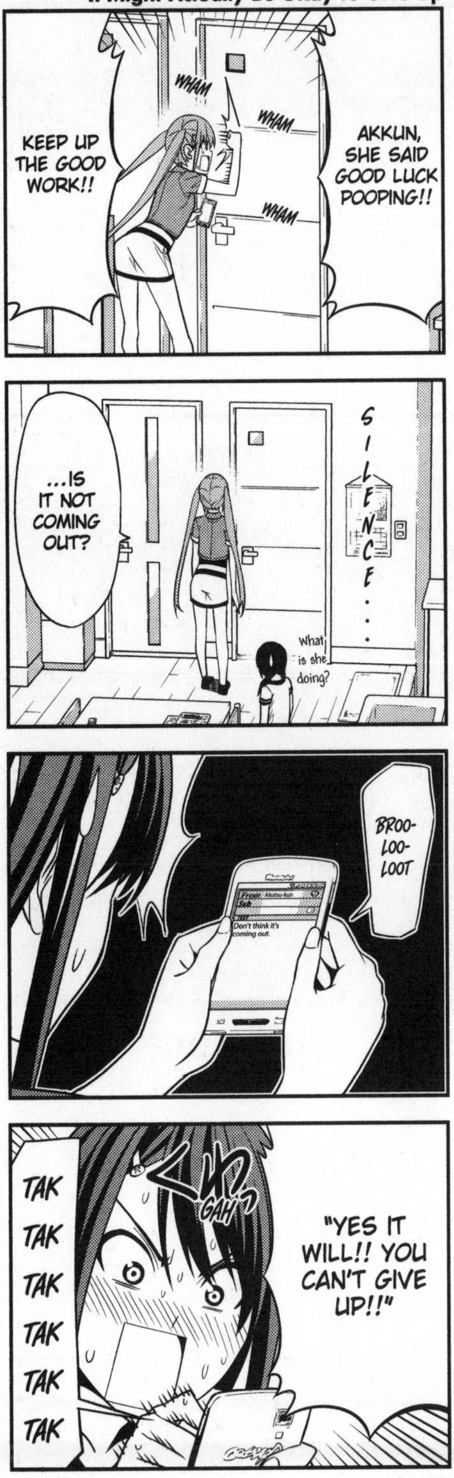
WHAM
WHAM
WHAM
AKKUN, SHE SAID GOOD LUCK POOPING!!
KEEP UP THE GOOD WORK!!
SILENCE...
What is she doing?
...IS IT NOT COMING OUT?
BROO-LOO-LOOT
From Akutsu-kun
Sub
Don't think it's coming out.
"YES IT WILL!! YOU CAN'T GIVE UP!!"
くわっ
GAH
TAK
TAK
TAK
TAK
TAK
TAK

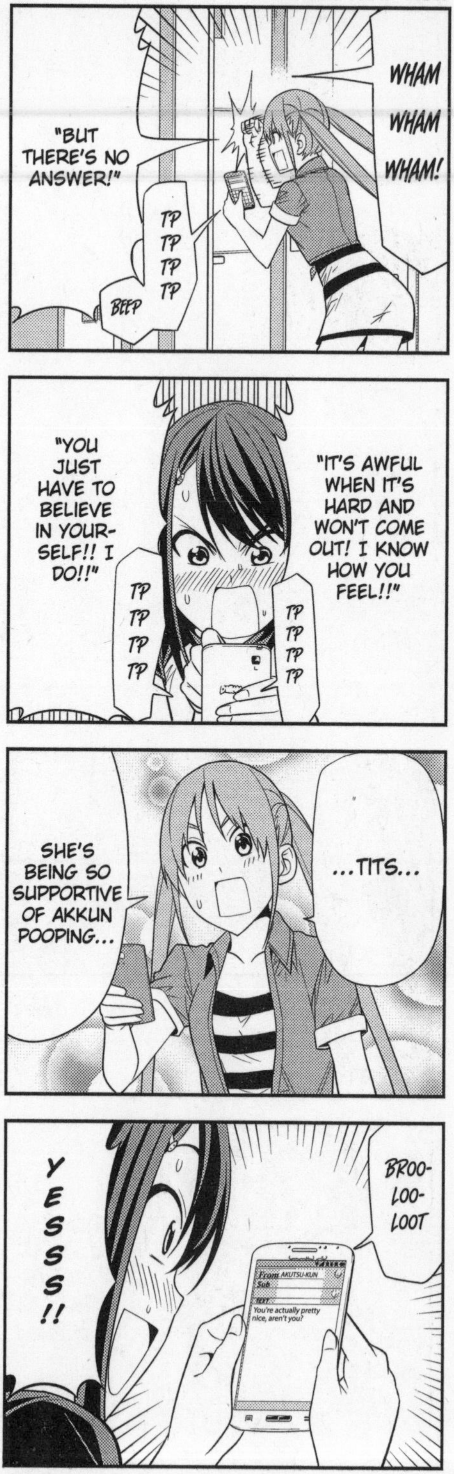
WHAM
WHAM
WHAM!
"BUT THERE'S NO ANSWER!"
TP TP TP TP
BEEP
"IT'S AWFUL WHEN IT'S HARD AND WON'T COME OUT! I KNOW HOW YOU FEEL!!"
TP TP TP TP
"YOU JUST HAVE TO BELIEVE IN YOURSELF!! I DO!!"
TP TP TP TP
...TITS...
SHE'S BEING SO SUPPORTIVE OF AKKUN POOPING...
BROO-LOO-LOOT
YESSS!!
From AKUTSU-KUN
Sub
TEXT
You're actually pretty nice, aren't you?

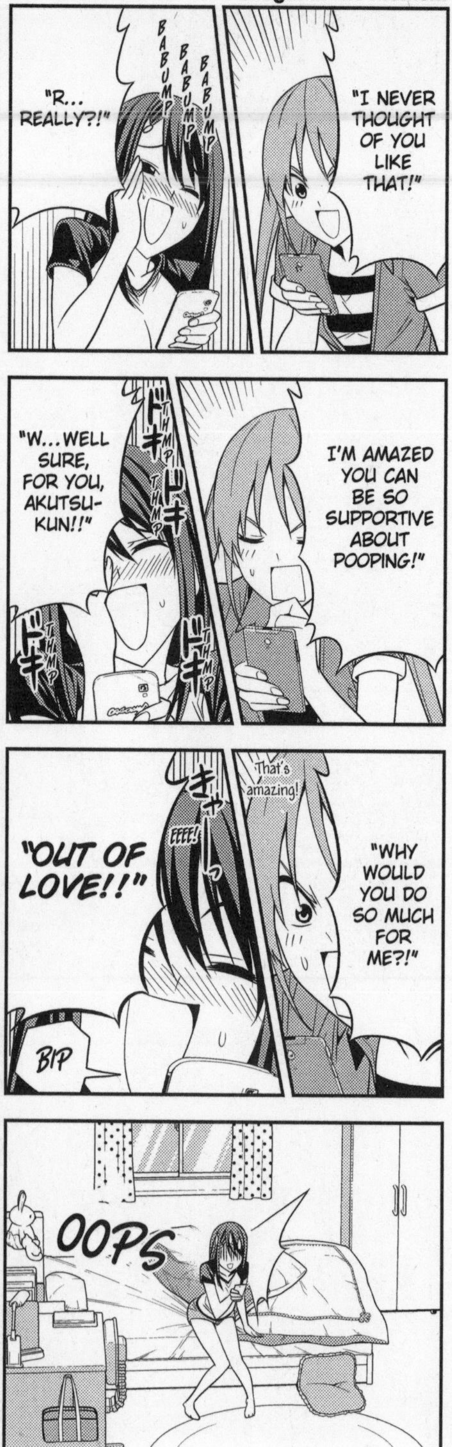
"I NEVER THOUGHT OF YOU LIKE THAT!"
BABUMP BABUMP BABUMP
"R... REALLY?!"
"I'M AMAZED YOU CAN BE SO SUPPORTIVE ABOUT POOPING!"
ドキ THMP ドキ THMP ドキ THMP ドキ THMP
"W...WELL SURE, FOR YOU, AKUTSU-KUN!!"
That's amazing!
"WHY WOULD YOU DO SO MUCH FOR ME?!"
きゃーっ EEEE!
"OUT OF LOVE!!"
BIP
OOPS

Didn't Mean That

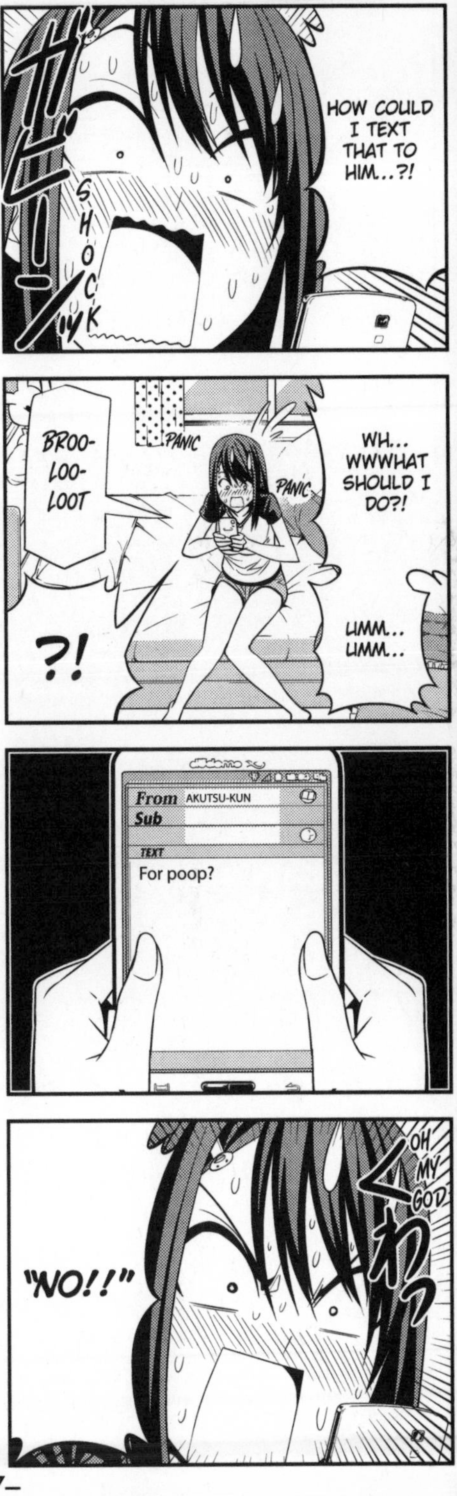
HOW COULD I TEXT THAT TO HIM..?!
SHOCK
WH... WWWHAT SHOULD I DO?!
PANIC
PANIC
BROO-LOO-LOOT
UMM... UMM...
?!
From AKUTSU-KUN
Sub
TEXT
For poop?
OH MY GOD
くわっ
"NO!!"

Last Chance

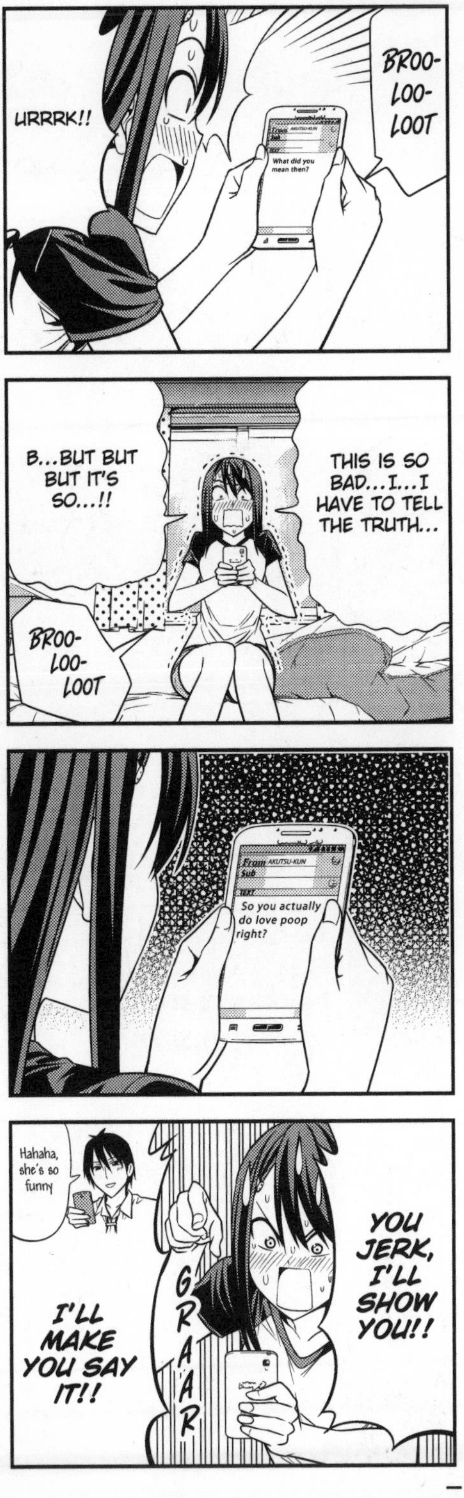
BROO-LOO-LOOT
From AKUTSU-KUN
Sub
What did you mean then?
URRRK!!
THIS IS SO BAD...I...I HAVE TO TELL THE TRUTH...
B...BUT BUT BUT IT'S SO...!!
BROO-LOO-LOOT
From AKUTSU-KUN
Sub
TEXT
So you actually do love poop right?
YOU JERK, I'LL SHOW YOU!!
GRAAR
Hahaha, she's so funny
I'LL MAKE YOU SAY IT!!

When You Try Too Hard for a Joke

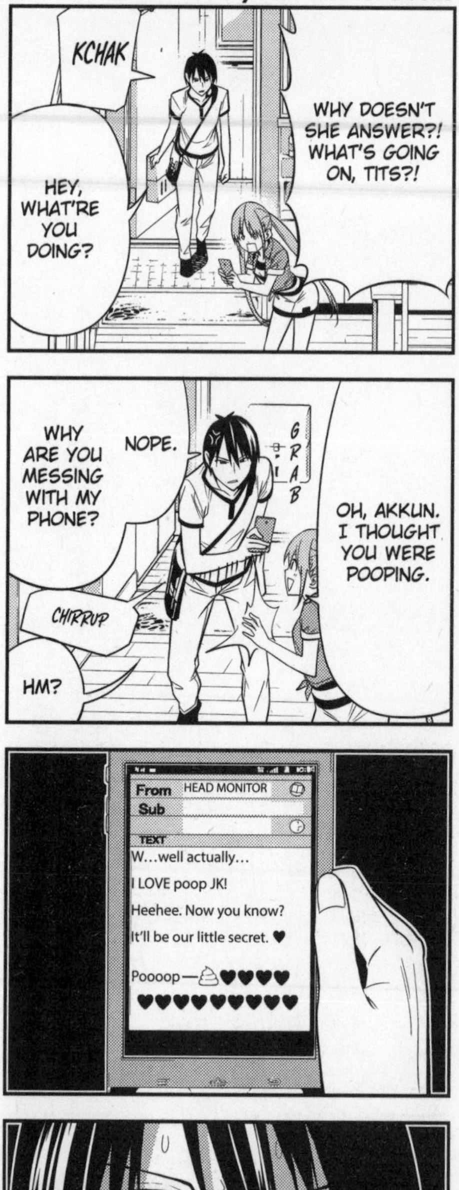
WHY DOESN'T SHE ANSWER?! WHAT'S GOING ON, TITS?!
KCHAK
HEY, WHAT'RE YOU DOING?
OH, AKKUN. I THOUGHT YOU WERE POOPING.
GRAB
NOPE.
WHY ARE YOU MESSING WITH MY PHONE?
CHIRRUP
HM?
From HEAD MONITOR
Sub
TEXT
W…well actually…
I LOVE poop JK!
Heehee. Now you know?
It'll be our little secret. ♥
Poooop— ♥♥♥♥
♥♥♥♥♥♥♥♥♥
SERIOUSLY, WHAT IS WRONG WITH THAT GIRL…?

Cling to Dreams and Disappointment Awaits

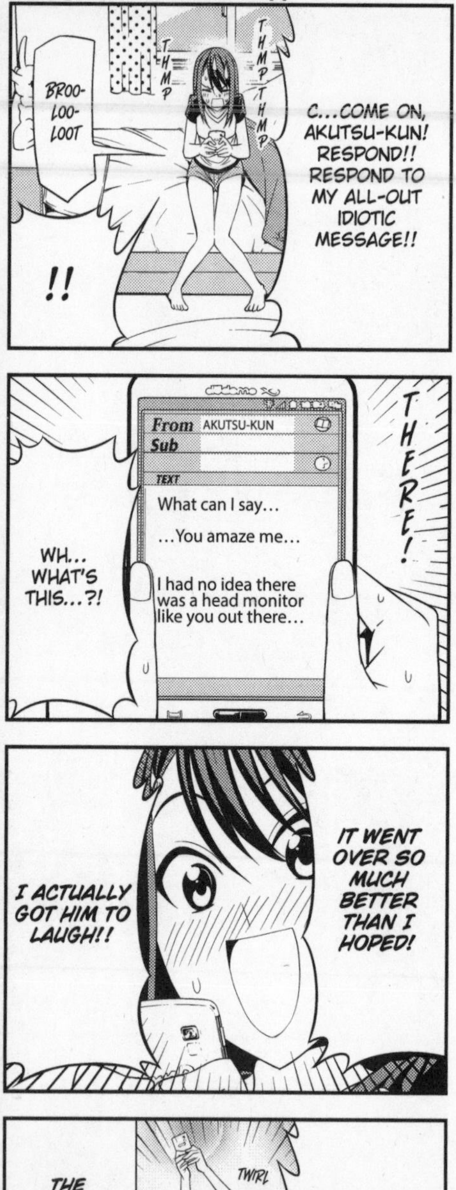
C…COME ON, AKUTSU-KUN! RESPOND!! RESPOND TO MY ALL-OUT IDIOTIC MESSAGE!!
THMP THMP THMP
THMP THMP
BROO-LOO-LOOT
!!
THERE!
From AKUTSU-KUN
Sub
TEXT
What can I say…
…You amaze me…
I had no idea there was a head monitor like you out there…
WH… WHAT'S THIS…?!
IT WENT OVER SO MUCH BETTER THAN I HOPED!
I ACTUALLY GOT HIM TO LAUGH!!
HE'S GONNA LIKE ME SOOO MUCH MOOORE!!
TWIRL
TWIRL
TWIRL
TWIRL
THE REALITY WAS MUCH HARSHER, BUT AT LEAST SHE WAS HAPPY.

You Talk to Yourself Too Much!

BA-BUMP BA-BUMP
S...SO AKUTSU-KUN THOUGHT OF ME AS SO SERIOUS AND PURE...
BUT NOW HE KNOWS I HAVE A SENSE OF HUMOR, TOO...!!
BA-BUMP BA-BUMP BA-BUMP
ドキドキドキ
THIS IS INCREDIBLE!!
IT REALLY IS.

(Every time I come home home, my wife is always)

Aho-Girl

\ˈahôˌgərl\ *Japanese , noun.*
A clueless girl.

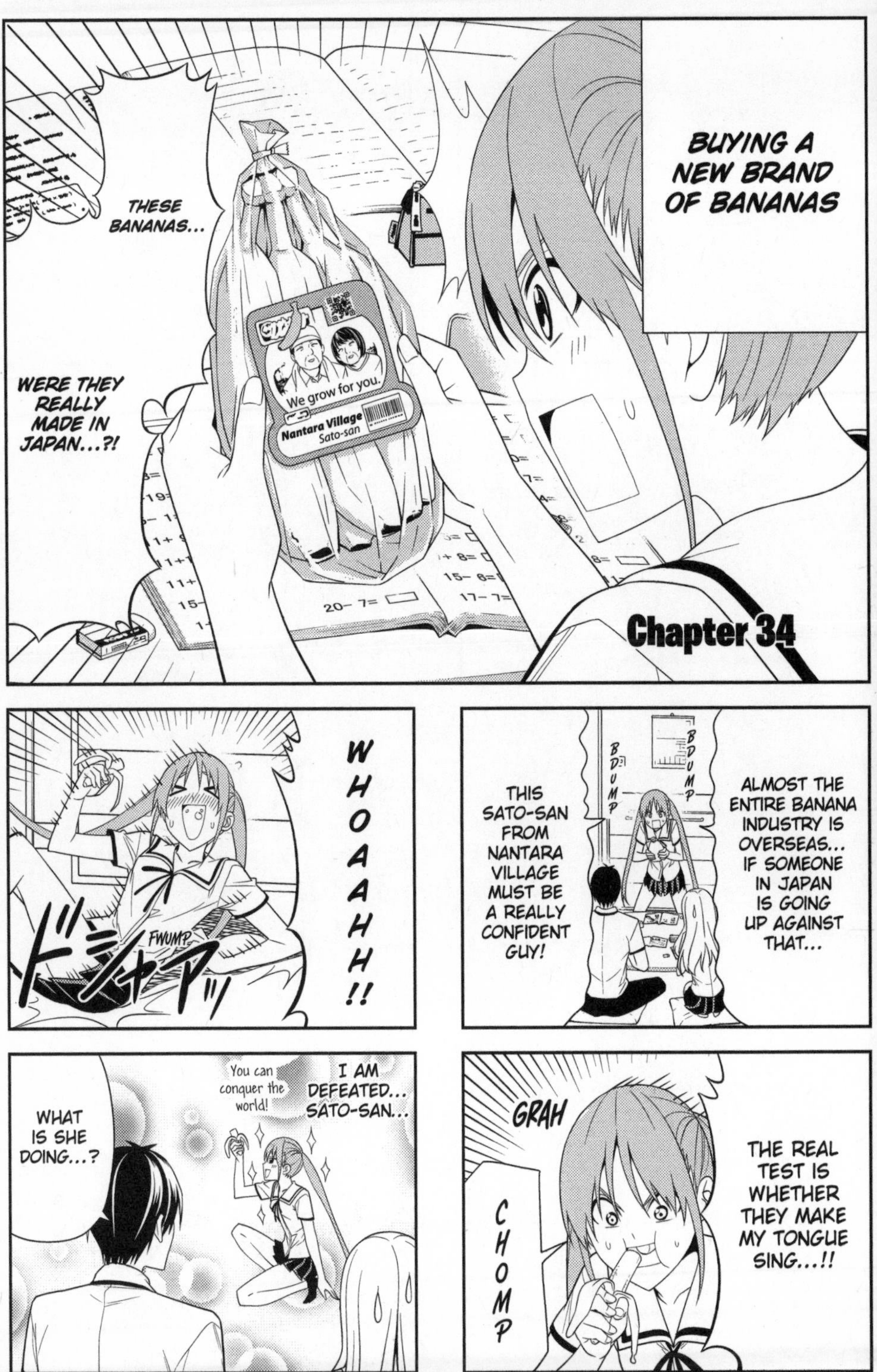
BUYING A NEW BRAND OF BANANAS
Chapter 34
THESE BANANAS...
We grow for you.
Nantara Village
Sato-san
WERE THEY REALLY MADE IN JAPAN...?!
BDUMP
BDUMP
ALMOST THE ENTIRE BANANA INDUSTRY IS OVERSEAS... IF SOMEONE IN JAPAN IS GOING UP AGAINST THAT...
THIS SATO-SAN FROM NANTARA VILLAGE MUST BE A REALLY CONFIDENT GUY!
WHOAAAHH!!
FWUMP
ドシャアッ
GRAH
THE REAL TEST IS WHETHER THEY MAKE MY TONGUE SING...!!
CHOMP
I AM DEFEATED... SATO-SAN...
You can conquer the world!
WHAT IS SHE DOING...?

The Legend of Sato

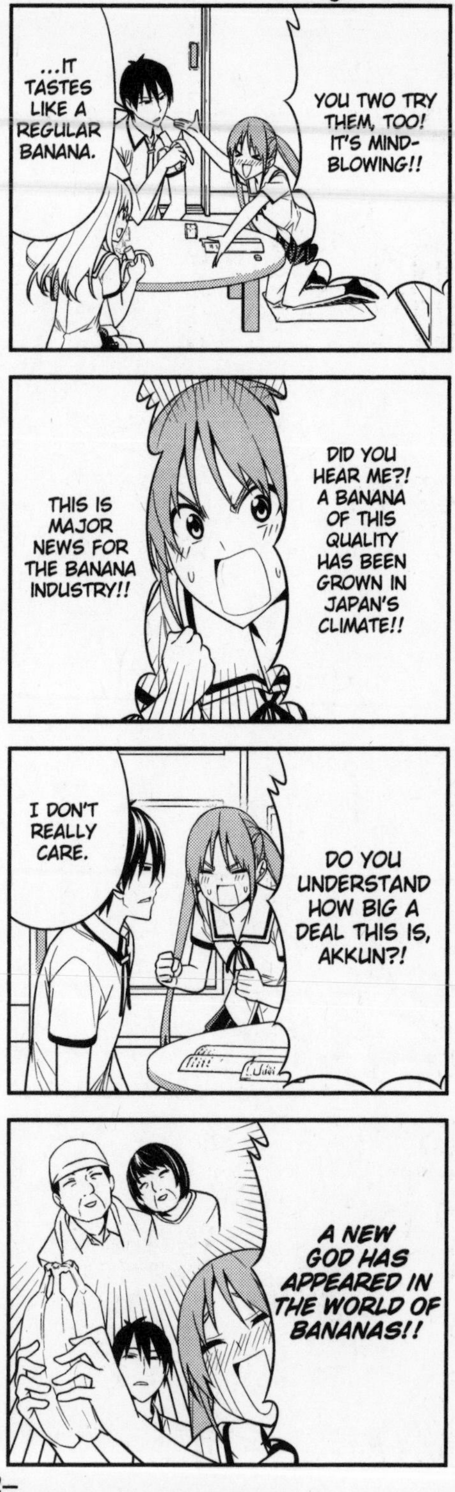
YOU TWO TRY THEM, TOO! IT'S MIND-BLOWING!!
...IT TASTES LIKE A REGULAR BANANA.
DID YOU HEAR ME?! A BANANA OF THIS QUALITY HAS BEEN GROWN IN JAPAN'S CLIMATE!!
THIS IS MAJOR NEWS FOR THE BANANA INDUSTRY!!
DO YOU UNDERSTAND HOW BIG A DEAL THIS IS, AKKUN?!
I DON'T REALLY CARE.
A NEW GOD HAS APPEARED IN THE WORLD OF BANANAS!!

I'm Going to Go Meet Them

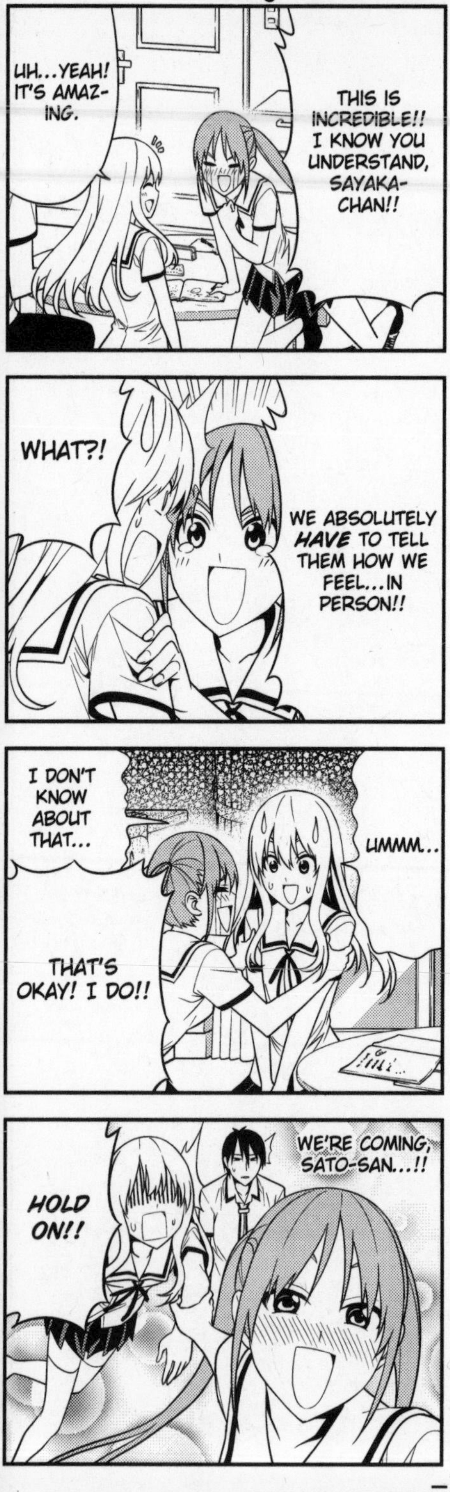
THIS IS INCREDIBLE!! I KNOW YOU UNDERSTAND, SAYAKA-CHAN!!
UH...YEAH! IT'S AMAZ-ING.
WE ABSOLUTELY *HAVE* TO TELL THEM HOW WE FEEL...IN PERSON!!
WHAT?!
UMMM...
I DON'T KNOW ABOUT THAT...
THAT'S OKAY! I DO!!
WE'RE COMING, SATO-SAN...!!
HOLD ON!!

No Way

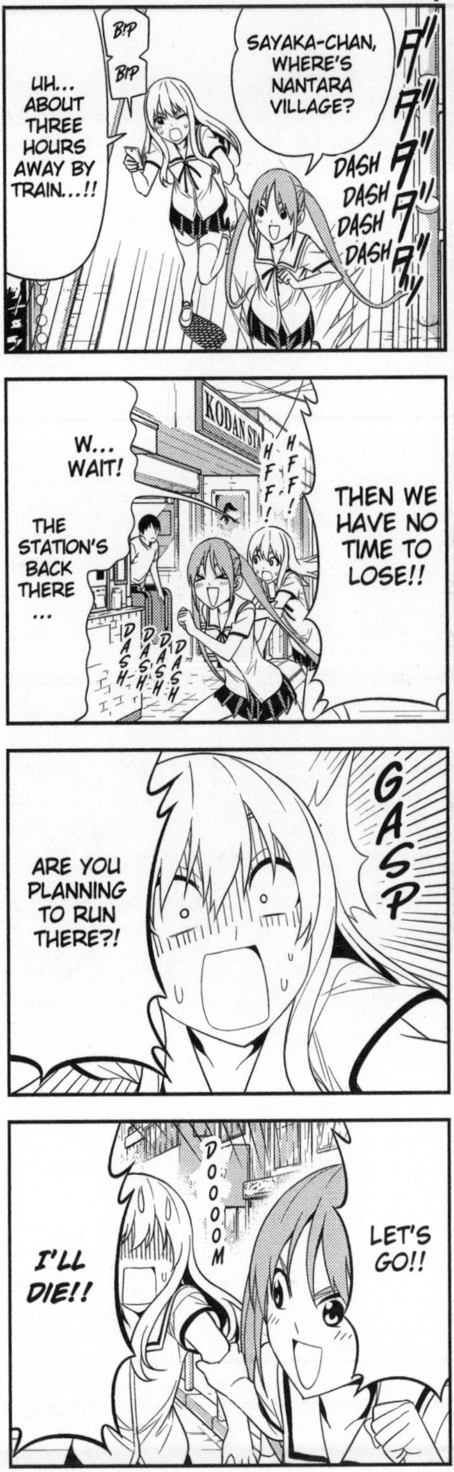
SAYAKA-CHAN, WHERE'S NANTARA VILLAGE?
DASH DASH DASH DASH
BIP BIP
UH... ABOUT THREE HOURS AWAY BY TRAIN...!!
KODAN STA
THEN WE HAVE NO TIME TO LOSE!!
HFF! HFF!
W... WAIT!
THE STATION'S BACK THERE ...
DASH DASH DASH DASH
GASP
ARE YOU PLANNING TO RUN THERE?!
LET'S GO!!
DOOOOOM
I'LL DIE!!

Sayaka Is Desperate

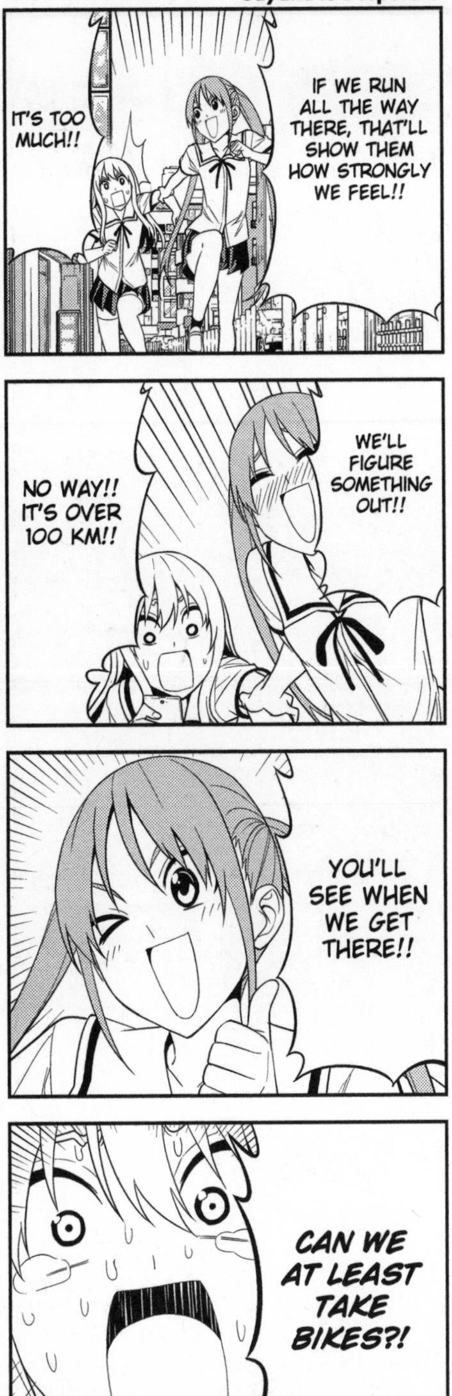
IF WE RUN ALL THE WAY THERE, THAT'LL SHOW THEM HOW STRONGLY WE FEEL!!
IT'S TOO MUCH!!
WE'LL FIGURE SOMETHING OUT!!
NO WAY!! IT'S OVER 100 KM!!
YOU'LL SEE WHEN WE GET THERE!!
CAN WE AT LEAST TAKE BIKES?!

Pay You Back When We Get Home...

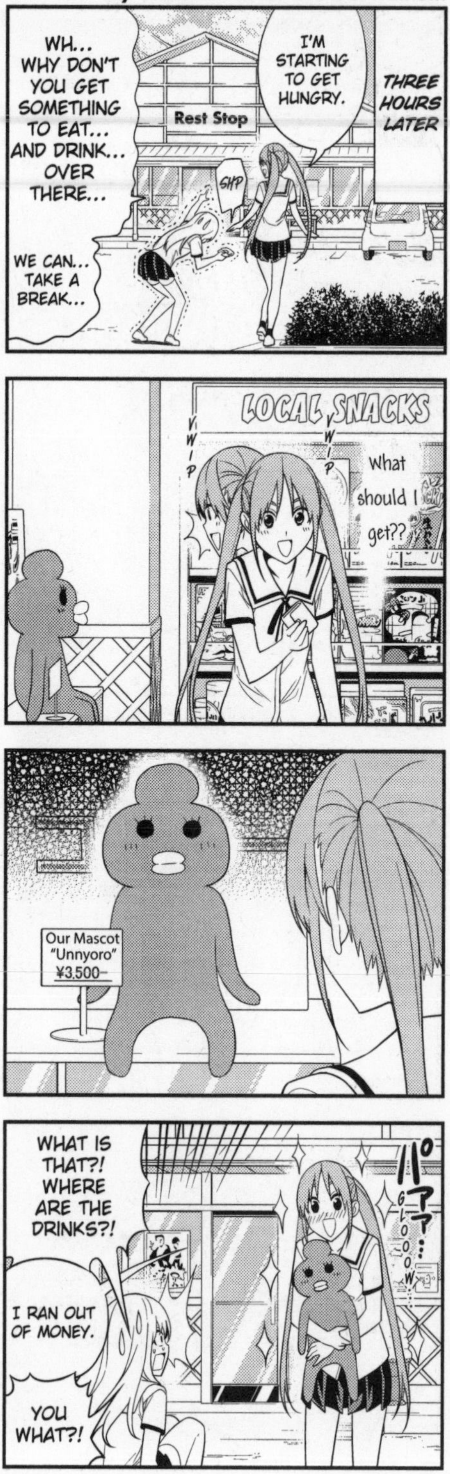
THREE HOURS LATER
I'M STARTING TO GET HUNGRY.
Rest Stop
WH... WHY DON'T YOU GET SOMETHING TO EAT... AND DRINK... OVER THERE...
SHP
WE CAN... TAKE A BREAK...
LOCAL SNACKS
VWIP
VWIP
What should I get??
Our Mascot "Unnyoro" ¥3,500–
パァァ... GLOOOOW
WHAT IS THAT?! WHERE ARE THE DRINKS?!
I RAN OUT OF MONEY.
YOU WHAT?!

Acquiring Friends

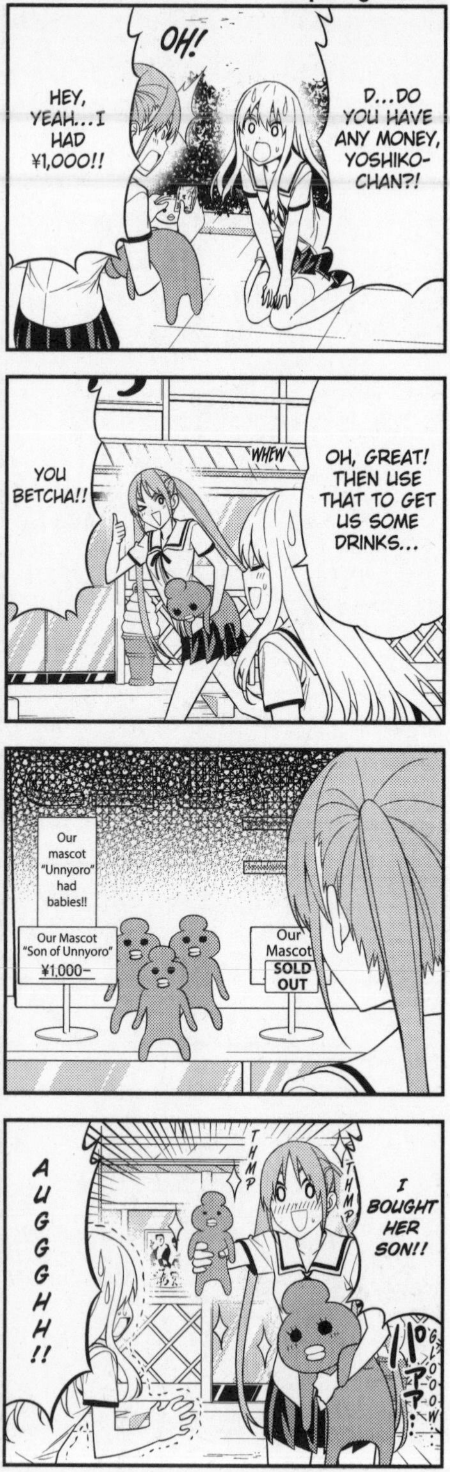
OH!
D...DO YOU HAVE ANY MONEY, YOSHIKO-CHAN?!
HEY, YEAH...I HAD ¥1,000!!
OH, GREAT! THEN USE THAT TO GET US SOME DRINKS...
WHEW
YOU BETCHA!!
Our mascot "Unnyoro" had babies!!
Our Mascot SOLD OUT
Our Mascot "Son of Unnyoro" ¥1,000–
I BOUGHT HER SON!!
THMP
THMP
パァァ GLOOOOW
AUGGGHH!!

Despair, Sayaka

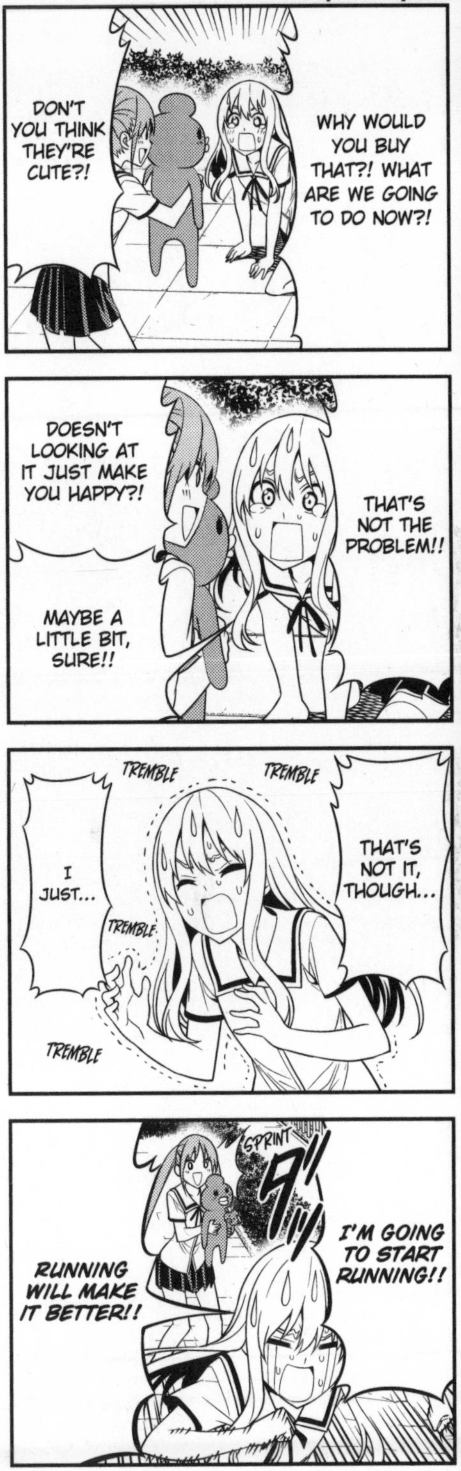
WHY WOULD YOU BUY THAT?! WHAT ARE WE GOING TO DO NOW?!
DON'T YOU THINK THEY'RE CUTE?!
THAT'S NOT THE PROBLEM!!
DOESN'T LOOKING AT IT JUST MAKE YOU HAPPY?!
MAYBE A LITTLE BIT, SURE!!
TREMBLE
TREMBLE
THAT'S NOT IT, THOUGH...
I JUST...
TREMBLE
TREMBLE
I'M GOING TO START RUNNING!!
SPRINT
RUNNING WILL MAKE IT BETTER!!

RUN, Sayaka, RUN

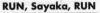

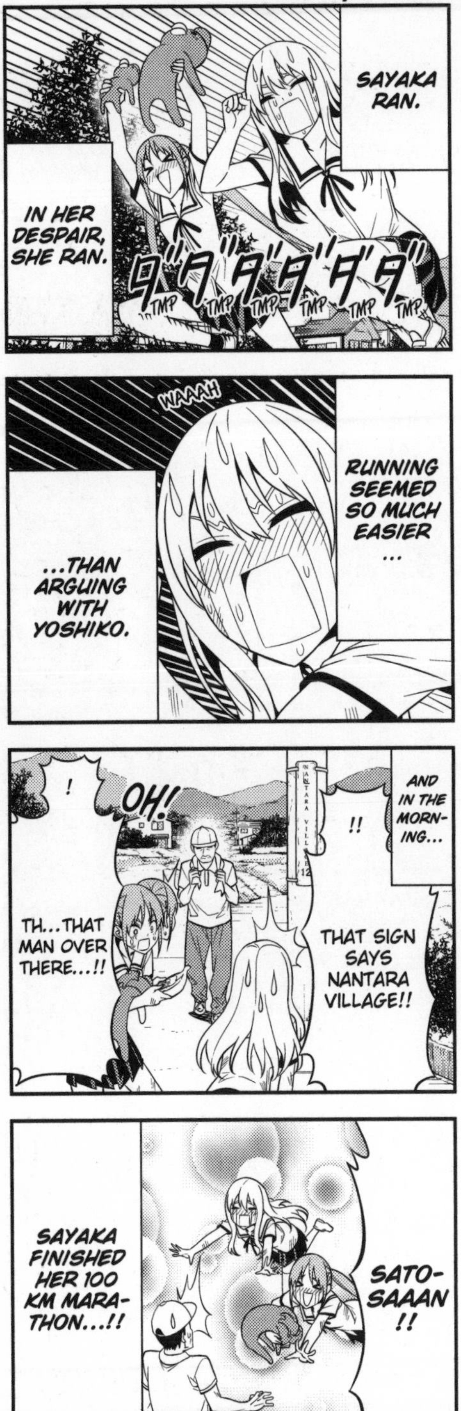
SAYAKA RAN.
IN HER DESPAIR, SHE RAN.
TMP TMP TMP TMP TMP TMP
RUNNING SEEMED SO MUCH EASIER ...
WAAAH
...THAN ARGUING WITH YOSHIKO.
AND IN THE MORN-ING...
!!
OH!
!
THAT SIGN SAYS NANTARA VILLAGE!!
TH...THAT MAN OVER THERE...!!
SATO-SAAAN !!
SAYAKA FINISHED HER 100 KM MARA-THON...!!

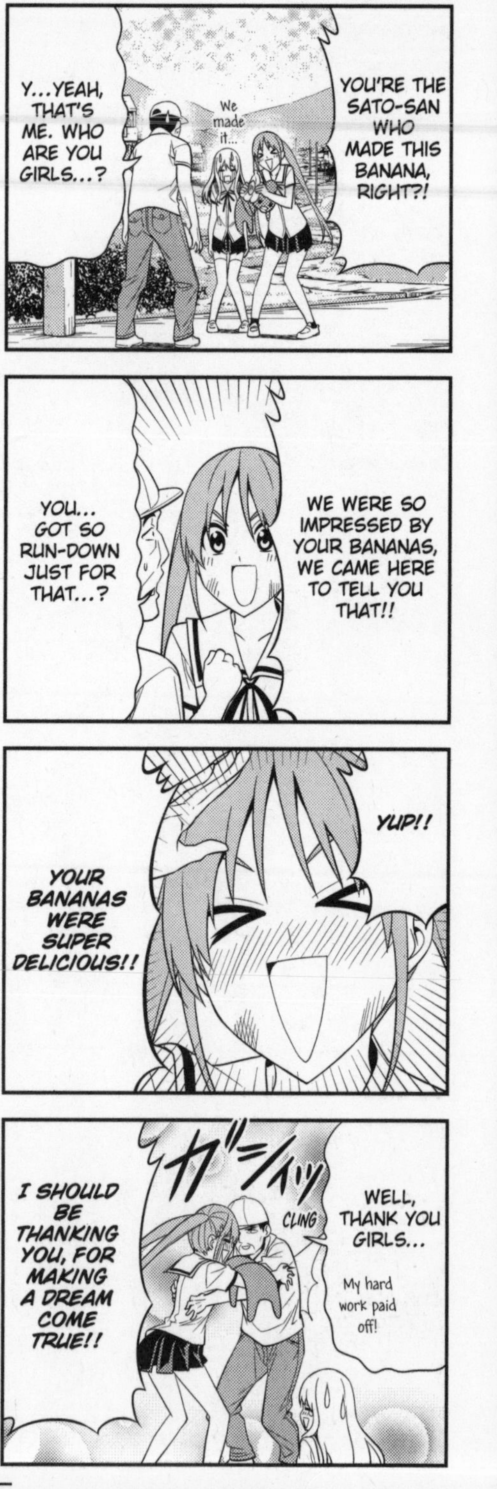
YOU'RE THE SATO-SAN WHO MADE THIS BANANA, RIGHT?!
We made it...
Y...YEAH, THAT'S ME. WHO ARE YOU GIRLS...?
WE WERE SO IMPRESSED BY YOUR BANANAS, WE CAME HERE TO TELL YOU THAT!!
YOU... GOT SO RUN-DOWN JUST FOR THAT...?
YUP!!
YOUR BANANAS WERE SUPER DELICIOUS!!
ガシィッ
WELL, THANK YOU GIRLS...
CLING
My hard work paid off!
I SHOULD BE THANKING YOU, FOR MAKING A DREAM COME TRUE!!

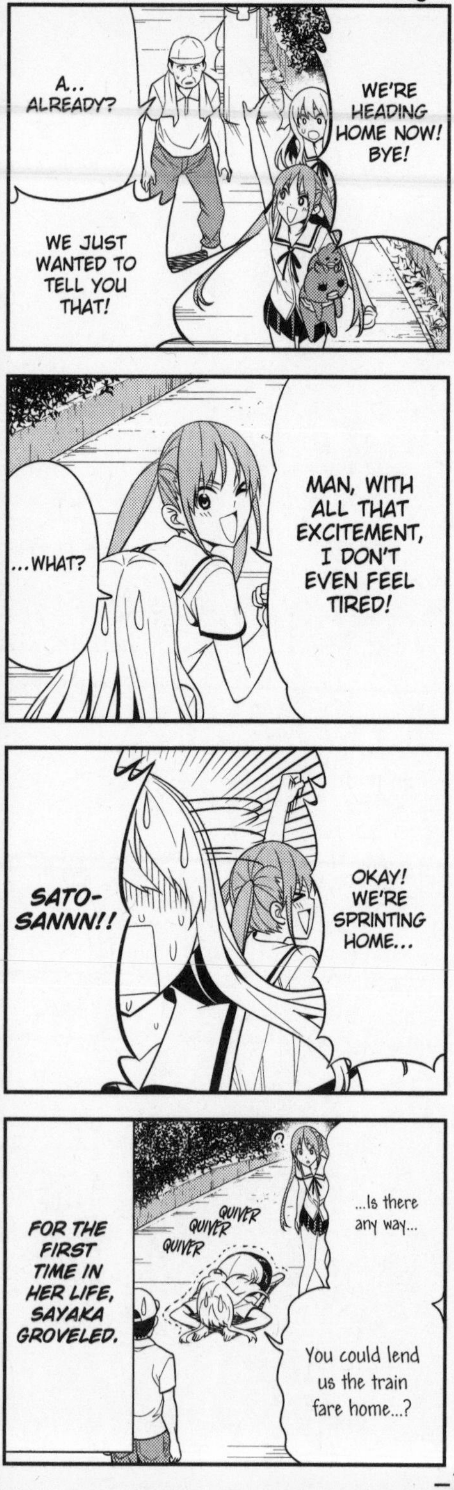
WE'RE HEADING HOME NOW! BYE!
A... ALREADY?
WE JUST WANTED TO TELL YOU THAT!
MAN, WITH ALL THAT EXCITEMENT, I DON'T EVEN FEEL TIRED!
...WHAT?
OKAY! WE'RE SPRINTING HOME...
SATO-SANNN!!
...Is there any way...
QUIVER
QUIVER
QUIVER
You could lend us the train fare home...?
FOR THE FIRST TIME IN HER LIFE, SAYAKA GROVELED.

She Just Says It

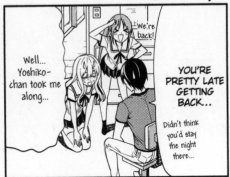

We're back!
YOU'RE PRETTY LATE GETTING BACK...
Didn't think you'd stay the night there...
Well... Yoshiko-chan took me along...
...And we ran 100 km to get there...
YOU DID WHAT?!

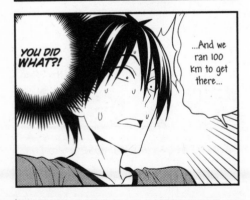

(Let the wind carry us across the land)

Aho-Girl

\'ahô,gərl\ *Japanese , noun.*

A clueless girl.

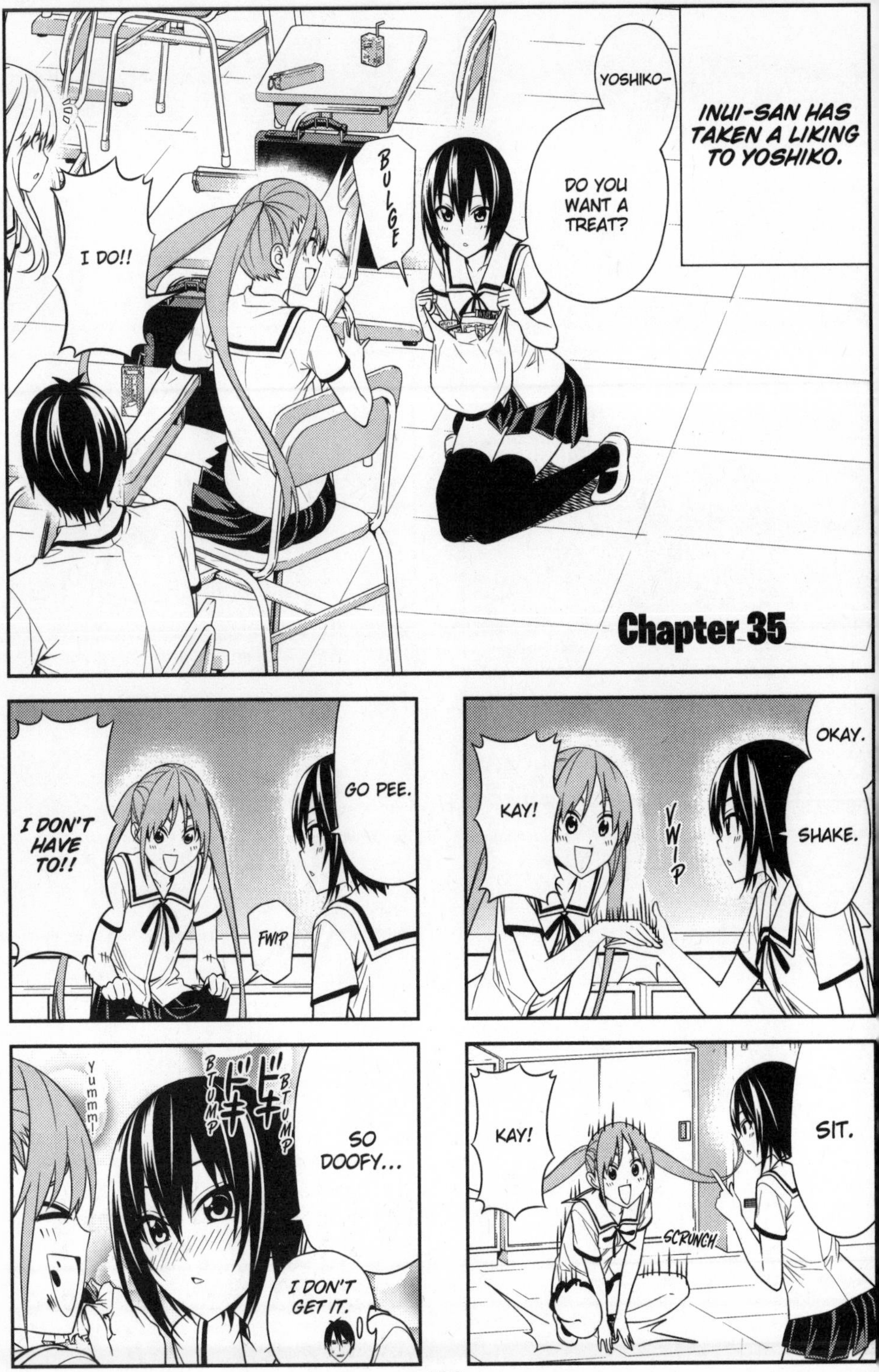

INUI-SAN HAS TAKEN A LIKING TO YOSHIKO.
YOSHIKO—
DO YOU WANT A TREAT?
BULGE
I DO!!
Chapter 35
OKAY.
SHAKE.
VWIP
KAY!
GO PEE.
FWIP
I DON'T HAVE TO!!
SIT.
KAY!
SCRUNCH
SO DOOFY...
BTUMP BTUMP
Yummm!
I DON'T GET IT.

The Conscience of This Manga

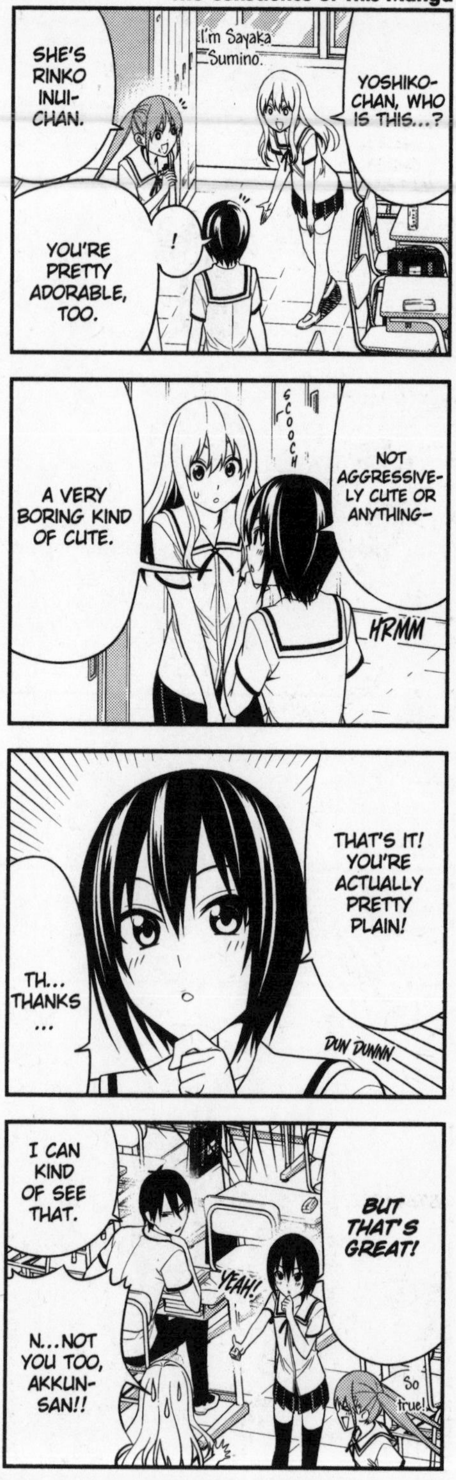
YOSHIKO-CHAN, WHO IS THIS...?
I'm Sayaka Sumino.
SHE'S RINKO INUI-CHAN.
!
YOU'RE PRETTY ADORABLE, TOO.
NOT AGGRESSIVE-LY CUTE OR ANYTHING-
SCOOCH
HRMM
A VERY BORING KIND OF CUTE.
THAT'S IT! YOU'RE ACTUALLY PRETTY PLAIN!
DUN DUNNN
TH... THANKS ...
BUT THAT'S GREAT!
I CAN KIND OF SEE THAT.
YEAH!
So true!
N...NOT YOU TOO, AKKUN-SAN!!

There's a Boom Coming

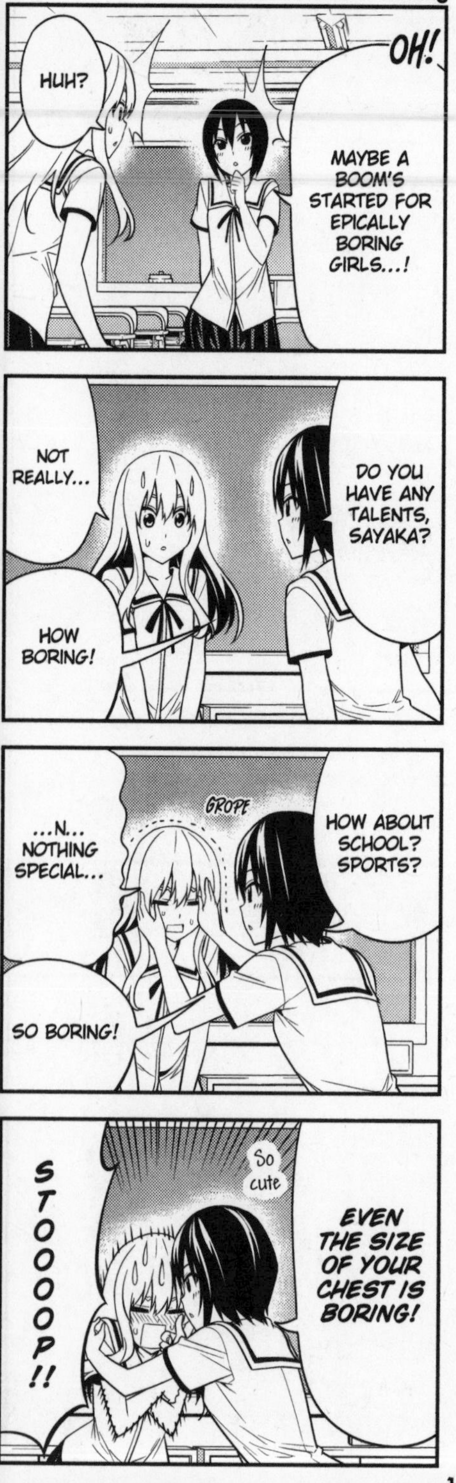
OH!
MAYBE A BOOM'S STARTED FOR EPICALLY BORING GIRLS...!
HUH?
DO YOU HAVE ANY TALENTS, SAYAKA?
NOT REALLY...
HOW BORING!
HOW ABOUT SCHOOL? SPORTS?
GROPE
...N... NOTHING SPECIAL...
SO BORING!
EVEN THE SIZE OF YOUR CHEST IS BORING!
So cute
STOOOOOP!!

WEIRD

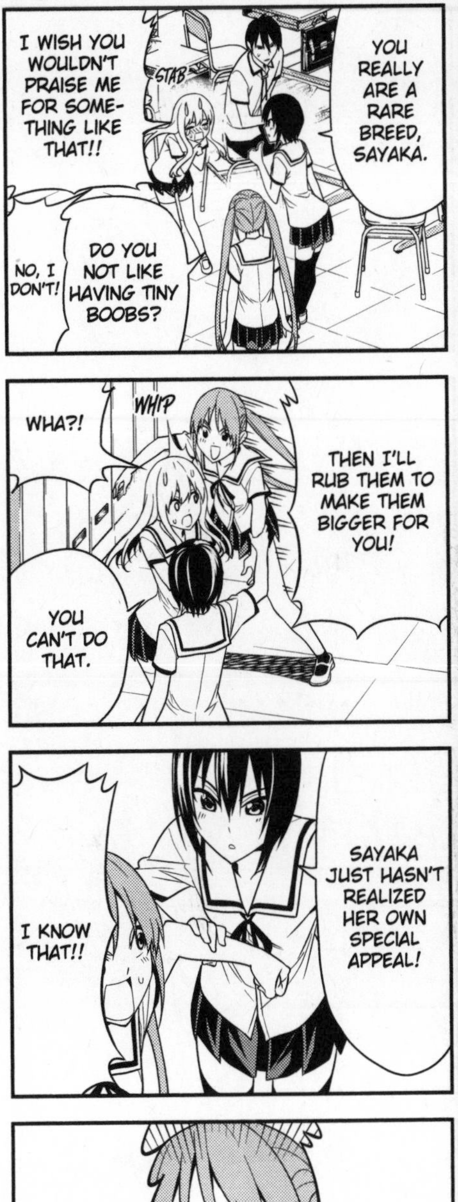
YOU REALLY ARE A RARE BREED, SAYAKA.
I WISH YOU WOULDN'T PRAISE ME FOR SOME-THING LIKE THAT!!
STAB
DO YOU NOT LIKE HAVING TINY BOOBS?
NO, I DON'T!
THEN I'LL RUB THEM TO MAKE THEM BIGGER FOR YOU!
WHIP
WHA?!
YOU CAN'T DO THAT.
SAYAKA JUST HASN'T REALIZED HER OWN SPECIAL APPEAL!
I KNOW THAT!!
IF SAYAKA-CHAN HAD HUGE BOOBS...
...IT'D BE WEIRD!!
WEIRD?!

Grant My Wish

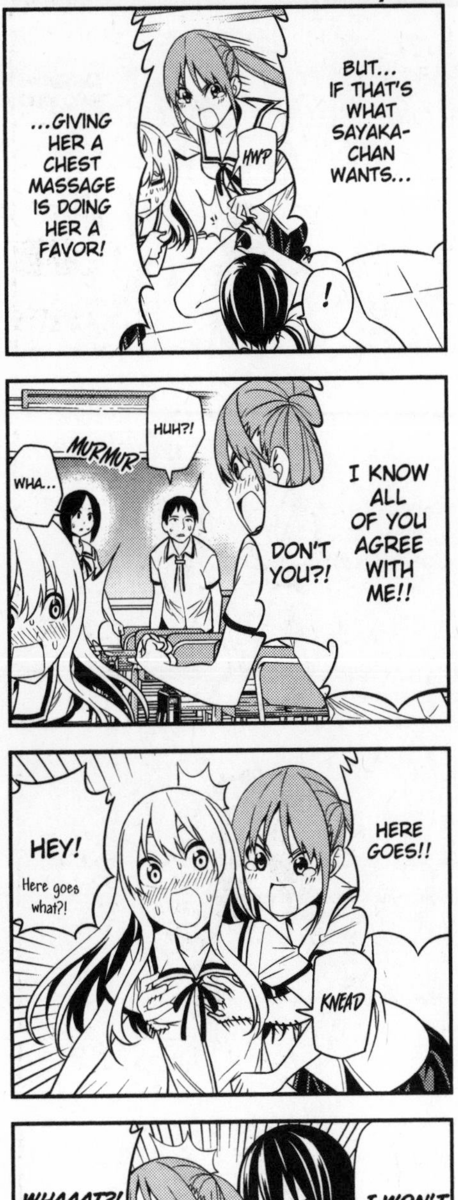
BUT... IF THAT'S WHAT SAYAKA-CHAN WANTS...
HWP
...GIVING HER A CHEST MASSAGE IS DOING HER A FAVOR!
!
I KNOW ALL OF YOU AGREE WITH ME!!
DON'T YOU?!
HUH?!
MURMUR
WHA...
HERE GOES!!
HEY!
Here goes what?!
KNEAD
I WON'T LET YOU DO THAT!
WHAAAT?!
SQUEEZE

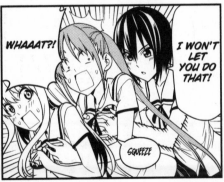

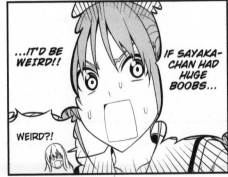

Medium Boobs

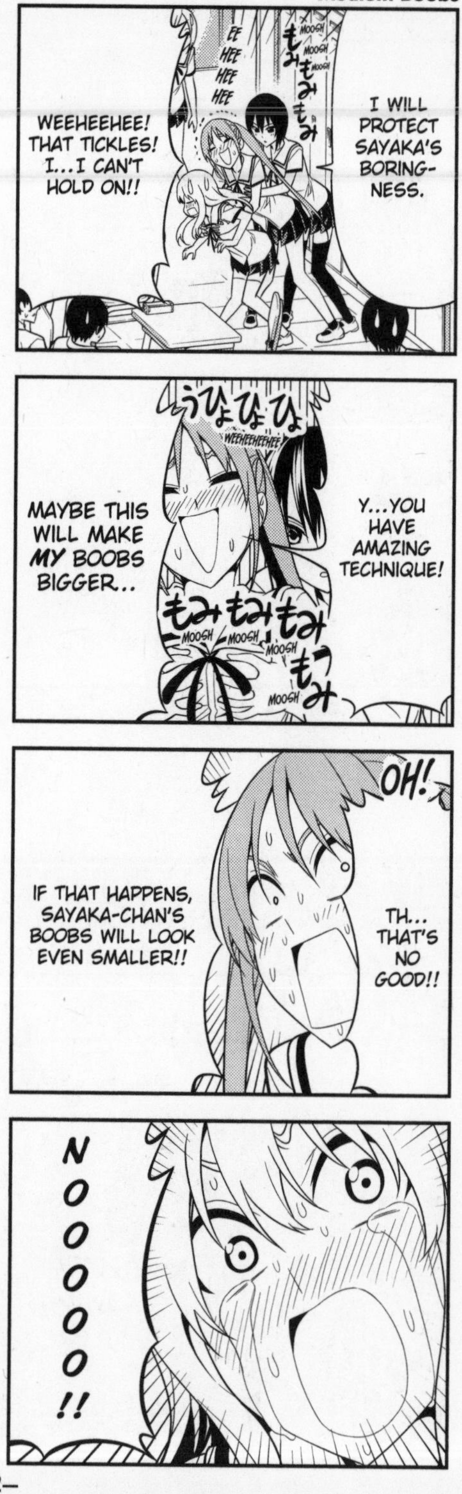
I WILL PROTECT SAYAKA'S BORING-NESS.
もみもみもみ
MOOSH MOOSH MOOSH
EE HEE HEE HEE
WEEHEEHEE! THAT TICKLES! I...I CAN'T HOLD ON!!
うひょひょひょ
WEEHEEHEEHEE
Y...YOU HAVE AMAZING TECHNIQUE!
MAYBE THIS WILL MAKE MY BOOBS BIGGER...
もみもみもみもみ
MOOSH MOOSH MOOSH MOOSH
OH!
TH... THAT'S NO GOOD!!
IF THAT HAPPENS, SAYAKA-CHAN'S BOOBS WILL LOOK EVEN SMALLER!!
NOOOOOOO!!

Massage Train

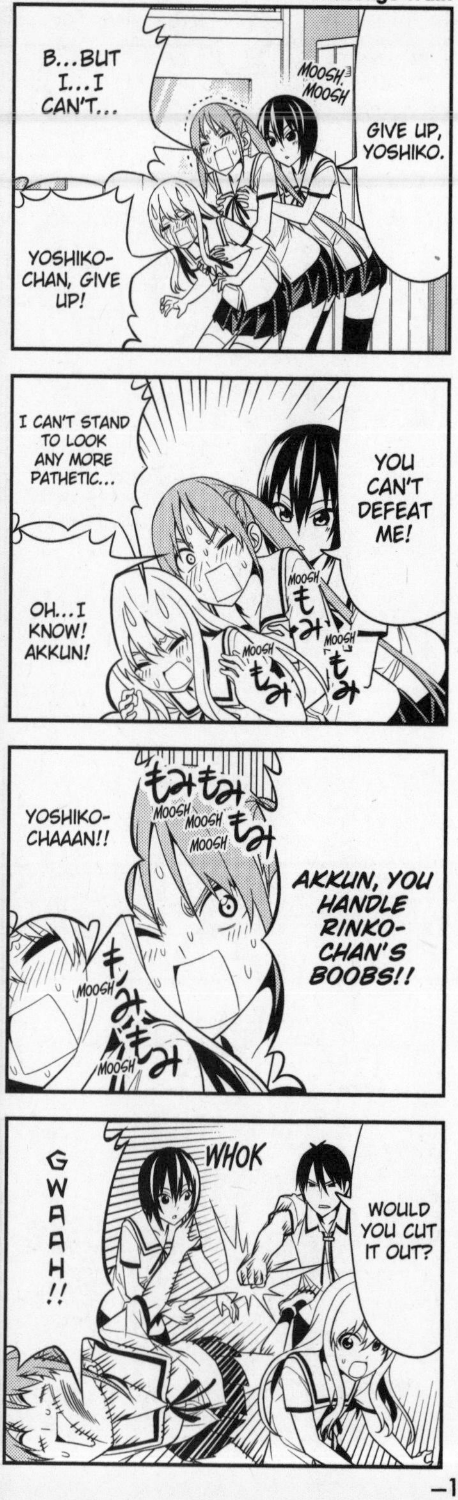
GIVE UP, YOSHIKO.
MOOSH MOOSH
B...BUT I...I CAN'T...
YOSHIKO-CHAN, GIVE UP!
YOU CAN'T DEFEAT ME!
I CAN'T STAND TO LOOK ANY MORE PATHETIC...
もみ MOOSH
もみ MOOSH
もみ MOOSH
OH...I KNOW! AKKUN!
AKKUN, YOU HANDLE RINKO-CHAN'S BOOBS!!
もみもみもみ
MOOSH MOOSH MOOSH
YOSHIKO-CHAAAN!!
もみもみ
MOOSH MOOSH
WOULD YOU CUT IT OUT?
WHOK
GWAAH!!

You Can't Do That

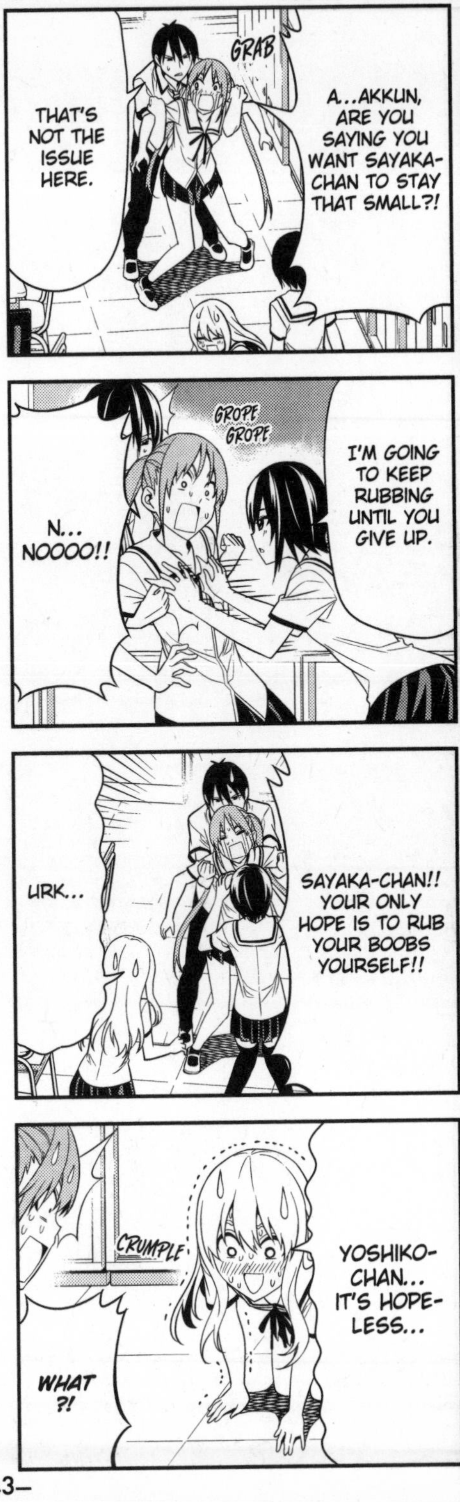
A...AKKUN, ARE YOU SAYING YOU WANT SAYAKA-CHAN TO STAY THAT SMALL?!
GRAB
THAT'S NOT THE ISSUE HERE.
GROPE GROPE
I'M GOING TO KEEP RUBBING UNTIL YOU GIVE UP.
N... NOOOO!!
SAYAKA-CHAN!! YOUR ONLY HOPE IS TO RUB YOUR BOOBS YOURSELF!!
URK...
YOSHIKO-CHAN... IT'S HOPE-LESS...
CRUMPLE
WHAT ?!

Confession...Why She Gave Up

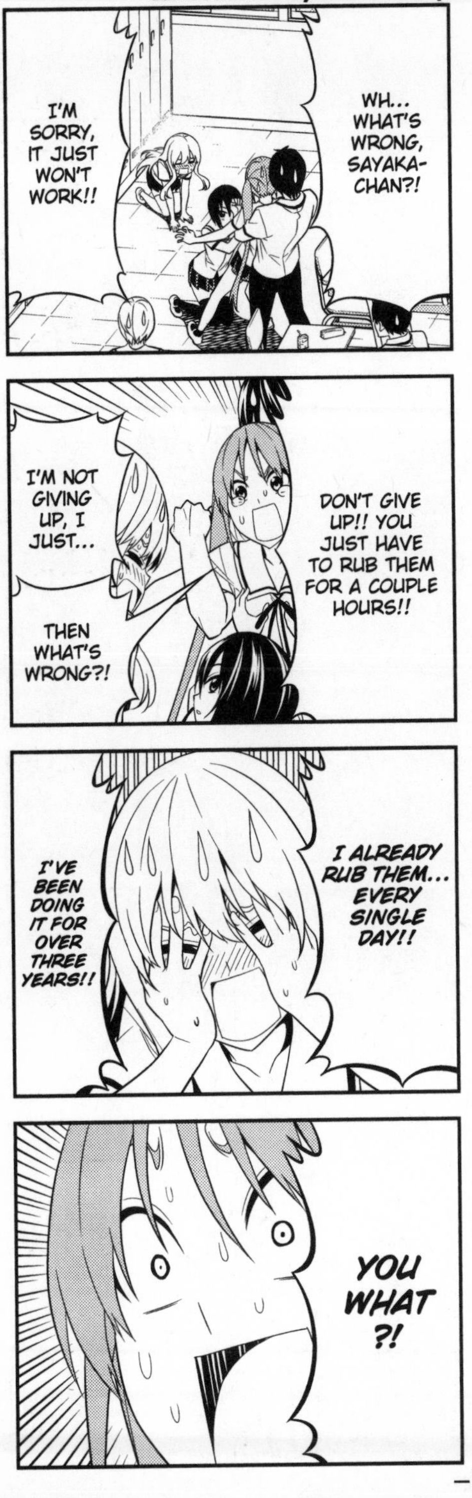
WH... WHAT'S WRONG, SAYAKA-CHAN?!
I'M SORRY, IT JUST WON'T WORK!!
DON'T GIVE UP!! YOU JUST HAVE TO RUB THEM FOR A COUPLE HOURS!!
I'M NOT GIVING UP, I JUST...
THEN WHAT'S WRONG?!
I ALREADY RUB THEM... EVERY SINGLE DAY!!
I'VE BEEN DOING IT FOR OVER THREE YEARS!!
YOU WHAT ?!

Proof of True Friendship

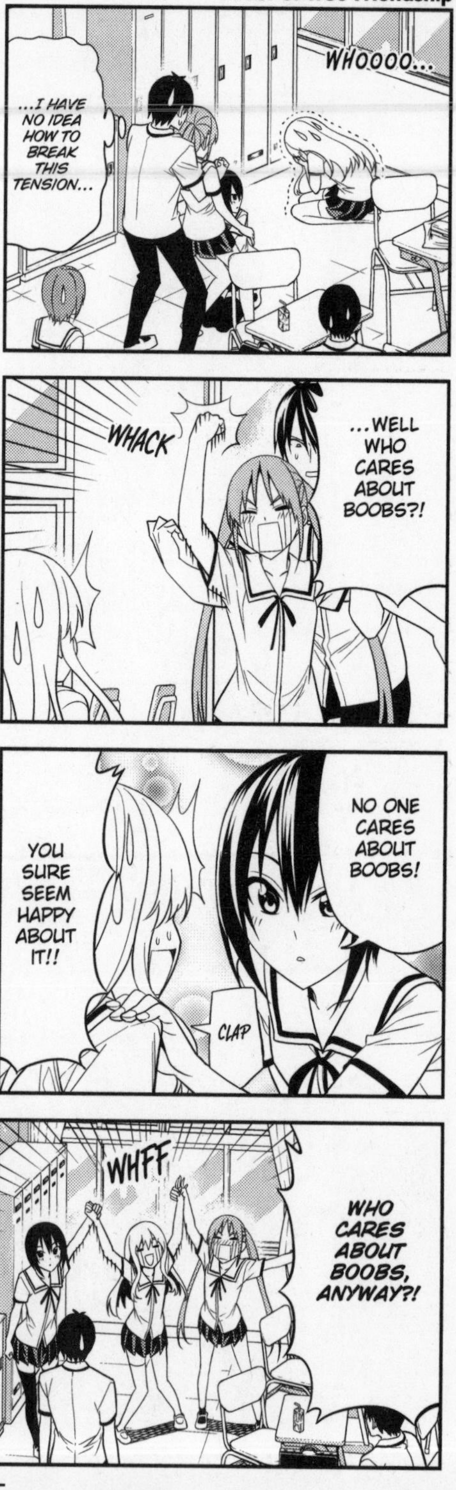
WHOOOO...
...I HAVE NO IDEA HOW TO BREAK THIS TENSION...
...WELL WHO CARES ABOUT BOOBS?!
WHACK
NO ONE CARES ABOUT BOOBS!
YOU SURE SEEM HAPPY ABOUT IT!!
CLAP
WHFF
WHO CARES ABOUT BOOBS, ANYWAY?!

Not Going Along with It, of Course

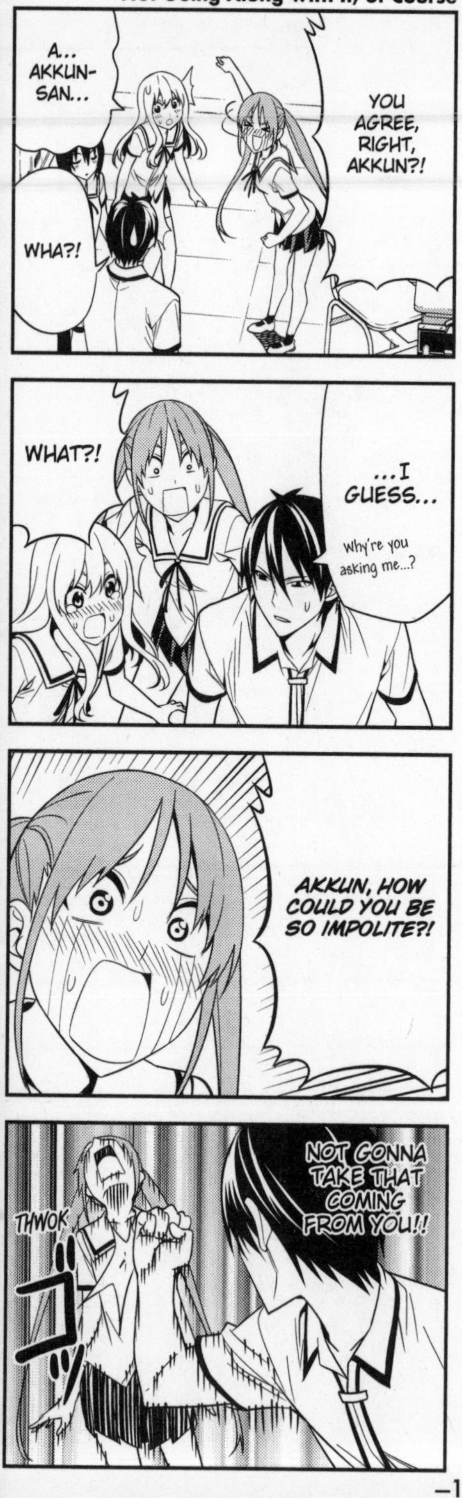
YOU AGREE, RIGHT, AKKUN?!
A... AKKUN-SAN...
WHA?!
...I GUESS...
Why're you asking me...?
WHAT?!
AKKUN, HOW COULD YOU BE SO IMPOLITE?!
NOT GONNA TAKE THAT COMING FROM YOU!!
THWOK
ゴッ

THREE YEARS AGO

TWO YEARS AGO

ONE YEAR AGO

THIS YEAR

(She can have chunibyo as long as she's cute)

Aho-Girl

\'ahô,gərl\ *Japanese , noun*.

A clueless girl.

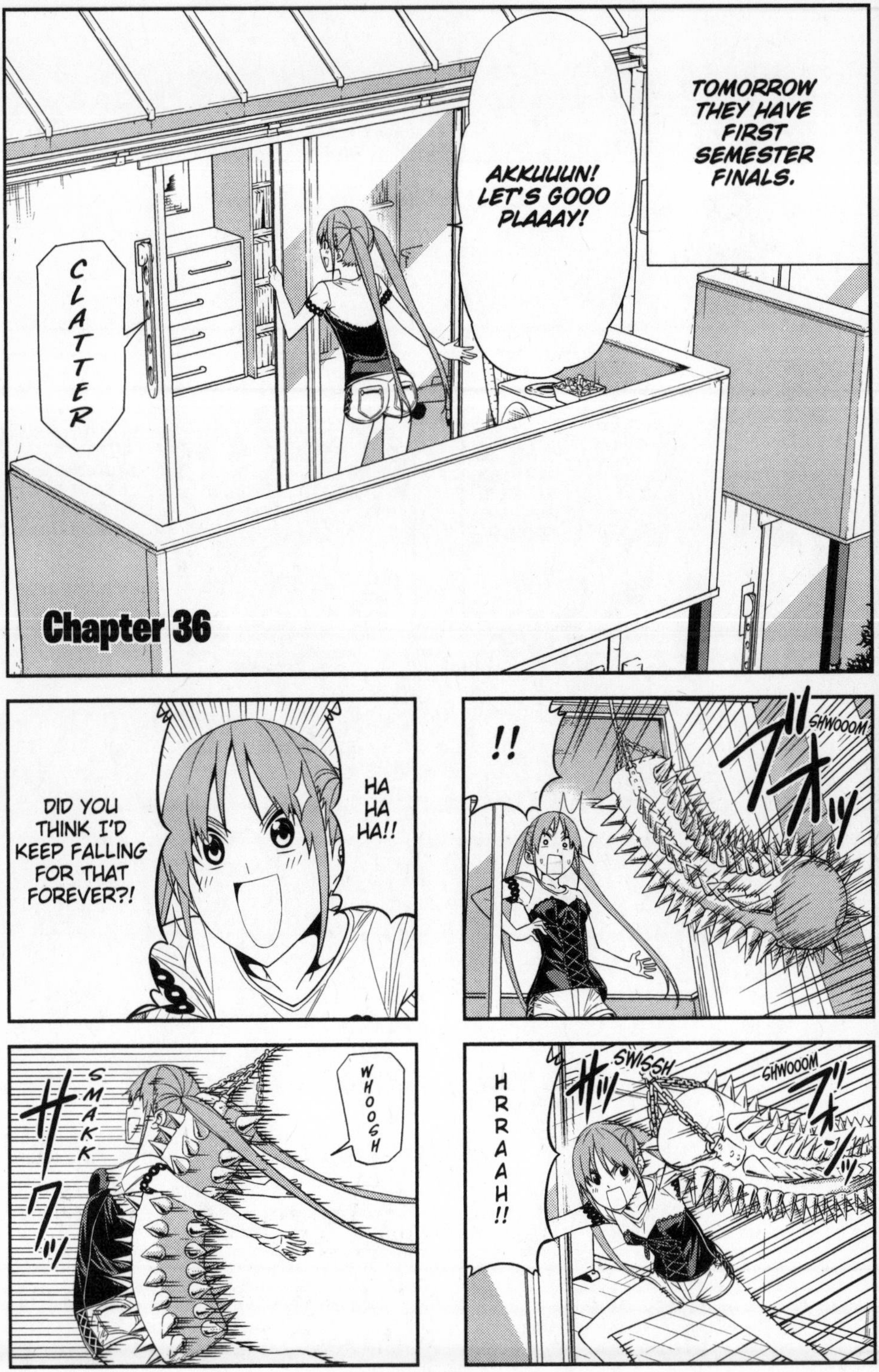
TOMORROW THEY HAVE FIRST SEMESTER FINALS.
AKKUUUN! LET'S GOOO PLAAAY!
CLATTER
Chapter 36
!!
SHWOOOM
ブオッ
HA HA HA!!
DID YOU THINK I'D KEEP FALLING FOR THAT FOREVER?!
HRRAAH!!
SWISSH
ザッ
SHWOOOM
WHOOSH
SMAKK

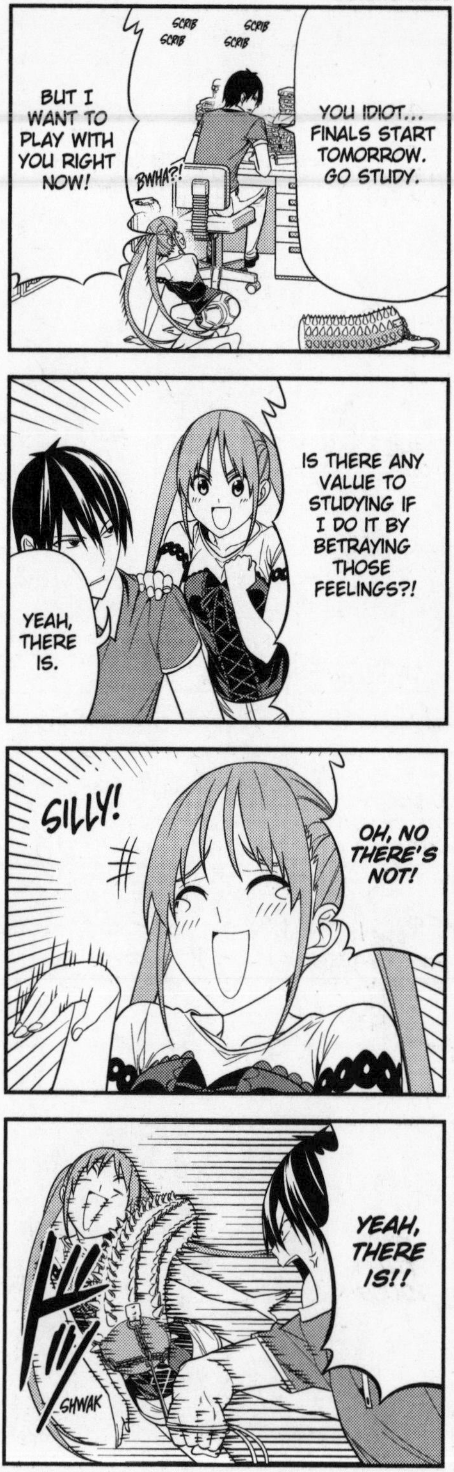
SCRIB SCRIB SCRIB SCRIB
YOU IDIOT... FINALS START TOMORROW. GO STUDY.
BUT I WANT TO PLAY WITH YOU RIGHT NOW!
BWHA?!
IS THERE ANY VALUE TO STUDYING IF I DO IT BY BETRAYING THOSE FEELINGS?!
YEAH, THERE IS.
OH, NO THERE'S NOT!
SILLY!
YEAH, THERE IS!!
SHWAK

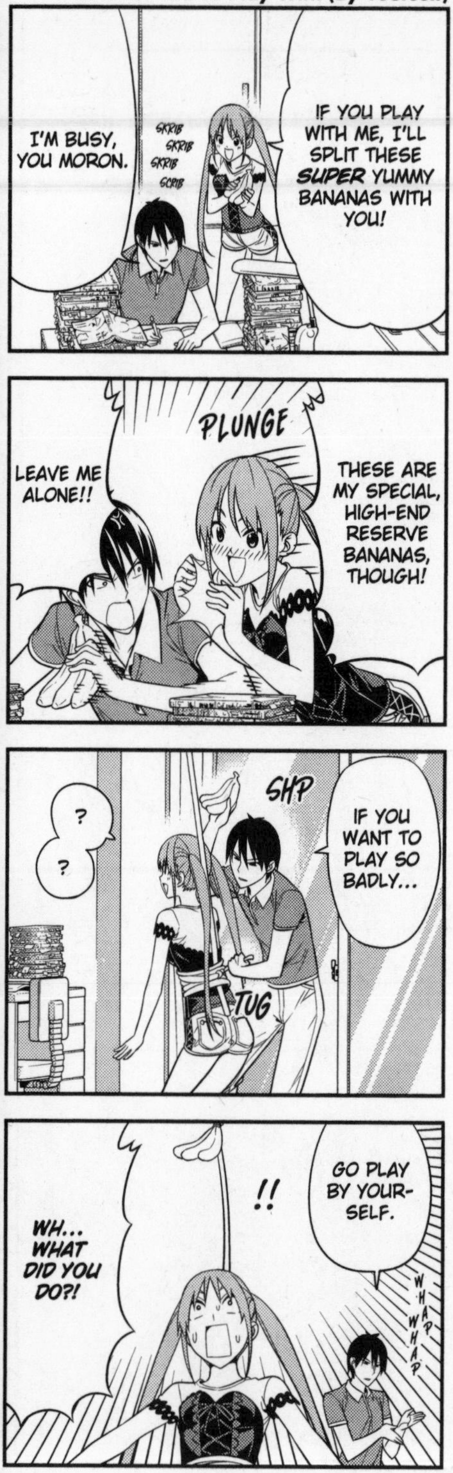
IF YOU PLAY WITH ME, I'LL SPLIT THESE SUPER YUMMY BANANAS WITH YOU!
SKRIB SKRIB SKRIB SCRIB
I'M BUSY, YOU MORON.
THESE ARE MY SPECIAL, HIGH-END RESERVE BANANAS, THOUGH!
PLUNGE
LEAVE ME ALONE!!
IF YOU WANT TO PLAY SO BADLY...
SHP
TUG
? ?
GO PLAY BY YOUR-SELF.
WHAP WHAP
!!
WH... WHAT DID YOU DO?!

It's Incredible

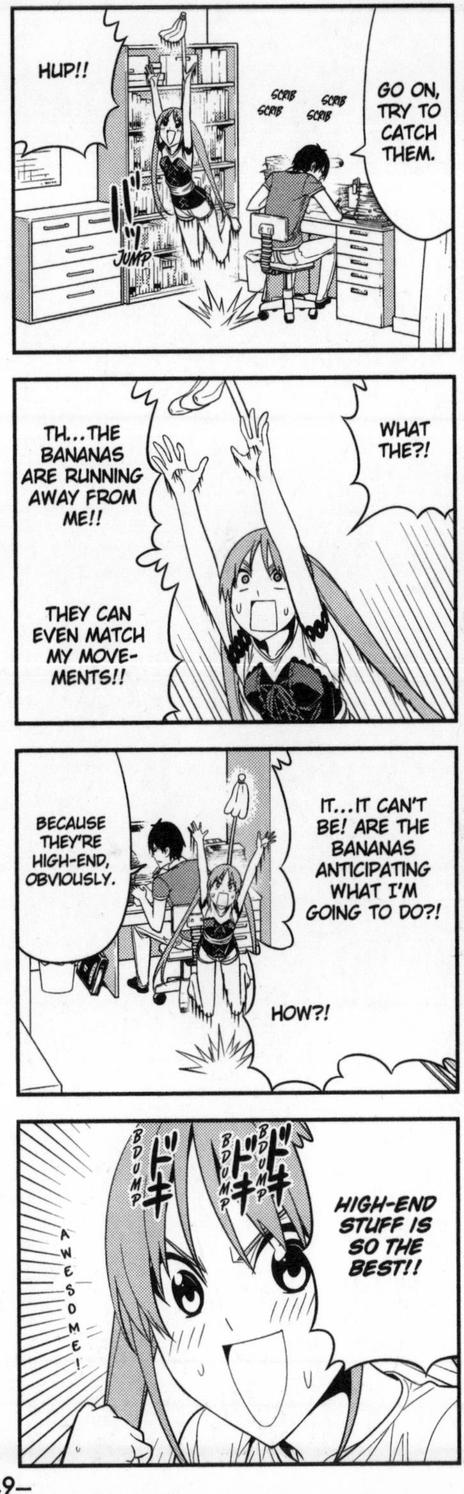
GO ON, TRY TO CATCH THEM.
SCRIB SCRIB SCRIB SCRIB
HUP!!
JUMP
WHAT THE?!
TH...THE BANANAS ARE RUNNING AWAY FROM ME!!
THEY CAN EVEN MATCH MY MOVEMENTS!!
IT...IT CAN'T BE! ARE THE BANANAS ANTICIPATING WHAT I'M GOING TO DO?!
HOW?!
BECAUSE THEY'RE HIGH-END, OBVIOUSLY.
ドキ ドキ ドキ
BDUMP BDUMP BDUMP
HIGH-END STUFF IS SO THE BEST!!
AWESOME!

Impressive...

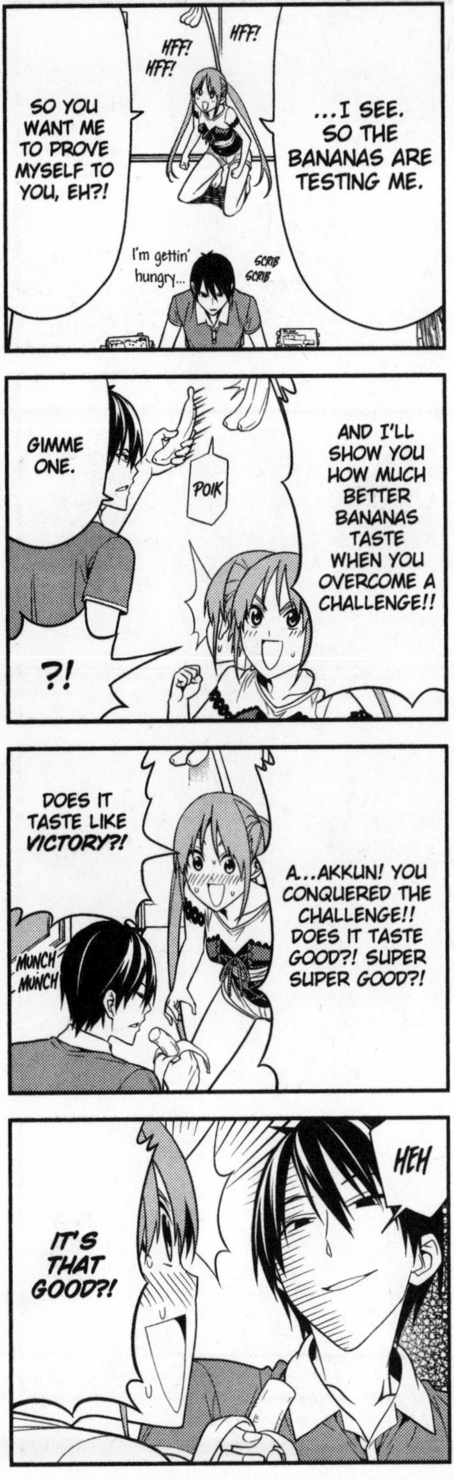
...I SEE. SO THE BANANAS ARE TESTING ME.
HFF! HFF! HFF!
SO YOU WANT ME TO PROVE MYSELF TO YOU, EH?!
SCRIB SCRIB
I'm gettin' hungry...
AND I'LL SHOW YOU HOW MUCH BETTER BANANAS TASTE WHEN YOU OVERCOME A CHALLENGE!!
POIK
GIMME ONE.
?!
A...AKKUN! YOU CONQUERED THE CHALLENGE!! DOES IT TASTE GOOD?! SUPER SUPER GOOD?!
DOES IT TASTE LIKE VICTORY?!
MUNCH MUNCH
HEH
IT'S THAT GOOD?!

You're Gonna Run Out

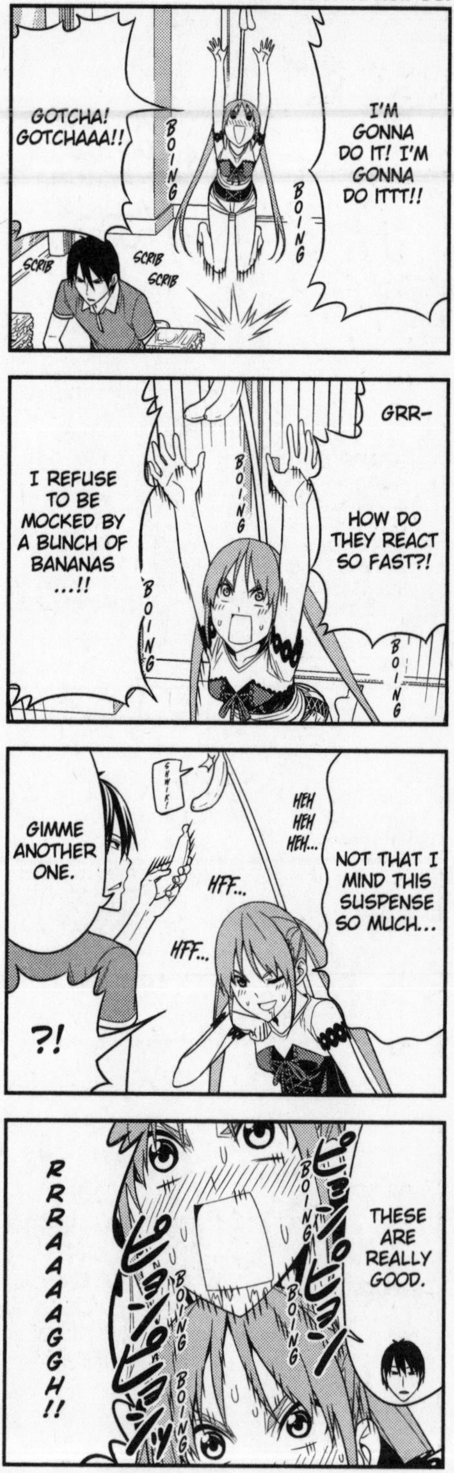
I'M GONNA DO IT! I'M GONNA DO ITTT!!
BOING
BOING
GOTCHA! GOTCHAAA!!
SCRIB SCRIB
SCRIB
GRR-
HOW DO THEY REACT SO FAST?!
BOING
BOING
I REFUSE TO BE MOCKED BY A BUNCH OF BANANAS ...!!
BOING
NOT THAT I MIND THIS SUSPENSE SO MUCH...
HEH HEH HEH...
SHWIK!
HFF...
HFF...
GIMME ANOTHER ONE.
?!
THESE ARE REALLY GOOD.
BOING
BOING
BOING
BOING
RRRAAAAAGGH!!

There It Goes!

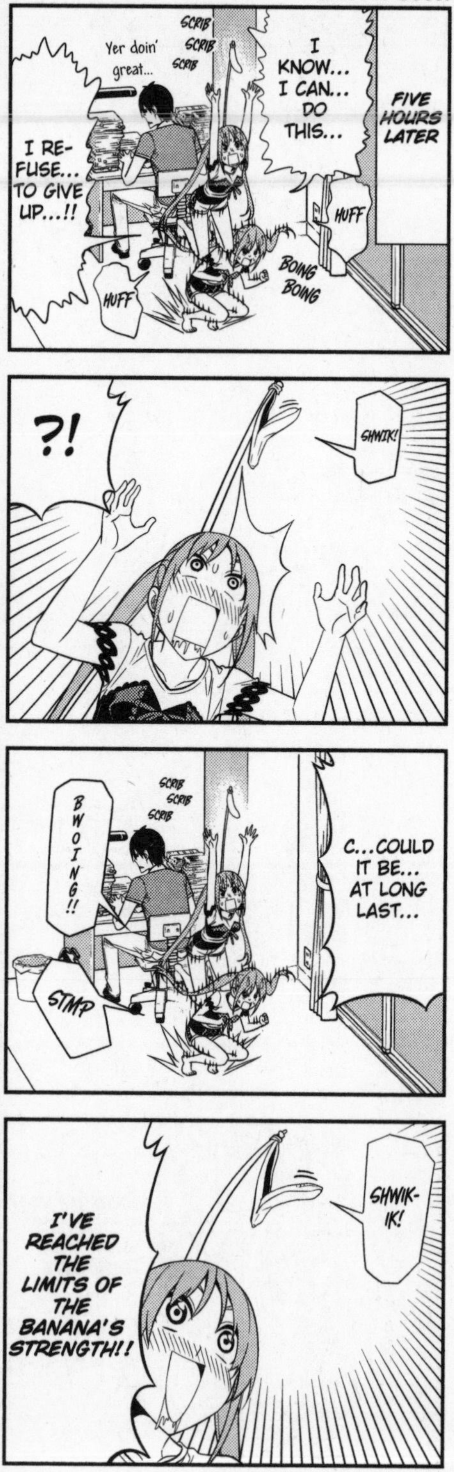
FIVE HOURS LATER
I KNOW... I CAN... DO THIS...
SCRIB SCRIB SCRIB
Yer doin' great...
I REFUSE... TO GIVE UP...!!
HUFF
BOING BOING
HUFF
SHWIK!
?!
C...COULD IT BE... AT LONG LAST...
SCRIB SCRIB SCRIB
BWOING!!
STMP
SHWIK-IK!
I'VE REACHED THE LIMITS OF THE BANANA'S STRENGTH!!

Nice Catch!

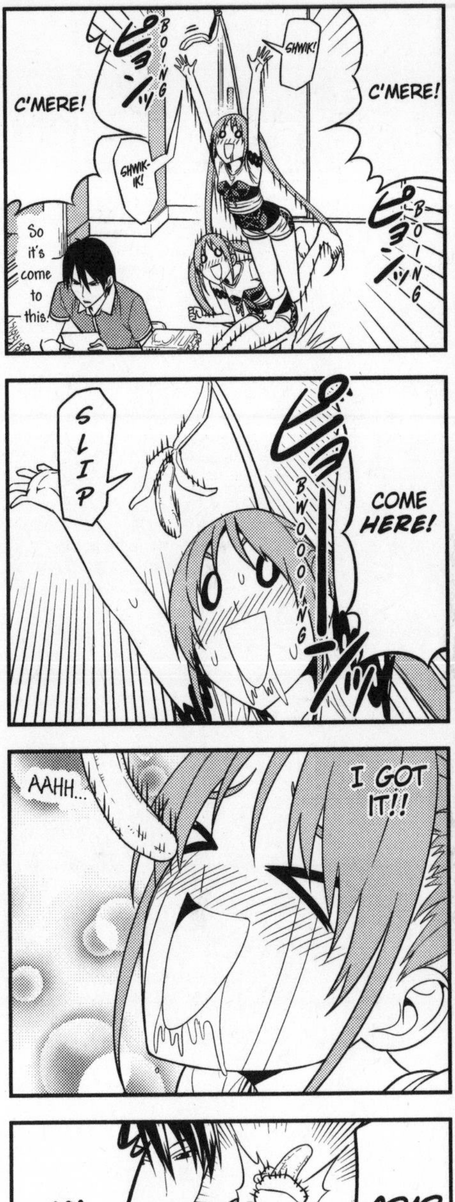
BOING
SHWIK!
C'MERE!
C'MERE!
SHWIK-IK!
So it's come to this.
BOING
COME HERE!
BWOOOING
SLIP
I GOT IT!!
AAHH...
GRAB
WHAT?!

Love

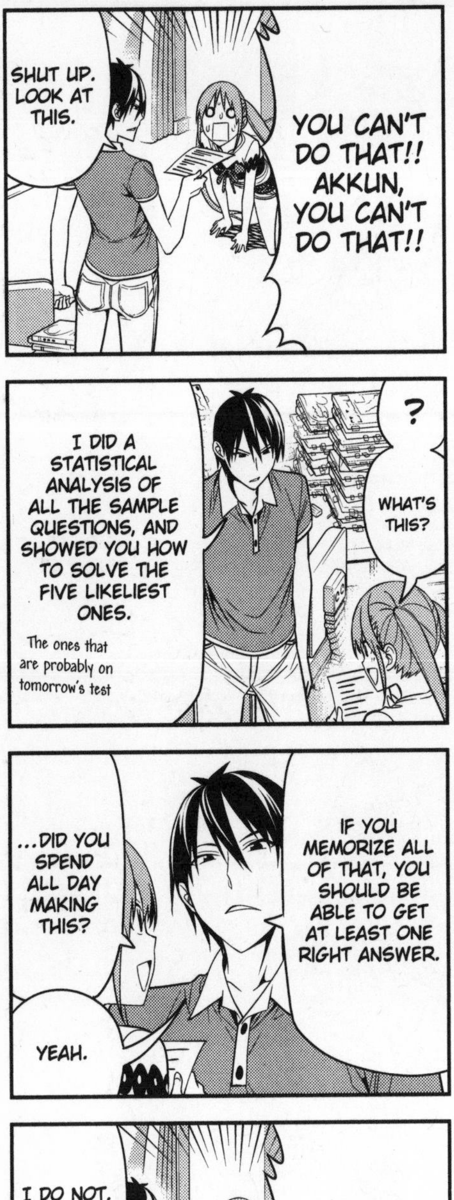
YOU CAN'T DO THAT!! AKKUN, YOU CAN'T DO THAT!!
SHUT UP. LOOK AT THIS.
?
WHAT'S THIS?
I DID A STATISTICAL ANALYSIS OF ALL THE SAMPLE QUESTIONS, AND SHOWED YOU HOW TO SOLVE THE FIVE LIKELIEST ONES.
The ones that are probably on tomorrow's test
IF YOU MEMORIZE ALL OF THAT, YOU SHOULD BE ABLE TO GET AT LEAST ONE RIGHT ANSWER.
...DID YOU SPEND ALL DAY MAKING THIS?
YEAH.
THAT'S LOVE! AKKUN, YOU LOVVVE MEEE!!
I DO NOT.
YOU'RE FINALLY WARMING UP! YAY!!
I'M GONNA KILL YOU.

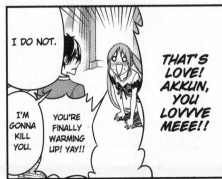

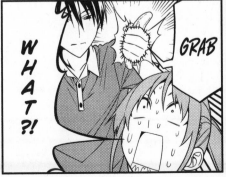

Love?

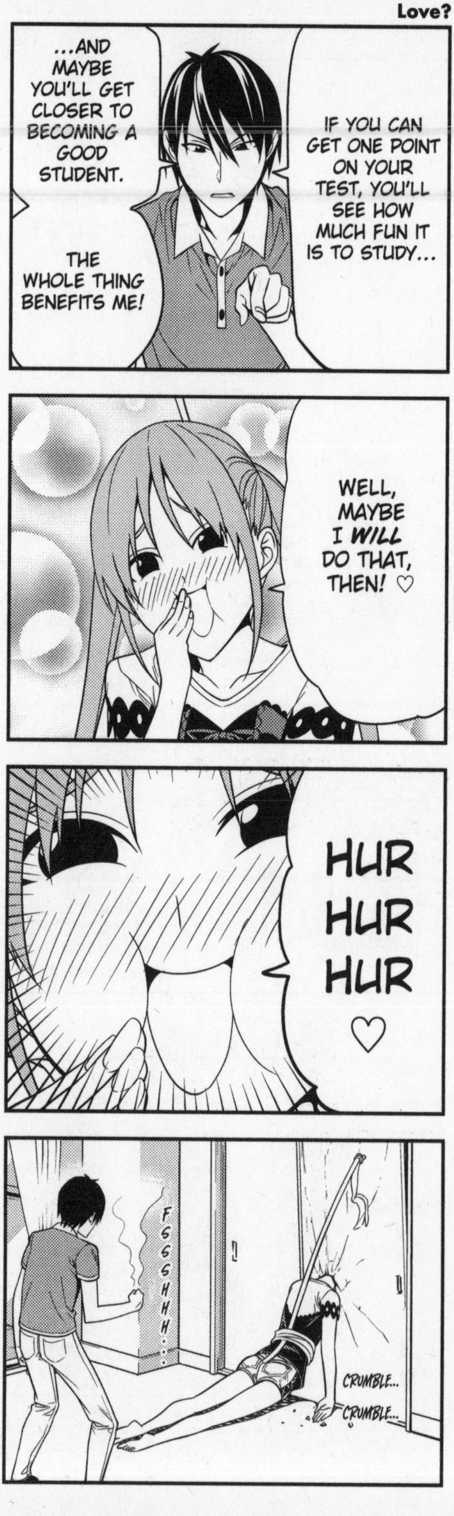
IF YOU CAN GET ONE POINT ON YOUR TEST, YOU'LL SEE HOW MUCH FUN IT IS TO STUDY...
...AND MAYBE YOU'LL GET CLOSER TO BECOMING A GOOD STUDENT.
THE WHOLE THING BENEFITS ME!
WELL, MAYBE I *WILL* DO THAT, THEN! ♡
HUR HUR HUR ♡
FSSSHHH...
CRUMBLE... CRUMBLE...

Results

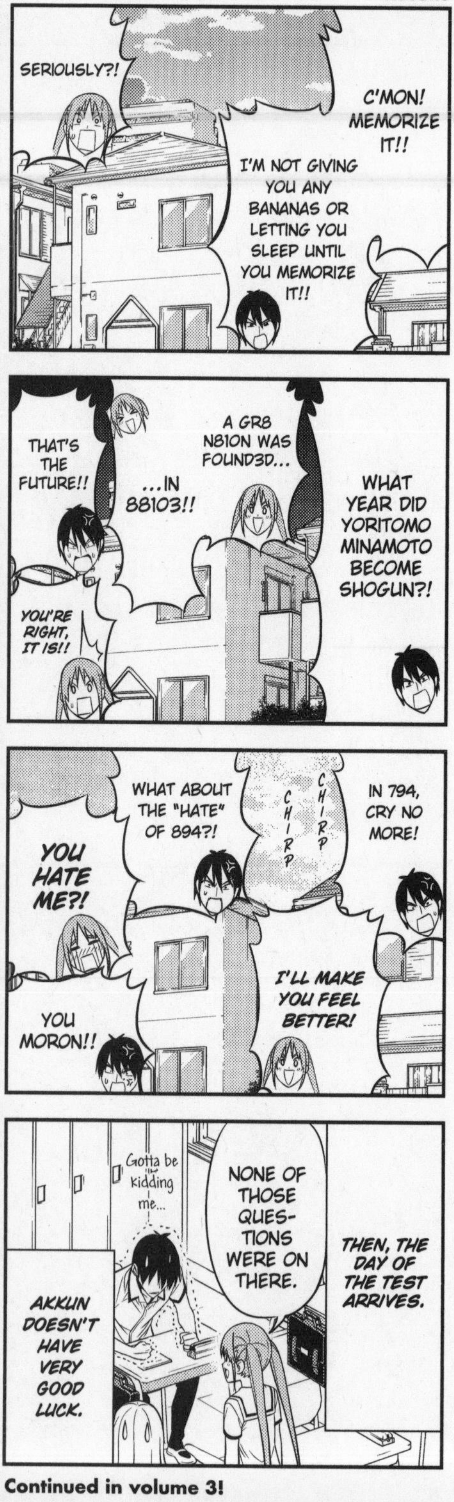
C'MON! MEMORIZE IT!!
I'M NOT GIVING YOU ANY BANANAS OR LETTING YOU SLEEP UNTIL YOU MEMORIZE IT!!
SERIOUSLY?!
WHAT YEAR DID YORITOMO MINAMOTO BECOME SHOGUN?!
A GR8 N810N WAS FOUND3D...
...IN 88103!!
THAT'S THE FUTURE!!
YOU'RE RIGHT, IT IS!!
IN 794, CRY NO MORE!
CHIRP CHIRP
WHAT ABOUT THE "HATE" OF 894?!
YOU HATE ME?!
I'LL MAKE YOU FEEL BETTER!
YOU MORON!!
THEN, THE DAY OF THE TEST ARRIVES.
NONE OF THOSE QUES-TIONS WERE ON THERE.
Gotta be kidding me...
AKKUN DOESN'T HAVE VERY GOOD LUCK.

Continued in volume 3!

Akkun—What a Klutz!

AND AS ALWAYS, AKKUN MISSED GETTING 100S IN ALL HIS CLASSES.

SHUT UP, YOU!!

DON'T GIVE UP, AKKUN!

(What happens twice will happen)

Aho-Girl

\'ahô,gərl\ *Japanese , noun.*

A clueless girl.

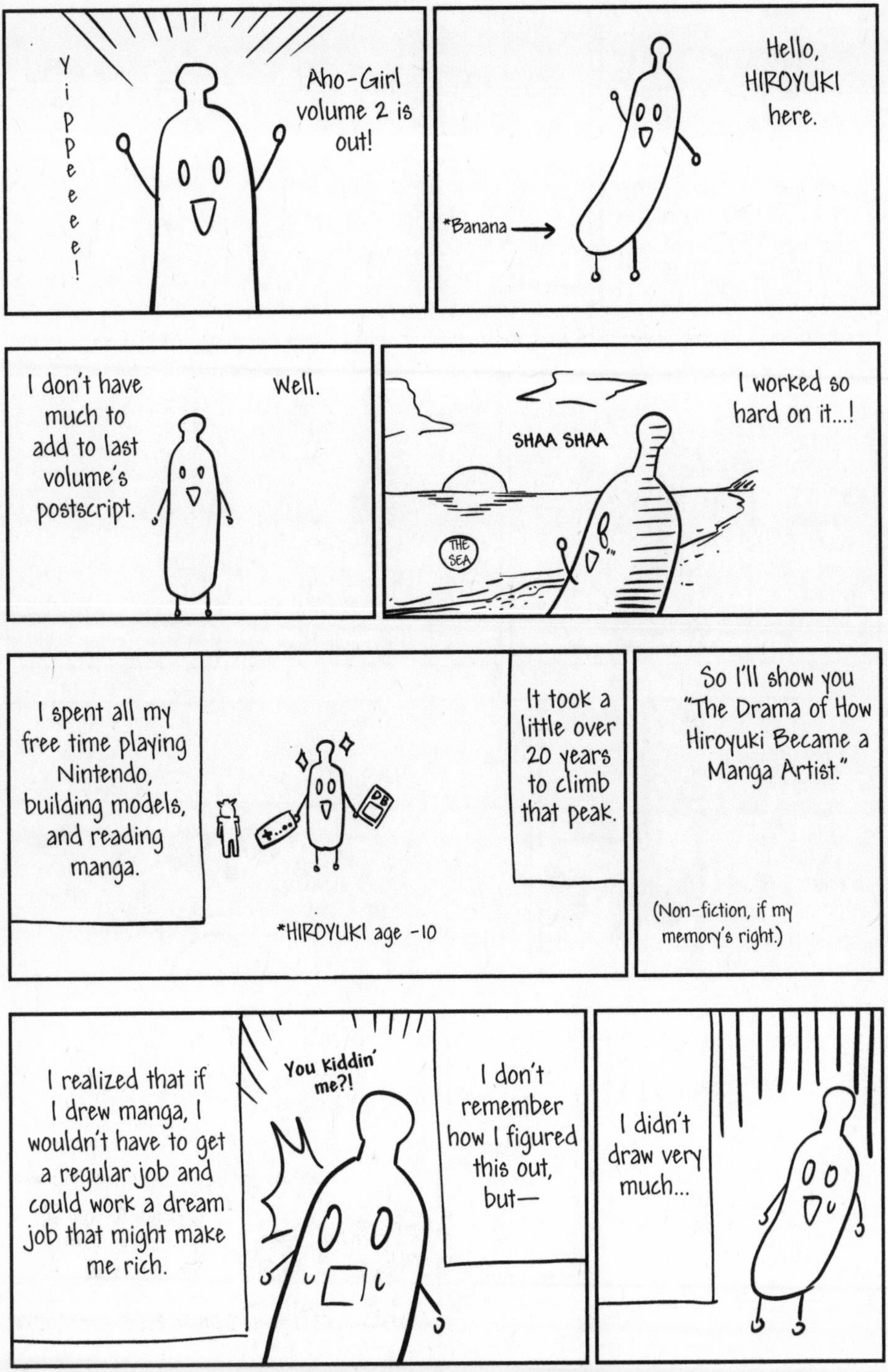
Hello, HIROYUKI here.
*Banana
Aho-Girl volume 2 is out!
Yippeeee!
I worked so hard on it...!
SHAA SHAA
THE SEA
Well.
I don't have much to add to last volume's postscript.
So I'll show you "The Drama of How Hiroyuki Became a Manga Artist."
(Non-fiction, if my memory's right.)
It took a little over 20 years to climb that peak.
I spent all my free time playing Nintendo, building models, and reading manga.
*HIROYUKI age -10
I didn't draw very much...
I don't remember how I figured this out, but—
You kiddin' me?!
I realized that if I drew manga, I wouldn't have to get a regular job and could work a dream job that might make me rich.

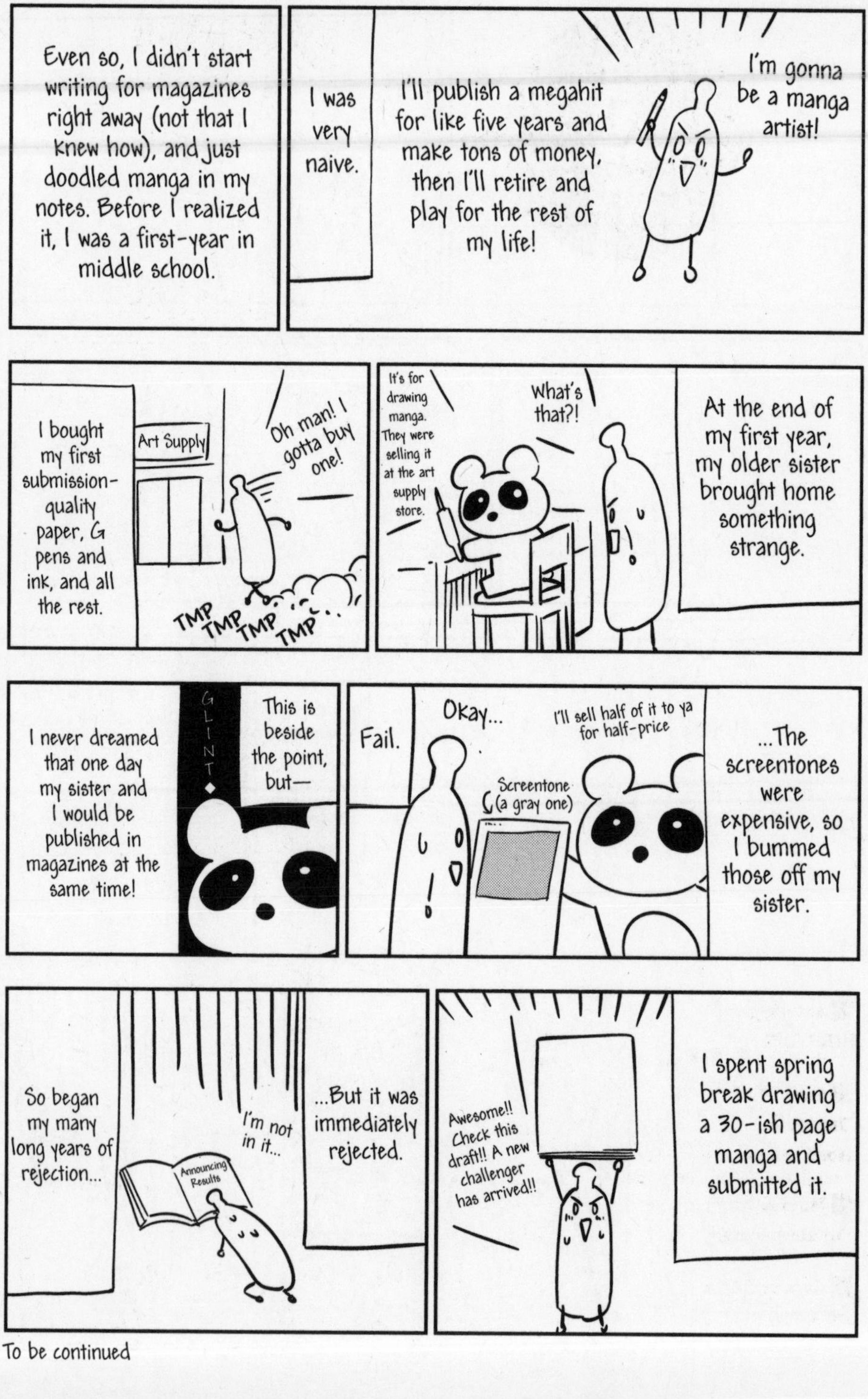
I'm gonna be a manga artist!
I'll publish a megahit for like five years and make tons of money, then I'll retire and play for the rest of my life!
I was very naive.
Even so, I didn't start writing for magazines right away (not that I knew how), and just doodled manga in my notes. Before I realized it, I was a first-year in middle school.
At the end of my first year, my older sister brought home something strange.
What's that?!
It's for drawing manga. They were selling it at the art supply store.
Oh man! I gotta buy one!
Art Supply
TMP TMP TMP TMP
I bought my first submission-quality paper, G pens and ink, and all the rest.
...The screentones were expensive, so I bummed those off my sister.
I'll sell half of it to ya for half-price
Okay...
Screentone (a gray one)
Fail.
This is beside the point, but—
GLINT
I never dreamed that one day my sister and I would be published in magazines at the same time!
I spent spring break drawing a 30-ish page manga and submitted it.
Awesome!! Check this draft!! A new challenger has arrived!!
...But it was immediately rejected.
I'm not in it...
Announcing Results
So began my many long years of rejection...

To be continued

AN EXTRA VALENTINE'S DAY COMIC THAT FIRST RAN IN KODANSHA'S *MAGAZINE SPECIAL.*

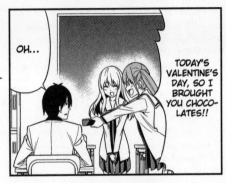

TODAY'S VALENTINE'S DAY, SO I BROUGHT YOU CHOCOLATES!!
OH...
BUT... THEY WERE SO YUMMY-LOOKING-
I COULDN'T STOP MYSELF. I ATE THEM ALL!!
WHAT?!
... AND?
THEY WERE SUPER!! YUMMY!!
I'M GLAD.

Magazine Special, 2013, issue no. 2

■ **Author**
HIROYUKI

■ **Staff**
Omae-san
Horikoshi-san

■ **Main Editor**
Fujikawa-sama

■ **Comics Editor**
Ito-sama

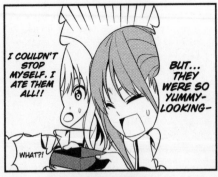

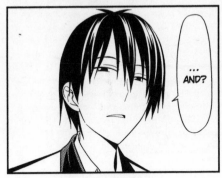

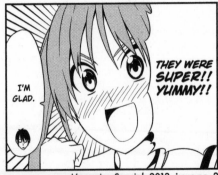

Translation Notes

Page 2
"Aggravated straight man"
This is an explanatory gloss of the Japanese term "tsukkomi." The tsukkomi and boke duo are a common trope in manzai-style stand-up comedy routines. The boke, like Yoshiko, draws over-the-top and just plain stupid conclusions to the tsukkomi's set-ups. The tsukkomi tries to remain calm and reasonable during the act, but is invariably pushed into extreme and sometimes violent reactions out of his frustration.

Page 6
"Solitaire Concentration"
This is the well-known card game where cards are placed face-down and a player or players must find a matching pair.

Page 8
"A Wild Yoshiko Appeared!"
"It's Super Effective!"
These titles refer to lines in the *Pokémon* series of video games. The first, "A Wild Yoshiko Appeared!" is displayed when a battle to capture a wild Pokémon begins. The second, "It's Super Effective!" is displayed during a battle when a particular attack hits a creature's weakness (such as a water attack against a fire creature).

Page 9
"So I Can Be Myself"
This is the title to the 1983 hit song "Boku ga boku dearu tame ni" by Yutaka Ozaki. The song was also used as the main theme song for a 1997 TV drama of the same name, starring the members of the pop group SMAP, which explores a group of high school friends who are reunited in their mid-20s and try to navigate their old friendships while remaining true to the people they've become in the intervening years. The song was also released with the English title "My Song"... but that wouldn't make much sense here, would it?

Page 10
"Stalemate"
In Japanese, the title actually says "no-side," which is a rugby term signaling the end of the game because no side (i.e., neither team) will have the next possession of the ball.

Page 12
"Men may be tortured, men may feel sadness, because of"
This quote is a reference to the manga and anime series Fist of the North Star. The inhumanly cruel Souther, one of the villains of the series, rose to power after becoming the sole successor to the Nanto Hōō Ken school. He uses his power to remorselessly commit atrocities and mundane cruelties against his subjects. When Kenshiro, the main character of the series, faces Souther in a climactic battle, Souther reveals that as a child he was adopted by the school's master Ogai, whom he loved as a father. Unfortunately, the Nanto Hōō Ken school of martial arts dictates that a master must be killed in order for the student to complete his training, and therefore Ogai tricked Souther into killing him so that Souther could achieve his destiny as master of the school. Having betrayed the man who raised him, the traumatized Souther renounces love in all its forms to protect himself from pain and sorrow. When Kenshiro uses a painless technique that will shortly kill Souther in their battle, Souther asks why Kenshiro allows himself to be burdened with the pain that love and other emotions cause. Kenshiro responds that despite the pain, love also brings joy and happiness. As he lies dying, Souther abandons his feelings of betrayal and reconciles with the spirit of his beloved master Ogai.

Page 15
"Pronunciation guide"
This refers to a convention in Japanese writing known as furigana. Furigana appears primarily over difficult kanji characters to help people pronounce the words correctly. It is also used to teach children how to read the different writing systems used in Japanese. A more sophisticated use of furigana is to provide subtext (literally!) in manga, lyrics, and other creative writing, showing a completely different word over the actual text. For example, a character might say "that idiot" while the furigana says "Yoshiko." The furigana is taken as what is spoken aloud, while the main text is taken as the implied meaning.

Page 17
"We're Not Making Oranges or Machines Here"
The title comes from a quote about teaching from the TV series Sannen B Gumi's lead character Kimpachi-sensei (played by Tetsuya Takeda): "We're not growing oranges or building machines here. We're building human beings, every day."

Page 23
"A Very Kibayashi-like Entrance"
Refers to manga writer Shin Kibayashi, who typically writes under a variety of pseudonyms. Some series he has worked on include *GetBackers*, *Kindaichi Case Files* (Kindaichi Shuunen no Jikenbo), and *PsychoBusters*.

the feudal lord of the old man's region and wins him further riches and acclaim.

Page 52
"¥30 million"
A little under $300,000 US.

Page 54
"This Twist Is Straight out of a Shonen Manga"
Shonen manga (i.e. "boys' comics") commonly features storylines with hand-to-hand fighting and other types of duels. In this case, Yoshiko's Mom's bra-stealing technique has been turned against her in the final moments of the battle, upping the tension as the brash upstart Head Monitor makes a resurgence from almost certain defeat.

Page 57
"Tanuki"
In English, a tanuki is properly called a "Japanese raccoon dog." They have a broad resemblance to raccoons, but are a separate and unrelated species. Fans of manga and anime are more likely familiar with the tanuki of Japanese folk lore, who is usually a trickster (though sometimes dull-witted) and a shapeshifter.

Page 64
"The other day, I met"
This is a reference to the children's song "The Other Day, I Met a Bear" (also known as "The Bear Song"). The lyrics are slightly different in Japanese, of course, and begins "The other day, deep in the forest," but the song is the same.

Page 65
"Pow-R Ranger"
This is a broad reference to all the various Super Sentai-type superhero TV shows, which along with the *Ultraman* and *Kamen Rider* series comprise the bulk of the Tokusatsu genre. The Japanese term used is here "Pachi Ranger," which we adapted as "Pow-R Ranger" in order to preserve the "P" on the rangers' masks. There happens to be a series of ads for pachinko parlors in Japan which also use characters called Pachi Rangers, but those characters more closely resemble a magical girl team than what is being invoked here.

Page 72
"Five stars, shining in the heavens! Five-Star Squadron!!"
This is the tagline to the Japanese TV series *Gosei Sentai Dairanger*, the seventeenth installment in the Super Sentai franchise which spawned the Power Rangers in the US. The title *Gosei Sentai Dairanger* is translated as

Page 32
"Body sushi"
The Japanese term for this is nyotaimori, which literally translates to "arrangement (on) a woman's body." It refers to eating sushi or sashimi off a woman's naked body. There is also a male version of this, called "nantaimori." The image of decadent nyotaimori arrangements was common during the bubble economy in the 1980s, although the actual practice remains rare and unsurprisingly disreputable.

Page 33
"Yakiniku"
Yakiniku is a Japanese dish in which a customer is presented with a plate of thinly sliced raw meats (usually beef) and vegetables, which they then cook to taste on a searing-hot griddle, grill, or hot plate at the center of the table. Yoshiko may think she's hot, but...yakiniku is ambitious.

Page 38
"She brings the city to life"
This is the opening line of a 1983 song by J-pop star Anri. The song, "Cat's Eye," was used as the opening theme of the anime of the same name, which follows the adventures of three sisters who are also art thieves.

Page 40
"Obasan"
This is a respectful form of address for an older (but not elderly) woman, literally meaning "aunt." Contrast to obaasan for "grandmother" and babaa for a more disrespectful term along the lines of "hag."

Page 41
"Mirin"
This is Japanese variety of sweet cooking wine, and it's part of what gives sushi rice its characteristic taste.

Page 42
"¥1000"
Equivalent to about $9 US.

Page 48
"Dig here"
This line is iconic of the Japanese fairy tale *Hanasaka-jiisan*, roughly rendered as "The Old Man Who Makes Flowers Bloom," wherein a childless old couple takes in a stray dog and pampers the dog like a child. In gratitude, the dog leads the old man out into a field and shows him a spot to dig. When the old man digs, he discovers a box of gold coins. When the dog is killed by a jealous neighbor, the dog's spirit tells his former master to burn his corpse and scatter his ashes over trees. Doing so causes the trees to spring into bloom, which impresses

into a very popular TV drama, and features the main character, a traveling businessman, making various perfunctory sales visits before heading to a nearby restaurant to revel in the food he finds there. Each installment focuses on a different restaurant or street vendor and different bit of cuisine. In the TV series, the main character visits real restaurants and eats meals that are offered on their real-life menus.

Page 122
"The Threat from Zeon is"
This is the title of an episode in *Mobile Suit Gundam* which aired in 1979. In the series, the Principality of Zeon is at war with the Earth Federation, and the episode takes place after the leader of Zeon has been killed. In response, the successor, Gihren Zabi, gives a speech rousing his beleaguered people to a renewed assault on the Earth Federation.

Page 128
"When a Person Clings to Dreams... Disappointment Awaits"
In Japanese, there is a well-known saying that "hito no yume to kaite, hakanai" (one literal translation being, "write a person's dream, and [it is] to no avail"). This saying is derived from the kanji used in the Japanese version of the sentence. When the kanji for "person" and "dream" are combined, they form a new kanji meaning "impermanent, transient, fickle, vain, empty," etc. Rather than try to fruitlessly encapsulate all this in a more literal translation, a looser translation of the sentiment is given instead.

Page 130
"Every time I come home, my wife is always"
In 2010, a question was posted on the Japanese version of Yahoo! Answers. The question was titled "Every time I come home, my wife always pretends to be dead." The OP goes on to explain that his wife concocts elaborate scenarios for him to stumble onto when he walks in the front door, such as splattering fake blood onto a t-shirt and lying on the ground, wearing a fake arrow through her head, putting a plastic bag over her head (though he could see it moving so he knew she could breathe), and even dressing up like a soldier and clinging to a gun as she lay sprawled on the floor. Obviously, the question became meme-ified, and there are several parody videos on YouTube reenacting these scenes. The original question (with one such video) can be seen here: https://tinyurl.com/y9kohf55.

Page 131
"Nantara Village"
The town's name, "Nantara," is written using very plau-

"Five-Star Squadron Dairanger."

Page 80
"Let it consume my body! x3"
In *Dragon Ball Z*, Goku uses a technique called "kaio-ken" that he alone has mastered. The technique takes a heavy toll on the user's ki and can badly damage the user's body. When fighting Vegeta, Goku realizes that his standard level kaio-ken will not be enough to win him the battle, and so he pumps even more of his physical resources into the attack, letting it consume him and unleashing the multiplied "kaio-ken x3."

Page 84
"Akutsu-sama"
Ryuichi has switched from calling Akkun "Akutsu-kun," which would be the standard form of address between age peer boys, to saying "Akutsu-sama." In this case, such a choice is an over-the-top expression of respect or admiration, putting Akkun on an almost god-like plane above Ryuichi.

Page 88
"Be-Bop High"
This refers to the classic manga *Be-Bop High School*, which features two ruffian high school boys who frequently get into fights with rivals and face other coming-of-age adversities. The manga series ran from 1983 to 2003 and led to several anime, live action, and video game adaptations.

Page 90
"Cutie Cure"
The title translated here as "Cutie Cure" is "Purichua," which is a reference to the *Pretty Cure* family of magical girl anime series (also known as "Purikyua," or PreCure). A recent incarnation of *Pretty Cure*, *Smile PreCure*, was adapted into a Netflix exclusive under the title *Glitter Force*. Rather than come up with a disguised version of "Glitter Force," it seemed more faithful to the feel of the "Purichua" term to use "Pretty Cure" as the starting point. Hence: "Cutie Cure."

Page 96
"We're messing around too much; we're children of summer"
This is a refrain in the song "Summer Nude" by the rock group the Magokoro Brothers, released in 1995. The song has been covered numerous times and has inspired a TV drama and a manga series.

Page 106
"When I'm eating—how should I put it? I'm"
This line is common in the manga series *Kodoku Gurume* ("The Solitary Gourmet"). The manga has been adapted

have to a system as robust in English as the Japanese system is the "l33t speak" transposition of numbers for look-alike letters. Since Yoshiko's answers are wildly wrong anyway, it isn't too much of a problem to substitute whatever numbers fit in English. However, for the curious, here are the original mnemonics Akkun tries to teach Yoshiko:

Japanese	Translation	Hidden Numbers
Ii kuni tsukuro	Let's build a great nation	1 9 2 2 9 6
Naku yo, uguisu!	Cry, nightingale!	7 9 4
(Yoshiko: I'll make you feel better!)		
Hakushi ni modosou!	Let's start over!	8 9 4
(Yoshiko: (You're giving me) A notice of divorce?!)		

Page 154
"What happens twice, will happen"
This is a Japanese saying that says, in full, "What happens twice, will happen thrice" ("nido aru koto ha sando aru"). Though intended in a more figurative "when it rains, it pours" sense, the meaning is often taken literally in a superstitious way. For example, if you bang your knee on a desk twice, someone is likely to tell you this and predict that the third time it happens will be the last time.

Page 156
"G pen"
A G pen is a type of pen nib favored by ink-drawing artists. It belongs to a subset of pen nibs that have come to be called "manga pen nibs," and requires the most skill to use effectively due to its flexibility and responsiveness to pressure and angle.

Aho-Girl
\\ˈahôˌgərl\\ Japanese , noun.
A clueless girl.

sible-seeming place name characters. However, the word "nantara" also means "whatever" or "so-and-so," so every time a character says "Nantara Village," it sounds in Japanese like they're saying saying "Something-or-other Village."

Page 133
"100 km"
About 62 miles.

Page 138
"Let the wind carry us across the land"
This refers to the title of a travel program that aired on Fuji TV from 1990 through 2000, which featured various hosts traveling to various places and interacting with people, visiting tourist spots, and so on to capture the allure of travel. The show's full title is "Kaze Makase – Shin/shokoku Manyuuki" ("Let the Wind Carry Us – A Tale of Travel to New and Varied Lands").

Page 146
"She can have chunibyo as long as she's cute"
"Chunibyo" (literally "eighth grade sickness") is a recent Japanese term referring to middle school students who go through a phase involving delusions of grandeur—believing they have magical powers, or a great destiny, or intellectual abilities far exceeding the mundane humans around them. Characters recovering from chunibyo were the subject of the recent anime Love, Chunibyo, and Other Delusions.

Page 148
"This is for you to play with (by yourself)"
A long-running children's TV show in Japan, airing from 1990 to 2013, was called "Tsukutte Asobo" ("Let's make (something) and play"). The philosophy of the show was to show children how to make things to exercise their creativity and learn good life skills. Here, the title of the show has been massaged somewhat to fit into English grammar, which requires pronouns such as "I" and "you" where Japanese can leave such words more ambiguous. HIROYUKI has also altered the title of the show slightly with the parentheticals, to more closely fit Akkun's intent.

Page 152
"A gr8 n810n was f0und3d…"
A common form of wordplay in Japanese is to assign numbers to replace homophone syllables in words to create a kind of code, which can be either playful shorthand, or can be used in a mnemonic (as it is here). Because Japanese has many different pronunciations for each number, the system is quite flexible. The only number that really functions this way in English is "8," as in "i h8 u," for example. The closest approximation we

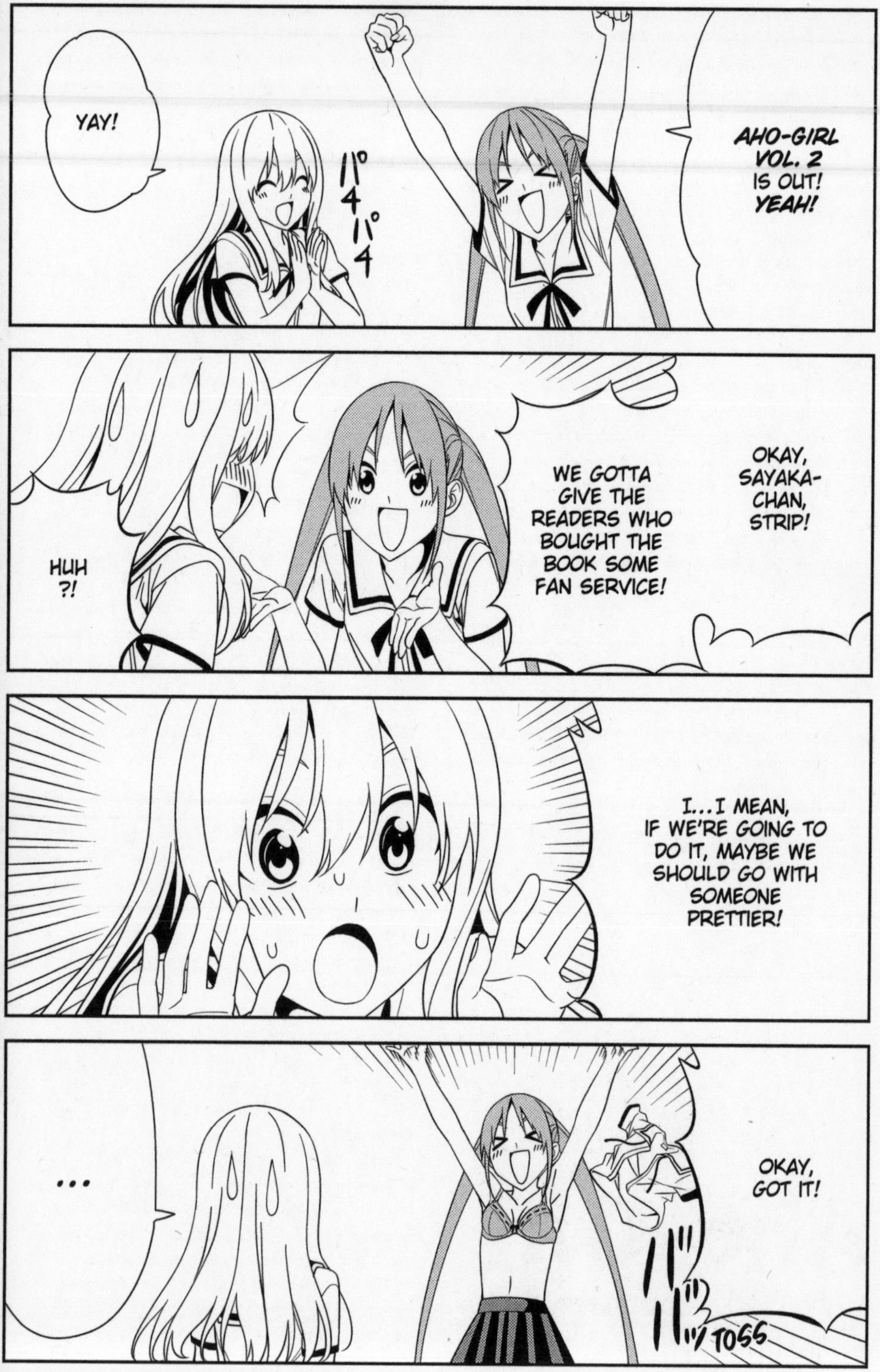
AHO-GIRL VOL. 2 IS OUT! YEAH!
パチパチ
YAY!
OKAY, SAYAKA-CHAN, STRIP!
WE GOTTA GIVE THE READERS WHO BOUGHT THE BOOK SOME FAN SERVICE!
HUH ?!
I...I MEAN, IF WE'RE GOING TO DO IT, MAYBE WE SHOULD GO WITH SOMEONE PRETTIER!
OKAY, GOT IT!
TOSS
...

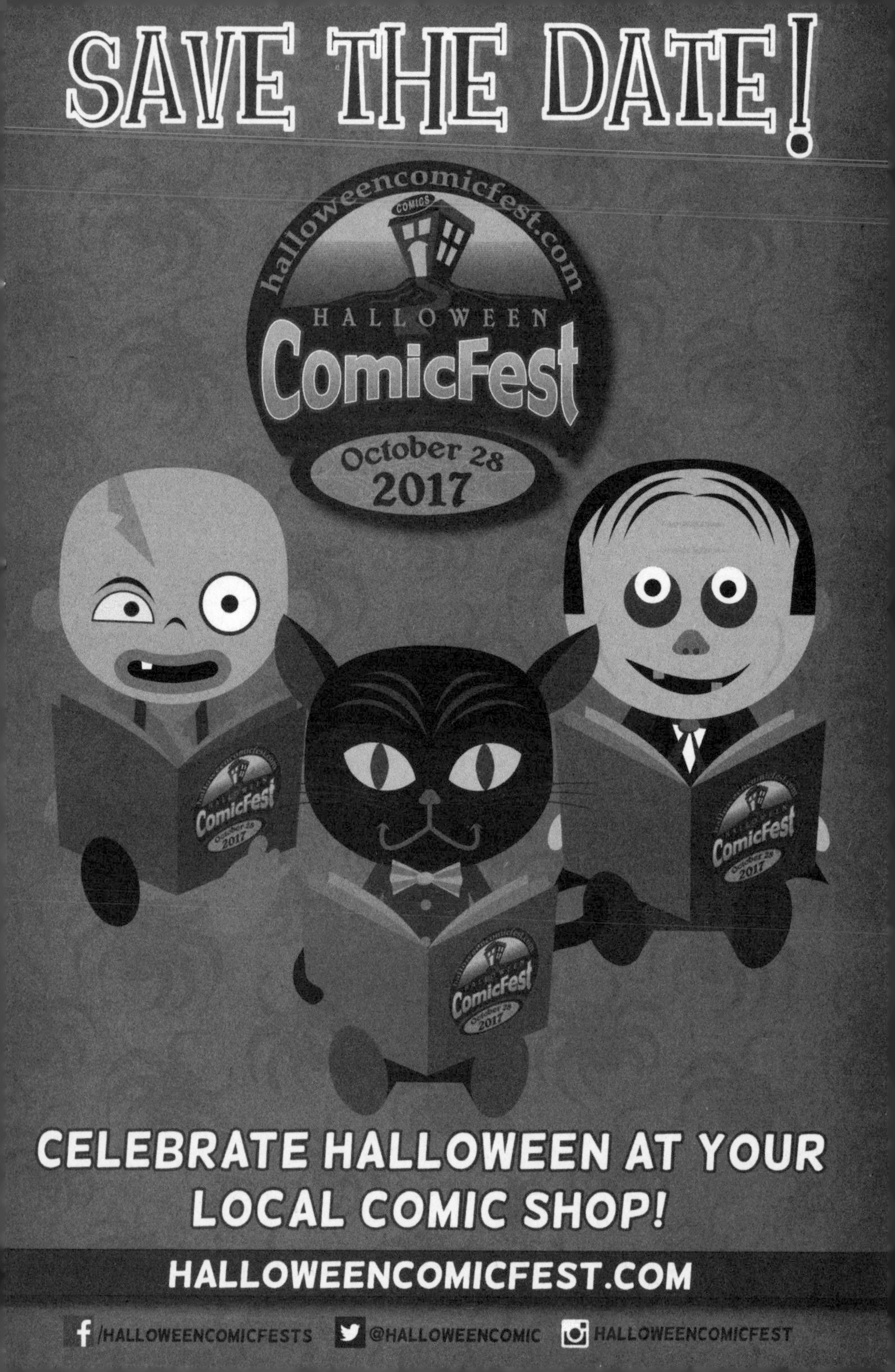
SAVE THE DATE!
halloweencomicfest.com
COMICS
HALLOWEEN
ComicFest
October 28
2017
CELEBRATE HALLOWEEN AT YOUR
LOCAL COMIC SHOP!
HALLOWEENCOMICFEST.COM
/HALLOWEENCOMICFESTS
@HALLOWEENCOMIC
HALLOWEENCOMICFEST

The award-winning manga about what happens inside you!

"Far more entertaining than it ought to be... what kid doesn't want to think that every time they sneeze a torpedo shoots out their nose?"
–Anime News Network

Strep throat! Hay fever! Influenza! The world is a dangerous place for a red blood cell just trying to get her deliveries finished. Fortunately, she's not alone…she's got a whole human body's worth of cells ready to help out! The mysterious white blood cells, the buff and brash killer T cells, even the cute little platelets— everyone's got to come together if they want to keep you healthy!

Cells at Work!

By Akane Shimizu

A new
series
from the
creator
of *Soul
Eater*, the
megahit
manga and
anime seen
on Toonami!

'Fun and lively...
a great start!"
-Adventures in
Poor Taste

FIRE FORCE

By Atsushi Ohkubo

The city of Tokyo is plagued by a deadly phenomenon: spontaneous human combustion! Luckily, a special team is there to quench the inferno: The Fire Force! The fire soldiers at Special Fire Cathedral 8 are about to get a unique addition. Enter Shinra, a boy who possesses the power to run at the speed of a rocket, leaving behind the famous "devil's footprints" (and destroying his shoes in the process). Can Shinra and his colleagues discover the source of this strange epidemic before the city burns to ashes?

The Black Museum: The Ghost and the Lady

By Kazuhiro Fujita

Deep in Scotland Yard in London sits an evidence room dedicated to the greatest mysteries of British history. In this "Black Museum" sits a misshapen hunk of lead—two bullets fused together—the key to a wartime encounter between Florence Nightingale, the mother of modern nursing, and a supernatural Man in Grey. This story is unknown to most scholars of history, but a special guest of the museum will tell the tale of The Ghost and the Lady...

Praise for Kazuhiro Fujita's *Ushio and Tora*

"A charming revival that combines a classic look with modern depth and pacing... **Essential viewing both for curmudgeons and new fans alike.**" — Anime News Network

"**GREAT!** The first episode of Ushio and Tora captures the essence of '90s anime." — IGN

Japan's most powerful spirit medium delves into the ghost world's greatest mysteries!

Story by Kyo Shirodaira, famed author of mystery fiction and creator of *Spiral*, *Blast of Tempest*, and *The Record of a Fallen Vampire*.

Both touched by spirits called yôkai, Kotoko and Kurô have gained unique superhuman powers. But to gain her powers Kotoko has given up an eye and a leg, and Kurô's personal life is in shambles. So when Kotoko suggests they team up to deal with renegades from the spirit world, Kurô doesn't have many other choices, but Kotoko might just have a few ulterior motives...

IN/SPECTRE

STORY BY **KYO SHIRODAIRA**
ART BY **CHASHIBA KATASE**

HAPPINESS

—ハピネス—

By Shuzo Oshimi

From the creator of *The Flowers of Evil*

Nothing interesting is happening in Makoto Ozaki's first year of high school. His life is a series of quiet humiliations: low-grade bullies, unreliable friends, and the constant frustration of his adolescent lust. But one night, a pale, thin girl knocks him to the ground in an alley and offers him a choice. Now everything is different. Daylight is searingly bright. Food tastes awful. And worse than anything is the terrible, consuming thirst...

Praise for Shuzo Oshimi's *The Flowers of Evil*

"A shockingly readable story that vividly—one might even say queasily—evokes the fear and confusion of discovering one's own sexuality. Recommended." —The Manga Critic

"A page-turning tale of sordid middle school blackmail." —Otaku USA Magazine

"A stunning new horror manga." —Third Eye Comics

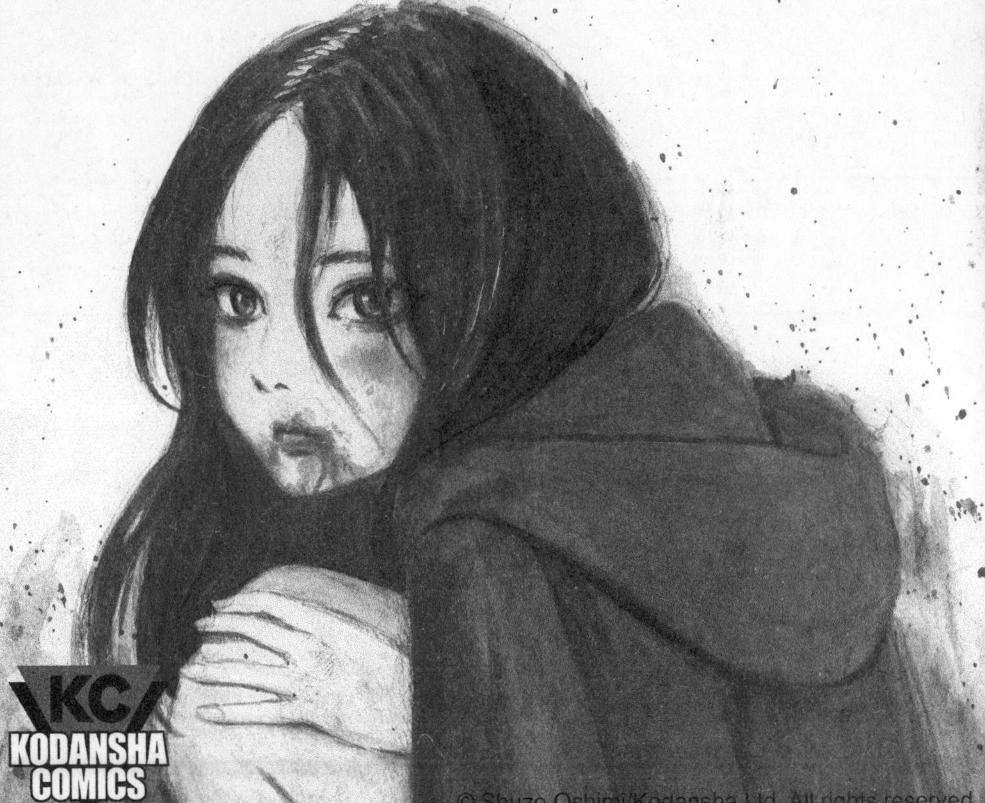

KC KODANSHA COMICS

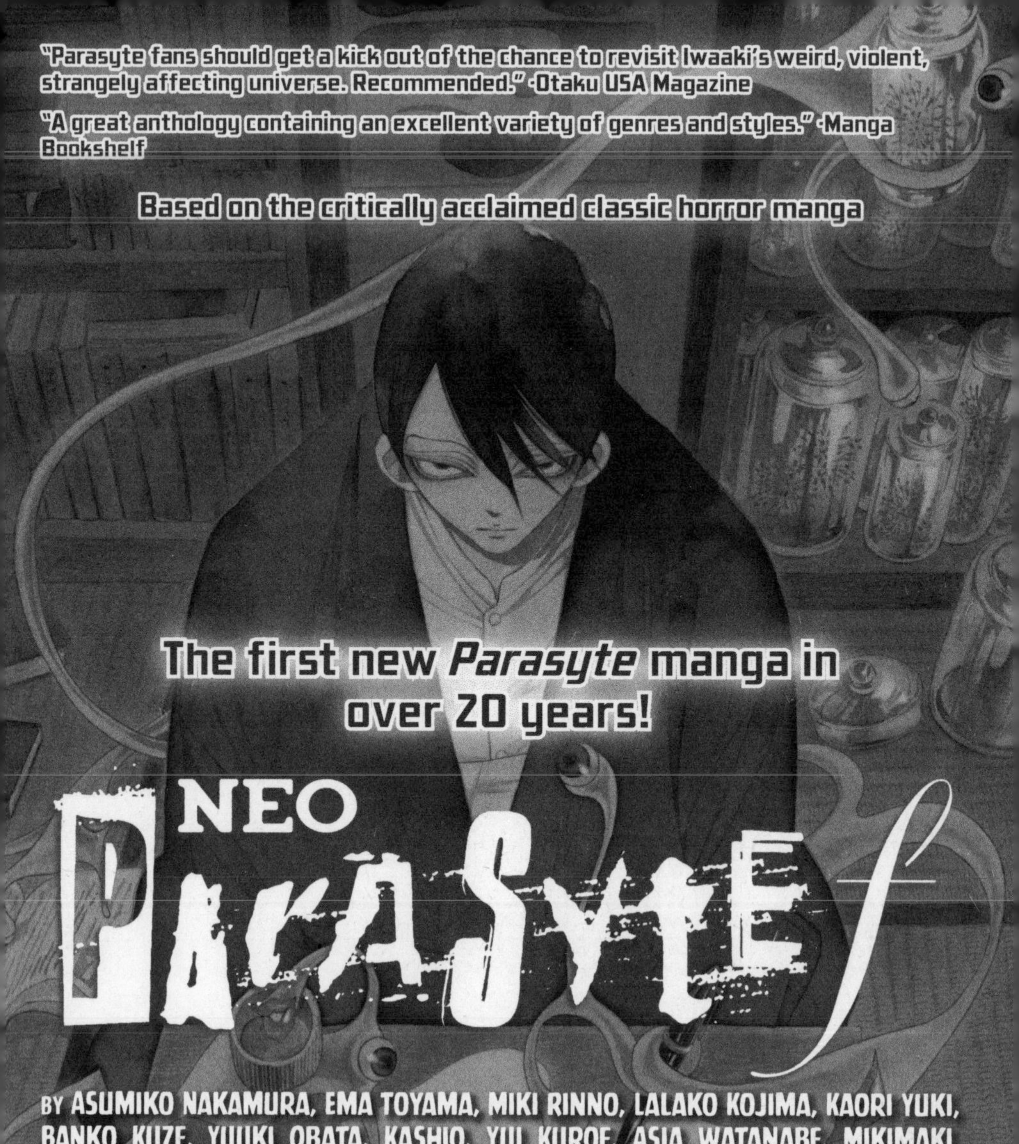
"Parasyte fans should get a kick out of the chance to revisit Iwaaki's weird, violent, strangely affecting universe. Recommended." -Otaku USA Magazine
"A great anthology containing an excellent variety of genres and styles." -Manga Bookshelf
Based on the critically acclaimed classic horror manga
The first new Parasyte manga in over 20 years!
NEO PARASYTE f
BY ASUMIKO NAKAMURA, EMA TOYAMA, MIKI RINNO, LALAKO KOJIMA, KAORI YUKI, BANKO KUZE, YUUKI OBATA, KASHIO, YUI KUROE, ASIA WATANABE, MIKIMAKI, HIKARU SURUGA, HAJIME SHINJO, RENJURO KINDAICHI, AND YURI NARUSHIMA

A collection of chilling new *Parasyte* stories from Japan's top shojo artists!

Parasites: shape-shifting aliens whose only purpose is to assimilate with and consume the human race... but do these monsters have a different side? A parasite becomes a prince to save his romance-obsessed female host from a dangerous stalker. Another hosts a cooking show, in which the real monsters are revealed. These and 13 more stories, from some of the greatest shojo manga artists alive today, together make up a chilling, funny, and entertaining tribute to one of manga's horror classics!

KODANSHA COMICS

KODANSHA COMICS

New action series from Hiroyuki Takei, creator of the classic shonen franchise Shaman King!

In medieval Japan, a bell hanging on the collar is a sign that a has a master. Norachiyo's bell hangs from his katana sheath, but he nonetheless a stray — a ronin. This one-eyed cat samurai travels acros dishonest world, cutting through pretense and deception with his blac

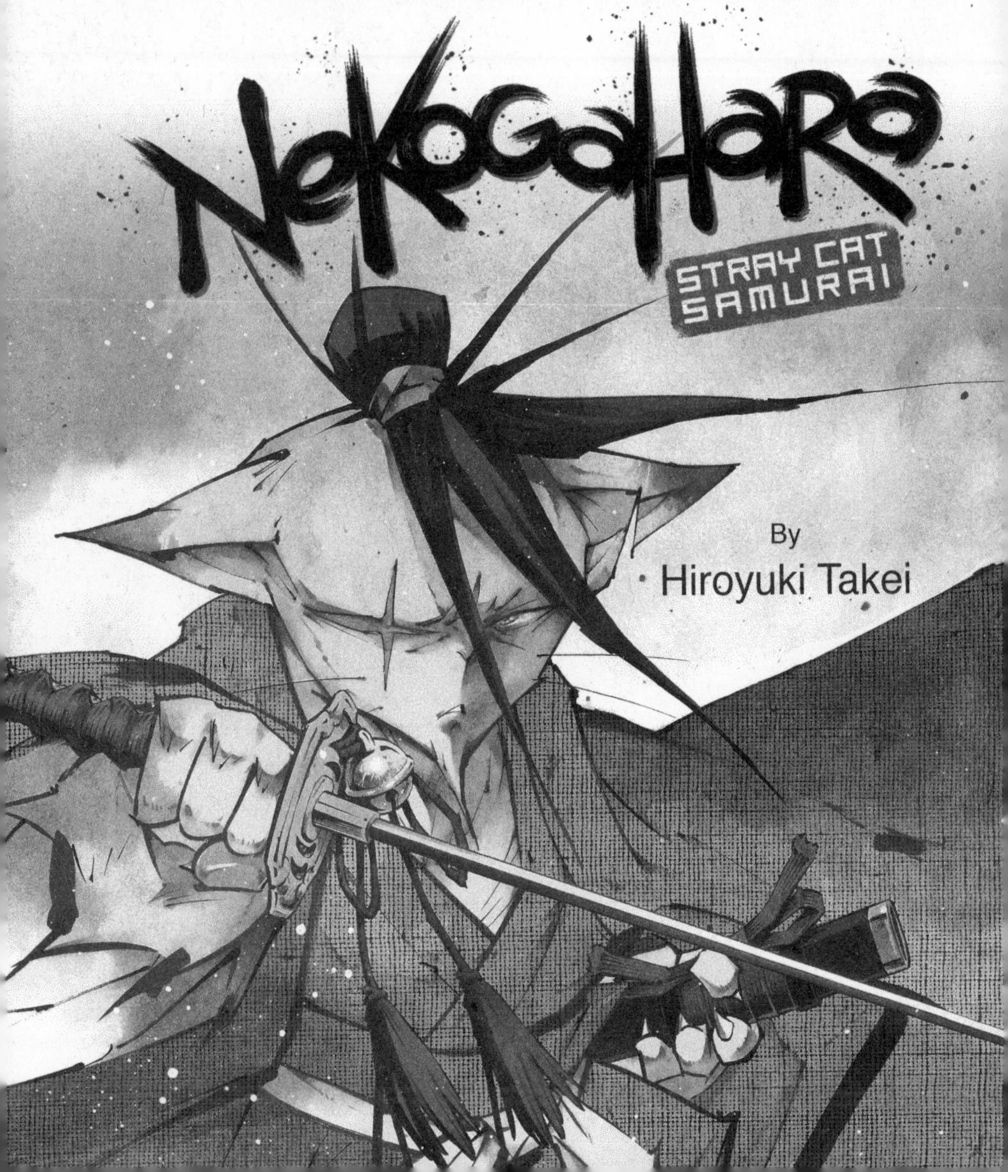
NEKOGAHARA
STRAY CAT SAMURAI
By
Hiroyuki Takei

Having lost his wife, high school teacher Kōhei Inuzuka is doing his best to raise his young daughter Tsumugi as a single father. He's pretty bad at cooking and doesn't have a huge appetite to begin with, but chance brings his little family together with one of his students, the lonely Kotori. The three of them are anything but comfortable in the kitchen, but the healing power of home cooking might just work on their grieving hearts.

"This season's number-one feel-good anime!" —Anime News Network

"A beautifully-drawn story about comfort food and family and grief. Recommended." —Otaku USA Magazine

sweetness & lightning

By Gido Amagakure

KC
KODANSHA COMICS

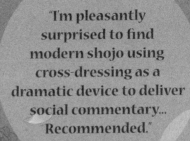

"I'm pleasantly surprised to find modern shojo using cross-dressing as a dramatic device to deliver social commentary... Recommended."

-Otaku USA Magazine

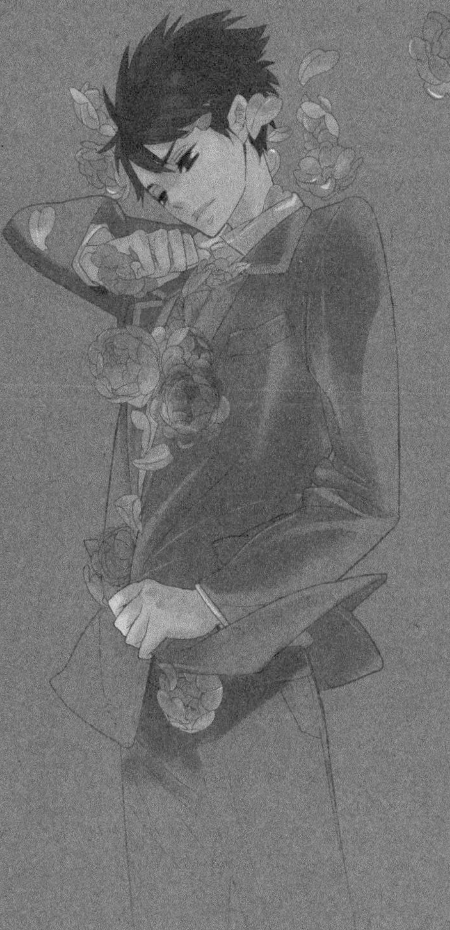

The prince in his dark days

By Hico Yamanaka

A drunkard for a father, a household of poverty... For 17-year-old Atsuko, misfortune is all she knows and believes in. Until one day, a chance encounter with Itaru–the wealthy heir of a huge corporation–changes everything. The two look identical, uncannily so. When Itaru curiously goes missing, Atsuko is roped into being his stand-in. There, in his shoes, Atsuko must parade like a prince in a palace. She encounters many new experiences, but at what cost...?

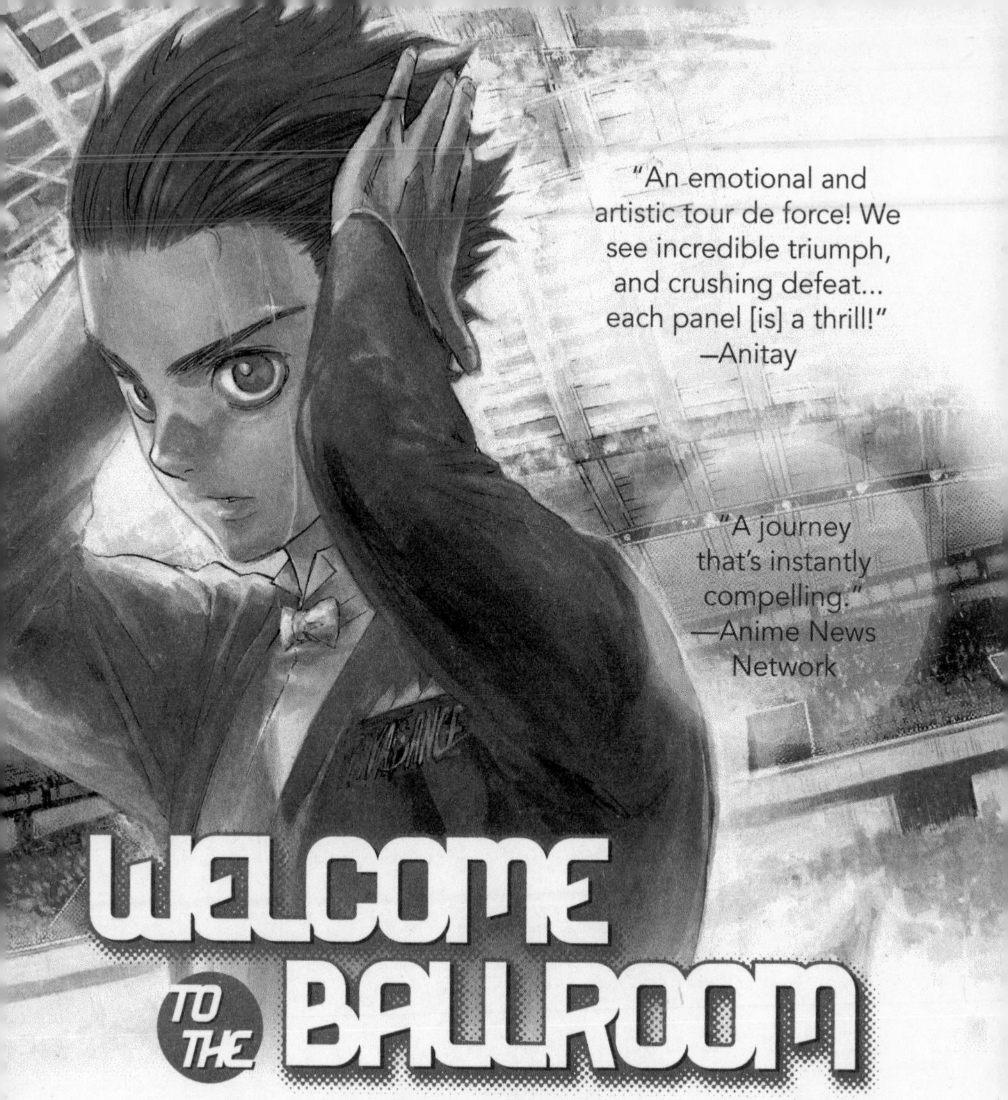

"An emotional and artistic tour de force! We see incredible triumph, and crushing defeat... each panel [is] a thrill!"
—Anitay

"A journey that's instantly compelling."
—Anime News Network

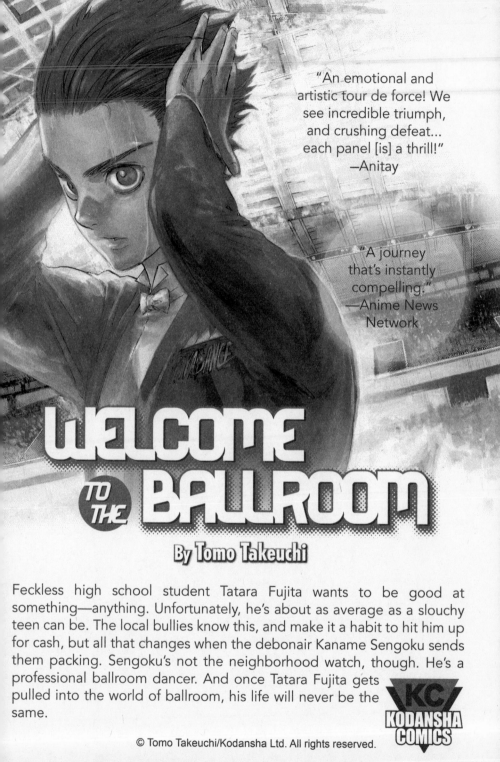

WELCOME TO THE BALLROOM

By Tomo Takeuchi

Feckless high school student Tatara Fujita wants to be good at something—anything. Unfortunately, he's about as average as a slouchy teen can be. The local bullies know this, and make it a habit to hit him up for cash, but all that changes when the debonair Kaname Sengoku sends them packing. Sengoku's not the neighborhood watch, though. He's a professional ballroom dancer. And once Tatara Fujita gets pulled into the world of ballroom, his life will never be the same.

KC KODANSHA COMICS

A Kodansha Comics Trade Paperback Original.

Aho-Girl volume 2 copyright © 2013 Hiroyuki
English translation copyright © 2017 Hiroyuki

Published in the United States by Kodansha Comics, an imprint of Kodansha USA Publishing, LLC, New York.

Publication rights for this English edition arranged through Kodansha Ltd., Tokyo.

First published in Japan in 2013 by Kodansha Ltd., Tokyo, as *Aho Gaaru* volume 2.

ISBN 978-1-63236-458-6

Printed in the United States of America.

www.kodanshacomics.com

9 8 7 6 5 4 3 2 1

Translator: Karen McGillicuddy
Lettering: Maggie Vicknair
Editing: Paul Starr
Kodansha Comics edition cover design by Phil Balsman